Introduction to Interdisciplinary Studies

Second Edition

To my wife, children, and grandchildren

"The greatest force in the world is an idea whose time has come."

Introduction to Interdisciplinary Studies

Second Edition

Allen F. Repko

University of Texas at Arlington (Retired)

Rick Szostak

University of Alberta, Edmonton, Canada

Michelle Phillips Buchberger

Miami University

Los Angeles | London | New Delhi
Singapore | Washington DC | Melbourne

FOR INFORMATION:

SAGE Publications, Inc.
2455 Teller Road
Thousand Oaks, California 91320
E-mail: order@sagepub.com

SAGE Publications Ltd.
1 Oliver's Yard
55 City Road
London, EC1Y 1SP
United Kingdom

SAGE Publications India Pvt. Ltd.
B 1/I 1 Mohan Cooperative Industrial Area
Mathura Road, New Delhi 110 044
India

SAGE Publications Asia-Pacific Pte. Ltd.
3 Church Street
#10–04 Samsung Hub
Singapore 049483

Acquisitions Editor: Helen Salmon
Editorial Assistant: Chelsea Pearson
eLearning Editor: John Scappini
Production Editor: Bennie Clark Allen
Copy Editor: Diane Wainwright
Typesetter: C&M Digitals (P) Ltd.
Proofreader: Wendy Jo Dymond
Indexer: Jean Casalegno
Cover Designer: Michelle Kenny
Marketing Manager: Susannah Goldes

Printed in the United States of America

Library of Congress Cataloging-in-Publication Data

Names: Repko, Allen F. | Szostak, Rick, 1959- author. | Buchberger, Michelle Phillips, author.

Title: Introduction to interdisciplinary studies / Allen F. Repko, University of Texas at Arlington (retired), Rick Szostak, University of Alberta, Edmonton, Canada, Michelle Phillips Buchberger, Miami University.

Description: Second edition. | Los Angeles : Sage, [2017] | Includes bibliographical references and index.

Identifiers: LCCN 2016023303 | ISBN 9781506346892 (pbk. : alk. paper)

Subjects: LCSH: Interdisciplinary approach to knowledge. | Social sciences.

Classification: LCC Q180.55.I48 R473 2017 | DDC 300—dc23
LC record available at https://lccn.loc.gov/2016023303

This book is printed on acid-free paper.

16 17 18 19 20 10 9 8 7 6 5 4 3 2 1

Brief Contents

Detailed Contents

Preface

The purpose of this book is to provide instructors and students in entry-level interdisciplinary courses and thematic programs with a comprehensive introduction to interdisciplinary studies. This book introduces students to the cognitive process that interdisciplinarians use to approach complex problems and eventually arrive at more comprehensive understandings of them. Put another way, students in these courses will learn to think like interdisciplinarians. By the end of an introductory course in which this book is used, students should be able to differentiate between disciplinary and interdisciplinary approaches to learning and research, follow and critique interdisciplinary arguments, understand interdisciplinary process, and assess the quality of their own work.

Interdisciplinary courses and programs continue to proliferate in higher education, even during the current economic retrenchment. Bestcolleges .com, a website that ranks various university programs, had this to say about interdisciplinary studies in 2016:

> Interest in integrative studies programs has risen as academics, organizations and students recognize the value of engaging in multidisciplinary and interdisciplinary learning. These types of degrees equip students with a wide-range of knowledge as well as the critical and analytical skills needed to be successful in the workforce.
>
> Rather than focusing on a single discipline, students can tailor their studies to their academic interests and professional goals. The result is an integrative learning experience that leads to personal fulfillment, a greater awareness of social responsibility and a thoughtful approach to modern issues. (Bestcolleges.com, paras. 1, 2)

This growing interest in interdisciplinary studies is reflected in the development of new programs. For example, East Stroudsburg University of

Pennsylvania established the Department of Intercultural and Interdisciplinary Studies in 2007. Franklin University created explicitly interdisciplinary core courses for its new interdisciplinary studies program in 2009. The next year, Southern Utah University announced that it was making interdisciplinarity and a first-year interdisciplinary course the centerpiece of its redefined mission as a public liberal arts and sciences institution. In 2011, Seattle University took an existing Liberal Studies program and overhauled the curriculum to become Interdisciplinary Liberal Studies. This involved adding three new required foundational courses for a total of five, which were phased in from 2011–2012. In Australia, the University of Melbourne is intensifying its undergraduate emphasis on interdisciplinary learning and research, believing that its graduates should be "knowledgeable across disciplines" and graduate with the ability to "examine critically, synthesize and evaluate knowledge across a broad range of disciplines." As evidence of its commitment, it has added two theme-based courses that are "explicitly interdisciplinary" (Golding, 2009, p.1).

The number of interdisciplinary undergraduate programs such as global studies, environmental studies, and human ecology has more than doubled over the past 3 decades—from fewer than a thousand programs in 1975 to more than 2,200 in 2000 (Brint, Turk-Bicakci, Proctor, & Murphy, 2009). More than 30,000 baccalaureate degrees in interdisciplinary-oriented programs were awarded in 2005, an increase of 70% from the previous decade (National Center for Education Statistics, 2007).

Entry-level courses in interdisciplinary studies and thematic programs that include interdisciplinarity as one of their foci have undergone significant changes in recent years in terms of content coverage, orientation, and teaching practice. Unlike a traditional discipline such as sociology, which has long had a recognized core of knowledge that is common to almost all introductory courses and textbooks, the field of interdisciplinary studies is just developing consensus about the principles (i.e., concepts, theories, or method) of the field. This emerging consensus is reflected, for example, in Repko and Szostak's (2016) *Interdisciplinary Research: Process and Theory* (3rd ed.).

The Need for This Book

Until recently, it was common practice for entry-level courses, whether in interdisciplinary studies or thematic interdisciplinary programs, to be taught by teams of disciplinarians who had no formal training in interdisciplinarity. Shrinking budgets have made this practice a luxury that few institutions can afford. Today, the responsibility for teaching an introductory course is more commonly the responsibility of a single instructor who often is more familiar with the disciplinary literature pertaining to the course or program theme than with the extensive literature on interdisciplinarity and the principles and best practices of the field. In this circumstance, the instructor is faced with the dual challenge of developing adequacy in the disciplines relevant to the course issue or theme as well as adequacy in the principles and best practices of interdisciplinarity. The single instructor approach will likely be the norm in coming years. The implication of this trend is that instructors, more now than ever, need a comprehensive textbook that introduces students to the principles of interdisciplinarity, prepares them to produce quality interdisciplinary work, and develops their ability to work with complex issues, problems, or questions that span multiple disciplines.

The authors' experience in designing and teaching entry-level interdisciplinary courses points to the need for a core or supplemental textbook that introduces students to the basic elements of this diverse and maturing field. This book (1) identifies the "drivers" of interdisciplinary learning and research and relates these to students' preparation for the rapidly changing job market of the new millennium; (2) situates interdisciplinary studies as part of the history of knowledge formations and the differentiation of knowledge into disciplines; (3) offers an integrated definition of interdisciplinary studies that helps students articulate the nature, value, and characteristics of interdisciplinary studies to friends, parents, and prospective employers; (4) helps students understand what it means to be interdisciplinary in terms of the cognitive abilities, values, and traits and skills that exposure to interdisciplinary studies fosters; (5) explains the role of the disciplines in the university and how interdisciplinary studies differs from, yet builds upon, the disciplines; (6) examines the diverse forms of interdisciplinary studies in terms of their assumptions, theories, commitment to epistemological pluralism, and perspectives on reality; (7) facilitates students' ability to think critically about real-world problems and intellectual questions that span a range of disciplines and interdisciplinary fields in the undergraduate curriculum; (8) presents models commonly used by practitioners for addressing issues that are complex; (9) introduces a rubric that enables students to assess the quality of interdisciplinary work by others as well as their own; (10) integrates discussions concerning intellectual autobiographies, student portfolios, and service learning; (11) presents material that is consistent with a constructivist and pragmatic approach to learning; and (12) prepares students for advanced interdisciplinary study.

The Intended Audiences

The book is intended for multiple audiences. Programs that are explicitly interdisciplinary and that offer an entry-level course will find the book particularly useful as a primary text that offers a comprehensive overview of the field and develops students' ability to begin thinking like interdisciplinarians. These courses are taught under a variety of titles such as "introduction to liberal studies," "interdisciplinary perspectives," and "introduction to interdisciplinary studies." Their focus is on presenting the basic principles of interdisciplinarity, exposing students to writings by the field's leading practitioners, and developing the ability to critically analyze the work of practitioners and students like themselves. Because this book is thoroughly grounded in the field's extensive literature, students using it will be well prepared to pursue more advanced study. For courses that include a short paper or culminating project that demonstrates achievement of interdisciplinary learning outcomes, the book includes chapters that explain how to apply the easy-to-follow, steplike process described in the "Broad Model" of interdisciplinary process to researching and writing papers. These chapters also include a rubric, based on the Broad Model, that students can fruitfully use to assess the interdisciplinary work of others as well as their own.

This book will also be useful as a supplemental text for entry-level courses in thematic multidisciplinary "studies" programs that focus on a single issue or theme. These programs include non-Western cultural studies (Asian area studies, Latin American area studies, African area studies, Middle Eastern studies), race and ethnic studies (African American studies, ethnic and race studies, Chicano/Hispanic studies, American Indian studies, Asian American studies), Western studies (European studies, North American studies, Western period history studies, European origin studies, Western studies, Canadian studies), environmental studies, international and global studies (international relations, global, peace, conflict studies, political economy), civic and government studies (urban studies, public affairs and public policy, legal studies), women's studies, American studies (American culture or studies, U.S. regional studies), and brain and biomedical studies (cognitive, neuroscience, biomedical, biotechnology, medical technology). Other programs include literary studies (and the rapidly expanding "digital" humanities), film studies, liberal studies, gerontology, Judaic studies, science and technology, arts management, health management, folk studies, ethics and values studies, and sexuality studies.[1]

---

1. Data compiled from College Catalog Study Database. Brint, Turk-Bicakci, Proctor, & Murphy (2008). Original publication of the table, copyright held by publisher the Johns Hopkins University Press: Brint, S. G., Turk-Bicakci, L., Proctor, K., & Murphy, S. P. "Expanding the Social Frame of Knowledge: Interdisciplinary, Degree-Granting Fields in American Colleges and Universities, 1975–2000." *Review of Higher Education*, 2009, 32(2), 155–183.

Many of these programs claim interdisciplinary status, which means that they probably subscribe to the core principles of interdisciplinarity discussed in this book. The majority of the readings used in introductory courses to these programs focus primarily on the topic of the course and only secondarily on interdisciplinarity, which is referenced in class discussion during the semester. However, these courses need to introduce students to the basics of interdisciplinarity as well as to the substantive content of the theme. After all, thematic programs typically build on disciplinary courses from several disciplines. Students can use the information in this book to understand, for example, the concept of disciplinary perspective, when to use an interdisciplinary approach, how to identify disciplines that are most relevant to the course theme (even if these are preselected), and how to critically analyze disciplinary insights using interdisciplinary techniques. Systematic coverage of this and other relevant information in this book will enhance the coherence and rigor of these courses.

As it is, considerable overlap exists between multidisciplinary and interdisciplinary approaches to learning and research. This book addresses instances of overlap but is careful to distinguish between these two broad approaches and to show how interdisciplinary approaches build on multidisciplinary approaches. The book identifies and explains the principles of interdisciplinarity *without being prescriptive concerning how these principles should be applied in a particular context of interdisciplinary learning.* This flexible approach enables instructors to strike a balance between introducing students to the substantive content of their course, say the environment, and the principles of interdisciplinarity.

This book will also be useful to general education programs. The great deficiency of many general education programs is their lack of cohesion and identifiable learning outcomes. This is remedied, in part, by structuring the program around a unifying issue, problem, or question that connects it to the disciplines participating in the common core curriculum and labeling it "interdisciplinary." However, the critical element that is lacking is an introductory course or cohort experience that prepares students to understand what a university is, the role that disciplines and interdisciplinary programs play in it, and how to make connections among knowledge areas that are epistemologically distant. All general education programs, therefore, need some basic understanding of interdisciplinarity. Even if the program merely requires students to take a menu of courses from participating disciplines, there should be an introductory course or entry-level cohort experience that introduces students to the disciplines constituting the common core.

To Instructors

There are at least five major problems that you face when designing and teaching an introductory-level interdisciplinary course. The first is "making do" with materials that typically do not reflect recent advances in the burgeoning literature on interdisciplinary studies. The unfortunate result is that interdisciplinary instructors are often unwittingly teaching and modeling multidisciplinarity, not interdisciplinarity. Faulty course design and the absence of rigorous learning outcomes that are explicitly interdisciplinary misinform students about the principles of the field and ill prepare them for advanced interdisciplinary course work. This book reflects the significant advances in interdisciplinary practice and theory over the past decade. Research shows that repeated exposure to interdisciplinary learning contexts fosters the development of certain cognitive abilities such as perspective taking and thinking critically about conflicting information on an issue or problem from multiple knowledge sources. The book also draws on the experience and wisdom of instructors in the field, many of whom have published valuable insights.

The second problem is how to structure the course and sequence the content so that it helps students advance cognitively from merely collecting and recalling information to creatively applying it. The organization of this book will aid instructors in designing their courses.

The third problem is how to engage and sustain student interest in multidisciplinary and interdisciplinary learning and research. Here the challenge is to engage students cognitively and introduce them to new ways of addressing complexity, diversity, and conflict. This book will help them develop the capacity to address pressing real-world problems, prepare them to make decisions about how to approach these problems, equip them to assess solutions to problems, and enrich them intellectually. Importantly, it will also inform them of the value in their future careers and lives of being able to perform interdisciplinary analysis.

The fourth problem is how to meaningfully assess the quality of student work. In recent years, assessment has become a major focus of the field of interdisciplinary studies. Consequently, the book draws on the research of leading authorities on interdisciplinary learning and assessment including Veronica Boix Mansilla and Lana Ivanitskaya. The last chapters of the book feature the Broad Model Rubric developed for the introductory course I designed and taught at the University of Texas at Arlington for many years and that I have presented at numerous workshops on assessment. The rubric may be flexibly applied to a broad range of entry-level student work.

The fifth problem is how to introduce students to the concept of interdisciplinary integration and the process that makes integration possible. The book presents theories of interdisciplinary integration and helps students to recognize the integrative work of practitioners who draw on multiple disciplines. However, the book does not explain the *process* of integration, believing that it should be reserved for advanced course work in interdisciplinary studies. Experience has shown that when students are thoroughly grounded in the material presented in this book, they will be ready to engage in this challenging process. Instructors who want their students to learn *how* to create common ground and integrate should use the follow-on text, *Interdisciplinary Research: Process and Theory* (3rd ed.).

Test questions and PowerPoint slides for each chapter can be found on the Instructor side of the accompanying website at www.sagepub.com/repkointrois2e.

To Students

You face three major obstacles in an entry-level multidisciplinary or interdisciplinary course. The first is comprehending subject matter that differs markedly from your prior exposure to disciplinary learning and thinking. This book helps you transition from disciplinary to interdisciplinary approaches to learning, problem solving, and research. The second is that you often bring into the course misperceptions about interdisciplinarity learned from other students or from disciplinary instructors who may have given the impression that such courses and programs are superficial or not have appreciated that employers increasingly look for interdisciplinary skills. This book corrects these misconceptions and explains how to effectively counter these criticisms. The third obstacle that you face is how to articulate what interdisciplinary studies is. This book develops your ability to understand interdisciplinarity so that you can clearly articulate its meaning and value to your family, peers, and potential employers.

The Approach Used and Style of Presentation

The style of presentation is succinct, conceptual (i.e., theory-based), *and* eminently practical. It reflects widely recognized approaches to interdisciplinary learning and assessment while also offering concrete practical examples and strategies of how to engage in interdisciplinary work.

Distinctive approaches to topic coverage include a cognitive development approach on how to become interdisciplinary. This is facilitated by a step-by-step approach to problem solving or meaning making that includes appropriate feedback loops, decision points, and opportunities for reflection as students explore the course theme individually, as an in-class collaborative effort, or cohort experience.

The book adopts Boix Mansilla's neo-Piagetian constructivist and pragmatic approach to teaching, which emphasizes that learners need to be actively involved in the learning process and that deep learning occurs when students are challenged to produce something of value. This book asks students to reflect on what they are learning and experience cognitive conflict as they struggle to reconcile alternative perspectives and conflicting insights.

Design Features and Benefits

The book addresses the major teaching and student learning challenges noted earlier by doing the following:

- To overcome the problem of students' possible difficulty in comprehending subject matter that differs so markedly from their repeated exposure to disciplinary learning, the book creatively uses a variety of visual aids (graphics, figures, tables, cartoons, and photographs) and other devices to make complex and unfamiliar concepts clear and understandable.

- To engage and sustain student interest in the material, the book provides both practical and cognitive features. To engage students practically, the book presents examples of professional and student work, pictures, and stories (such as the fable of the elephant house) that are woven into the narrative. To engage students cognitively, the book includes in-text "Challenge Questions" and end-of-chapter "Critical Thinking Questions," "Applications and Exercises," "Case Studies," and other active learning devices.

- To overcome possible student and parental apprehension about the marketability of an interdisciplinary program or degree, the book includes Chapter 1, which discusses factors that are propelling and sustaining interdisciplinarity as a mode of learning.

- To overcome student difficulty in articulating what interdisciplinarity is, the book presents an easy-to-understand definition of interdisciplinary studies in Chapter 3 that will enable them to explain this often misunderstood concept to parents, friends, and prospective employers.

- To inform students about how they benefit from interdisciplinary studies, the book devotes Chapter 4 to identifying the abilities, values, skills, and traits that interdisciplinarity fosters.

- To counter criticism that interdisciplinary studies are superficial and a poor substitute for disciplinary depth (i.e., a traditional disciplinary major), the book emphasizes the foundational importance of the disciplines, examines their perspectives, identifies their defining elements, and critically analyzes their approach to learning, meaning making, and creation of new knowledge.

- To demonstrate that interdisciplinary studies is a maturing academic field, the book introduces students to the assumptions, theories, approaches to research, epistemology, and perspectives that undergird the field and give it credibility, coherence, and rigor.

- To present a balanced approach to the complex concept of interdisciplinarity, the book acknowledges counterviews on several points of controversy.

- To introduce students to interdisciplinary thinking and help them recognize quality interdisciplinary work, the book presents the "Broad Model," which integrates commonly used approaches to conducting interdisciplinary research. This model presents an easy-to-follow step-by-step approach to the interdisciplinary research process that emphasizes the importance of personal reflection on each STEP taken. This model leads students through the early STEPS of interdisciplinary process but stops short of those STEPS that call for creating common ground and integrating insights.

- To empower students to examine a complex problem from multiple disciplinary perspectives, the book presents a theory-based approach to perspective taking and applies it to a variety of contexts using examples from student and professional work.

- To address the widespread use of student intellectual autobiographies, student portfolios, and service learning, the text references these approaches and follows them up with detailed discussions in the appendixes.

- To meet the need of students whose instructors require an interdisciplinary product or paper rather than just walking students through the interdisciplinary process as an in-class collaboration, the last three chapters of the book present easy-to-follow STEPS that are applicable to a variety of group or individual projects.

- To address the need for increased rigor and coherence in the field, especially at the entry level, the book includes a "Broad Model Rubric" that students can use to assess examples of interdisciplinary work, as well as their own, as they engage in each STEP of the process called for in the Broad Model.

Changes in the Second Edition

This second edition is completely revised and updated to reflect both the comments we received from several scholars who had read and/or taught from the first edition as well as the insights of dozens of works published since the first edition. We rearranged material, moving the new Chapter 2 forward in the book, and moving discussions of natural science, social science, the humanities, and the fine and performing arts from Chapter 1 to the new Chapter 2. And we made numerous additions to the text:

- In Chapter 1, we added more information on career prospects for interdisciplinary students, the value of the skills achieved in interdisciplinary education, and the evaluation of interdisciplinary programs. We also added discussions of the nature of the academy, community development, interdisciplinary analysis of electronic medical records, and the integration of personal identity.

- In Chapter 2, we redrafted the discussion of the history of disciplines and interdisciplinarity. Later on we added discussions of globalization and media studies.

- In Chapter 3, we clarified our discussion of transdisciplinarity and drew connections across interdisciplinary metaphors.

- In Chapter 4, we added a discussion of several additional key values, especially intellectual courage, and discussed how interdisciplinarity allows us to applaud diversity while also pursuing particular values. We added brief discussions of the importance of interdisciplinary values and skills beyond the academy and workplace, and of blogging as an alternative to the e-portfolio.

- In Chapter 5, we more clearly distinguished insights from perspectives (we did so again in Chapter 7). And we stressed that the various elements of disciplinary perspective are mutually reinforcing. We added a paragraph on academic peer review. And we discussed the different types of scholarly theory.

- The main changes in Chapter 6 involved brief extensions and clarifications of the assumptions underlying interdisciplinary studies.

- In Chapter 8, we clarified the distinction between assumptions and conclusions, and added a brief discussion of evidential validity.

- Though it is not the purpose of this book to discuss the entire interdisciplinary research process as outlined in Repko and Szostak (2016), we recognize that students will be curious about the later steps of this process. We have thus added a brief discussion of strategies for integration to Chapter 9 and of developing disciplinary adequacy in Chapter 12. In Chapter 9, we also extended our discussion of connections between poetry and mathematics.

- In Chapter 10, we provided more detailed advice on how students should perform STEPS 1 and 2 of the Broad Model in written work.

- In Chapter 11, we added brief discussions of the nature of interdisciplines, the creative value of diagrams, and the importance of terminology in interdisciplinary searching.

- In the Appendixes, we added a discussion of blogging in Appendix B, added an example of student work in Appendix D, and provided answers for new critical thinking questions in Chapters 10 and 11 in Appendix E.

- We have ensured that there are critical thinking questions at the end of each chapter. We have revised the wording of questions to ensure that students cannot just answer "yes" or "no." And we have identified for each chapter questions particularly well suited to group work.

Contents

The book is divided into three parts, each organized around a theme that addresses a key aspect of interdisciplinary studies as described in this book.

Part I: Understanding Interdisciplinary Studies

The theme of Part I is understanding interdisciplinary studies as a diverse, dynamic, and growing field. It includes six chapters that explain the emergence of the interdisciplinary idea and its defining elements while presenting counterviews along the way. Chapter 1 contextualizes interdisciplinary studies in the real world and identifies factors propelling its continuous advance inside and outside the academy. Chapter 2 draws on widely accepted but contrasting definitions of interdisciplinary studies and presents an integrated definition. Chapter 3 examines the abilities, values, traits, and skills that interdisciplinary studies fosters and introduces students to the intellectual autobiography, the portfolio, and service learning. Chapter 4 traces the rise of interdisciplinarity as a corrective to disciplinary dominance. Chapter 5 examines the defining elements of the disciplines and explains how these are of importance to interdisciplinarians. Chapter 6 presents the "DNA" of interdisciplinary studies, which are the assumptions, theories, epistemology, and perspectives that provide coherence and rigor to the field.

Chapter 1: Interdisciplinary Studies in the Real World

The emergence of interdisciplinary studies and its demonstrated ability to sustain itself as a recognized approach to learning and research is no accident. There are powerful "drivers" of the field's continued advance. The chapter begins by asking why interdisciplinary studies matters and identifies six drivers of interdisciplinary learning and research. The chapter discusses how each of these is relevant to students who are both intellectually concerned about our world and practically concerned about preparing themselves for work in the new century. The chapter summarizes the case for interdisciplinary studies and discusses its implications for students' career development.

Chapter 2: The Rise of the Modern Disciplines and Interdisciplinarity

The genesis of the interdisciplinary idea and its demonstrated ability to sustain itself as a recognized approach to learning and research is actually rooted in the history of the modern disciplines. The chapter begins by discussing why the past matters and explains that the disciplines (e.g., art history, psychology, and chemistry) have existed for less than 200 years. Understanding why knowledge came to be differentiated into disciplines and why they have come to dominate the contemporary university is foundational to understanding why interdisciplinarity came about and why it is able to adapt to new challenges. The chapter surveys developments in the natural sciences, social sciences, humanities, and fine and performing arts. This chapter also explains the emergence of interdisciplinarity as a logical response to disciplinary reductionism, dualism, and hegemony. Specifically, it identifies interdisciplinary studies' six criticisms of the disciplines and disciplinary specialization.

Chapter 3: Interdisciplinary Studies Defined

"Interdisciplinary studies," "interdisciplinary learning," and "integrative learning" are terms that have become part of the vocabulary of higher education. This chapter begins by explaining "why definitions matter." It defines the terms "interdisciplinary" and "interdisciplinarity" and presents widely recognized definitions of "interdisciplinary studies." It then deconstructs these definitions to identify their commonalities and key concepts before presenting an integrated definition of interdisciplinary studies. The chapter explains the difference between critical and instrumental interdisciplinarity and how the concepts of "disciplinarity," "multidisciplinarity," "transdisciplinarity," and "interdisciplinarity" differ. The chapter closes with a critical analysis of useful and not so useful metaphors to describe interdisciplinary studies.

Chapter 4: The Interdisciplinary Studies "Cognitive Toolkit"

Advocates of interdisciplinary studies claim that it fosters the development of certain abilities, values, traits, and skills. Research on cognition and learning shows that exposing students to interdisciplinarity fosters cognitive abilities that are distinctive to interdisciplinary studies and do not occur naturally in disciplinary contexts. And while all disciplines and fields boast of teaching critical thinking skills, interdisciplinary studies and interdisciplinary fields do so of necessity, employing distinctive strategies.

Additionally, interdisciplinary learning promotes certain competencies and values and emphasizes the development of certain traits and skills that will serve students well as they venture forth into the world outside the academy. The chapter explains how students can apply this "cognitive toolkit" by creating intellectual autobiographies, developing portfolios or blogs, and participating in service-learning projects, which are discussed more fully in the appendixes.

Chapter 5: Academic Disciplines

The disciplines are the foundational units of learning and knowledge production in most university settings. Since most interdisciplinary activity draws on the disciplines and their insights, it is of fundamental importance for students to understand the disciplines. The chapter acknowledges counterviews of the role of disciplines in interdisciplinary work, presents definitions of "discipline," examines commonalities shared by these definitions, and presents an integrated definition. The chapter also discusses disciplines as epistemic, social, and organizational structures, and presents a taxonomy of disciplines, fields, and professions. Most important for interdisciplinary work, the chapter discusses the key concept of disciplinary perspective, defines this all-important concept, explains how perspective taking is used in multidisciplinary and interdisciplinary contexts, examines misconceptions about disciplinary perspective, and identifies the defining (and mutually reinforcing) elements of a discipline's perspective. Perspectives are carefully distinguished from disciplinary insights.

Chapter 6: The "DNA" of Interdisciplinary Studies

All disciplines and knowledge formations are undergirded by certain assumptions, theories, epistemologies, and perspectives on reality. This is inherently true of the field of interdisciplinary studies, which, despite its great diversity, is knit together by certain assumptions. Many in the field embrace certain theories, such as theories on complexity, perspective taking, common-ground creation, integration, and production of interdisciplinary understandings or cognitive advancements. The chapter acknowledges counterviews on many of these points. In addition, the field shares an epistemology or way of knowing that goes against the mainstream approaches of reductionism and dualism. In combination, these intellectual currents provide the field with a distinctive perspective on reality that motivates its pedagogy and research.

Part II: Thinking Critically About Interdisciplinary Studies

The theme of Part II is how to think critically as interdisciplinarians about disciplinary and interdisciplinary approaches to complex problems. This theme is explored in three chapters: Chapter 7 explains how to recognize and think critically about disciplinary perspectives; Chapter 8 examines how to recognize and think critically about disciplinary insights; and Chapter 9 focuses on how to recognize and think critically about interdisciplinary integrations and understandings.

Chapter 7: Thinking Critically About Disciplinary Perspectives

Thinking critically in interdisciplinary studies begins with developing a sophisticated conception of knowledge and truth so that we can make sense of the multiple and often conflicting disciplinary perspectives on problems that are complex and multidimensional. The chapter challenges students to reflect on their present epistemological position (i.e., how one determines whether something is true), assess their tolerance for multiplicity, and move toward critical pluralism. By moving toward critical pluralism, students are equipped to interrogate (i.e., critically analyze) disciplinary perspectives as these bear on the problem or issue under study. There are several practical benefits of interrogating disciplinary perspectives: It is an interdisciplinary move that is necessitated by complexity; it is a prerequisite for turning multidisciplinary work into interdisciplinary work; it enables us to see the relevance of other perspectives; it illuminates our understanding of the problem *as a whole*; it reduces the possibility of making poor or narrow decisions; and it exposes the strengths and limitations of each perspective. The chapter then examines the work of practitioners and students to demonstrate how interdisciplinarians interrogate disciplinary perspectives.

Chapter 8: Thinking Critically About Disciplinary Insights

Students, especially early in their college education, often wonder how they can be expected to critically evaluate books or articles written by disciplinary experts. Since the author knows so much more about the subject than the student does, how can the student presume to critique? Interdisciplinary students may have an advantage here, for as this book contends, disciplinary authors provide an incomplete analysis of any complex problem. Students familiar with the material in earlier chapters will, in other words, know that there is a downside to expertise: Experts may ignore much that is beyond their experience. But this lesson has broader import: Since no work is perfect, *all* works need to be critically evaluated. The objective of this chapter is to provide practical advice on how to critically evaluate any text, whatever the disciplinary or interdisciplinary orientation of its authors. One important technique in critical analysis is to map an author's arguments. The chapter explains how to map arguments and concludes by mapping the scholarly enterprise.

Chapter 9: Thinking Critically About Integration and Its Results

Thinking critically in interdisciplinary studies extends to integration and its result. The chapter describes three commonly used approaches to perform interdisciplinary integration—contextualization, conceptualization, and problem centering. Examples of each approach are presented along with analyses of their respective strengths and limitations. The chapter then introduces the "Broad Model," which subsumes these approaches and presents examples of how practitioners creatively apply the model to problems spanning the disciplines, professions, and applied fields. Techniques of interdisciplinary integration are introduced. The chapter concludes by discussing the difference between "partial" and "full" integration, the result of integration, and the core premises that underlie the concept of more comprehensive understanding.

Part III: Interdisciplinary Research and Writing

The theme of Part III is applying interdisciplinary processes in contexts where students, whether working in cohorts or individually, are asked to produce products that are explicitly interdisciplinary. These products may assume many forms, such as posters, plays, or video productions. But they should also include a written component that confirms student understanding of interdisciplinary concepts, theory, and research process and the ability to apply these to a concrete project. Part III includes three chapters that present interdisciplinary process as a steplike and reflexive research road map called the Broad Model and explain how to apply its easy-to-follow STEPS. These chapters also introduce and apply the "Broad Model Rubric," based on the Broad Model, which establishes easy-to-understand criteria for each STEP, allowing students to evaluate their work as they go.

Chapter 10: An Interdisciplinary Research "Road Map"

Being educated includes understanding the importance of research and having the ability to gather information on subjects of interest. This chapter compares disciplinary and interdisciplinary approaches to research and explains the utility of the Broad Model's approach to the interdisciplinary research process. The chapter examines the model's first two STEPS: defining the problem or stating the research question (STEP 1) and justifying using an interdisciplinary approach (STEP 2). It then explains how to evaluate practitioner and student work using the Broad Model Rubric so that students can assess their understanding of key concepts and the quality of their work.

Chapter 11: Identifying Relevant Disciplines and Gathering Information About the Problem

Because interdisciplinary studies is rooted in the disciplines, the interdisciplinary process involves drawing on disciplinary perspectives and their insights when addressing complex problems. This chapter presents strategies for identifying disciplines that are relevant to the problem under study (STEP 3) and gathering information about the problem (STEP 4). The chapter also demonstrates how to apply the Broad Model Rubric to examples of practitioner and student work to prepare students to assess their performance of these STEPS.

Chapter 12: Analyzing Insights and Reflecting on Process

This chapter completes our discussion of the STEPS of the Broad Model and the application of the Broad Model Rubric with examples of practitioner and student work. The chapter demonstrates how to assess practitioner and student attempts to critically analyze disciplinary insights and locate their sources of conflict (STEP 5). It discusses how students can achieve and demonstrate "disciplinary adequacy." It also assesses examples of practitioner and student reflection on how using the interdisciplinary process described in this book has enlarged their understanding of the problem (STEP 6).

Website

To enhance your use of the book, visit www.sagepub.com/repkointrois2e for additional resources.

Allen F. Repko

Rick Szostak

Michelle Phillips Buchberger

Acknowledgments

The authors and SAGE Publishing thank the following scholars who gave detailed advice on how the second edition might be improved:

Simeon Dreyfuss, *Marylhurst University*

Quincy A. Edwards, *University of South Florida*

Mallory Koci, *Emporia State University*

Michele Parker Randall, *University of Central Florida*

David Sidore, *Middle Georgia State University*

About the Authors

 **Allen F. Repko**, PhD, is the former director of the interdisciplinary studies program in the School of Urban and Public Affairs at the University of Texas at Arlington, where he developed and taught the program's core curriculum for many years. The program is one of the largest in the United States. Repko has written extensively on all aspects of interdisciplinary studies, has twice served as coeditor of the interdisciplinary journal *Issues in Integrative Studies,* and has served on the board of the Association for Interdisciplinary Studies (AIS). Though recently "retired," he continues to write and speak at AIS conventions, where he conducts annual workshops on interdisciplinary program development and assessment. He can be contacted at allenrepko@att.net.

 **Rick Szostak**, PhD, is a professor of economics at the University of Alberta, where he has taught for 31 years. He is the author of a dozen books and 50 articles, all of an interdisciplinary nature. Several of his publications address how to do interdisciplinary research, teach interdisciplinary courses, administer interdisciplinary programs, or organize information in order to facilitate interdisciplinarity. As an associate dean, he created the Office of Interdisciplinary Studies at the University of Alberta, the Science, Technology and Society program, an individualized major, and two courses about interdisciplinarity. He has twice served as coeditor of the interdisciplinary journal *Issues in Integrative Studies.* He was president of the Association for Interdisciplinary Studies (AIS) from 2011 to 2014. He can be contacted at rszostak@ualberta.ca.

Michelle Phillips Buchberger, PhD, is an assistant professor of integrative studies at Miami University. She previously proposed, developed and chaired the B.S. Interdisciplinary Studies program at Franklin University, which is taught in both traditional and online formats. A fairly recent convert to interdisciplinarity, she has worked as co-coordinator (with Pauline Gagnon) of the Alpha Iota Sigma international honors society for interdisciplinary studies and has presented and written on topics including teaching interdisciplinary studies online, working with nontraditional students, and creative thinking in interdisciplinary studies. She teaches several courses about interdisciplinarity, including electronic portfolios, theories and methods of interdisciplinary studies, creative thinking, and the interdisciplinary studies capstone course. She has a PhD in English Literature, which she also teaches. She can be contacted at buchbem@miamioh.edu.

Understanding Interdisciplinary Studies

The theme of Part I is understanding interdisciplinary studies as a diverse, dynamic, and growing field. Its six chapters explain what is driving the field's steady advance, offer an integrated definition of this often misunderstood concept, and discuss the intellectual capacities, values, traits, and skills that interdisciplinary studies fosters. The chapters explain the rise of the modern disciplines and the emergence of interdisciplinary studies. They also identify the defining elements of disciplines; describe them as epistemic, social, and organizational communities; and discuss the key concept of disciplinary perspective. Part I closes with a detailed examination of the "DNA" of interdisciplinary studies in terms of its assumptions, theories, epistemology, and perspectives.

Chapter 1 Objectives

This chapter explains why interdisciplinary studies is now considered basic to education, problem solving, professional practice, and innovation. Interdisciplinarity provides a time-tested practical way to address the inherent complexity of real-world problems, including those problems arising in the workplace. The overall objective of this chapter is to spark your interest in interdisciplinary studies and help you appreciate the real-world significance of interdisciplinarity that is set out in the chapters ahead. Related objectives include understanding why interdisciplinary studies is considered basic to education and research, the factors driving the advance of interdisciplinary studies, and the relevance of interdisciplinary studies to your career development.

Interdisciplinary Studies in the Real World

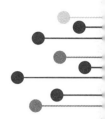

Now that you are in university and enrolled in an interdisciplinary studies (IDS) course or program, you need to understand how IDS can help you achieve your long-term career goals. We begin by explaining why IDS matters and what is driving this innovative approach to learning and problem solving today. We then discuss the academic benefits of IDS and explain how IDS aids your career development.

Why Interdisciplinary Studies Matters

We desire to have our lives count for something, to do something meaningful, to make a contribution to society. Thus, we come to the university to learn how to make a difference in the world. There are many ways to do this: educating our children, becoming responsible workers and citizens, protecting the environment, combating poverty, reducing crime and violence, creating new art forms, discovering cures for diseases, developing new technologies, starting new businesses, improving public policies, and promoting peace, justice, and security. To make such a difference, we must prepare for the realities of life in the twenty-first century with its growing complexities and new challenges. This requires developing the skills to make connections, solve complex problems, develop leadership skills, engage in strategic

Learning Outcomes

By the end of this chapter, you will be able to:

- Demonstrate an understanding of why interdisciplinary studies is considered basic to education, problem solving, professional practice, and innovation

- Describe the "drivers" of interdisciplinary studies today

- Identify and describe new and emerging interdisciplinary fields of study and their significance

- Explain why systems thinking and contextual thinking are increasingly viewed as important

- Explain why a knowledge society needs both disciplinary specialization and interdisciplinary breadth

- Explain the academic benefits of pursuing an interdisciplinary studies degree

- Explain the relevance of interdisciplinary studies to your career development

thinking, communicate effectively, practice analytical thinking, and work collaboratively. IDS helps you to develop these skills.

What Is Driving Interdisciplinary Studies Today

For over two decades, major scientific organizations, funding agencies, and prominent educators have advocated the need for interdisciplinary studies. The current interest in interdisciplinarity is widespread and increasing in intensity, motivated by the belief that it is now basic to education and research. To meet this perceived need, educators have developed a wide range of interdisciplinary courses and "studies" programs. Interdisciplinarity, it is fair to say, is becoming an integral part of higher education.

There are solid reasons for this development with which you, as an educated and responsible citizen, should be familiar. These reasons or "drivers" are the subject of several recent reports by leading scientific and educational organizations and are the focus of this chapter: (1) the complexity of nature, society, and ourselves; (2) the complexity of the globalized workplace; (3) the need for systems thinking and contextual thinking; (4) the changing nature of university research; (5) the public world and its pressing needs; and (6) a knowledge society's need for *both* disciplinarity *and* interdisciplinarity. Combined, these drivers make a powerful case for interdisciplinary studies.

The Complexity of Nature, Society, and Ourselves

The first driver of interdisciplinary studies is the complexity of nature, society, and ourselves—all amazingly complex systems. A subject or problem is complex when its multiple parts require study by different disciplines. These parts interact in important ways, but the disciplines by their nature fail to study the interactions. For example, the subject of illegal immigration is complex because it has multiple parts, each of which is studied by a different discipline: the immigrant's home country (history, sociology, cultural anthropology), proximity of home country to country of destination (Earth science), immigration policies of country of destination (political science), and economic opportunity (economics). However, studying each part in isolation of the others and ignoring their interactions will not explain the cause or the effects of illegal immigration. What is required is an interdisciplinary approach that views the subject as a complex system with multiple interacting parts. An interdisciplinary approach critically analyzes the relevant disciplinary insights (i.e., what experts have written) and attempts to create common ground among them in order to produce a more comprehensive understanding or propose a holistic solution.

Razmak and Bélanger (2016) study the question of why electronic medical records have been adopted so slowly in North America. They suggest that several factors, studied by different disciplines, are important: psychological resistance among some medical staff, managerial challenges, complex political decision-making processes, financial limitations, and problems in software application. They argue that only interdisciplinary research can address such a complex problem (and they follow the research steps that are outlined in the later chapters of this book), or indeed a host of problems in the area of business/management studies.

The Complexity of the Globalized Workplace

A second driver of interdisciplinary studies is the complexity of the globalized workplace where effective communication requires sensitivity to diverse cultures. Today, the need to understand this complexity is more urgent than ever before, especially since the human population has reached the 7 billion mark, further straining our planet's limited resources. In the past decade, the world economy has undergone radical change, raising the question of what knowledge is needed by college graduates in the new globalized workplace. Pulitzer Prize–winning columnist Thomas Friedman and foreign policy expert Michael Mandelbaum (2011) describe this change in their book *That Used to Be Us* (see Box 1.1).

Box 1.1   The Changing Workplace

The merger of globalization and the IT revolution that coincided with the transition from the twentieth to the twenty-first century is changing everything—every job, every industry, every service, every hierarchical institution. It is creating new markets and new economic and political realities practically overnight. This merger has raised the level of skill a person needs to obtain and retain any good job, while at the same time increasing the global competition for every one of those jobs. It has made politics more transparent, the world more connected, dictators more vulnerable, and both individuals and small groups more empowered.

All of these dramatic changes in the workplace, coming in rapid-fire succession, have left a lot of people feeling up in the air and asking, "Where do I fit in? How do I stay relevant in my job? And what kind of skills do I need to learn at school?" The short answer is that the workplace is undergoing a fundamental restructuring that every educator, parent, and worker needs to understand. (Friedman & Mandelbaum, 2011, pp. 54, 72)

This fundamental restructuring of the economy and the workplace demands a new type of worker with a new set of skills. This is a person who can understand, use, and integrate knowledge, technology, and methods, as well as collaborate with persons from diverse cultural backgrounds with diverse disciplinary training. This person must be able to work with intangible information to produce a tangible product. Most tangible products are the result of integrating information from multiple and diverse knowledge domains, and they require working in teams. For example, designing an "app" for the Apple iPhone requires, at a minimum, the ability to integrate software, art, math, gaming, English grammar, marketing, law, database management, finance, and interpersonal communication—everything that goes into an application. In other words, designing an app requires a lot more training and creativity than just writing software code.

The world of business is becoming increasingly interdisciplinary because business is transacted within an increasingly fast-paced and complex environment that demands interdisciplinary skills to address this complexity. Among these skills, the ability to integrate knowledge from multiple disciplinary sources is critical. Jan Rivkin (2005), a professor in the Strategy Unit of the Harvard Business School, identifies the skills that are crucial for today's managers (see Box 1.2).

Box 1.2 Integrative Skills

Integrative skills are crucial. Managers who possess them can spot the core of an innovative strategy, grasp the implications for other parts of the company, and build out the idea relentlessly until it comes to pervade a company's entire value chain. They see, for instance, how improvements in a retailer's information system have implications for store location, store manager autonomy, pricing policy, and vendor relations. (Rivkin, 2005, p. 42)

The Need for Systems Thinking and Contextual Thinking

A third driver of interdisciplinary studies is the need for systems thinking and contextual thinking. Reduced to its most basic meaning for the purposes of this book, **systems thinking** is the ability to break a problem down into its constituent parts to reveal internal and external factors, figure out how each of these parts relates to the others and to the problem as a whole, and identify which parts different disciplines address. The ability to analyze systems is thus a key component of the increased job complexity discussed earlier. Addressing pressing public policy problems such as climate change or inner-city poverty also require systems thinking.

Everything we do takes place within systems. Examples of systems in which we operate daily include the environment, the economy, and transportation. It is useful to understand how complex systems function and how their various parts interrelate so we can understand how they affect our lives. We also need to understand the operation of complex systems so we can figure out which public policies to support.[1]

An example of a complex system is the U.S. economy. A key component of an economy is its central bank (e.g., the Federal Reserve, the "Fed," in the United States) and its power to set interest rates. By lowering the prime interest rate, the Fed impacts the U.S. economy in multiple ways, economic as well as noneconomic. First, a lower prime rate lowers the cost of loans to consumers, such as car loans (which has a positive effect on the economy by stimulating car sales and thereby increasing the number of cars produced, which means that manufacturers should eventually have to hire more workers). But a lower prime rate also lowers the interest rate that banks can pay on savings (which is negative because it reduces the interest income that retirees depend on to purchase things such as cars). There are also the unexpected political impacts of a reduction in the prime rate. For example, China (which already holds a substantial amount of U.S. national debt) may be less interested in purchasing more debt because of the lower rate of interest it would receive. So if you ask the question, "What interest rate *should* the nation's central bank charge?" answering it requires input from several disciplines including political science (which studies government policies and international relations), economics (which studies consumer behavior), philosophy (which studies ethics and logic), and possibly history (which studies historical patterns).

In addition to being able to apply systems thinking upon entering the globalized workplace, students need to be prepared to apply contextual thinking to complex problems. **Contextual thinking** is the ability to view a subject from a broad perspective by placing it in the fabric of time, culture, or personal experience. This kind of thinking, which is a primary focus of interdisciplinary learning, "is characterized by wholeness, by the relationship between parts, and by the assumption that knowledge changes" (King & Kitchener, 1994, p. 40).

---

1. Systems are arguably simple or complicated, not just complex, but all systems involving humans arguably are complex.

However, contextual thinking is not a primary learning outcome of traditional disciplinary majors. After completing their general requirements (which vary from university to university), many undergraduates specialize or "major" in a traditional discipline. As they proceed in their major, they are prone to develop a **silo perspective**, meaning the tendency to see the university and the larger world through the narrow lens of that major (see Figure 1.1). What a traditional major typically fails to provide is context—the context of the whole system—and the ability to view reality through multiple disciplinary lenses and make connections across different knowledge formations (see Figure 1.2).

In contrast, undergraduates pursuing an interdisciplinary field such as environmental studies, cultural studies, American studies, urban studies, and health management studies are taught to relate the smallest parts of the system they are studying to the whole. A hallmark of interdisciplinary studies is relating the particular to the whole by drawing on multiple disciplinary perspectives that are relevant to a specific problem or question. This feature is one of the reasons interdisciplinary studies is becoming a key component in liberal arts programs across the United States and elsewhere.

A liberal education fosters both systems thinking and contextual thinking. It develops the "integrative arts" necessary for meeting the challenges of our globalized world (Schneider, 2003). A liberal education helps you to learn how to learn, draw on multiple sources of knowledge, apply theory to practice in various settings, critically analyze information, integrate diverse and even conflicting points of view, collaborate with others in problem solving, and understand issues and positions contextually. A liberal education that emphasizes integrative and interdisciplinary learning—the ability to make connections—is well worth pursuing (Huber, Hutchings, & Gale, 2005, pp. 4–5).

Box 1.3 The Nature of the Academy

Students are rarely—even in general education programs—given a sense of how the academy as a whole is organized. The modern university has generally been structured around discipline-based departments. These departments usually have considerable autonomy in decisions about who to hire and what to teach. As we shall see in Chapter 4, disciplines are each characterized by a set of research questions, theories, and methods (and other characteristics). Universities may thus encompass scholars with expertise on every phenomenon that scholars study and every type of theory and method that they employ, but the university has no master strategy for best communicating this knowledge to students. Indeed, university presidents do not even have a visual map of what theories, methods, and subjects are addressed across their various departments (though it is possible to construct such a map). Universities may use their general education programs to achieve some broad overview of the scholarly project, but general education programs themselves often defer to departments and thus simply require students to take courses from several disciplines without providing much advice on how to draw connections across these courses. The various "studies" programs noted above have emerged in recent decades to allow insights from diverse disciplines into a common theme to be gathered (but not always integrated). Universities are still experimenting with the best way of achieving interdisciplinary understandings within an organizational structure designed with disciplines in mind. Should "studies" programs be freestanding departments, or should they employ faculty that are also appointed to a disciplinary department? How can general education programs best be structured so that students gain some sense of the academy as a whole and an idea of how to integrate insights from different disciplines? This book, and the literature on interdisciplinarity in which it is grounded, provides important input into these debates regarding the organization of the academy by showing that there is a coherent body of understanding about interdisciplinarity itself that all students should be exposed to.

It deserves emphasis that general education programs that expose students to different disciplinary perspectives but provide no encouragement toward integrating these can inadvertently encourage a narrow disciplinary focus. Students can become understandably frustrated when experts reach different conclusions about the same issue. They are then guided—likely subconsciously—to cling to the consensus within their disciplinary major. An exposure to interdisciplinary thinking—that there are reasons that experts disagree, that undergraduate students can understand these reasons and learn to evaluate and integrate differences in insights across disciplines—can transform frustration into excitement. Students should see coping with complexity as a challenge: It is not always easy, but there are techniques for proceeding toward a more comprehensive understanding. This book can only explore some of these techniques, but we hope nevertheless to fire students' excitement toward addressing complex questions.

The Changing Nature of University Research

A fourth driver of interdisciplinary studies is the changing nature of university research. Leaders of major U.S. scientific organizations are emphasizing the importance of increased interdisciplinarity. The reason, explains Rita Colwell (1998), former director of the National Science Foundation (NSF), is that "interdisciplinary connections are absolutely fundamental" because "it is at the interfaces of the sciences where the excitement will be most intense."

Figure 1.1   View From Inside a Silo

Source: ©iStockphoto.com/Michael Westhoff.

Emphasizing more interdisciplinary research is both financially and scientifically sensible, says Columbia University Professor Mark C. Taylor, because graduates are becoming too specialized to find employment due to the unsustainable nature of department-based hierarchies (Baskin, 2012). In 2011, the NSF dispatched one of its top officials and University of Michigan Professor Myron P. Gutmann to college campuses to promote the need for greater interdisciplinary research if they wish to win NSF grants. Gutmann notes that such research has yielded rapid advances in various fields, such as health care applications of atomic-scale science and the study of extreme weather events through analysis of both natural and social variables (see Box 1.4).

Similarly, the U.S. National Institutes of Health (2012) describes how interdisciplinary connection making is essential to the advancement of health research (see Box 1.5).

Box 1.4   Interdisciplinary Social Research

The social, behavioral, and economic sciences—familiarly known as the "SBE sciences"—increase fundamental understanding of human social development and interaction and of human behavior, as individuals and as members of groups and more formal organizations. Our sciences contribute knowledge that has societal relevance and can inform critical national areas such as job creation, health care, education, public safety, law enforcement, and national security, among others. NSF's SBE directorate is unique in that it houses a mosaic of related programs enabling fundamental research in crosscutting topics by combinations of economists, political scientists, sociologists, psychologists, linguists, neuroscientists, anthropologists, and other social and behavioral scientists. This focus on fundamental research allows us to collaborate effectively with our colleagues in other directorates and federal agencies to address problems that range from coastal flood response to the needs of an aging population to preparing our military with the insights they need to understand behavior in a changing world (Gutmann, 2011).

Box 1.5 Interdisciplinary Health Research

Health research traditionally has been organized much like a series of cottage industries, lumping researchers into specialty areas, where their efforts remain disconnected from the greater whole by artificial barriers constructed by technical and language differences between different disciplines and departmentally based specialties. But, as science has advanced over the past decade, two fundamental themes are apparent: The study of human biology and behavior is a wonderfully dynamic process, and the traditional divisions within health research may in some instances impede the pace of scientific discovery.

The broad goal for the [Interdisciplinary Research] Program, therefore, is to change academic research culture, both in the extramural research community and in the intramural program at the NIH, such that interdisciplinary approaches are facilitated. The . . . Program includes initiatives to dissolve academic department boundaries within academic institutions and increase cooperation between institutions, train scientists to cultivate interdisciplinary efforts, and build bridges between the biological sciences and the behavioral and social sciences. Collectively, these efforts are intended to change academic research culture so that interdisciplinary approaches and team science are a normal mode of conducting research and scientists who pursue these approaches are adequately recognized and rewarded. (U.S. National Institutes of Health, 2012, Overview section, para. 2)

Increasingly, the significant advances in knowledge production are occurring at the interdisciplinary borderlands between established disciplines and fields. (On team research, see Cooke & Hilton, 2015.)

Interdisciplinary Borderlands This perceived need to cross disciplinary boundaries in order to advance scientific progress is reflected in the results of the national survey of interdisciplinary programs at 222 colleges and universities conducted in 2006 by the Social Science Research Council (SSRC; see Table 1.1).

The Public World and Its Pressing Needs

The public world and its pressing needs is a fifth driver of interdisciplinary studies. The need to resolve problems of a general public interest is noted by the National Academy of Sciences (2005; see Box 1.6).

These public interest problems cannot be adequately addressed by individual disciplines because they require drawing on expertise from multiple disciplines: Should we genetically modify plants and animals? Is an affordable university

Table 1.1 Top 10 Interdisciplinary Majors and Percentage of Institutions Offering Major	
Top 10 Interdisciplinary Majors	**Percentage of Institutions Offering Major**
Intercultural studies*	13.08
Latin American studies*	16.82
African American and Africana studies***	21.50
International relations*	28.04
Asian and East Asian studies*	31.78
Biochemistry and molecular biology**	33.64
American studies*	36.45
Neuroscience and psychobiology**	36.45
Women's and gender studies***	44.86
Environmental studies and science** (could also be ***)	63.55

Source: Rhoten, D., Boix-Mansilla, V., Chun, M., & Klein, J. T. (2006). Interdisciplinary education at liberal arts institutions. Brooklyn, N.Y.: Social Science Research Council, 2006.

Note: that of the top 10 interdisciplinary majors, more than half are in global or area studies (*), three follow a biology-plus model (**), and the most popular are in areas often considered advocacy/activism fields (***). Also striking is that two thirds of respondents expected to increase interdisciplinary offerings over the next 5 years. "The most commonly cited motivation was research, based on the belief that the kinds of questions students and faculty are investigating today often require the expertise of scholars from more than one discipline" (Klein, 2010, p. 43).

Box 1.6 Interdisciplinarity and Technology

Human society depends more than ever on sound science for sound decision making. The fabric of modern life—its food, water, security, jobs, energy, transportation—is held together largely by techniques and tools of science and technology. But the application of technologies to enhance the quality of life can itself create problems that require technological solutions. Examples include the buildup of greenhouse gases (hence global warming), the use of artificial fertilizers (water pollution), nuclear power generation (radioactive waste), and automotive transportation (highway deaths, urban sprawl, and air pollution). (National Academy of Sciences, 2005, p. 34)

education a civic right? What is the meaning of populist movements such as the Tea Party and Occupy Wall Street? What are some of the causes of income inequality, and should we be concerned about it?

When addressing problems of general public interest, it is often necessary (and even preferable) to draw on expertise from public stakeholders. Such a **stakeholder** is a person or an entity outside the academy who is interested in and may have a material stake in the outcome of a particular societal issue. For example, community development projects in urban areas typically recruit expertise from relevant disciplines as well as from community institutions and interest groups. They join forces around complex societal issues of mutual concern such as homelessness, gang violence, affordable housing for low-income families, green spaces for recreation, public transportation, small business development, and venues for artists and musicians.

Community Development Interdisciplinarity has implications not just for global challenges such as climate change but for a host of more local concerns. Butterfield and Korazim-Korosy (2007) discuss both how and why to pursue community development in an explicitly interdisciplinary fashion. They argue that experts trained in many fields need to work collaboratively with community members. There are thus two types of collaboration and integration involved: among disciplines and between academy and community. Butterfield and Korazim-Korosy note that these disciplinary experts generally lack training or encouragement to support interdisciplinary interactions. Social work in particular is, like all professions, inherently interdisciplinary, but interdisciplinary techniques are not always taught to social work students.

Interdisciplinary courses often have a community-service-learning component, where students can apply their interdisciplinary skills (see Box 1.7). Students can then engage with the community and draw upon information from multiple disciplines in order to help develop community initiatives. Many students in interdisciplinary programs have an interest in addressing community challenges, and enter careers or volunteer roles later in life where they can apply interdisciplinary understandings in the pursuit of novel community programs.

Successful Intelligence and Integrative Thinking It is tempting to suppose that revolutionary insights and generative technologies come only from a gifted few such as a Bill Gates, a Steve Jobs, or a Mark Zuckerberg, or from massive government programs such as the Manhattan Project that produced the atomic bomb. Not so. Revolutionary insights and generative technologies require what Robert J. Sternberg (1996) calls "**successful intelligence**." Sternberg,

Box 1.7 Integrative Studies

Many colleges and universities these days have "Integrative Studies" initiatives that look beyond integrating academic material. They hope to connect students' course work with their residence life, volunteer activities, and more. These programs provide further evidence that integrative skills have value far beyond one's course work. And these programs find indeed that the integrative challenges students face outside the classroom are similar to and can be addressed in similar ways to the integrative challenges addressed within interdisciplinary courses. See Hughes, Munoz, and Tanner (2015).

one of the world's leading researchers and authorities on intelligence, says that successfully intelligent people think well in three different ways: creatively, analytically, and practically.

Sternberg describes the three types of intelligence that together make for "successful intelligence":

- **Creative intelligence** formulates ideas and makes connections.
- **Analytical intelligence** breaks a problem down into its component parts, solves problems, and evaluates the quality of ideas.
- **Practical intelligence** applies an idea in an effective way, whether in business or in everyday life.

What makes for successful intelligence, says Sternberg, is keeping these three ways of thinking in balance and knowing how and when to use each way of thinking.

Interdisciplinary learning fosters the development of all three components of "successful intelligence." First, it helps to build the creative thinking tools of observing, imaging, abstracting, recognizing patterns, forming patterns, analogizing, empathizing, modeling, transforming, and integrating. Second, it stresses the importance of breaking a problem down into its component parts and connecting each part (if applicable) to a discipline. Third, it values applying the result of the interdisciplinary project in a way that is practical and critical.

Producing revolutionary insights and generative technologies requires the ability to think integratively as illustrated in Figure 1.2. **Integrative thinking**, a defining characteristic of interdisciplinary learning, is the ability to knit together information from different sources to produce a more comprehensive understanding or create new meaning. Integrative thinking is a subject of Howard Gardner's *Five Minds for the Future* (2008).

The mind that is able to integrate and communicate complex ideas is one of the five minds that the fast-paced future will demand as described by Gardner in Box 1.8.

The rapidly changing workplace that Gardner describes highlights the need for interdisciplinary studies. Increasingly, workplaces need people who are educated in multiple disciplines, who know how to gather and integrate

Figure 1.2 Integrative Thinking

Source: ©iStockphoto.com/danleap.

Box 1.8 The Interdisciplinary Mind

Against all odds, individuals seek synthesis. . . . [The] most ambitious form of synthesis occurs in *interdisciplinary work* [emphasis added]. Biochemists combine biological and chemical knowledge; historians of science apply the tools of history to one or more fields of science. In professional life, interdisciplinarity is typically applied to a team composed of workers who have different professional training. In a medical setting, an interdisciplinary team might consist of one or more surgeons, anesthesiologists, radiologists, nurses, therapists, and social workers. In a business setting, an interdisciplinary or cross-functional team might feature inventors, designers, marketers, the sales force, and representatives drawn from different levels of management. The cutting-edge interdisciplinary team members are granted considerable latitude on the assumption that they will exit their habitual silos and engage in the boldest forms of connection making. (Gardner, 2008, p. 54)

knowledge from those disciplines, and who know how to apply that knowledge to complex problems. Because the pace of job destruction and job creation is increasing, students entering today's workforce will not only need to change jobs several times in the course of their working life but also need to change careers. According to Andrew Ross (2012), "no one, not even in the traditional professions, can any longer expect a fixed pattern of employment in the course of their lifetime." This means that you must learn to be flexible and develop a broad range of cognitive and technical skills that you can apply as your jobs and careers change. Interdisciplinary learning provides you with the cognitive abilities and values that will enable you to integrate information and synthesize new solutions.

A Knowledge Society Needs
Both Disciplinarity and Interdisciplinarity

A sixth driver of interdisciplinary studies is the awareness that a knowledge society needs *both* disciplinarity and interdisciplinarity. Science and society now recognize that disciplinarity and interdisciplinarity are not mutually exclusive but are complementary within a knowledge society (Frodeman & Mitcham, 2007, p. 1).

A **knowledge society** is one in which the development and creative application of knowledge is the primary engine of economic growth, prosperity, and empowerment of all developing sectors of society. According to Robert Frodeman and Carl Mitcham (2007),

> Knowledge *production* today has a tendency to swamp knowledge *use systems* [emphasis added] at both the individual and institutional levels. Overwhelmed by knowledge, we find it increasingly difficult to make good decisions—or, Hamlet-like, any decision at all. . . . [P]oliticians, [for example], when faced with difficult problems, often call for more research as a way to stall for time. (p. 2)

In addition to data overload, Frodeman and Mitcham assert that our knowledge society is increasingly characterized by a disconnect between knowledge production and knowledge utilization (see Box 1.9).

Box 1.9 Knowledge Production Versus Utilization

This disconnect is in part the result of the sheer volume of information being produced. Disciplines pursue more and more specialization and detail, crowding out awareness of ends or purposes. Interdisciplinary efforts are often characterized as shallow, but this is true only in comparison with the [silo] narrowness of depth in disciplinary detail and specialization. It's equally the case that the disciplines are unable to offer any width and breadth of contextualization. Moreover, no epistemological justification is offered for why we should prioritize the vertical as compared to the horizontal dimensions of knowledge. In what sense does a PhD know something more valuable than a person with three masters? As important as disciplinary depth is, [equally important is] knowledge of the overall topographic landscape of human affairs. (Frodeman & Mitcham, 2007, pp. 2–3)

The Academic Benefits of Pursuing an Interdisciplinary Studies Degree

Fortunately, once close-minded disciplines and applied fields are beginning to recognize that interdisciplinarity is necessary for four practical reasons. (1) Interdisciplinarians—that is, scholars familiar with strategies for integrating insights from diverse disciplines—are uniquely equipped to ask and answer questions about complex issues that transcend the confines of single disciplines. (2) By placing complex issues in a broad context, interdisciplinarians raise

additional questions that often challenge societal values. For example, addressing environmental sustainability raises questions about human freedom and responsibility and the proper roles of the public and private sectors.
(3) Interdisciplinarity offers a process that enables you to effectively integrate knowledge drawn from relevant disciplines. *This process enables you to go as deep into as many disciplines as is necessary or appropriate to grasp the essentials of the problem, to see the problem in the broadest possible context, to integrate expert insights into it, and to construct a more comprehensive understanding of it.* (This process is the subject of Part III of this book.) (4) Pursuing interdisciplinary studies empowers you in five ways:

a. To deal with complex societal problems. Interdisciplinary courses and programs typically focus on complex subjects such as the environment, sustainability, rights, politics, justice, and public health. These are *civic issues* in that they impact society as a whole. Interdisciplinary pedagogies (i.e., methods of teaching) prepare you for civic engagement by creating a classroom experience that encourages openness, dialogue, and mutual respect. Civic engagement flows from a sense of empathy and ethical consciousness.

b. To effectively translate your education to new contexts, new problems, and new responsibilities. Civic engagement means using political as well as nonpolitical means to affect the quality of life in a community. Civic engagement is advanced as you appreciate diversity, tolerate ambiguity, and develop a sense of responsibility for the community *as a whole*.

c. To think and act *effectively* on complex problems without getting overwhelmed or cowed by disciplinary experts or resorting to digging in your heels. It is OK to acknowledge that people with whom you disagree make valid points because you know how to proceed toward integration in the face of disagreement.

d. To know how to find and evaluate information relevant to the complex problems you will face in life. In an age of information overload, you need to know how to look for information and then to assess its reliability.

e. To develop a more holistic understanding of your personal identity (see Box 1.10).

An extensive assessment of student learning outcomes at the University of North Dakota found that interdisciplinary learning (and participation in interdisciplinary learning communities) significantly enhanced both academic achievement and degree completion. The assessment exercise also found that interdisciplinary students were more engaged and showed higher skill achievement. These results are likely connected to improved academic achievement (see Carmichael & LaPierre, 2014). We return to the question of skills in Chapter 4.

Box 1.10   Integrating Personal Identity

Our colleagues at Norfolk State University have an intriguing assignment in their Introduction to Interdisciplinarity course. They have students create videos in which they take an interdisciplinary approach to the question of personal identity (drawing on Crenshaw's 2014 research on intersectionality). Personal identities are complex, with multiple meanings, and intersect across race, class, gender, and sexuality, while reflecting experiences of family, government, economy, education, and religion. Increasingly, technology serves as a highly relevant vehicle or tool for crafting a cohesive identity. Note that these various aspects of who we are need not always align: We may, for example, have aspirations that are quite different from what our parents want(ed) us to do. Interdisciplinarity can help us, then, to achieve a more holistic understanding of who we are. Moreover, this project provides a space for students to reflexively engage interdisciplinarity and subsequently illustrates that interdisciplinary understandings are useful for far more than just integrating across disciplines. We are happy to report that through utilizing technology, students often incorporate interdisciplinarity as part of their identity.

Interdisciplinary Studies and Your Career Development

Recently, Bloomberg Business published a study of skills across U.S. industries that recruiters considered "most important" and "hardest to find." The study included the graphic shown in Figure 1.3, which is divided into four quadrants as follows: The upper left are skills "less common, less desired"; the upper right are skills "less common, more desired"; the bottom left are skills "more common, less desired"; the bottom right are skills "more common, more desired" (Levy & Cannon, 2016, p. 2).

Figure 1.3 The Skills Gap

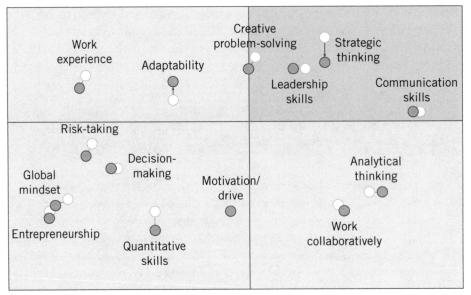

Less common, less desired   **Less common, more desired**

Work experience

Adaptability

Creative problem-solving

Strategic thinking

Leadership skills

Communication skills

Risk-taking

Global mindset

Decision-making

Entrepreneurship

Motivation/drive

Quantitative skills

Analytical thinking

Work collaboratively

More common, less desired   **More common, more desired**

Source: The Skills Gap (2016). [Interactive graphic showing desirable traits by industry]. "The Bloomberg Job Skills Report 2016: What Recruiters Want" by Francesca Levy and Christopher Cannon, February 9, 2016. http://www.bloomberg.com/graphics/2016-job-skills-report/. Used with permission of Bloomberg L.P. Copyright© 2016. All rights reserved.

We could hardly ask for better evidence that interdisciplinarity education aids employability: The skills identified by recruiters are independently identified as outcomes in studies of interdisciplinary programs. Strategic thinking blends creativity, analysis, and practical understanding as discussed above. And by encouraging students to see issues from multiple perspectives— and communicate—interdisciplinarity prepares students for teamwork and leadership. We discuss the other three more desired skills in more detail here.

Communication. IDS programs typically emphasize the skills of effective communication and productive collaboration. The communication in view here is of two kinds. The first is the ability to communicate across interdisciplinary boundaries. This communication is possible because, despite the differences in jargon, there is overlap among the assumptions, concepts, theories, and methods used by the disciplines as well as underlying recurring patterns in both natural phenomena and human behavior that are perceived across disciplines. In many cases, each of the disciplines is saying something similar about the nature of the world, only in a different language. The second is the ability to engage in productive communication with students and coworkers who hold a variety of interests, beliefs, and mind-sets, even if some of these sharply conflict with and differ from yours. IDS programs typically promote this skill by involving students in team work, which fosters the skill of working collaboratively.

Creative problem solving. Interdisciplinarity advances creative approaches to solving complex intellectual and practical problems. In interdisciplinary work, **creativity** involves bringing together different perspectives and previously unrelated ideas, discovering commonalities among them, and combining them into a more comprehensive understanding. This new understanding should be both novel and useful, the defining characteristics of a creative solution.

Analytical thinking. Interdisciplinarity typically emphasizes analytical thinking that is required to evaluate the quality of ideas and solve complex problems, whether intellectual or practical. Developing this skill begins in the classroom and is then transferable to real-world settings. Outside of the academy, problems are of the real-world variety. For example, in a research lab, scientists do not work on problems whose solutions can be readily discovered simply and mechanistically by applying known formulas. Instead, they tackle problems whose solutions are yet unknown and must be found. Solutions to these real-world problems require analytical as well as intuitive and speculative strategies that work sometimes but not other times. Innovative companies such as Apple, Google, and Facebook value people who think analytically and creatively. As one transformative product is being introduced to the market, another is already under development. Analytical thinking is required to know the market for a product, while creative thinking is what produces products in the first place and keeps them coming out (Sternberg, 1996, pp. 136, 141).

Our colleagues at West Virginia University survey graduates in the years following their interdisciplinary and multidisciplinary studies programs. In the survey in 2014, 112 of 118 respondents (95%) reported that they were employed. They provided a wide range of occupations: 39% were in customer-related areas of business such as real estate and sales, 20% were in other areas of business such as human resources, 23% were in education, 13% in health care, and 9% in government service. Importantly, satisfaction with the degree—an impressive 84% and rising as the program is developed—varied little across careers. While we must be careful in drawing conclusions from one survey at one university, the indication is that graduates of interdisciplinary studies programs find their education useful across a wide range of occupations.

CRITICAL THINKING QUESTIONS

1. How is globalization affecting your education, and how you are preparing for life after university?

2. Why is the ability to engage in systems thinking, contextualization, perspective taking, and integrative thinking important when it comes to addressing complex problems?

3. Why is interdisciplinary connection making essential to the advancement of knowledge?

4. After reading Box 1.8, explain how the humanities can aid our understanding of problems traditionally considered to fall within the research

domain of the sciences, such as genetically modifying animals or public funding for educating special needs children.

5. How does interdisciplinary studies foster the development of creative intelligence?

6. Identify a generative technology (other than the iPhone or iPad) and explain how it is likely the product of integrating knowledge from multiple sources.

7. Explain why major funding agencies that support faculty research and thus shape the agenda of higher education are increasingly emphasizing the importance of interdisciplinarity.

APPLICATIONS AND EXERCISES

1. From your reading of this chapter, comment on this statement: "Today's graduates will *not* be entering a career that lasts a lifetime but a lifetime of multiple careers." How should you prepare academically for this new reality?

2. Other than the economy and the university, what other system is impacting your life, and how?

3. Of Sternberg's three types of "successful intelligence," which type(s) do you believe you already possess, and which do you believe you need to develop further? Explain why.

4. If you know what career or profession you plan to pursue, describe how it has changed in recent years. Identify the critical skills that the career/profession requires. If you are undecided about your future career or profession, select one that you think might interest you. In either case, do you feel that your present abilities and skills "fit" the job or profession? How might the abilities and skills that interdisciplinarity fosters improve the "fit"?

5. Identify an unresolved complex problem at your place of work (or the place of work of someone you know) and explain how an interdisciplinary approach could possibly aid its resolution.

6. Much has happened in our world since the list of popular majors appearing in Table 1.1 was constructed. Given the realities of the world today and the trends discussed in this chapter, what changes in this list do you anticipate 5 years from now?

7. What are the key elements of your personal identity, and are there challenges in integrating these?

Note: Any of these questions, but perhaps especially 4, 5, and 6, could also be used to motivate group discussions on the value of interdisciplinarity. Students could seek to identify and appreciate the perspectives of others in their group.

Chapter 2 Objectives

In any university (whether physical or virtual), you will definitely encounter the disciplines in the general education core or in a traditional major or in a theme-based multidisciplinary or interdisciplinary studies program. The disciplines are powerful and pervasive approaches to learning and knowledge production. They shape our perceptions of the world, our ability to address complexity, and our understanding of others and ourselves. Less than 200 years old in their modern form, they have come to dominate the ordering, production, and communication of knowledge.

Today, disciplinary dominance is being challenged by interdisciplinarity. This chapter addresses three key questions. First, how did the modern disciplines develop and come to have the near-monopoly status on learning and research that they presently enjoy? Second, how do we account for the emergence of interdisciplinarity, its great diversity, and rapid growth? Third, what, specifically, are interdisciplinary studies' criticisms of the disciplines and disciplinary specialization? Though the chapter draws on many European thinkers, space does not allow us to trace the institutional rise of interdisciplinarity in countries where there has been increased interest in interdisciplinarity in recent decades.

The Rise of the Modern Disciplines and Interdisciplinarity

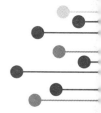

Why the Past Matters

One of the most important but overlooked buildings in Washington, D.C., is the National Archives.

Engraved in its stonework in bold letters is this motto: "The past is prologue." This quote from Shakespeare's *The Tempest* (Act III, Scene 1) has a meaning that is both simple and profound: The past affects the present. The motto is appropriate to this building because it holds the three original documents that formed the United States, defined its government, and still inform the exercise of government today: the Declaration of Independence, the Constitution, and the Bill of Rights. It also exhibits other original documents of great importance, including Lincoln's Emancipation Proclamation. These documents communicate the timeless values of "equality," "inalienable rights," and "freedom" that illumine the present and animate the worldwide movement toward freedom and democracy.

Learning Outcomes

By the end of this chapter, you will be able to:

- Explain the rise of the modern disciplines and how they have come to enjoy near-monopoly status in learning and research

- Explain the rise of interdisciplinarity, its great diversity, and rapid growth

- Understand interdisciplinary studies' critique of the disciplines and disciplinary specialization

The past, whether it concerns a nation's founding values, the prevailing system of learning and knowledge production, or the emergence of the concept of interdisciplinarity, is relevant for four practical reasons:

- The past shapes our identity and the core of our humanity.
- Probing the past enables us to discover roots, detect change, and discern trends.
- Reflecting on the past enables us to reconstruct cause and effect and act in the world as moral agents.
- Studying the past makes the present comprehensible.

More specifically, understanding the past is relevant to those in the natural sciences whose climate models, for example, must include data on past conditions to place present climate conditions in broad historical context. For those in the social sciences, understanding the past is essential to understanding the root causes of present societal problems. For those in the humanities, a full understanding of objects and texts is possible only by placing them in historical context. For those in the fine and performing arts, the past is always present in new forms of dance, theater, and music. And for those in applied fields such as criminal justice, public health, or business, studying past laws, practices, and business models shows what has worked and not worked.

Understanding why things are the way they are is foundational to learning. The present dominance of the disciplines is rooted in the past. It would be easy to look at the modern academy and assume that it had always been organized around disciplines. But we shall see that disciplinarity in general, as well as the shape of individual disciplines, is the result of fairly recent historical processes. Discovering how the modern disciplines gained institutional structure and power and why they now dominate learning and knowledge production is foundational

Figure 2.1 The National Archives of the United States

Source: Photograph of the United States National Archives Building, Washington D.C. by David Samuels, http://en.wikipedia.org/wiki/File:US_National_Archives_Building.jpg. Licensed under the Creative Commons Attribution-Share Alike 3.0 unported license. https://creativecommons.org/licenses/by-sa/3.0/us/.

to understanding why the contemporary university is organized around the disciplines. Studying the past also explains the rise of interdisciplinarity and how this transformational concept has been able to challenge disciplinary dominance and sustain itself as a recognized approach to learning and knowledge production.

The Rise of the Modern Disciplines

As a preview of this brief probing of the past, we offer a list of the far-reaching effects that the historical shift in knowledge production and teaching toward disciplinarity produced. Since interdisciplinary studies arose in response to these developments, you should understand the factors that caused knowledge to be divided into disciplines in the first place:

- *Specialization, fragmentation, and* **reductionism** (the strategy of dividing a thing into its constituent parts and studying them separately)

- *Empiricism* (the basis for new knowledge in factual evidence derived from sensory inputs, not in conjecture, faith, or imagination)

- *Professionalization* (the need to apply education to specific sectors of society)

- *Legitimatization* (the granting of academic degrees)

- *Departmentalization* (the forming of specialized functioning areas in the university)

You should look for these factors as you read the following discussion.

The Origin of the Concept of Disciplinarity

We stress developments in the West because these had a direct bearing on the development of interdisciplinarity. The term "discipline" was introduced as "disciplina" by the Romans. But in both Roman and medieval times it was applied to a limited set of professions such as the law and medicine, in recognition of the fact that these required the learning of specialized information (Klein, 1990). Note that only some professions received attention in universities of the Middle Ages: Though engineers and artists existed, there were no "disciplines" of agricultural or mechanical or military engineering or theatre arts (Saffle, 2005). Not until the twentieth century would these fields be absorbed into the academic curriculum of the Western university, and some of them play a role in the history of interdisciplinarity. Outside of the professions, all students received the same broad general education.

The Scientific Revolution of the sixteenth through eighteenth centuries is associated with an increased insistence on testing theories through careful observation or experiment. The revolution also became associated with scientific specialization. As the body of received theory and observation in separate fields such as astronomy or chemistry or botany grew, it became increasingly difficult for any one person to keep abreast of more than one field of inquiry. The very first academic journals, which emerged in the seventeenth century (creatures of the British and French Royal Scientific Societies), were general in coverage but nevertheless encouraged increasingly separate discussions of different fields of inquiry. While the idea of science as a unified endeavor was still embraced, in practice most scientists knew only one field of inquiry well.

Between 1750 and 1800, the disciplines consolidated their hold on the teaching and production of knowledge by embracing three new revolutionizing learning techniques: writing, grading, and examinations. These practices were introduced in three new teaching settings: the seminar (beginning in the German universities around 1760), the laboratory (beginning in the French *Grandes Écoles* before the Revolution), and the classroom (beginning in Scotland around 1760). The doctorate, originated at the Humboldt University of Berlin in the early nineteenth century, was adopted by Yale University in 1861, and soon thereafter by other American universities. From the United States, the doctorate spread to Canada in 1900, then to the United Kingdom in 1917, and today has become common in large parts of the world.

The university and the disciplines became an engine of knowledge production that far outstripped any other method of learning devised by any previous civilization. There would be major advances in understanding across a wide range of disciplines in the nineteenth and twentieth centuries. These practices have been so successful that today they are used the world over.

The Professionalization of Knowledge

The academic disciplines of today and the modern concept of disciplinarity are largely the product of developments in the late nineteenth and early twentieth centuries. This period saw the formation of new categories of knowledge. Natural philosophy was divided into physics, chemistry, and mathematics, whereas natural history became biology.

By the middle of the nineteenth century, the social sciences were fragmenting into anthropology and political economy, out of which were formed economics and political science. The disciplines of psychology, sociology, and history soon followed. These disciplines arose to address new social conditions and applied a scientific and distinctively empirical approach to studying the problems of a rapidly industrializing and urbanizing society (Easton, 1991, p. 11).

The disciplines that became known as the humanities—philosophy, classical and modern languages, history, art history, and religious studies—"formed a rump of knowledge" that was left over after the other new specialties were formed (Easton, 1991; Frodeman & Mitcham, 2007, p. 4). Since few humanist scholars protested the rise of disciplinarity and the emphasis on research, the humanities soon accommodated themselves to the new order of knowledge production.

Along with the rise of scientific specialties came increased competition for university resources, so universities began to organize themselves around the disciplines. This academic revolution was led by a small number of visionaries. In 1869, Harvard University president Charles William Elliot introduced the concept of the major and the elective system for undergraduates, which began replacing the general studies degree.

These developments were accompanied by the emergence of new professional societies in the United States. National organizations emerged in history in 1884, economics in 1885, political science in 1903, and sociology in 1905 (Hershberg, 1981). The Modern Language Association was founded in 1883 (Moran, 2010) and remains one of the leading organizations dedicated to the study and teaching of literature and language.

Disciplinary journals allowed geographically isolated specialists to keep abreast of the latest research and also gave them a forum for presenting their own research. Specialists did not need to consider perspectives other than those of their own specialty (Swoboda, 1979).

As the modern research university took shape, disciplinarity was reinforced in two major ways. First, the disciplines recruited students to their ranks to produce a new generation of teachers and researchers. Second, industries demanded and received specialists from the universities (Klein, 1990). The trend toward specialization, especially in the sciences, was further propelled by increasingly more expensive instrumentation, elaborately equipped laboratories, and highly trained personnel.

The increased emphasis by universities on research in the late nineteenth century reflected in turn the fact that many of the natural sciences had become economically useful. The link between science and useful technology had been tenuous through much of history, but in the late nineteenth century, developments in chemistry (dyes and pharmaceuticals) and physics (various electrical products) in particular had direct implications for technology. This era thus marked the transition to an economy increasingly dependent on scientific research and the end of the "tinkerer tradition" of innovators such as Thomas Edison and Henry Ford. A related development that would have far-reaching implications for the future of higher education was the integration that was occurring not between knowledge specialties but between industry and education (see Figure 2.2). For example, discipline-based studies in service of industrial concerns were (and remain) a major part of chemistry's history. As for the social sciences and humanities, the Progressive Movement in the United States held out hope that society could be improved through better understanding; the link between social science and public policy was not as strong as the link between natural science and technology but could be used to justify specialized research in the social sciences and humanities as well. The traditional role of the university in providing a shared body of knowledge to students became increasingly focused on the humanities: The disciplines of history, literature, and philosophy were each called upon to celebrate the inheritance of "Western Civilization."

Figure 2.2   Scientists in a Chemical Laboratory

Source: ©iStockphoto.com/&#169 Alexander Raths.

Only in the last decades of the nineteenth century, then, do we see disciplines with three key characteristics: deciding what is taught through the departmental structure, deciding what is good research through dedicated journals managed by disciplinary associations, and deciding who gets hired and promoted through decisions by both departments and journals. It is these three characteristics that we can associate with the word *disciplinarity*. Note that the third characteristic reinforces the first two: Individuals will only be hired and promoted if they broadly concur with the research and teaching emphases of the discipline.

It should be stressed that disciplines slowly evolve over time as new research questions, theories, and methods are embraced. In the discipline of economics, for example, one can detect several important changes over the last century and a half, including the development of a different approach to the study of the aggregate economy from that used to study individual markets in the aftermath of the Great Depression, insistence on mathematical expression of research results in the early postwar period, and a more recent willingness to relax an assumption that humans behave rationally.

Concerns About Overspecialization

Not everyone, however, saw greater disciplinary specialization as a positive development. Already in the early 1700s, the Italian thinker Giambattista Vico called for a new approach to learning. He claimed that the ascendancy of science and mathematics in the curriculum had led to a neglect of broad education in favor of specialized knowledge. He argued that the "human sciences" such as history, philosophy, and law can achieve knowledge and understanding "from within" and in fact are superior to the natural sciences, which can only describe the external phenomena in nature (Moran, 2010). Nevertheless, Vico's call for less specialization and a more comprehensive approach to learning largely fell on deaf ears. His critique was the forerunner of many critiques, including those that contributed to the formation of the field of interdisciplinary studies two centuries later.

The proliferation of academic disciplines from the late nineteenth century naturally increased concerns regarding overspecialization, in particular how these new disciplines were connected to issues of power and self-interest. Late nineteenth-century German philosopher Friedrich Nietzsche and early twentieth-century Spanish philosopher José Ortega y Gasset saw the new disciplines as symptoms of a more general phenomenon: the growing *interdependence* of government, business, and education. Driving this interdependence was an economic system that increasingly depended on the availability of specialists and professionals. Under this system, the disciplines and the universities served two vital functions: They trained persons for careers in government and business, and they gave these new professions legitimacy and status by providing them with academic credentials (Moran, 2010).

The Rise of Interdisciplinarity

Once the disciplines were established by the end of the nineteenth and the early twentieth centuries, it was only logical that interest in interdisciplinarity would begin to develop. "Seen in the broad sweep of Western civilization," writes Newell (2010b), "interdisciplinarity is the latest response to the dominant Western intellectual tradition of rationality and reductionism that is ultimately grounded in dichotomous [i.e., either–or] thinking" (p. 360). In the United States, the advance of the interdisciplinarity concept began after World War I with the quest for an integrated educational experience by influential education leaders. It gained momentum in the 1960s with the development of experimental colleges; achieved legitimacy as part of the liberal mainstream in the 1980s as honors, women's studies, and environmental studies programs embraced it; emerged in the 1990s as a small but normal part of university education; and achieved "fad" status in the first decade of the new millennium (p. 361). At each stage, how interdisciplinarity was understood and practiced changed.

The Quest for an Integrated Educational Experience

The story of the interdisciplinary idea in the United States begins with the movement to reform general education after World War I. This effort was a response to two problems besetting American culture and education at the time. The first was the perceived lack of national cultural unity resulting from the massive influx of immigrants in previous decades. The second was the eroding cohesiveness of university education produced by disciplinary specialization (Boyer, 1981). The belief animating the general education reform movement was that both these problems could be solved by creating an integrated educational experience that prepared students for modern life (see Box 2.1).

There were differing conceptions of the kind of reform needed. One emphasized the importance of passing on the classical and secular ideals of Western culture through a common core of "great books" (see Figure 2.3).

Box 2.1 General Education

Without a general education, human beings tend to be somewhat parochial. We are disinclined to think beyond the scope of direct human experience—to factors or forces that operate on different scales of time or space, that function systematically rather than individually, or that have multiple causes; nor are we inclined to see a problem from other perspectives (be they grounded in cultures, religions, or disciplines). Even well-educated humans have some difficulty moving back and forth between the general and the specific, theory and application, the abstract and the concrete. Interdisciplinary studies provide an approach in which such skills become habits of mind; they fall naturally out of the interdisciplinary process. (Newell, 2010b, p. 361)

The second conception focused on historically situated problems of society such as racism. John Dewey sought to balance the need to pass on the Western cultural heritage with the need to critique its failings. Dewey advocated engaging students in discussing pressing social and political issues by exposing them to different perspectives (Newell, 2010b, p. 362). What these conceptions held in common was the notion that general education is "the place where all the parts would add up to a cohesive whole" (Hutcheson, 1997, pp. 109–110).

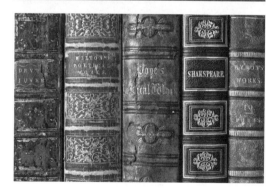

Figure 2.3 Examples of Great Books of the Western Intellectual Tradition

Source: ©iStockphoto.com/221A.

Interdisciplinarity in the 1960s and 1970s

After World War II, a second general education reform movement emerged, triggered by the 1945 Harvard report *General Education in a Free Society*. The report called for a new general education curriculum based on the sciences and writings of the European humanist tradition. Against the backdrop of the spread of communism and the growing power of the Soviet Union, proponents intended the curriculum to provide a common core of knowledge, beliefs, and values centered on the ideals of freedom and democracy—in short, a national ideology that could oppose Soviet totalitarianism and communist ideology (Bender, 1997).

Against this backdrop of ideological conformity, criticism of the disciplines intensified and focused on two themes. The first was the enormous power that the disciplines had accumulated since the turn of the century. Influenced by Friedrich Nietzsche, French philosopher Michel Foucault argued in the 1960s that the disciplines are not just a way to produce knowledge; they are a sophisticated mechanism for regulating human conduct and social relations. He found the examination to be the "quintessential practice that epitomizes both the modern power of knowledge and the modern practice of meticulous disciplinary control" (Hoskin, 1993, p. 277). (See Box 2.2.)

Box 2.2   Disciplinary Power

[Normalization] has become one of the major functions of our society. The judges of normality are present everywhere. We are in the society of the teacher-judge, the doctor-judge, the educator-judge, the "social worker"-judge; it is on them that the universal reign of the normative is based; and each individual, wherever he may find himself, subjects to it his body, his gestures, his behavior, his aptitudes, his achievements. . . .

The carceral [i.e., prison-like] texture of society assures both the real capture of the body and its perpetual observation [and characterizes] the new economy of power. . . . [T]he instrument of knowledge that this very economy needs [and] its most indispensable condition [is the] activity of examination. (Foucault, 1975, pp. 304–305)

Challenge question: How does Foucault's critique of "normalization" apply to traditional education? How does interdisciplinary studies challenge the "normal" in education today?

The second criticism focused on the deepening isolation of the disciplines from each other. The disciplines had marginalized the notion of holistic thinking in favor of reductionist thinking. Tony Becher (1989) uses the anthropological metaphor of tribes to describe the disciplines, each having its own culture and language (see Box 2.3).

Interdisciplinarity in the 1960s and 1970s was part of a radical rejection of traditional education. The critique of the disciplines was strengthened by the confluence of three

Box 2.3   Disciplinary Tribes

Men of the sociology tribe rarely visit the land of the physicists and have little idea what they do over there. If the sociologists were to step into the building occupied by the English department, they would encounter the cold stares if not the slingshots of the hostile natives. . . . The disciplines exist as separate estates, with distinctive subcultures. (Becher, 1989, p. 23)

major developments: civil tensions over the issue of race, political tensions over the Vietnam War, and social tensions over marginalized groups. Combined, these tensions and conflicts served as a catalyst from which emerged calls for more holistic forms of education and experimental programs and new thinking about how the academy should relate to society (Mayville, 1978).

Challenge question: How does interdisciplinary studies and/or the theme-based program you are in challenge disciplinary tribalism with each discipline having its own culture and language?

This new thinking included calls for radical university reforms, one central element of which was the elimination of the traditional academic disciplines in favor of more holistic notions of training that were closer to the practical problems of life (Weingart, 2000). The reason was obvious: The disciplines and the scholarship that they produced had failed to explain, or had ignored, the great social movements and ideological struggles that characterized the period (see Figure 2.4). To that generation of students and young faculty, "the disciplines seemed increasingly irrelevant or even obstructionist to their quest to understand, address, and solve the great issues of the day" (Katz, 2001). By contrast, interdisciplinarity became a programmatic, value-laden term that stood for reform, innovation, progress, and opening up the university to all kinds of hitherto marginalized publics (Weingart, 2000).

The radicalism of the 1960s and 1970s spawned the creation of new fields such as African American ("Black," at first) studies, women's studies, and ethnic studies, and new topics such as environmental studies, development studies, and urban studies. During the 1970s, researchers with an interdisciplinary orientation began tackling problems such as poverty and social medicine. At the same time, interdisciplinarity became identified with the development of experimental colleges and radical curricular experiments within more traditional institutions. However, within the young field,

Figure 2.4 Civil Rights March

Source: ©PhotoQuest/ArchivePhotos/Getty Images.

> tensions were increasing between those who wanted to embrace
> the disciplines and then transcend them, and those who
> rejected the legitimacy of disciplines; and those who sought
> rigor in interdisciplinarity, and those who saw interdisciplinarity
> as freedom; and those who strove for intentionality in
> integration, and those who embraced serendipity. (Newell,
> 2010b, p. 363)

By the late 1970s, when the social struggles had subsided and mundane academic routine had returned to the universities, the call for interdisciplinarity became much less urgent. "What had seemed progressive only a few years earlier appeared outdated, if not quaint" (Weingart, 2000). Nevertheless, a legacy tradition was established.

Interdisciplinarity Acquires Academic Legitimacy in the 1980s and 1990s

In the early 1980s, interdisciplinarity began to acquire academic legitimacy when, for example, the National Collegiate Honors Society declared that "honors" was "synonymous" with interdisciplinarity, thus linking it with quality and rigor. Women's studies programs asserted that they were interdisciplinary by their very nature, which, in this instance, linked interdisciplinarity with critiques of the academy in general and the disciplines in particular. Environmental studies also embraced the interdisciplinary impulse by seeking to pull together insights from a variety of disciplines to form holistic conceptions such as ecosystems (Newell, 2010b, p. 362).

While such developments helped to legitimize interdisciplinarity, they also encouraged "divergent views about the relationships between the disciplines and interdisciplinarity (are they complementary or antagonistic?) and perpetuated the impression that the nature of interdisciplinarity is self-evident" (Newell, 2010b, p. 362). To counteract this thinking and clarify the nature and practice of interdisciplinarity, interdisciplinarians founded professional associations such as INTERSTUDY (in the sciences and research) and the Association for Integrative Studies (AIS), which changed its name to the Association for Interdisciplinary Studies in 2013. The AIS founded a journal, *Issues in Integrative Studies* (which changed its name to *Issues in Interdisciplinary Studies* in 2013), that for over three decades has facilitated a focused conversation about the form that interdisciplinary teaching and research should take.

In the 1990s, two developments converged to affect interdisciplinarity in both a positive and a negative way. The first was that interdisciplinarity received further legitimacy as educators widely viewed it as part of a package of curricular and pedagogical innovations. These included collaborative learning, multicultural education, learning communities, inquiry- and problem-based learning, writing across the curriculum, civic education, service learning, and study abroad. While the antagonism between interdisciplinarity and the disciplines was being reduced, a second, more subtle, development occurred: Interdisciplinarity was being accepted by a wider range of discipline-based faculty who were unfamiliar with its origins and character. By the new millennium, the historic roots of interdisciplinarity were lost and the range of conceptions of interdisciplinarity had grown wider and fuzzier (Newell, 2010b, p. 363). Many faculty naively assumed that "we are *all* doing interdisciplinarity." This "anything goes" attitude prompted one critic of interdisciplinarity to complain in the prestigious *Chronicle of Higher Education* that interdisciplinarity has become "so fuzzy that a university's commitment to it is close to meaningless" (Wasserstrom, 2006, p. B5).

We have stressed above the emergence of interdisciplinary *teaching* in the twentieth century. But this development—and especially the casual acceptance of interdisciplinarity by many in disciplines—owed much to an increased recognition of the value of interdisciplinary *research*. As we saw in Chapter 1, there has been an increased recognition in recent decades that a range of complex problems—climate change, inner-city poverty, racism—require interdisciplinary analysis. The development of interdisciplinary teaching would always have been a challenge within the modern research-oriented university (and indeed often proceeded fastest in smaller liberal arts college which prioritized teaching) unless supplemented by an interest in interdisciplinary research. But as university presidents and research-granting agencies came to laud interdisciplinary research, the incentive grew to claim that one was interdisciplinary without reflecting on what this means.

These faculty who embraced an "anything goes" attitude to interdisciplinarity were largely unaware of the burgeoning literature that was clarifying the nature of interdisciplinarity and preparing it to enter the new millennium on a coherent and rigorous footing. The tireless and prolific work of interdisciplinarians such as Julie Thompson Klein, William H. Newell, and Rick Szostak was reinforced by a flurry of highly visible national reports by prestigious groups and path-breaking books and articles by key interdisciplinary scholars revealing the details of an emerging consensus about the fundamentals of the field that Newell summarizes in Box 2.4.

Box 2.4 Fundamentals of Interdisciplinarity

An interdisciplinary study has a specific substantive focus that is so broad or complex that it exceeds the scope of a single perspective; interdisciplinarity is characterized by an identifiable process that draws explicitly on disciplines for insights into the substantive focus; those insights must be integrated; and the objective of integration is instrumental and pragmatic—to solve a problem, resolve an issue, address a topic, answer a question, explain a phenomenon, or create a new product. (Newell, 2010b, p. 363)

Interdisciplinarity Practice in the New Millennium

Developing competence in interdisciplinarity includes not only understanding the historical roots of the field but also being familiar with current interdisciplinary advances in the following academic sectors. We discuss developments in both interdisciplinary teaching and research here but focus on implications for interdisciplinary learning.

Natural Science Investigations of real-world problems of interest to the natural sciences have become increasingly interdisciplinary. Real-world complexity often defies using a single disciplinary approach and requires drawing on research and using tools from multiple natural science disciplines (e.g., physics, chemistry, biology, and Earth science) and possibly other disciplines and fields interested in the problem. Complex natural systems such as the Earth's climate cannot be fully understood without considering all major subsystems that contribute to it, including ocean currents, the formation and destruction of polar ice caps and mountain glaciers, solar radiation, land use, land cover, and the processes governing the transportation of microscopic particles, such as carbon, through the air. Investigating questions such as climate change, for example, also involves understanding the role that increased carbon dioxide emissions play in the grand system of Earth's climate. One aspect of this system is the relationship between these emissions and increasing ocean acidification as shown in Figure 2.5.

We noted earlier an increased connection between natural science and technology in the late nineteenth century. In the late twentieth century there has been increased collaboration between life sciences and medicine and between physical sciences and engineering (Klein, 2010, p. 17). For example,

Figure 2.5   Ocean Acidification: Consumption of Carbonate Ions Impedes Calcification

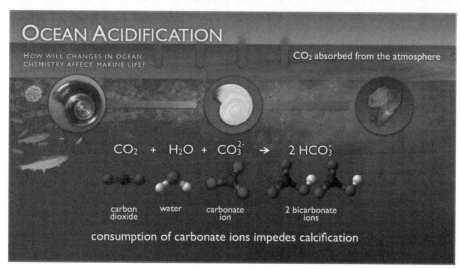

Source: Pacific Marine Environment Laboratory, NOAA.

Elias Zerhouni, former director of the National Institutes of Health, reports that what is needed to understand the molecular events that lead to disease is the integration of disciplinary expertise and new technologies (2003, pp. 63–64). Klein (2010) cites three boundary-crossing developments occurring in the sciences and technology: (1) the quiet daily flow of borrowing methods, concepts, and tools between disciplines; (2) the application of "knowledge from one discipline in order to contextualize another, akin to the engineering profession's inclusion of social contexts of practice"; and (3) "the emergence of new communities of practice" where individuals and groups work together to solve problems of mutual interest (pp. 18–19).

A prime example of interdisciplinary natural science with technological implications is the human-genome mapping project described in Box 2.5.

Box 2.5 The Human-Genome Matching Project

The human-genome mapping project was a complex undertaking that depended on extensive collaboration across many fields, including the biological and computational sciences. Basic questions of life—how living beings grow, how the brain functions, why many animals need to sleep, how retroviruses function—share the characteristic of complexity, and understanding them, even in part, depends on multiple disciplines. Gaining such understanding will almost certainly require deep expertise both at the subsystem level and at the interdisciplinary level—and the integration of these two levels. It is important to note that depth in research is not confined to single-discipline investigations. Statistical mechanics, for example, unites physicists and mathematicians in studies of substantial depth. (Kafatos & Eisner, 2004, p. 1257)

The implication of increased boundary crossing for interdisciplinary studies is this: You need to *understand how different disciplines view the object or phenomenon under study.* For example, an organism "is simultaneously a physical (atomic), chemical (molecular), biological (macro-molecular), physiological, mental, social, and cultural object" (Klein, 2010, p. 20).

In natural science and technology, then, we see three broad trends:

- Much of scientific interdisciplinary work today is instrumental and motivated by practical problem solving (Weingart, 2000).

- Disciplines have become more porous and multidisciplinary (Repko & Szostak, 2016).

- Faculty are incorporating new knowledge about genetics, cognition, and the cosmos into the science curriculum and organizing courses around complex technical and social problems and topics. They are also including introductory courses that integrate elements of mathematics, physics, chemistry, and biology (Klein, 2010).

In one interdisciplinary science program, students studied the possible environmental consequences of a large tract of farmland and forest near their university being developed as a subdivision and shopping center. The subject was appropriate for interdisciplinary study because it had multiple parts that interacted with each other and that required studying both the parts and the system as a whole from multiple disciplinary perspectives: the pond and stream that watered and drained the site (Earth science and hydrology), the trees and plants that absorbed carbon dioxide and produced oxygen (chemistry), and wildlife that depended on the pond, stream, and forest (biology and ecology). (Note: One could also integrate social science insights into such a project.)

The Social Sciences The social sciences (which traditionally include anthropologists, economists, political scientists, psychologists, and sociologists) deal with systems, issues, problems, and questions that are even more complex. This has resulted in the development of a large and growing number of interdisciplinary fields and programs that span the social sciences and connect to the natural sciences and the humanities. In 2011, the National Science Foundation (NSF) and Directorate for Social, Behavioral and Economic Sciences (SBE) issued a report on research priorities for the next decade. Among its conclusions were the following:

- "Future research will be interdisciplinary, data-intensive, and collaborative" (p. 5).

- "Interdisciplinary training [is needed] in new research methods, including integration and synthesis across data, methods, and disciplines" (p.5).

- The NSF/SBE will concentrate "on more focused planning activities" that will "enhance interdisciplinary research" with initial preference given to four areas: population change; disparities; communication, language, and linguistics; technology, new media, and social networking (p. 5).

The problems social scientists study are usually concerned with the cause(s) of something or the effect(s) of something on other things. Examples of hypothetical student research involving primarily the social sciences include the cause(s) of childhood obesity, the effects of undocumented immigration on health care and education, and the cause(s) of gang formation.

The two most influential developments in the social sciences since the end of World War II are area studies (e.g., the Middle East) and quantitative research methodology (i.e., measurement using numerical data and statistical analysis). These movements reveal the intent to develop a comprehensive understanding of concrete patterns of social life, the hope that scientific knowledge can help solve domestic social problems, and the expectation that social science can become an effective source of objective knowledge that can inform government policy (Calhoun & Rhoten, 2010).

Area studies and quantitative research methodology can be seen as occupying opposite ends of a continuum. On one end, area studies with its focus on people as embedded in culture, institutions, and history represents the humanistic approach to social science; on the other, quantitative research methodology with its focus on statistics and data sets represents the scientific approach.

Area studies such as American studies bring together different disciplinary perspectives in order to achieve a richer, more complete view of a society or culture in its particular historical or geographical setting. By bringing together all relevant knowledge of its particular focus, area studies attempt to be holistic. By contrast, quantitative research methodology does not attempt to illuminate the whole but rather to identify causal relationships within individual aspects of society. It insists that the study of these specific causes can and should be based on numerical information (Calhoun & Rhoten, 2010).

"Globalization" is a topic that has attracted considerable attention in recent decades. The concern here is with how different regions of the world interact increasingly in the economic, political, and cultural spheres. Connections among economic, political, and cultural interactions can only be explored in an interdisciplinary fashion. Sociologists may study the effect of American movies on French culture, while economists explore the reasons for the increasingly global marketing of songs and movies, and political scientists examine the political responses to these transformations.

Interdisciplinary fields in the social sciences typically focus on issues of public concern. For example, business is a "social problem" in that social science can contribute insights into management education and offer methods on how to research organizational behavior.

Three implications for interdisciplinary learning follow from this discussion:

- The pursuit of a comprehensive view of social life requires understanding different disciplinary perspectives.

- The pursuit of innovation must be based on developing learning skills and borrowing tools from other disciplines.

- The pursuit of a truly comprehensive understanding of a particular social problem that is of public concern requires integrating insights from relevant disciplines (Calhoun & Rhoten, 2010).

The New Humanities In contrast to the natural and social sciences, the humanities (art history, history, literature, music education, philosophy, and religious studies) are not necessarily attracted to the study of systems or the identification of cause–effect relationships. Rather, they tend to concern themselves with artifacts (music, plays, operas, paintings, sculpture, ballets, videos, installations, etc.) that express the human experience. The humanities explore and find ways to articulate the emotions, probe values, ponder meaning, ask "big" questions, unleash imagination, or critique the human condition. The humanities engage the complexity of real-world problems by focusing on expression, effect, values, meaning, and how the stuff natural and social sciences study plays out in human lives (i.e., lived experience). Because human beings, human culture, and human experience are all exquisitely complex, the humanities benefit greatly from interdisciplinary study. One leading author explains interdisciplinary practice in the humanities (see Box 2.6).

Box 2.6 Interdisciplinary Humanities

[The humanities disciplines are] paying increasing attention to . . . the contexts of aesthetic works and the responses of readers, viewers, and listeners. . . . Close reading of a text or technical analysis of a painting or a musical composition may be combined with psychoanalytical, sociological, semiotic, deconstructionist, or feminist approaches. Disciplinary categories [have] broadened to encompass more subject matter, conditions of artistic production, social science methods and concepts, and previously marginalized groups and other cultures. This development [is] reinforced by heightened interests in history, sociology, politics, and an anthropological definition of culture. (Klein, 2010, pp. 30–31)

Examples of topics, themes, and questions that require drawing primarily on the humanities include the following: How have significant aspects of the human experience been articulated using different media, and how has this process changed over time? What causes civilizations to collapse? Is the American Dream still valid? What does it mean to be a global citizen? Such questions draw upon multiple humanities disciplines.

In recent years, the humanities have embraced what Klein (2010) calls "the new generalism," which challenges both the modern system of disciplinarity and the older humanities model of unified knowledge and culture. She describes "the new generalism" as "not a unified paradigm" but "a cross-fertilizing synergism in the form of shared methods, concepts, and theories about language, culture, and history" (p. 30). The new humanities, reports Klein (2010), is doing the following:

- It is *deconstructing* (i.e., disassembling) disciplinary knowledge and learning while *raising political questions* concerning their value and purpose. This trend is especially evident in cultural studies, women's and ethnic studies, and literary studies.

- It is paying increasing attention to the *contexts* of aesthetic works and the response of readers, viewers, and listeners to them.

- It is combining psychoanalytical, sociological, semiotic, deconstructionist, and/or feminist approaches.

- It is broadening the meaning of "the humanities." This category of disciplines now encompasses social science methods and concepts, as well as previously marginalized groups and other cultures.

- It is heightening interest in history, sociology, politics, and an anthropological definition of culture.

A new and rapidly growing subfield within the new humanities is digital humanities, which investigates how new technologies influence and reflect scholarship (especially) in the humanities and artistic expression. Three examples illustrate the creativity, diversity, and importance of this field. John Sparrow combines the creative talents of the fine artist with the manipulation of digital data to transform old texts into new art in interactive works like *Birdsong Compliance* (http://itchaway.net/poetry/birdsong-compliance/). Second, an image was produced by the OPTE project (http://www.opte.org/) representing the Internet connections of one computer in one month during 2003. Although the purpose of the project was to map Internet growth and identify gaps in the infrastructure, as well as analyze the effects of natural and man-made disasters on Internet usage, the images produced were so startling and beautiful that they were displayed at the Museum of Modern Art in New York, thus challenging (as modern art does constantly) the boundaries between knowledge domains. Third, early attempts at digital imaging to preserve copies of deteriorating ancient manuscripts leveraged imaging technologies from medicine and aviation before it became more commonplace in the late 1990s (Prescott, 2012).

One area of the humanities where a systems approach may prove invaluable is the growing field of media studies. The last century has witnessed a series of technological developments—radio, television, Internet, smart phone, and more—that have changed the way that people receive (and increasingly produce) information and entertainment. These technologies are shaped by cultures, institutions, and governments, and in turn have a huge effect on how people live. Media studies grapples with this series of complex transformations and explores the question of how individuals and societies do and could interact with new media. (Note that here, as elsewhere, there is scope for an even broader interdisciplinary purview with insights from social and natural science.)

These changes have several implications for interdisciplinarity in general, and for programs that focus on the humanities and on the fine and performing arts (see the next section) in particular:

- They blur the limits of the conventional distinction between disciplinarity and interdisciplinarity.

- They involve **informed borrowing**, selecting one path to understanding while "bracketing" others. In photography, "bracketing" involves taking numerous versions of the same photograph using various exposure settings.

- They invite learners, listeners, viewers, or readers to actively participate in constructing the more comprehensive understanding themselves rather than to passively accept one produced by an expert.

- While instrumental interdisciplinarity is still important in the humanities, critical interdisciplinarity is more often embraced.

The Fine and Performing Arts There are real and distinct differences between the fine and performing arts and the humanities. The fine and performing arts (art, dance, music, creative writing, theater, and voice) produce many of the artistic artifacts that are studied by the humanities. They thus stress the perfection and execution of skills in order to produce or collaborate on creative work but also analyze and discuss the strengths and weaknesses of existing works of art. In contrast, the humanities often *study* the work produced by fine and performance artists (and, increasingly, productions from a much wider sphere of artistry) and discuss and interpret the purpose and meaning of these productions; perhaps considering how these works fit into historical, social, political, or cultural contexts; how particular works reflect or anticipate major shifts in political power and/or major catastrophes (wars, revolutions, and genocides, for example); how and why particular works are innovative; and the effects of works on their respective audiences.

The fine and performing arts engage the complexity of real-world problems by providing insights that express, interpret, exemplify, or respond effectively to such problems. For example, they can contribute to our understanding of anger among minority youth by analyzing the anger motif expressed in rap lyrics. And they can sensitize us to the plight of AIDS victims by creating a theatrical or film production that dramatizes the life of a person with AIDS. The arts are concerned with techniques of expression that elicit responses, especially subjective or emotional ones, to aspects of the human condition in all its complexity. There has been increased interest in recent years in connecting different art forms.

Problems at the Human–Nature Interface Many real-world problems cut across the categories of knowledge, and like the problems mentioned earlier, are the kinds of problems that interdisciplinary studies is uniquely equipped to address. Almost all environmental problems (as distinct from natural disasters such as volcanic eruptions) take place where the human and natural worlds meet and interact. For example, the problem of the causes of fresh water scarcity involves drawing on disciplines from the natural sciences *and* the social sciences. Certain problems arising from our interactions with each other require that we cut across disciplinary categories. For instance, issues relating to social justice require drawing on disciplines in the social sciences *and* the humanities. And the issue of reconciling how to clone humans with what it means to be human involves drawing on disciplines in the natural sciences *and* the social sciences *and* the humanities. These types of complex issues have given rise to numerous interdisciplinary fields that are designed to engage in border-crossing activity to develop understandings and offer solutions that are more comprehensive than those generated by single disciplines.

An example of one new field that spans the natural sciences, social sciences, and humanities is aural architecture, pioneered by Barry Blesser (see Box 2.7). This refers to auditoriums, places of worship, or digital simulations of virtual spaces that are sonically complex.

Box 2.7 Aural Architecture

I had not appreciated the artistic, social, historical, and philosophical context of my isolated activities. . . . I could have framed the discussion solely in terms of the physical and mathematical properties of sound waves that contribute to the aural experience of a concert hall. . . . Rather, I have chosen to explore the broad phenomenon of auditory spatial awareness without regard to a single discipline [or] culture. . . . In dealing with a musical space, a composer sees one aspect of the phenomenon, whereas architects, archeologists, anthropologists, audio engineers, psychophysical scientists, and blind individuals see other aspects. When we have access to multiple views, each with its own biases and limitations, we acquire greater understanding of the phenomenon. . . . The union of diverse viewpoints, like multiple shadows from an object that we cannot see, allows us to form an image of the phenomenon, which by definition always remains inaccessible. (Blesser & Salter, 2007, pp. ix–x)

The implication for interdisciplinary learning is that it will often be necessary to draw on disciplines from across the natural sciences, social sciences, and humanities.

The Growth of Interdisciplinarity The growth and diversity of interdisciplinary studies is truly remarkable, attesting to its adaptability to new trends and important issues. Table 2.1 is based on a 2009 study of data compiled from the College Catalog Study Database, which sampled 293 institutions.

From this brief survey of the emergence of interdisciplinarity and its growing diversity, it is possible to identify five prominent lines of development that are relevant to interdisciplinary learning. First, interdisciplinarity is about change, not for the sake of change but for the purpose of achieving more comprehensive understandings of scientific, technological, social, and intellectual subjects that span multiple disciplines. Second, interdisciplinary work requires familiarity with the perspectives and tools of relevant disciplines. Third, interdisciplinarity may assume either a critical or an instrumental "form" depending on the topic and purpose of the study. Fourth, interdisciplinarity has been diversifying at a dizzying pace. And fifth, interdisciplinarity is likely to gain even more in importance.

Table 2.1 Fields Typically Organized as Interdisciplinary Programs, 2000–2001

Interdisciplinary Field
Non-Western Cultural Studies
Asian area studies
Latin American area studies
African area studies
Middle Eastern studies
Race and Ethnic Studies
African American studies
Ethnic and race studies
Chicano, Hispanic studies
American Indian studies
Asian American studies
Western Studies
European, North American studies
Western period history studies
European origin studies
Western studies
Canadian studies
Environmental Studies
International and Global Studies
International relations, global
Peace, conflict studies
Political economy
Civic and Government Studies
Urban studies
Public affairs, public policy
Legal studies

Interdisciplinary Field
Women's Studies
American Studies
American culture or studies
U.S. regional studies
Brain and Biomedical Science
Cognitive, neuroscience
Biological psychology
Biomedical, biotechnology
Medical technology
Other
Interdisciplinary studies
Communication
Film studies
Media Studies
Liberal studies
Gerontology
Judaic studies
Science and society
Arts management
Folk studies
Ethics, values
Sexuality studies

Source: Brint, S. G., Turk-Bicakci, L., Proctor, K., & Murphy, S. P. (2009). Expanding the social frame of knowledge: Interdisciplinary, degree-granting fields in American colleges and universities, 1975–2000. *Review of Higher Education* 32(2), Table 2, pp. 164–165. © 2008 Association for the Study of Higher Education. Reprinted with permission of The Johns Hopkins University Press.

A more recent survey of degree programs at 286 colleges and universities in the United States provides some information on how interdisciplinary programs are distributed across fields. Note that this survey defines "interdisciplinary teaching programs" in part as programs that draw on teaching staff from more than one department. The survey thus likely underestimates the importance of interdisciplinary studies programs taught within dedicated departments. It surely underreports "communications" programs that are often taught in schools of communication. Nevertheless, the survey is useful in highlighting the importance of area studies programs and in capturing the importance of interdisciplinary programs across the social sciences, humanities, natural sciences, and performing arts. It is notable that interdisciplinary programs are also found across a range of professional programs. The survey proceeds to break these broad classes into hundreds of distinct interdisciplinary programs such as African American studies.

Interdisciplinarity's Criticism of the Disciplines

Interdisciplinarity emerged as a much needed supplement to and corrective of disciplinarity's monopoly on learning and knowledge production. But what is it *exactly* about the disciplines that so concerns advocates of interdisciplinarity? The answer to this question is found in the discussion of the interdisciplinary critique of the disciplines. This critique touches on six (overlapping) limitations of disciplinary specialization. Competence in studies includes your understanding of these limitations.

Specialization Can Blind Us to the Broader Context

Disciplinary specialization can blind us to the broader context. **Context** refers to the circumstances or setting in which the problem, event, statement, or idea exists. This criticism is implicit in a bit of dialogue found in *The Little Prince* by Antoine de Saint-Exupéry (Excerpt translated from the French by Richard Howard. Copyright © 1943 by Houghton Mifflin Harcourt Publishing Company. Copyright renewed 1971 by Consuelo de Saint-Exupery; English translation copyright © 2000 by Richard Howard, reproduced by permission of Houghton Mifflin Harcourt Publishing Company. All rights reserved.):

> "Your planet is very beautiful," [said the little prince]. "Has it any oceans?"
>
> "I couldn't tell you," said the geographer. . . .
>
> "But you are a geographer!"
>
> "Exactly," the geographer said. "But I am not an explorer. I haven't a single explorer on my planet. It is not the geographer

who goes out to count the towns, the rivers, the mountains, the seas, the oceans, the deserts. The geographer is much too important to go loafing about. He does not leave his desk." (pp. 45–46)

Table 2.2	Distribution of Interdisciplinary Programs by Primary Field, 2011
• General, individualized studies 5.4%	
• Visual and performing arts 3.8%	
• Humanities 13.1%	
• Communications 1.4%	
• American ethnic studies 11.4%	
• International, area studies 20.4%	
• Social science 19.4%	
• Natural science, mathematics 14.0%	
• Health 2.6%	
• Engineering, technology 2.2%	
• Education 0.8%	
• Business 2.3%	
• Agriculture 1.2%	
• Miscellaneous 0.6%	
• Home economics 0.4%	
• Physical education, recreation, and leisure 0.4%	
• Human services 0.7%	
• Unknown 0.1%	
• Total 14,760 100%	

Source: Brint, S. G., Turk-Bicakci, L., Proctor, K., & Murphy, S. P. (2009). Expanding the social frame of knowledge: Interdisciplinary, degree-granting fields in American colleges and universities, 1975–2000. *Review of Higher Education* 32(2). 2008 Association for the Study of Higher Education.

The lesson of this story is that specialization—that is, "not leaving [your] desk" to see what's outside your area of specialization—can blind you to the broader context of a situation. Specialized thinking makes it less likely that you will be able to answer the larger, more important, practical questions of life. Advocates of interdisciplinary learning believe that *specialization alone* will not enable us to master the pressing problems facing humanity today. The more specialized the disciplines become, the more necessary interdisciplinarity becomes.

Specialization Tends to Produce Tunnel Vision

Disciplinary specialization can produce consequences much like what tunnel vision produces. In natural eyesight, tunnel vision means that the eye has only a small area of focus, with the rest of the field of view beyond the lens being unfocused or blurry, as shown in Figure 2.6. When it comes to approaching a complex problem, the specialist is able to focus only on the part of the problem that is familiar to the specialist, not on other parts that fall outside the specialist's area of expertise.

Figure 2.6   Tunnel Vision

Source: Tunnel vision imitation by Скампецкий http://en.wikipedia.org/wiki/File:Tunnel_vision_sc.png licensed under the Creative Commons Attribution-Share Alike 3.0 Unported license. https://creativecommons.org/licenses/by/3.0/deed.en.

Focusing on only part of a complex problem can produce serious unintended consequences. For example, the experts who designed the system of hydroelectric dams on the Columbia and Snake River systems were certain that these dams would not harm the many salmon species that spawned in the rivers' tributaries. But the experts were wrong. Today, despite the extensive building of fish ladders and other costly efforts to mitigate the effects of these dams on the native fish populations, several species are on the verge of extinction and an industry that employed tens of thousands of workers is in ruins. In this world of specialists, even highly educated individuals can be unaware of the social, ethical, economic, and biological dimensions of a policy or an action. Indeed, a person may know a great deal about a particular subject but be unable to calculate its possible impacts.

Specialization Tends to Discount or Ignore Other Perspectives

Interdisciplinarity faults the disciplines for sometimes failing to consider other perspectives. **Perspective in an interdisciplinary sense** refers to a discipline's unique view of that part of reality that it is typically most interested in. For example, psychology sees human behavior as reflecting the cognitive constructs *individuals* develop to organize their mental activity. "Individuals" is italicized to emphasize that psychology is not interested in groups as sociology is, or in religious institutions and faith traditions as religious studies is. So when cognitive psychology studies a complex behavior such as terrorism, it studies only the mental life of individual terrorists, not groups of terrorists, and not their religious beliefs because it tends to discount the influence of religion on individual behavior. Consequently, when investigating the causes of terrorism, psychology tends to discount or even ignore the perspectives of sociology, economics, or religious studies.

Specialization Can Hinder Creative Breakthroughs

Specialization can sometimes hinder creative breakthroughs by its inability to bring previously unrelated ideas from other disciplines together. **Creative breakthroughs** often occur when different disciplinary perspectives and unrelated ideas are brought together (Sill, 1996). Noted British scientist and novelist C. P. Snow (1964) says, "The clashing points of two subjects, two disciplines, two cultures—or two galaxies, so far as that goes—ought to produce creative changes. In the history of mental activity that has been where some of the breakthroughs came" (p. 16).

For example, Moran (2010) reports that "interdisciplinarity has produced some of the most interesting intellectual developments in the humanities over the past few decades" (p. 180). These include areas of literary theory such as narratology, the analysis of narratives, led by thinkers such as Gérard Ginette, whose work spans the late 1960s to the early 2000s. Narratology considers all stories equally worthy of study, from Shakespeare to gossip, and attempts to deconstruct each narrative into its component parts, often revealing emergent and interestingly consistent patterns. Narratology is interdisciplinary because it integrates what it draws from texts outside of those studied traditionally as part of a literature or even a popular culture class. Any exchange where a story is shared is worthy of study. Also, its methods draw on disciplines that include anthropology, linguistics, literature, and sociology.

Jacques Derrida (a French philosopher active from the 1960s to his death in 2004) and the poststructuralist theory with which he is closely associated also emerged from the interdisciplinary humanities. Derrida challenged the ability of language to communicate consistent and verifiable statements about reality and human existence because of the unstable relationship that exists between a word in any language and what it represents to the users of that language. Poststructuralism, and its close relative, postmodernism, had dramatic and wide-reaching effects on numerous disciplines, both inside and outside of the humanities. It challenged all scientific and objective attempts to articulate reality, including the assumptions that had dominated and underpinned knowledge since the Enlightenment. The implication is that interdisciplinarity is more likely than specialization to advance the production of knowledge.

Specialization Fails to Address Complex Problems Comprehensively

The nature of a complex problem is that, like a diamond, it has many facets. Interdisciplinarity faults disciplinary specialization for its tendency to focus on a particular facet or component of a complex problem rather than addressing the problem comprehensively. For example, global warming has many facets: biological, chemical, political, and economic. Biologists may address global warming from a biological perspective and hypothesize about the effect of increased production of carbon dioxide, a greenhouse gas, on ocean temperatures and coral reefs. While this specialized research is necessary and helpful, it does not provide a comprehensive understanding of global warming. Such an understanding would have to also consider the effects of climate warming on, say, the supply of fresh water for agriculture and food prices in particular regions. Each disciplinary contribution can be valuable, but none of them provides the truly comprehensive perspective on the problem that the public and policy makers really need. On too many issues of public importance, the disciplines tend to talk past each other. Disciplinarians act as though the part of the problem they analyze is the whole problem and simply ignore other aspects.

Specialization Imposes a Past Approach on the Present

Critics of disciplinary specialization point out that it is a product of a bygone era that was very different from today's world of increasing complexity and rapid social change. The structure of the disciplines and their silo approach to learning and problem solving reflect the form and the level of knowledge achieved in an earlier historical period. Consequently, it is unreasonable to expect that the disciplines *by themselves* will be capable of providing the comprehensive understandings of, or solutions to, contemporary issues and social problems.

Conversely, the rise of interdisciplinary research and learning reflects the need to ask new questions, try new approaches, produce new technologies, and develop new intellectual orientations. We can never entirely dispense with the disciplines as a means of organizing knowledge, says Moran (2010), but we can use them to create new intellectual configurations of knowledge. Critics of the disciplines readily admit that interdisciplinarity *by itself* is no panacea for the world's problems. Rather, they believe that the disciplines *and* interdisciplinary studies working together might produce creative breakthroughs that would otherwise not be possible using traditional approaches.

Summary of the Interdisciplinary Criticism of Disciplinary Specialization

Most interdisciplinarians do not seek the end of the disciplines; they fully appreciate the invaluable contributions that specialization has made in the production of knowledge. They believe, however, that although the disciplines are useful for producing, organizing, and applying knowledge, a purely specialized approach to learning and knowledge production comes at a very high price:

- Specialization can blind us to the broader context.
- Specialization tends to produce tunnel vision.
- Specialization tends to discount or ignore other perspectives.
- Specialization can hinder creative breakthroughs.
- Specialization fails to address complex problems comprehensively.
- Specialization imposes a past approach on the present.

For these reasons, interdisciplinary learning strives to balance disciplinary specialization with interdisciplinary integration. Happily, most interdisciplinarians and many disciplinarians view the disciplines and interdisciplinarity as complementary ways to learn, produce knowledge, and solve complex problems.

CRITICAL THINKING QUESTIONS

1. Of the several concerns about overspecialization that the chapter discusses, which ones seem most applicable today, and why?

2. Explain why interdisciplinarity is advancing in the natural sciences, the social sciences, the humanities, the fine and performing arts, and the applied fields.

3. From your reading of Chapters 1 and 2, describe the relationship between interdisciplinarity and the disciplines.

APPLICATIONS AND EXERCISES

1. Reflect on how an important past event has shaped your self-understanding, or has motivated you to pursue an undergraduate degree.

2. Explain how your brief study of the origins of the disciplines and the rise of interdisciplinarity has made the system of learning you are experiencing at your college or university more comprehensible.

3. Select an article on a controversial public policy issue from a major publication such as the *New York Times*, the *Wall Street Journal*, or some other publication recommended by your instructor. Ask these questions of the author of the article, being careful to provide "in text" evidence to support your analysis (Note: This can be pursued as a group project):

   a. Does the author place the issue in a broad context? How?

   b. Does the author suffer from tunnel vision?

   c. Does the author discount or ignore other perspectives on the issue?

   d. Does the author propose a creative solution to the issue?

   e. Does the author address the issue comprehensively?

   f. How might an interdisciplinary approach improve the author's treatment of the issue?

Source: ©iStockphoto.com/Andrea Scala.

 # Chapter 3 Objectives

"Interdisciplinary studies" is a common term in the vocabulary of higher education. But scholars differ in their understanding of what it involves and, thus, how to define it. One of the objectives of this chapter is to define this important approach to learning and research. The first part of the chapter presents several widely recognized definitions of interdisciplinary studies, and in typical interdisciplinary fashion, identifies commonalities that they share. From these commonalities, we construct an integrated definition. Other objectives are to explain the differences between disciplinarity, multidisciplinarity, interdisciplinarity, and transdisciplinarity; examine critical and instrumental approaches to interdisciplinarity; and critically analyze metaphors commonly used to describe interdisciplinary studies.

Interdisciplinary Studies Defined

Why Definitions Matter

Before defining interdisciplinary studies and other important terms, it is useful to explain why definitions matter. How you define a word is critical to any effort you make to understand it. For example, the word *justice* is defined, and thus understood, very differently depending on your politics, values, or faith tradition. Similarly, the concept "sustainability" has a different meaning to an economist than it does to a biologist or historian. Interdisciplinary students and scholars need to be careful to identify the different meanings attached to key terminology by scholars in different disciplines. These differences do not mean that one understanding is right and others are wrong. Rather, they reveal the reality that experts from different disciplines are trained to view the world and to approach problem solving in quite different ways. Definitions matter when individuals or groups use the same word but have different understandings of its meaning. For example, two opposing groups (see Figure 3.1) may describe their respective proposed tax policies as "fair." But what does each group mean by "fair"? For one group, "fair" may mean a tax policy that requires "the wealthy" (another problematic concept) to pay more in taxes in order to fund popular social programs. But for the other group, a "fair" tax policy may mean one that spreads the tax burden more evenly so that those who earn the most can retain most of what they have earned. Obviously, defining "fair" in the context of competing tax policies is problematic because each group attributes conflicting values to the concept. Underlying these conflicting notions of fairness are disciplinary worldviews about democracy, capitalism, and the role of government.

Learning Outcomes

By the end of this chapter, you will be able to:

- Define *interdisciplinary* and *interdisciplinarity*

- Understand the differences between disciplinarity, multidisciplinarity, interdisciplinarity, and transdisciplinarity

- Understand the differences between critical and instrumental forms of interdisciplinarity and recognize examples of each

- Understand the usefulness and limitations of metaphors descriptive of interdisciplinarity

Figure 3.1   Fair Tax Rally

Source: Florida Fair Tax, Marion County–2009 Supporters; http://www .fairtax.org/site/Clubs?club_id=1060& sid=4730&pg=photo.

Some people might prefer an alternative to any precise definition. But interdisciplinarians, who want to aid communication across groups, disciplines, and political divides, recognize the importance of clarifying the definition that is applied to a concept.

Defining Interdisciplinary Studies

The term *interdisciplinary studies* refers to the field as a whole. *Interdisciplinary* denotes a particular approach to study that is distinct from disciplinary approaches. For example, a disciplinary approach to a particular environmental problem would be to study it through the narrow lens of, say, biology, whereas an interdisciplinary approach would be to study the same problem by drawing on biology and other disciplines relevant to the problem. The next term **interdisciplinarity** refers to the "intellectual essence" of the field. This "essence" refers *both* to its "defining elements" *and* to the "process" it uses to engage in the scholarly enterprise. "Defining elements" refer to the basic principles of the field that give it coherence. We address both defining elements and process in the following:

Interdisciplinary studies approaches complex problems using a process, the crux of which is integration of disciplinary *insights*. **Insights** are scholarly contributions to the clear understanding of a complex problem, object, or text. Insights may be found in published books or articles, or in papers delivered at scholarly conferences. For example, it is necessary to draw on insights from multiple disciplines to produce a more comprehensive understanding of the causes of school violence. *Integration* refers to blending or synthesizing. For instance, insights from cognitive psychology, religious studies, and political science can be integrated to construct a more comprehensive understanding of the causes of certain forms of terrorism.

Widely Recognized Definitions of Interdisciplinary Studies

This discussion introduces five definitions of interdisciplinary studies that have gained wide acceptance and represent some degree of consensus among scholars.

As you read them, identify what these definitions have in common: for example, their use of the same terms or similar phrasing. More particularly, record each definition's understanding of (a) the focus or purpose of interdisciplinary (ID) study, (b) the process used in ID study, and (c) the outcome or product of ID study. As you gather this information, it is useful to create a table similar to Table 3.1 to capture your observations and categorize the information gathered. This exercise will help you learn how to integrate insights that appear to be quite different. (Note: These definitions contain concepts that may be unfamiliar to you but are explained later in this chapter.)

1. Julie Thompson Klein and William H. Newell (1997) in "Advancing Interdisciplinary Studies":

   Interdisciplinary studies is a process of answering a question, solving a problem, or addressing a topic that is too broad or complex to be dealt with adequately by a single discipline or profession. . . . [It] draws on disciplinary perspectives and integrates their insights through the construction of a more comprehensive perspective. (pp. 393–394)

2. Diana Rhoten, Veronica Boix Mansilla, Marc Chun, and Julie T. Klein (2006) in *Interdisciplinary Education at Liberal Arts Institutions*:

   [Interdisciplinary studies] is a mode of curriculum design and instruction in which individual faculty or teams identify, evaluate, and integrate information, data, techniques, tools, perspectives, concepts, or theories from two or more disciplines or bodies of knowledge to advance students' capacity to understand issues, address problems, and create new approaches and solutions that extend beyond the scope of a single discipline or area of instruction. (p. 3)

3. Veronica Boix Mansilla (2005) in "Assessing Student Work at Disciplinary Crossroads":

   [Interdisciplinary studies gives] the capacity to integrate knowledge and modes of thinking drawn from two or more disciplines to produce a cognitive advancement—for example, explaining a phenomenon, solving a problem, creating a product, or raising a new question—in ways that would have been unlikely through single disciplinary means. (p. 16)

4. National Academy of Sciences, National Academy of Engineering, and Institute of Medicine (2005) (hereafter referred to as the National Academies):

Interdisciplinary [studies] integrates information, data, techniques, tools, perspectives, concepts, and/or theories from two or more disciplines or bodies of specialized knowledge to advance fundamental understanding or to solve problems whose solutions are beyond the scope of a single discipline or area of research practice. (p. 26)

5. Carol Geary Schneider (2004), "Liberal Education and Integrative Learning":

Integrative learning is a shorthand term for teaching a set of capacities—capacities we might also call the arts of connection, reflective judgment, and considered action—that enables graduates to put their knowledge to effective use. . . . It should also lead students to connect and integrate the different parts of their overall education, to connect learning with the world beyond the academy, and above all, to translate their education to new contexts, new problems, new responsibilities. (pp. 1–2)

Because the wording of each definition varies considerably from the others, a superficial reading of the definitions might lead you to conclude that they have little in common. But close reading reveals that they share several commonalities. Identifying these commonalities will enable you to develop a deeper understanding of this concept and construct a more comprehensive definition

Table 3.1 Five Definitions of Interdisciplinary Studies			
Definition	Purpose of ID Study	Process of ID Study	Product of ID Study
Klein & Newell			
Rhoten et al.			
Boix Mansilla			
National Academies			
Schneider (Association of American Colleges and Universities)			

of interdisciplinary studies. **Close reading** calls for careful analysis of a text that begins with attending to individual words, sentence structure, and the order in which sentences and ideas unfold.

Commonalities Shared by These Definitions

One way to identify commonalities in two or more texts (or definitions) is to isolate key words or phrases that appear in each text. Most of the terms italicized in the list are active verbs; three are nouns that have a verb form—*process* and *construction* in Definition No. 1 and *teaching* in Definition No. 5.

- "*Process*" (Def. No. 1)

- "*Draws on* disciplinary perspectives" (Def. No. 1)

- "*Integrates* their insights" (Def. No. 1)

- "*Construction* of a more comprehensive understanding" (Def. No. 1)

- "*Identify*, *evaluate*, and *integrate* information . . . from two or more disciplines or bodies of knowledge" (Def. No. 2)

- "*Advance* students' capacity to *understand* issues" (Def. No. 2)

- "*Create* new approaches and solutions that extend beyond the scope of a single discipline or area of instruction" (Def. No. 2)

- "The capacity to *integrate* knowledge and modes of thinking *drawn* from two or more disciplines" (Def. No. 3)

- "*Produce* a cognitive advancement" (Def. No. 3)

- "*Integrates* information, data, techniques, tools, perspectives, concepts, and/or theories from two or more disciplines or bodies of specialized knowledge" (Def. No. 4)

- "*Advance* fundamental understanding or to *solve* problems" (Def. No. 4)

- "*Teaching* a set of capacities" (Def. No. 5)

- "*Connect and integrate* the different parts of their overall education" (Def. No. 5)

- "*Connect* learning with the world beyond the academy" (Def. No. 5)

- "*Translate* their education to new contexts, new problems, new responsibilities" (Def. No. 5)

This exercise in close reading enables us to identify the core ideas and key concepts that each definition advances about the nature of interdisciplinarity. From this list, it is then possible to categorize these key words or phrases under three broad headings: *purpose*, *process*, and *product* of interdisciplinary studies. Some of these words or phrases may be applicable to more than one category. It is now relatively easy to summarize the key ideas under each heading. (Note: These commonalities are discussed only briefly here and are examined in greater detail elsewhere in this book.)

The Purpose of Interdisciplinary Studies The purpose of interdisciplinary studies is to develop your "capacity" to integrate knowledge, modes (i.e., manner or method) of thinking, and education experience, and apply your education to the world beyond the university. **Capacity** refers to your "cognitive" or "intellectual" ability to think, perceive, analyze, create, and solve problems. Interdisciplinary studies prepares you to engage the real-world complexities referenced in Chapter 1.

The Process of Interdisciplinary Studies Interdisciplinary studies, as noted earlier, involves using a process. This process, strategy, or procedure is an interdisciplinary approach to critically analyzing the problem before engaging in integration. This process is the focus of Part III of this book.

Developing competency in interdisciplinary process does not happen quickly; it happens over time. How much time depends on the extent to which you encounter situations that provide opportunities to apply your newly acquired understanding and capacities. As a process, interdisciplinarity develops your cognitive capacities in several ways that include, but are not limited to, those listed in Table 3.2. These capacities are the foci of much of this book.

The Product of Interdisciplinary Studies The product of interdisciplinary studies is a more comprehensive understanding of a problem. This understanding assumes many forms such as a new insight, a solution, an account, an explanation. The understanding is achieved by integrating knowledge and modes of thinking from two or more disciplines to create products, solve problems, and offer explanations in ways that would not be possible using single disciplinary means (Repko & Szostak, 2016). The product or cognitive gain of interdisciplinary studies, then, is a combination of *cognition* and *application*, of understanding and taking action.

Table 3.2 Cognitive Capacities Developed by Interdisciplinary Studies

Cognitive Capacities

Identify issues, problems, or questions appropriate for interdisciplinary inquiry.

Deconstruct the problem to reveal its several disciplinary parts and how these parts relate to each other.

Place the problem within a larger context (i.e., "contextualize" the problem).

Understand how interdisciplinarians gather and evaluate information.

Empathize with (but not fully embrace) expert viewpoints that may conflict.

Detect the assumptions, biases, values, and disciplinary training of experts (e.g., know how they think).

Reflect on your own biases and values.

Understand how interdisciplinarians discover or create common ground between different and conflicting viewpoints.

Understand how interdisciplinarians integrate knowledge that is contrasting and conflicting. (Note: This book introduces the concept of integration and facilitates your understanding of integration. A detailed discussion of how to actually perform integration and construct more comprehensive understandings is reserved for the follow-on text, *Interdisciplinary Research: Process and Theory*, 3rd edition, 2016.)

Understand how interdisciplinarians construct more comprehensive understandings of complex problems.

An Integrated Definition of Interdisciplinary Studies

It is now possible to present an integrated definition of interdisciplinary studies:

> Interdisciplinary studies is a cognitive process by which individuals or groups draw on disciplinary perspectives and integrate their insights and modes of thinking to advance their understanding of a complex problem with the goal of applying the understanding to a real-world problem.

This definition contains five ideas that you can easily commit to memory and use to construct your own definition of interdisciplinary studies:

- Cognitive process of drawing on disciplinary perspectives (a discipline's unique view of reality)

- Integrate insights

- Advance understanding

- Complex problem (*An interdisciplinary "problem" can be stated as a problem, an issue, a question, a hypothesis, or an imagined or projected world.)

- Apply the understanding

This definition is both purposeful and practical. Interdisciplinary work is not so much an end in itself as a means to achieve a result that can assume many forms—some abstract (such as a new understanding) and some concrete (such as a new product).

The Premise of Interdisciplinary Studies

The underlying premise of interdisciplinary studies is that the disciplines are themselves the necessary precondition for and foundation of the interdisciplinary enterprise. *Precondition* means prerequisite; it also implies preparation. In other words, developing competence in interdisciplinarity involves understanding the disciplines, their character, and their approach to problem solving. *Foundation* means the basis on which something stands, like a house standing on a foundation. The disciplines are foundational to interdisciplinary studies because they have produced the perspectives and insights that contribute to our ability as humans to understand our world. Even with the many shortcomings of the disciplines, we need to take them seriously and learn from them as much as we can. In our quest for more comprehensive understandings of, and ultimately solutions to, the many complex problems confronting the worlds of nature and human society, *the disciplines are the place where we begin but not where we end.* This premise is explicit in the integrated definition of interdisciplinary studies. Three examples illustrate this premise:

- To write a textbook on technology and American society since its colonial beginnings, the authors had to consult literature from multiple disciplines including history, art (to illustrate technological advances), economics, and the interdisciplinary fields of American studies and science, technology, and society.

- To explain the complex phenomenon of autism, researchers had to be deeply informed by disciplinary expertise from psychology, genetics, the visual arts, and music education.

- To design an interactive museum display of the life and presidency of Gerald R. Ford, curators had to consult expertise from several disciplines and fields including American literature, history, communications, education, race and ethnic studies, and civic and government studies.

Differences Between Disciplinarity, Multidisciplinarity, Interdisciplinarity, and Transdisciplinarity

Developing competence in interdisciplinary studies requires knowing the differences between disciplinarity, multidisciplinarity, interdisciplinarity, and transdisciplinarity. Reading Lawrence Wheeler's "The Fable of the Elephant House" provides a useful backdrop for making these very different approaches clear.

The Fable of the Elephant House

Once upon a time a planning group was formed to design a house for an elephant. On the committee were an architect, an interior designer, an engineer, a sociologist, and a psychologist. The elephant was highly educated too . . . but he was not on the committee.

The five professionals met and elected the architect as their chairman. His firm was paying the engineer's salary, and the consulting fees of the other experts, which, of course, made him the natural leader of the group.

At their *fourth* meeting they agreed it was time to get at the essentials of their problem. The architect asked just two things: "How much money can the elephant spend?" and "What does the site look like?"

The engineer said that precast concrete was the ideal material for elephant houses, especially as his firm had a new computer just begging for a stress problem to run.

The psychologist and the sociologist whispered together and then one of them said, "How many elephants are going to live in this house?" . . . It turned out that *one* elephant was a psychological problem but *two* or more were a sociological matter. The group finally agreed that though *one* elephant was buying the house, he might eventually marry and raise a family. Each consultant could, therefore, take a legitimate interest in the problem.

The interior designer asked, "What do elephants do when they're at home?"

"They lean against things," said the engineer. "We'll need strong walls."

"They eat a lot," said the psychologist. "You'll want a big dining room . . . and they like the color green."

"As a sociological matter," said the sociologist, "I can tell you that they mate standing up. You'll need high ceilings."

So they built the elephant a house. It had precast concrete walls, high ceilings, and a large dining area. It was painted green to remind him of the jungle. And it was completed for only 15% over the original estimate.

The elephant moved in. He always ate outdoors, so he used the dining room for a library . . . but it wasn't very cozy.

He never leaned against anything, because he had lived in circus tents for years, and knew that walls fall down when you lean on them.

The girl he married *hated* green, and so did he. They were *very* urban elephants.

And the sociologist was wrong too. . . . They didn't stand up. So the high ceilings merely produced echoes that greatly annoyed the elephants. They moved out in less than six months!
(Wheeler & Miller, 1970)

It is doubtful that you will be called upon to serve on a committee to build a house for an elephant. But it is highly likely that you will be involved in addressing a complex problem where disciplinary experts will approach the problem from their narrow perspectives.

Disciplinarity

In the fable, the disciplinary experts "saw" the problem of building a house for the elephant through the narrow lens of their particular discipline and proposed solutions that reflected their narrow understanding. A **discipline** is a branch of learning or body of knowledge such as physics, psychology, or history. **Disciplinarity** refers to the system of knowledge specialties called disciplines, which is little more than a century old. The disciplinary approach to addressing a complex problem is to focus on a problem or the part of a problem that the discipline is interested in. In "The Fable of the Elephant House," the committee of disciplinary experts broke the building project problem down into its various parts with each disciplinary expert focusing only on that part of the problem that corresponded to his area of expertise.

The committee's action reflected the "divide and conquer" strategy of **disciplinary reductionism**, which reduces complex things to simpler or more fundamental things. Disciplinary reductionism *assumes* that by dividing a complex problem, object, or behavior into its constituent parts and studying them separately, the knowledge produced by narrow specialties can be readily combined into an understanding of the phenomenon as a whole. In the case of the elephant house, reductionism is evident by the conversation between the psychologist and sociologist about the possible number of elephants that might inhabit the house: Psychologists study individuals whereas sociologists study groups. Since they were unsure about the number of elephants that would ultimately inhabit the house, they agreed that both disciplines had a legitimate interest in the problem.

Disciplinary reductionism has produced much of what we know about our world and ourselves. However, disciplinary reductionism does not always produce positive results, as is evident in the case of the series of dams that were built on the Columbia and Snake Rivers. This extensive (and expensive) system of dams, tragically, resulted in the destruction of the salmon fishery industry in the region and the near extinction of several species of salmon. The reason: Narrow disciplinary perspectives dominated the planning process. In disciplinary work, a single discipline (shown as the dark puzzle piece in Figure 3.2) approaches the problem. No effort is made to involve other disciplines.

Figure 3.2 Disciplinarity

Source: ©iStockphoto.com/t_kimura.

Multidisciplinarity

Multidisciplinarity is the placing side by side of insights from two or more disciplines without attempting to integrate them (see Box 3.1).

"The Fable of the Elephant House" illustrates a multidisciplinary approach to solving a complex problem because the disciplinary experts (i.e., committee members) speak with separate voices and their perspectives on the problem are presented in serial fashion: The engineer focused on building strong walls; the sociologist was concerned about the number of elephants that would live in the house; the psychologist focused on the eating habits and color preferences of elephants. But notice that no one questioned the project as a whole or the process by which the house was being designed and built. In multidisciplinary work, each participating discipline retains its separate identity, as shown in Figure 3.3.

Box 3.1 Multidisciplinarity

Multidisciplinary studies proceeds from combined disciplinary provinces, and its methods differ little from the traditional ones. Through a multidisciplinary framework, one may consider the humanities sequentially through literature, then psychology, then biology; but these separate disciplines never intersect upon a well-defined [point]. Multidisciplinary examinations may be characterized as a juxtapositioning of disciplines. The clearly distinguished and sequential studies simply provide consecutive disciplinary views of the [question]. (Cluck, 1980, p. 68)

Interdisciplinarity

Missing from the fable of the elephant house is an interdisciplinarian who would have suggested that the committee develop a comprehensive description of shelters preferred by elephants. The interdisciplinarian is trained to recognize disciplinary perspectives and can readily detect how disciplinary assumptions can skew understanding.

Interdisciplinarity *subsumes* (i.e., includes or absorbs) multidisciplinarity and *transcends* it (i.e., goes beyond its limits) by means of integration. This is reflected in our integrated definition of interdisciplinary studies: "a cognitive process by which individuals or groups draw on disciplinary perspectives and integrate their insights and modes of thinking to advance their understanding of a complex problem with the goal of applying the understanding to a real-world problem."

Figure 3.3 Multidisciplinarity

Source: ©iStockphoto.com/alexsl.

Two Metaphors As "The Fable of the Elephant House" contains no example of an interdisciplinary approach, two metaphors are introduced to draw a sharp contrast between multidisciplinary and interdisciplinary approaches. A **metaphor** is a figure of speech in which a word or phrase, a story, or a picture is likened to the idea that you are trying to communicate.

> *The Bowl of Fruit.* Multidisciplinarity can be compared to a bowl of fruit containing a variety of fruits, each fruit representing a discipline and being in close proximity to the others. The number of fruits used and the proportions of each in the bowl may not be based on anything more than visual appeal, as shown in Figure 3.4.

An example of a multidisciplinary approach to understanding a complex problem is an environmental science program where instructors from two different disciplines present their perspectives on a particular topic in serial fashion. Though readings by experts from each field are provided, it is left to the students to make connections between the two disciplinary perspectives. Without clear instruction on what interdisciplinary studies involves and how the interdisciplinary process works, students are unable to make sense of the conflicting disciplinary views on the problem let alone integrate their insights. Sadly, this approach is common on many campuses. The relationship between the disciplines in a multidisciplinary context is merely one of proximity, as in the bowl of fruit.

Figure 3.4 The Bowl of Fruit Illustrating Multidisciplinarity

Source: ©iStockphoto.com/MaxRiesgo.

The Smoothie. Moti Nissani (1995) compares interdisciplinarity to a "smoothie." The smoothie is finely blended so that the distinctive flavor of each fruit is no longer recognizable, yielding instead the delectable experience of the smoothie, as shown in Figure 3.5.

To transform the environmental studies course from a multidisciplinary to an explicitly interdisciplinary one, the following would need to occur:

- Students would be introduced to the interdisciplinary process and learn that it is an overarching process that does not privilege particular disciplines or their methods.

- Students would be introduced to the concept of disciplinary perspective and learn how to use it to identify disciplines potentially relevant to the problem.

- Students would examine the participating disciplines for their perspective on reality and their assumptions,

Figure 3.5   The Smoothie Illustrating Interdisciplinary Integration

Source: ©iStockphoto.com/AWEvans.

epistemologies, theories, key concepts, and research methods and learn how these influence disciplinary experts' understanding of the problem.

- Students would critically evaluate expert insights and locate their sources of conflict.

- Students would be introduced to the concept of common ground and learn to use techniques to create it as well as to recognize integrations that are deeply informed by disciplinary expertise.

- Students would be introduced to the concept of interdisciplinary understanding and learn how to recognize understandings that could be evaluated against the specific goal of the interdisciplinary project.

The difference between multidisciplinarity and interdisciplinarity is illustrated in Figure 3.6.

Figure 3.6   The Difference Between Multidisciplinarity and Interdisciplinarity

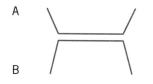

A   A   **Multidisciplinary**

B   B   Insights into a common problem from two disciplines (A + B) are consulted but no integration occurs

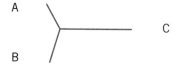

A   **Interdisciplinary**

B   C   Insights into a common problem from two disciplines (A + B) are integrated to construct a more comprehensive understanding

Source: Reprinted with permission from *Integrating Interdisciplinary Research* (2004, p. 29), by the National Academy of Sciences, courtesy of the National Academies Press, Washington, D.C.

The Difference Between Multidisciplinarity and Interdisciplinarity Summarized

- Multidisciplinarity is the study of a complex issue, problem, or question from the perspective of two or more disciplines by drawing on their insights but *making no attempt to integrate them*. Insights are juxtaposed (i.e., placed side by side) and are added together but not integrated.

- Interdisciplinarity is the study of a complex issue, problem, or question from the perspective of two or more disciplines by drawing on their insights and *integrating them*. The interdisciplinary process is used to construct a more comprehensive understanding of the problem. The object of inquiry may be an intellectual question or a real-world problem.

You should not conclude that multidisciplinary approaches are inferior to interdisciplinary approaches. There are many instances where multidisciplinary approaches are appropriate because all that is desired (or even needed) is to place insights from two or more disciplines side by side for the limited purpose of comparing them. A multidisciplinary approach would be adequate, for instance, for the limited purpose of comparing two plans for starting a business, two approaches to developing an urban space, or two bills that address a public policy issue.

Note that in these situations, the challenge is to select the better plan and reject the other, because both plans are already comprehensive—they each address the entire problem. But when the problem is complex, none of the alternative plans is comprehensive; each addresses only one aspect of the problem. In this case, an interdisciplinary approach is required, and the challenge is not to select one plan and reject the others but to select insights from each plan and then integrate them into a new, more comprehensive plan. Thus, when a problem is simple or multifaceted but not complex, a multidisciplinary approach should suffice, but when it is complex, a multidisciplinary approach is never adequate—an interdisciplinary approach is necessary.

Transdisciplinarity

Transdisciplinarity is an approach related to multidisciplinarity and interdisciplinarity but different from them. The term *transdisciplinarity* once signaled the pursuit of a unified theory of everything. Today, especially in Europe, it means research that integrates not just across disciplines but across nonacademic sources of insight from stakeholders and practitioners. A transdisciplinary environmental research program would thus involve local farmers, not as subjects but as participants. Stakeholders may include local businesses, government (local, state, or federal) agencies, nonprofit organizations, and various interest groups (Gibbons et al., 1994). Practitioners in this context are those who must implement the policy after it is developed. Practitioners may be politicians, bureaucrats, NGOs, public administrators, and so forth. Transdisciplinarity is thus associated with a team approach to research and an emphasis on case studies: environmental degradation in a particular locality rather than in general. It can thus be considered to be a type of interdisciplinarity with extra defining characteristics: nonacademic participation, teams, and case studies. Transdisciplinarians (see Box 3.2) propose democratic solutions to controversial problems such as environmental sustainability and risks of technological modernization such as nuclear power plants (Transdisciplinary Net, 2009).

Box 3.2 Transdisciplinarity

We define *transdisciplinarity* as involving academic researchers from different unrelated disciplines as well as nonacademic participants, such as land managers, user groups, and the general public, to create new knowledge and theory and delve into a common question. Transdisciplinarity thus combines interdisciplinarity with a participatory approach. (G. Tress, Tress, & Fry, 2007, p. 374)

This definition gives us a glimpse into what would be involved in going beyond interdisciplinary studies as we have defined it. Transdisciplinarity seeks to integrate the insights of academic researchers *and* nonacademic participants as part of the research process. It also seeks to use the more comprehensive understanding constructed by interdisciplinary studies to design and implement real-world policy. As used in this book, **transdisciplinarity** is the cooperation of academics, stakeholders, and practitioners to solve complex societal or environmental problems of common interest with the goal of resolving them by designing and implementing public policy.

Two Conceptions of Interdisciplinarity

Klein (1996) presents two conceptions of interdisciplinarity: instrumental and critical. These can be viewed not as mutually exclusive but as occupying opposite ends of a spectrum: At one end is instrumental interdisciplinarity, which sees interdisciplinarity as a way to solve complex practical problems; on the other end is critical interdisciplinarity, which sees interdisciplinarity as a theoretical problem (see Box 3.3).

Box 3.3   Bridge Building and Restructuring

Solving social and technological problems and borrowing tools and methods exemplify instrumentalism. The search for unified knowledge and critique exemplify the other end of the spectrum. The difference is embodied in two metaphors . . . bridge building and restructuring. . . . Bridge builders do not tend to engage in critical reflection on problem choice, the epistemology of the disciplines being used, or the logic of disciplinary structure. In contrast, restructuring changes parts of disciplines. It often embodies, as well, a critique of the state of the disciplines being restructured, and, either implicitly or explicitly, the prevailing structure of knowledge. (Klein, 2005, pp. 10–11)

While we focus on instrumental interdisciplinarity in this book, developing competence in interdisciplinary studies requires understanding both conceptions and recognizing how their approaches differ but also interact, as in the field of environmental studies.

Critical Interdisciplinarity

Critical interdisciplinarity questions disciplinary assumptions and ideological underpinnings. In some cases, it aims to replace the existing structure of knowledge (i.e., the disciplines) and the system of education based upon it (Klein, 2010, p. 23). A radical form of critical interdisciplinarity is "anti-disciplinary" and asserts that the disciplines are constructed by oppressors and are imbued with their values and way of thinking, so if one rejects oppression, then one must also reject disciplines. Examples of fields that have strong critical imperatives include women's studies, development studies, environmental studies, post-colonial studies, and cultural studies. These fields were formed and grew "on waves of public concern for specific societal problems, and were sometimes the 'academic arm' of social or 'rights' movements" (Mollinga, 2008, p. 8).

Critical interdisciplinarity adopts an attitude of suspicion and calls into question not only research data but also the researcher, the research design, and the interpretation of findings. Every part of the research process comes under critical scrutiny, exposing its taken-for-granted assumptions that may serve elite interests or that may produce findings that reinforce the status quo. Critical interdisciplinarity rejects the belief that research can be apolitical, objective, and value neutral (Alvesson & Sköldberg, 2000, p. 110).

Critical interdisciplinarians are also suspicious of holism and integration (Lattuca, 2001, p. 246). They fault instrumentalists for merely integrating disciplinary insights without advocating the transformation of the disciplines themselves. Rather than building bridges between disciplines for practical problem-solving purposes as instrumentalists do, critical interdisciplinarians seek to dismantle boundaries of all kinds and challenge existing power structures, demanding that interdisciplinarity respond to the needs and problems of oppressed and marginalized groups (Kann, 1979, pp. 187–188). Canadian studies scholar Jill Vickers makes the case for critical interdisciplinarity in Canadian studies (see Box 3.4). Her analysis is similar to critiques in race and ethnic studies, non-Western cultural studies, peace and conflict studies, and women's studies.

Box 3.4 Critical Interdisciplinarity

Certainly, for many advocates of I-D, the motive is to put back together things which disciplinary methods of analysis broke into parts. . . . The Asia Studies scholar wants her students to understand China or Japan in their complexity, not as fragmented expertise. Educators in the professions want their students to learn social work or engineering as a carefully structured synthesis of the knowledge from the different disciplines they will need to counsel clients or design computers. . . .

[The] assertion that interdisciplinarity is *essentially* a process for achieving integrative synthesis is problematic, however, because it ignores the most important issues about the nature of knowledge raised by the "four posts" [i.e., post-modernism, post-positivism, post-colonialism, post-structuralism]. Both post-modernists and post-colonialists would assert that [the instrumentalist] goal of integration and synthesis is an attempt to impose (or retain) a totalizing account of difference, since integration usually involves the absorption of the weaker by the stronger. . . .

(Continued)

(Continued)

As practiced by most scholars and students in Canada, I-D Canadian Studies is a field of self-studies which emerged partly in opposition to European dominance and partly in opposition to U.S. dominance. . . . The concept of *critical interdisciplinarity* captures . . . two forces at work—the *integrative* tendency . . . and a self-asserting, *disintegrative* tendency which tries to draw the focus away from the centre of existing knowledge systems, away from the Western-centered towards the indigenous, away from the male-centered towards women-centered, and so on. . . .

This must involve us in the question of what different kinds of cognitive communities consider evidence or its equivalent in terms of what makes one "bit" of knowledge persuasive to us while other "bits" are not persuasive. Here the answers among the different types of cognitive communities are very different. In women's studies, for example, testimonial ("lived experience") plays a crucial role. In native studies, traditional knowledge preserved over the centuries through an oral tradition and interpreted by Elders is central. (Vickers, 1998, pp. 21–23)

Instrumental Interdisciplinarity

The more common conception of interdisciplinarity is **instrumental interdisciplinarity**. This is a pragmatic conception of interdisciplinarity that focuses on research, borrowing (from disciplines), and practical problem solving in response to the demands of society (Weingart, 2000, p. 39). The instrumental approach embraces the full diversity of authors and perspectives rather than rejecting their legitimacy, or as Vickers indicates, "drawing the focus away from those with which one disagrees, as critical interdisciplinarity does." Instead, instrumentalists seek to create commonalities between conflicting disciplinary insights, integrate these, and construct more comprehensive understandings of complex problems. Though pragmatic, instrumental interdisciplinarity necessitates questioning the disciplines but does so without being hostile to them. Instrumental interdisciplinarians are aware that disciplinary understandings are biased but believe that these can be carefully evaluated in order to reveal less-biased insights that can then be integrated into a more holistic understanding. Marilyn R. Tayler (2012) provides an example of an instrumental approach in which she focuses primarily on which disciplines are relevant to her subject in terms of their perspectives or worldview and how occasional "overlapping" of these perspectives complicates the research process (see Box 3.5).

Box 3.5   The Nature of Disciplines

The term "discipline," in the context of interdisciplinary research, encompasses subdisciplines, schools of thought and interdisciplinary fields. . . . What they all have in common is that each is characterized by its own perspective or world view. . . . The potentially relevant fields for this study include religion, religious studies, political science, law, history, sociology and cultural studies. (Taylar, 2012, p. 26)

Some interdisciplinarians combine instrumental with critical approaches. For example, Michan Andrew Connor (2012) describes how a purely instrumental approach fails to integrate the multiple, overlapping, and occasionally conflicting elements of the essential relationship between places and social life. In his case study of "the metropolitan problem" (i.e., suburban sprawl) exemplified in the city of Lakewood in Los Angeles County, California, Connor critiques the effects of "metropolitanization" on two levels: on "a deeply practical one that resonates with public policy and social justice issues," and on a scholarly one that takes experts to task for failing to develop "self-consciously integrative and interdisciplinary methods" (see Box 3.6).

Box 3.6   Metropolitanization

Over the course of the 20th century, the United States became a metropolitan nation. In 1910, only 28% of Americans lived in cities or their surrounding suburbs, but by 2000, 80% of Americans lived in metropolitan areas, and in 37 of 50 states, the majority of the population lived in metropolitan areas (Hobbs & Stoops, 2002, pp. 1, 7).

Suburban population (31% of Americans) had nearly reached parity with urban (32%) in 1960. By 2000, just over half of the U.S. population lived in suburbs, while only three in ten Americans lived in cities (Hobbs & Stoops, 2002, p. 33). This ongoing process of metropolitanization is important because social benefits and problems are not evenly distributed in space; residential location ties individuals and families to spatial patterns of distribution. Sections of metropolitan areas can be described as "communities of opportunity" (Reece, Rogers, Gambhir, & Powell, 2007), and differences in opportunity organized spatially can have tremendous effects. Local living environments influence life

(Continued)

(Continued)

chances; shape perceptions, political views, and values; and structure political, economic, social, and ecological conflicts. On one level, then, the problem of metropolitan formation is a deeply practical one that resonates with public policy and social justice issues.

But the metropolitan problem is also a scholarly problem, in the sense that efforts to understand metropolitan areas have been incompletely developed and inadequately integrated. Though there is evidence that "metropolitan studies" (as distinct from "urban" or "suburban" studies) is emerging as a multidisciplinary scholarly endeavor, its practitioners to date have not developed self-consciously integrative and interdisciplinary methods. More often, metropolitan scholars continue to address similar, though not wholly congruent, sets of problems and issues using characteristically disciplinary methods and theoretical approaches. In this chapter, adapted from a larger research project, the application of a purposefully interdisciplinary research process is considered as a demonstration of one possible interdisciplinary synthesis for metropolitan studies. (Connor, 2012, pp. 53–54)

Connor's pioneering work in the interdisciplinary field of American studies demonstrates that the distinctions between instrumental and critical interdisciplinarity are not absolute and unbridgeable. *All* interdisciplinary problems require critical assessment of the insights of disciplines and of the assumptions underlying them. What interdisciplinary problems don't *require* is questioning of disciplinarity, which is the focus of critical interdisciplinarity.

The approach to interdisciplinary studies set out in this book is instrumental, seeing interdisciplinarity as a way to approach complex problems, but the authors are receptive to any constructive challenges to the interdisciplinary process (including ways to improve the evaluation of disciplinary insights and the identification and assessment of assumptions underlying them) provided by critical interdisciplinarians.

Useful Metaphors of Interdisciplinary Studies

Metaphors are important to interdisciplinary studies in three ways: (1) They help us visualize an unfamiliar concept, (2) they help us contrast this mode of learning with disciplinary modes of learning, and (3) they help us communicate to others what interdisciplinary studies is about. To this end, three metaphors are presented, each of which communicates one or more key aspects of interdisciplinarity.

The Metaphor of Boundary Crossing

The metaphor of boundary or border crossing compares disciplines to territories, countries, or spaces. Boundaries exist in many forms, including geographical, social, economic, political, religious, gender, educational, legal, and ethnic. We are surrounded by boundaries. However, we are mostly unaware of their existence until we happen to find one blocking our progress. An example of an economic boundary is attempting to purchase a luxury car without having the money necessary to pay for it, insure it, and maintain it.

The metaphor depicts the process of moving from one discipline or knowledge formation to another, say, from sociology to economics. Interdisciplinary studies typically involves investigating a boundary-overlapping issue where you have to draw on expert views from two or more disciplines. The issue of human cloning, for example, requires crossing the boundaries between biology, religion, ethics, and law. The problem of how to fund public education calls for crossing the boundaries between education, economics, sociology, and political science. The question of how to interpret the meaning of a poem or painting or song lyrics involves crossing the boundaries between communication, psychology, and several disciplines in the humanities such as literature, art history, and music.

The metaphor of boundary crossing is useful for communicating two aspects of interdisciplinarity: its *focus on the disciplines* as sources of expert information on a particular problem and its *description of the action* required to access expertise.

By its focus on the disciplines, the metaphor of boundary crossing implies that they are similar to foreign countries with well-defined borders and carefully guarded points of entry such as the U.S.–Mexico border crossing shown in Figure 3.7. It is true that disciplines historically staked out their differences, claims, and activities and built institutional structures to define and protect their knowledge practices and source of funding. In universities, these structures typically are called academic departments.

The metaphor of boundary crossing also says something about the action required to access this expertise. Interdisciplinary learners are like travelers who move from Country A to Country B to Country C in search of knowledge relevant to the problem under study. To search productively, the "traveler" must learn the language of each "country." For interdisciplinarians, crossing disciplinary boundaries is necessary to access disciplinary expertise.

Figure 3.7   U.S.–Mexico Border Crossing

Source: ©iStockphoto.com/TrevorSmith.

This territorial metaphor suffers from three deficiencies. First, it conveys the notion that disciplines are static rather than dynamic and evolving entities. The reality is that within each discipline there are those who challenge and erode the boundaries of their discipline. The second is the notion that language poses a significant or even insurmountable barrier to accessing expertise in unfamiliar disciplines. While language poses a challenge, it is a manageable one, requiring only that the interdisciplinarian learn enough of a discipline's language to work productively in it. Third, this metaphor leaves the impression that the boundary itself remains unchanged by the act of crossing it. Our next metaphor will suggest, instead, that the act of integration affects the territories it connects.

Becoming interdisciplinary involves seeing yourself as a traveler in search of knowledge from disciplines that will help you to develop a useful program of study and solve specific problems. Becoming interdisciplinary also involves your learning to communicate productively with others who are different from you.

The Metaphor of Bridge Building

The metaphor of bridge building is a useful way to communicate another important aspect of interdisciplinary learning: *the idea of connecting knowledge from two or more disciplines in order to advance understanding*. The purpose of a bridge is to connect two points of land that are divided by some impassable obstacle such as a river or ravine. A bridge makes communication possible.

There are two attractions to this metaphor. The first is the idea that interdisciplinarity is something that takes place between two disciplines. Accordingly, the disciplines are like the land on either side that the Golden Gate Bridge connects (see Figure 3.8). Each shore offers depth of specialized knowledge on particular topics. Interdisciplinarity is like the bridge that makes it possible for you to draw on disciplinary expertise and make connections between two or more knowledge formations. The boundary between the two disciplines becomes porous.

The second attraction of this metaphor is the idea that interdisciplinary studies has an applied orientation. Making connections between different knowledge domains is not merely a stimulating intellectual exercise but a practical way to deepen and broaden your understanding of a complex topic that would not be possible using a single disciplinary approach as well. For example, connecting the views of authors from psychology and political science on the complex problem of the causes of terrorism can provide new insights into this troubling phenomenon.

There are, however, limitations with using bridge building to describe interdisciplinary studies. Bridge building leaves the lands connected unchanged (though they get more traffic), whereas interdisciplinarity may influence the disciplines. Moreover, **critical reflection** is the process of analyzing, questioning, and reconsidering the activity (cognitive or physical) that you are engaged in and stands in contrast to the metaphor of bridging. This "looking back" serves several purposes:

- To revisit key decisions that were made
- To construct knowledge about yourself in terms of asking "why you made the decisions that you did"
- To view the project as a whole rather than as a series of separate parts and actions
- To make meaning of the experience for future reference

Figure 3.8   Golden Gate Bridge, San Francisco: View Across Bay

Source: ©iStockphoto.com/ c8501089.

In other words, *interdisciplinary studies cares as much about understanding the implications of the connections it makes as it does about the process of making connections.*

The designers of a bridge do not tend to engage in critical reflection on the project once it is under way. This is because civil engineers can design the whole bridge at the outset, before construction begins. They can do this because what they are constructing is simple, not complex. In contrast, there's a lot of simulation, experimentation, and trial and error in constructing a more comprehensive understanding. That's because a full understanding of a complex problem (unlike a bridge) yields an imprecise and shifting pattern (not an unvarying blueprint). There are right and wrong choices in engineering, whereas in interdisciplinary work the choices are between better and worse.

Furthermore, whereas physical bridges are built to handle a variety of vehicles, in interdisciplinary studies, the bridge between disciplines is designed only for the specific problem being studied. Shift to another problem, or even to a different combination of disciplines, and a new bridge will probably have to be built.

The Metaphor of Bilingualism

The metaphor of bilingualism offers another useful way to visualize the concept of interdisciplinarity. The focus of this metaphor is on communication through the use of language and compares disciplines to foreign languages. The attraction of this metaphor is that it recognizes that disciplines, like foreign languages, each have their own vocabulary that must be understood in order for individuals to be able to communicate with each other (see Figure 3.9). Unlike our previous metaphors, it appreciates that interdisciplinary integration is an ongoing process. One popular introductory-level sociology textbook lists over a hundred key terms

Figure 3.9 Difficulty in Communicating With Another Discipline

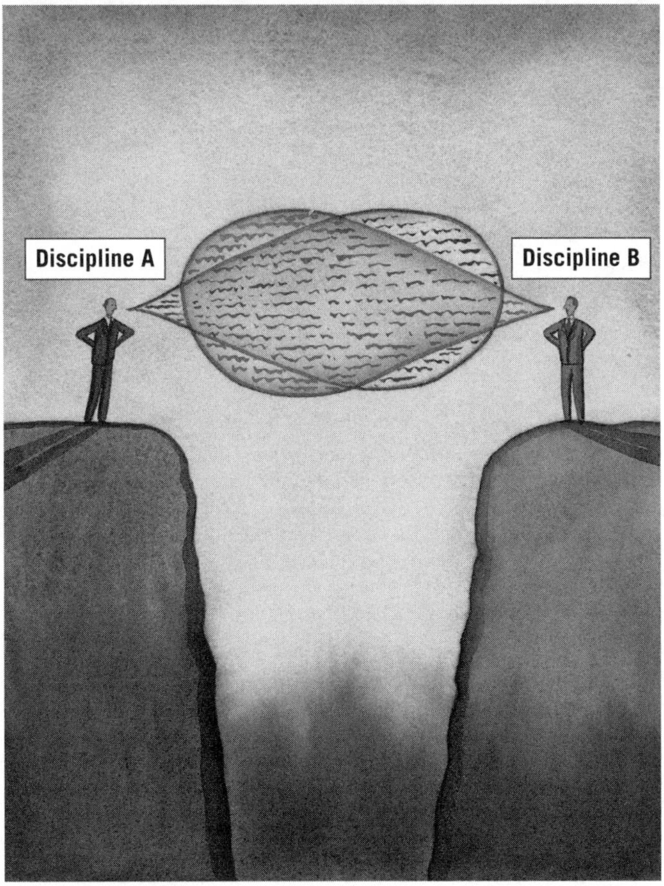

Source: ©Stockbyte/Getty Images.

that students are expected to learn, much like a foreign language. Imagine the linguistic challenge that you would face if, after having spent 2 years majoring in art history, you decided to major in biology in order to go to medical school. Or if after majoring in psychology, you decided to major in criminal justice to enter law enforcement. For many, developing proficiency in a new discipline is as difficult and time consuming as developing proficiency in a foreign language.

There are two limitations to the metaphor of bilingualism. First, because bilingualism means fluency in two languages, it implies that you cannot work in new disciplines without first mastering them. This is not the case. Rather than requiring mastery, interdisciplinary studies involves developing *adequacy*

Table 3.3 Summary of Aspects of Interdisciplinary Studies Provided by Each Metaphor

Aspects of Interdisciplinary Studies

Metaphor	Comparison	Useful Aspect(s)	Weakness(es)
Boundary Crossing	Compares interdisciplinary studies to crossing physical boundaries	1. Focuses on the disciplines as sources of expertise on a given topic 2. Describes the action required to access that expertise	1. Conveys the incorrect notion that disciplines are static rather than dynamic entities 2. Fails to describe the language barrier between disciplines
Bridge Building	Compares interdisciplinary studies to connecting two points of land	1. Interdisciplinary studies is something that takes place between two disciplines 2. Interdisciplinary studies has an applied orientation	1. The designers of a bridge do not tend to engage in critical reflection on the project once it is underway
Bilingualism	Compares interdisciplinary studies to learning foreign languages	1. Recognizes that, like foreign languages, each discipline has its own vocabulary that must be understood in order for individuals to be able to participate in a conversation with others from that discipline	1. Assumes that you must master each discipline before working in it 2. Bilingualism involves either/or thinking 3. Integrating disciplinary insights involves more than translation

in disciplines relevant to the problem such that you can access their insights and understand them. The preceding two metaphors did not imply that it was necessary to master each discipline.

There is a second and more serious limitation of the metaphor of bilingualism. It is often assumed that translation or merely sorting out disciplinary vocabularies is all that is required to engage in interdisciplinary work. But as noted earlier in the definition of interdisciplinary studies, a hallmark of interdisciplinarity is integration of insights from the relevant disciplines. Integration involves far more than translation. Even when the insights are expressed in the same language, they often conflict. So a basic competency of interdisciplinarity is the ability to recognize and address the sources of conflict in disciplinary perspectives.

CRITICAL THINKING QUESTIONS

1. From your close reading of the five definitions of interdisciplinary studies, explain how interdisciplinarity differs from disciplinarity in terms of (a) purpose, (b) process, and (c) product.

2. In "The Fable of the Elephant House," how could the narrative be altered to include (a) an interdisciplinary approach to the project and (b) a transdisciplinary approach?

3. Of the various metaphors used in this chapter to describe interdisciplinary studies, which one is closest to (a) the definition of interdisciplinary studies and (b) your understanding of interdisciplinarity? Why? Can you think of another metaphor that perhaps combines several of the useful aspects of the metaphors discussed?

APPLICATIONS AND EXERCISES

1. Develop your personal definition of interdisciplinary studies as it relates to the interdisciplinary field you are working in so that you can easily communicate it to friends, family, and potential employers. Discuss your definition with classmates or with family and friends.

2. In your opinion, how do you think interdisciplinary studies can add value to your college education? Again, this is a useful question for discussion.

3. Conduct separate interviews of four classmates and ask them to define "social justice" in a single sentence. Write down their responses word for word. Use close reading to identify any commonalities in their definitions. Then develop a comprehensive definition of "social justice." This could be a group exercise.

4. Read the following excerpt from a scholarly article and determine whether the authors are engaged in interdisciplinary or transdisciplinary work:

> Integration of disciplines and interest groups in landscape research projects is expected to contribute to a better understanding of landscapes and to solve problems related to land use, planning, and policy development. By *integration* in landscape research projects we mean that different disciplines and knowledge communities are bridged and their knowledge fused together to address a research question. (B. Tress, Tress, & Fry, 2005)

5. How might the instrumental approach to interdisciplinarity be used to provide creative and meaningful solutions to many of the complex problems that plague human society?

6. From your reading of the discussions of critical and instrumental interdisciplinarity, which approach would likely be more helpful to policy makers as they grapple with the following issues:

   a. The development of green energy technologies

   b. What to do about immigrants who are undocumented

   c. The preservation of fine and performing arts programs in public education during a time of severe budgetary constraints

7. For students working primarily in the fine and performing arts, explain how the popular techno aesthetic of "remixing" is a useful and not so useful metaphor for interdisciplinary studies.

Source: ©iStockphoto.com/Talaj.

Chapter 4 Objectives

Interdisciplinary studies fosters certain cognitive capacities, values, traits, and skills that are applicable to the complexities of life after graduation. This chapter introduces you to this "cognitive toolkit," which will empower you to deal with complex problems and approach your education with greater self-awareness of what you are learning and how your learning affects your intellectual development. This toolkit should prove useful in your chosen profession and enable you to be a productive citizen who makes a difference. This chapter also helps you understand the value of an intellectual autobiography, portfolio, and service-learning experience and how these can help you develop and apply the intellectual "toolkit" that interdisciplinary studies fosters.

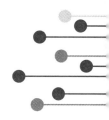

The Interdisciplinary Studies "Cognitive Toolkit"

How She Did It

The Vietnam Veterans Memorial in Washington, D.C., created by architect Maya Lin (2000) is world famous.

Located on the Mall along Constitution Avenue between the Lincoln Memorial and the Washington Monument, the memorial is a black granite wall that gently slopes downward below ground level. The first panels that visitors see are short with only a few soldiers' names. But as visitors walk along the wall descending below ground level, they see the panels grow in height and length and include an expanding list of soldiers' names carved into the stone. The names are in no particular order, becoming part of the mass

Figure 4.1   Vietnam Veterans Memorial

Source: U.S. Department of Defense photo by Linda Hosek; http://www.defense.gov/PhotoEssays/PhotoEssaySS.aspx?ID=2887.

Learning Outcomes

By the end of this chapter, you will be able to:

- Identify the cognitive capacities and values fostered by interdisciplinary studies, and understand how these are reflected in Maya Lin's work

- Identify the traits and skills fostered by interdisciplinary studies

- Understand the value of an intellectual autobiography, portfolio, and service-learning experience and how these can help you develop and apply the intellectual "toolkit" that interdisciplinary studies fosters

of names that are below the surface of the ground. Every panel is polished so that it reflects the viewer's own face and body, possibly reminding visitors of the human life behind every name. At its midpoint, the wall angles and begins ascending toward the ground above. The panels become smaller and the names become fewer with each passing step. The visitor leaves the scene at ground level again, reentering the world of the living and leaving the Vietnam War behind them.

The memorial happens to be a remarkable example of interdisciplinary work. The question is, "How exactly did Lin do it?" The following discussion answers this question by connecting Lin's work to the intellectual capacities, values, traits, and skills that interdisciplinary studies fosters.

Intellectual Capacities

Repeated exposure to interdisciplinary studies fosters the development of certain intellectual capacities, three of which are foundational to interdisciplinarity: perspective taking, critical thinking, and integration (Ivanitskaya, Clark, Montgomery, & Primeau, 2002, p. 95). **Perspective taking (interdisciplinary)** is the intellectual capacity to view a problem or subject or artifact from alternative viewpoints, including disciplinary ones, in order to develop a more comprehensive understanding of it (Baloche, Hynes, & Berger, 1996). That is, we come to understand not only how others view something in a particular way but also why they do so: You cannot really understand how another views things unless you have some idea as to why. We are not born with this capacity, which is why young children don't understand that other people have different feelings and experiences from their own. Perspective-taking capacity develops over time until it is quite sophisticated in adulthood. Research at Ohio State University suggests that reading fiction, which is one form of perspective taking, "changes us by allowing us to merge our own lives with those of the characters we read about" (Kaufman, 2012). Research in the fields of business management and social and developmental psychology strongly suggests that the capacity to take on multiple perspectives is important for a host of fundamental social and cognitive behaviors.

The painting *Two Men and a Donkey* (Figure 4.2), for example, suggests the need of the two men to understand each other's perspective of the problem of moving the donkey. Without such perspective taking, one or both men could be endangered, or at the least, moving the donkey could be a failed effort.

Other research suggests that perspective taking reduces stereotyping of those who are different from us, improves decision quality by enabling us to deal with multiple inputs, and increases creativity. It aids in recalling information by linking it to a specific perspective and facilitates the simultaneous processing of information from different perspectives when required to do so. It also enables us to adopt a broader perspective, improves efficiency when integrating information, and facilitates assembling new sets of potential solutions to a complex problem.

This research explains the importance that Lin attached to perspective taking at every stage of the design process. At no time did she allow any single perspective or ideological narrative to dominate her thinking. She consulted all relevant disciplines including architecture, art, Earth science, history, and psychology. She also consulted various community groups, including veterans and politicians. In good interdisciplinary fashion, she remained "apolitical" throughout the process: "I do not choose to overlay personal commentary on historical facts. I am interested in presenting factual information, allowing viewers the chance to come to their own conclusions" (Lin, 2000, p. 2:03). Lin's evenhanded approach is a model of how to produce quality interdisciplinary work.

Figure 4.2 *Two Men and a Donkey*

Source: © DEA / G. DAGLI ORTI/ De Agostini Picture Library/Getty Images.

The second intellectual capacity that involvement in interdisciplinary studies fosters is **critical thinking**. This is the capacity to analyze, critique, and assess (Halx & Reybold, 2006; Hatcher, 2006; Tsui, 2007). All disciplines and academic fields, including interdisciplinary studies, claim to teach their students how to think critically and analytically. In fact, disciplines in the liberal arts and the humanities typically claim "critical thinking" as an important learning outcome, as do the natural sciences and the applied fields. However, as Karri A. Holley (2009) explains, each discipline approaches critical thinking differently (see Box 4.1).

These widespread claims to promoting critical thinking raise the question: How does interdisciplinary studies contribute to the development of this key intellectual capacity in ways that are different from single-subject approaches? And do they have any advantages over single-subject approaches? We address this in more detail in Chapter 8 but note three differences here. One difference,

Box 4.1 Disciplines and Critical Thinking

Because academic contexts are frequently disciplinary in origin and because the cognitive vehicles of problem solving are positioned in a specific field, how students operationalize their analytical abilities varies widely. The task of deciphering financial statements as part of writing a business plan for a fledgling company requires analytical skills different from reading a sixteenth century text for modern-day implications. Students become socialized to particular models of analysis in their studies; as they progress through the required courses in their respective disciplines, this socialization assumes a universal way of knowing. "As we train ourselves to think in a particular way, that way of thinking becomes more and more entrenched as *our* way of thinking (and unfortunately, sometimes the *only* right way of thinking)" (Holley, 2009, p. 47).

argues Robert Toynton (2005), is that interdisciplinary studies students encounter "the approaches, products, and processes" of relevant disciplines "*from a detached and comparative viewpoint* [emphasis added]" (p. 110). Critical thinking of this kind occurs only in interdisciplinary contexts, where students are challenged to evaluate and integrate the conflicting assumptions and insights of disciplines concerning some complex issue such as the environment, which spans the natural sciences, the social sciences, and the humanities (Jones & Merritt, 1999, p. 336). A second way interdisciplinary studies contributes to the development of critical thinking is to foster **intellectual dexterity**, which is the ability to speak to (if not from) a broad spectrum of knowledge and experience (Huber, Hutchings, Gale, Miller, & Breen, 2007). Interdisciplinary studies contributes to the development of critical thinking in a third way: It shifts one's focus from a narrow disciplinary context to a broader interdisciplinary context. That is, we do not just apply a set of critical thinking tools designed for a particular disciplinary context but rather master critical thinking strategies with general applicability. This has direct application to the workplace of the new century where changes in technology have made the capacity to think critically more important than ever. According to Diane Halpern (1999),

> Better thinking is not a necessary outcome of traditional discipline-based instruction. However, when thinking skills are explicitly taught for transfer, using multiple examples from several disciplines, students can learn to improve how they think in ways that transfer across academic domains. (pp. 69–70)

For these reasons, critical thinking "can be taught most effectively in an interdisciplinary curricula" (Kelder, 1992, p. 10).

In creating and building the Vietnam Veterans Memorial, Maya Lin had to think critically about the project in ways that were both disciplinary and interdisciplinary. She had to carefully consider the contribution that each discipline and each stakeholder would make to the memorial but do so from a detached and comparative viewpoint so as to maintain balance among them:

> I spent much time researching the site—not just the physical aspects of the site but the cultural context of it as well: who will use the site, the history of the place, the nature of the people who live there. I spend the first few months researching a multitude of facts, history, and materials, not knowing if anything I am studying will be of use to me in the artwork. (Lin, 2000, p. 3:05)

The third intellectual capacity that interdisciplinary studies fosters is integration, which is at the heart of the interdisciplinary process. Integration involves critically evaluating disciplinary insights and locating their sources of conflict, creating common ground among them, and constructing a more comprehensive understanding of the problem. The "payoff" of integration is the new understanding. The payoff of Lin's integrative work was the Vietnam Veterans Memorial. Integration, in other words, produces the culmination of the interdisciplinary process.

In her design work, Lin was confronted with conflicts of all kinds, including contrasting views on the meaning of the war and how best to memorialize the dead. Finding common ground amid all of this conflict was a daunting challenge. In the end, Lin decided that the war should be memorialized as a scar etched as deeply into the earth as it was on the nation's psyche. Its physical expression is captured in the memorial's design, which involved a literal "cutting open of the earth—an initial violence that heals in time but leaves a memory, like a scar" (Lin, 2000, pp. 2:07, 4:15).

Values

Interdisciplinary studies fosters certain values that are guiding principles, mind-sets, or attitudes. These become more important when we address issues that deeply concern us. What should become clear as you examine these values is that engaging in interdisciplinary studies may affect the way you think about yourself, your community, your profession, and the world, if you allow it to. These values include empathy, ethical consciousness, humility, appreciation of diversity, tolerance of ambiguity, and civic engagement. As it happens, Lin's approach to her work manifested all of these values to a greater or lesser degree.

Empathy is identification with another's thoughts, pain, or situation in a way that can be communicated to others. Approaching individuals, groups, and cultures with empathy is part of what it means to become interdisciplinary. Empathy is an outcome of perspective taking (Gorenflo & Crano, 1998). Lin's capacity to engage in perspective taking enabled her to empathize with each group that would be affected by the memorial: the fallen soldiers, their loved ones, and those discordant groups who held strong but clashing views on war. Lin's memorial is not a statement for or against the war. In interdisciplinary work, empathy is limited to understanding the views of others; *it does not extend to adopting their views or acting to support them.* Otherwise, you engage in the practice common to disciplinary learning: taking sides or adopting a perspective rather than attempting to understand multiple perspectives. To be clear, interdisciplinarians are capable of taking firm positions despite empathy. But interdisciplinarians strive to ground their conclusions in critical thinking rather than perspectival bias. Empathy is needed in all interdisciplinary work, especially in contexts where persons or groups hold beliefs, engage in lifestyles, or express views very different from your own. Academic examples of these contexts include urban studies, race and ethnic studies, women's studies, and sexuality studies.

Ethical consciousness is self-knowledge that includes recognition of bias. It means being aware, for example, of the impact of a particular product on the environment and having this awareness affect your decision to purchase or boycott the product. Bias takes two forms here: disciplinary and personal. **Disciplinary bias** refers to favoring one discipline's understanding of the problem at the expense of competing understandings of the same problem offered by other disciplines. This is likely to occur simply because you are more familiar with a particular discipline than with others. One useful strategy here is to purposely seek to identify strengths in the insights of disciplines with which you have less familiarity and limitations in the insights of disciplines with which you have the greatest familiarity. **Personal bias** is often more subtle and refers to allowing your own point of view (e.g., your politics, faith tradition, cultural identity) to influence how you understand or approach the problem. Personal bias manifests itself through selecting materials that agree with your viewpoint while rejecting those that challenge it or by allowing a particular belief to shape your analysis of the problem. When this happens, the old expression "the fix is in" applies, meaning that the outcome is determined beforehand. Personal bias, no matter how well intentioned, is inconsistent with quality interdisciplinary work. Interdisciplinarity values diversity of perspective and seeks out relevant viewpoints, even those that conflict, or with which you disagree. Lin's ethical consciousness did not permit her to use the memorial as a vehicle for publicizing her personal view of the war. This ethical stance is necessary if interdisciplinarity is to produce understandings that are truly comprehensive and integrative, as Lin's work is. While interdisciplinarity develops your capacity to live with ideological diversity, conflict, and tension, this is not to say that "all points of view are equally valid," which amounts to extreme relativism. Rather, interdisciplinarians are realistic and tend to assume there is good and bad in each competing viewpoint. They both respect the views of others *and* critique those views, much as you would critique the view of a friend with whom you disagree.

Humility in the context of interdisciplinary studies is a positive attitude of mind that recognizes the limits of one's training and expertise and seeks to overcome these limits by drawing on expertise from multiple disciplines. It is the awareness that whatever comprehensive understanding you achieve is inevitably incomplete, limited in time and space, and likely to change as knowledge in the disciplines progresses. Lin was trained as an architect, not as a historian, psychologist, or sociologist. She was self-aware of how little she knew about the war and all of the complex factors surrounding its prosecution and aftermath. In Lin, we see humility combined with open-mindedness and respect for different views. Specifically, interdisciplinary humility is the awareness that the very complex nature of the problems studied means that the best you can strive to achieve is a general or rough understanding of the problem, not a complete or precise one. Still, you can have the satisfaction of knowing that as you move toward knowing more and more about the problem, you are accomplishing something that would be unlikely using a purely disciplinary approach. In short, interdisciplinary humility reflects awareness of both self and reality when confronted by complexity. It is evidenced to the extent that you see the weaknesses of the perspectives closest to your own and the strengths of other perspectives (Newell, 1989, p. 3).

Appreciation of diversity of ideas and people means being open to information from any and all relevant sources and having respect for people because of our common humanity. "Being open" does not mean agreeing with or abandoning a critical stance but being willing, even eager, to learn from different disciplines and other knowledge sources, as Lin was in designing the memorial. There is almost always some "kernel of truth," some valuable insight generated by the perspective of any group. One of the striking features of the memorial is its transcendence of differences and diversity. Sometimes, appreciating diverse ideas is easier than appreciating diverse people. Though we may hold different political views, adhere to different faith traditions, belong to different cultures, or have different ethnic or racial roots, we must acknowledge our commonality of being human. Recent advances in DNA research have shown that all humanity shares a common ancestry. The implication of this finding for interdisciplinarity is profound: We are not just individuals, but members of an incredibly large and very diverse human family. We are all equal, at least in this most basic way. As interdisciplinarians, we not only are (or should be) acutely aware of our common humanity but we also realistically address the differences that divide us. The great value of interdisciplinary studies is that it challenges us to confront these differences but to do so in a way that respects different viewpoints. This value is needed especially in collaborative learning and research contexts.

Tolerance of ambiguity means openness to more than one interpretation, depending on the immediate context. The Vietnam War certainly falls into the category of ambiguity. Lin designed her memorial in such a way that it left much of the ambiguity surrounding the war unresolved. She depicted the war as a fact, without passing judgment on it. Ambiguity is a useful tool in many fields, including literature and rhetoric. For example, Groucho Marx's classic joke depends on grammatical ambiguity for its humor: "Last night I shot an elephant in my pajamas. How he got in my pajamas, I'll never know." Ambiguity arises when you see that each discipline's perspective on an issue is grounded in compelling but different arguments (Newell, 1989, p. 3). Ambiguity, however, does not equate to relativism, and tolerance does not mean agreement. Interdisciplinarity recognizes that ambiguity can be unsettling, especially for those who have deeply held biases or demand clear-cut solutions to complex and controversial issues. But ambiguity is a fact of the complexity of life. Indeed, life's problems are problematic precisely because they involve uncertainty and ambiguity. They are often so complicated that it is impossible to learn everything that you need to understand them, let alone solve them. Becoming interdisciplinary means accepting that understanding any complex problem is an ongoing process and that complete understanding of it is elusive. Accepting that there is something more to know keeps you from becoming too settled in your understanding of a problem. You remain open to new perspectives and new information. You are willing to keep seeking an integrative understanding even though the shape of this is not immediately obvious.

Civic engagement is the use of nonpolitical as well as political means to affect the quality of life in a community. It flows from a belief that one can make a difference and indeed that one *can* and *should* play some role in the design or implementation of public policies. Issues such as environmental sustainability, human rights, and public health are civic issues because they impact society as a whole. Few of us will ever have the opportunity to design a world-class memorial that touches the lives of literally millions as Maya Lin has done. But we can touch people's lives in other ways that may be as effective, beginning with participating in a service-learning project. Civic engagement flows from a sense of empathy, ethical consciousness, and a heightened sense of responsibility for your community, nation, and the world *as a whole*. Working to make a difference in the civic life of your community involves developing the necessary knowledge, skills, and personal networks in the classroom and then applying these to the world outside the university. In practical terms, this means respecting the views of other people and groups because they are situated in a different location in society and have had different experiences and thus see issues from at least a slightly different perspective than you do. It is worth remembering that people to whom you accord respect are more likely to grant respect to your views.

Box 4.2 Ethics and Diversity

Note that we have earlier urged both a respect for diversity and a certain set of values. These two types of recommendation are often thought to be in conflict: If we embrace diversity, then we cannot advocate any particular values. But we can—and should—respect different perspectives without adopting every insight that might be generated by any perspective. It is our ability to integrate across the insights generated by different perspectives that allows us to embrace both a set of values and a strong appreciation of diversity.

Traits and Skills

Interdisciplinary studies also fosters the development of certain personality *traits*, which are distinguishing characteristics of a person, and *skills*, which are competencies in applying knowledge effectively or performing a task creatively. Admittedly, there is some overlap between the intellectual capacities discussed earlier and the skills typically associated with interdisciplinary studies.

Traits

The first trait is *entrepreneurship*, which involves taking risk to achieve a particular goal. The interdisciplinarian is like an entrepreneur in three ways.

Both are eager to venture into a space with which they are unfamiliar. For the entrepreneur, the space is a new market or a new product; for the interdisciplinarian, the space is a new discipline and new insights. Both are able to see possibilities that others do not see. The entrepreneur sees the possibility of meeting an unmet need through the creation of a new process or product; the interdisciplinarian sees the possibility of resolving a problem by creating common ground and integrating insights. And both are able to make connections between different things. The entrepreneur is able to connect, say, two different technologies to create a new product useful for a new purpose; the interdisciplinarian is able to creatively connect two different disciplinary insights in order to produce a more comprehensive understanding of a problem.

A second trait is *love of learning*, or excitement at the prospect of exploring new ideas, even if these ideas challenge one's own thinking. Interdisciplinarians are intensely interested in the world and welcome opportunities to view it and its problems from differing perspectives. Finding themselves in new and challenging work situations, they will seek to acquire a working knowledge of relevant terminology and the analytical skills necessary to develop an understanding of a given problem. Interdisciplinarians are not prisoners of bias (either personal or ideological), nor are they impressed by surface explanations of complex problems or simplistic solutions to them. Instead, they are willing to invest the time and intellectual energy to sort through and integrate conflicting viewpoints in order to achieve an understanding that is more comprehensive.

A third trait is *self-reflection*, which is self-conscious, careful thinking about your behavior and beliefs, why you made certain choices at various points, and how these choices have affected the outcome. Learning, in general, is a process of cognitive and personal transformation that relies heavily on self-reflection, which promotes a stronger self-concept and greater self-knowledge. Part of this process involves examining, perhaps in a reflective paper, your responses to an emotionally charged issue. The writing of an intellectual autobiography is a common method used in interdisciplinary studies and other programs to encourage self-reflection.

A fourth trait is *intellectual courage*. Recall our earlier discussion of empathy. It is far easier to ignore the suffering of others than to allow ourselves to feel it. More generally, it is easier to assume that our perspective is right than to recognize why others have different perspectives. And in the act of integrating, we inevitably produce comprehensive insights that are novel: It is generally easier in life to think as others do than to seek to justify novel ideas.

Interdisciplinarity requires a capacity, that is, for *independence of judgment*. Nor, as we shall see, is it always easy to produce novelty: We must have the courage to face a period in which we grapple with our ignorance. This in turn requires a certain degree of self-confidence, a degree of optimism, and an ability to abide incomplete and conflicting understandings. We hope in this book to increase your self-confidence and optimism by acquainting you with strategies that are useful in interdisciplinary exploration. It is of paramount importance that you appreciate that interdisciplinary integration is possible, if not always straightforward. You then need the intellectual strength to apply interdisciplinary strategies in order to achieve novel understandings. In a variety of ways, then, interdisciplinarity takes intellectual courage: We must be willing to experience some discomfort in order to achieve interdisciplinary understandings. The reward of achieving new understanding will generally far exceed the discomfort experienced along the way—just as our pleasure in a joke's punchline exceeds the cognitive tension associated with the joke's buildup—but we can only get the benefit if we are willing to face the cost. (Note here that the benefits will be larger if you have adopted values such as empathy and civic engagement and thus care about achieving superior understandings of societal challenges.)

Several other traits are implied in the foregoing. It is useful to be *patient*, as interdisciplinary examination of a question takes time. Interdisciplinary scholars and students need to *tolerate ambiguity* rather than seek one simple answer to every question. They need to *enjoy a challenge* and be able to laugh at mistakes they may make along the way. Interdisciplinarians should be *open minded*. This, we might note, is not a quality that is always appreciated in contemporary society: We expect our politicians to have a 10-second answer to every question, and our friends to have no doubt about which football team is best. Open-mindedness implies in turn a willingness to actually *listen* to what others are saying rather than always be focused on winning an argument at any cost.

It should be stressed here that an important part of the integrative process occurs subconsciously. This is true of creative acts more generally. Our subconscious minds are far better than our conscious minds at making new connections, at producing novelty. But our subconscious minds are also where our emotions reside. We may consciously aspire to courage and risk taking and self-reflection, and to acting to alleviate the problems of our time, but if we do not internalize such attitudes, our subconscious minds will not be as innovative as they could be. We will not be consciously aware that we are subconsciously shrinking from innovation. We need to really want to leave our comfort zone in order to be able to do so.

Skills

Among the skills that interdisciplinary studies fosters is that of *communicative competence*. This takes two forms. First, interdisciplinary studies fosters distinctive communicative competency regarding *what* is being communicated. Persuasive disciplinary communication typically sets out the strengths of one perspective and the limitations of other perspectives; it makes the case that one position is right and others are wrong. Persuasive interdisciplinary communication is concerned with balancing out competing claims, identifying strengths and limitations of every position, and instead of selecting one of the positions, it selects insights from each position to create a new position—one that is responsive to each of the contributing positions but dominated by none of them.

Next, interdisciplinary studies fosters distinctive communicative competency regarding the *differences* between those to whom you are communicating. Here the focus is on applying the intellectual capacities which we noted earlier: perspective taking, critical thinking, and integration. In the classroom, communicating in a manner that people from different disciplines will understand and find interesting involves describing the perspectives of interested disciplines on the complex problem under study and how each perspective illumines some aspect of the problem (the subject of Chapters 5 and 6). It also involves demonstrating critical thinking about the problem in terms of making interdisciplinary connections; comparing perspectives, interpretations, or theories; and evaluating these (the subject of Part II). In the workplace, communicative competence refers to your capability to apply the capacities, values, traits, and skills associated with interdisciplinary studies by constructively interacting with individuals whose disciplinary training, values, and beliefs differ from yours.

A second skill is *abstract thinking*, which is thinking characterized by mental adaptability and flexibility that enable you to use concepts and make generalizations. Abstract thinking is different from concrete thinking, which limits thought to what is right in front of you. The abstract thinker can conceptualize or generalize and understands that a concept may have different meanings in different disciplinary contexts. One example of this contrast would be the reactions of each type of thinker to a drawing of a woman holding a torch. The concrete thinker would simply interpret the drawing as a woman holding a torch to provide physical light, whereas the abstract thinker might interpret the drawing as representing the concept of freedom. Another example would be the possible reactions of disciplinarians and interdisciplinarians to the drawing. A political scientist might see the woman holding the torch as representing political freedom for oppressed individuals or groups, whereas the interdisciplinarian might see the woman as representing a broader and more inclusive conception of freedom that transcends narrow disciplinary conceptions. Abstract thinking is particularly important in interdisciplinary studies because it enables you to understand the *process* by which interdisciplinarians construct a more comprehensive understanding. Interdisciplinary studies requires a more challenging form of abstract thinking than the disciplines do because the objects of interdisciplinary study are complex (i.e., consist of multiple disciplinary parts).

A third skill is *creative thinking*, which is thinking that combines "previously unrelated ideas" or forms "a new relationship among ideas" (Davis, 1992). Creative thinking is often described as thinking "outside the box" (see Figure 4.3). The "box" refers to thinking about a complex problem in narrow disciplinary terms. Interdisciplinary studies *promotes* creative thinking by getting you to look at a problem in new ways, and by challenging you to ask yourself how conflicting insights into the problem might both contain "kernels of truth." Integrative understandings have to be *created*: They are necessarily novel combinations of preexisting ideas.

A fourth skill is **metacognition**, the awareness of your own learning and thinking processes, often described as "thinking about your thinking." It involves detaching yourself from your own worldview and attitudes as you think about how you have assembled your own thoughts about things. This is a key skill for interdisciplinarians to develop since interdisciplinary studies is, after all, *one large* metacognitive process. When you are engaging in interdisciplinary work, you must step back from each discipline that may be relevant to a complex problem and think metacognitively about it—identifying and critically evaluating the way each discipline thinks about the problem. This involves identifying each discipline's perspective, and in particular, its concepts and theories as well as the assumptions underlying them.

Figure 4.3   Thinking Outside the Box

"Thinking outside of the box is difficult for some people. Keep trying."

Source: Cartoon by Randy Glasbergen.

Though careers and professions differ considerably, the intellectual capacities, values, traits, and skills we have discussed are empowering to all of them in ways that are worth noting. First, *you are empowered to think and act effectively on complex problems without getting overwhelmed or cowed by disciplinary experts or resorting to digging in your heels.* It is OK to acknowledge that people with whom you disagree make valid points because you know how to proceed toward integration in the face of disagreement. Second, *you are empowered to address real-world complexity* in ways that others are unable to do. Third, *you are empowered to effectively apply your education to new contexts, new problems, and new responsibilities.* Careers are changing, so transfer/adaptability of these intellectual capacities, values, traits, and skills is crucial. As noted earlier, they will allow superior understandings of complex societal challenges, and thus will support you as a voter and member of the community. Many of the challenges we face in our social lives can be alleviated by understanding the perspectives of those we interact with and seeking shared understandings. By understanding the perspectives that are guiding behaviors, we are better able to identify *commonalities* rather than *compromises.*

Ways to Apply Your Interdisciplinary "Toolkit"

Interdisciplinary studies programs often include opportunities for you to apply and develop the tools in the "cognitive toolkit." Opportunities include writing an intellectual autobiography, preparing a portfolio of your work, and performing service learning. Though these opportunities are also available to students in disciplinary majors, they take on special significance for interdisciplinary studies students.

Writing an Intellectual Autobiography

While a biography is the story of someone's life and an autobiography is the story of your own life told from your own perspective, an **intellectual autobiography** is the story of your academic or intellectual journey told from your point of view. Writing an intellectual autobiography helps you to reinforce several of the traits and skills described in the toolkit as well as to make explicit your own journey toward becoming interdisciplinary. This exercise is broadly similar to Norfolk State's videos on personal identity mentioned in Chapter 1. (Note: Eric Stanley, an accomplished musician and graduate of the Interdisciplinary Studies program at Virginia Commonwealth University, has an interesting video on his intellectual journey at https://www.youtube.com/watch?v=XS04HN4myHc.) Menken and Keestra (2016, Chapter 13) provide some brief examples of autobiographical reflections by interdisciplinary researchers.

The most important reason for including an intellectual autobiography as part of your work in interdisciplinary studies is the "strong sense" critical thinking that such an endeavor demands. In **"strong sense" critical thinking**, your attention is directed *inward*, causing you to examine the assumptions and premises you have used to construct the logical argument presented in your work. Interdisciplinary work demands that you are aware of your own biases and values. Failure to identify such bias can result in a skewed approach to the interdisciplinary process. Also, such scrutiny of your own biases and values gives you practice in identifying and evaluating assumptions, which is foundational to the interdisciplinary approach to critical thinking, performing integration, and constructing a more comprehensive understanding.

By analyzing your life in the form of an intellectual autobiography, you may be able to identify how your choices of studies and/or your family background and other experiences have informed your perspectives and values. The intellectual autobiography may help you to identify future learning goals (Augsburg & Chitewere, 2013). Sometimes, just acknowledging that you have a particular worldview is an important starting point in the identification of the potential for bias. As Margaret K. Willard-Traub (2007) reminds us, our attitudes and worldviews often affect the way we approach and frame projects and problems, and intellectual autobiographies encourage us to become aware of our position on topics so that we are cognizant of our own tendencies to privilege certain approaches or ways of thinking about the world. As she writes, "[r]eflective texts have the potential for illuminating the subject position of the writer, the implications of that subject position as it shifts over time, and the impact such inevitable flux can have on how intellectual projects are framed and pursued" (p. 190).

In addition to critical thinking, the actual process of writing an intellectual autobiography is an exercise in *self-reflection* and *metacognition*, types of thinking used by interdisciplinarians as they approach complex problems. To clearly articulate your findings about your intellectual journey, you need to employ self-reflection (thinking about your behaviors and beliefs) and metacognition (thinking about your own thinking that is evidenced in your attitudes, behaviors, and experiences). It can be hoped that self-reflection becomes habitual (Augsburg & Chitewere, 2013). If you can use this same approach to think about disciplines relevant to a complex problem, you will find this important part of interdisciplinary work that much easier to accomplish.

Finally, as you assemble your intellectual autobiography, it can be quite reassuring to see how your own capacities, values, traits, and skills are common among interdisciplinarians. Having a sense of identity with a community of learners can be helpful, especially if you have experienced some difficulty in choosing a major, so that you can better understand what interdisciplinary studies actually is about and articulate your understanding to those around you. See Appendix A for the content and format of a sample intellectual autobiography.

Preparing a Portfolio

A portfolio is a collection of your work that is gathered in a form that can be shared with an audience. Portfolios are growing rapidly in popularity across higher education campuses, and especially in interdisciplinary studies programs, because they demonstrate students' ability to understand interdisciplinarity and apply the interdisciplinary process. *The process of preparing a portfolio of your university work begins with the entry-level interdisciplinary course you are in, which is why we introduce it here.*

Not everyone has heard of interdisciplinary studies, and as an interdisciplinarian entering the job market, this lack of awareness is something to anticipate and offset. Preparing a portfolio can help you document and explain interdisciplinary skills and illustrate how they are transferable to the workplace. You can organize your portfolio so as to provide some context for the work samples you select, explain how they provide evidence of interdisciplinary competencies or traits, and show how these competencies meet the demands of the workplace. The portfolio is much more than just a collection of your work; it shows how your work at university both developed and expressed (some of) the values, skills, and traits described earlier. You should take care not only in selecting work—for both the quality of the work and its role in the narrative you wish to provide—but in structuring a coherent narrative that connects these pieces.

The increasing turnover in the job market is a reality that interdisciplinarians can turn to their advantage, since an interdisciplinary education by definition does not silo you into one career path. In contrast, it equips graduates with key skills, many of which constantly appear at the top of employers' lists of desirable competencies. For example, the National Association of Colleges and Employers Job Outlook for 2012 notes the following as the top five "most sought-after skills on a student's resume" (in descending order): the ability to work in a team structure, the ability to verbally communicate with persons inside and outside the organization, the ability to make decisions and solve problems, the ability to obtain and process information, and the ability to plan, organize, and prioritize work. Preparing a portfolio can help you identify specific interdisciplinary competencies in a form that can be customized for specific career opportunities. Working from an advertisement for a job, you can showcase the competencies sought by an employer, depicting the correlation between the competencies and your own skills with a short narrative that makes the connection explicit.

Finally, preparing a portfolio is itself a process that develops *critical thinking* and *self-reflection*. Analysis and evaluation (critical thinking) are prerequisites for assembling an effective portfolio. You will be using criteria and astute judgment to evaluate your work so that you can choose the artifacts that best illustrate your achievements. The flexibility of the portfolio enables you to illustrate achievements over a period of time, indicating where and when improvements have occurred and *reflecting* on how these improvements were accomplished. Critiquing your own work and reflecting on how to improve it further are helpful life skills that will persist well beyond the completion of your portfolio and graduation.

Appendix B contains more information about portfolios, including a sample e-portfolio and grading rubric, and additional information on the kinds of e-portfolios available and what security issues you need to consider when creating an e-portfolio.

Box 4.3   Blogging

Many of the goals of an e-portfolio can be achieved in the less formal format—and one that is more familiar to most students—of blogging. Blogging allows the student to reflect intermittently on various issues. Individual blogs can be linked to more sustained work such as the materials prepared during your university career. Students can thus emphasize in their blogs ideas that they have encountered in their university career and relate these to the issues of the day or to their personal experiences. Since blogging is an ongoing activity, students can use their blogs to demonstrate intellectual growth as they develop new insights over time.

Performing Service Learning

A service-learning project provides you with an opportunity to apply your knowledge of interdisciplinarity in a real-world setting. Though these opportunities are typically reserved for students who are at least midway in their academic program, you need to prepare for them early on to receive the maximum benefit of what they have to offer.

There are at least two practical benefits of interdisciplinary studies for students who engage in service-learning projects. One is the opportunity to apply perspective taking to the task you are assigned and possibly to witness firsthand the limitations of narrow disciplinary approaches to a complex problem that exists or may arise. In this event, recall "The Fable of the Elephant House" in Chapter 2. Despite the abundance of disciplinary expertise available, the project failed because each of the disciplinary experts approached the complex problem of building the elephant house from his or her own narrow perspective.

A second benefit is the opportunity to apply, develop, and refine your intellectual toolkit. Here the focus is not so much on the task or complex problem but on the *people* with whom you are working. Contact with individuals who may hold beliefs, engage in lifestyles, and express views very different from your own presents both a challenge and an opportunity. Such experience should invite self-reflection, reveal bias, and foster the values we discussed earlier.

Service learning "is a teaching and learning strategy that integrates meaningful community service with instruction and reflection to enrich the learning experience, teach civic responsibility, and strengthen communities" (www.servicelearning.org). You should use service learning to encounter perspectives and life experiences of community members that are different from your own on issues that are addressed in your classes only from disciplinary "silo" perspectives. Perspectives from the community can offer insights that complement or challenge those drawn from disciplines. Either way, they enrich your understanding, making it more comprehensive (Newell, 2010a, pp. 6–11).

Interdisciplinary studies is not just about making connections with people who are different from you. While valuable, that is not empowering. What is empowering is being able to make sense of the contrasting or conflicting insights you encounter by integrating them into a more comprehensive understanding of the situation in its full complexity. Appendix C contains additional information on service learning, including grading rubrics.

CRITICAL THINKING QUESTIONS

1. Why is it important for you *not* to approach a controversial and complex issue with your mind already made up about it?

2. Explain how perspective taking allows us to

   - Consider previously ignored or submerged perspectives of individuals or groups

   - Improve decision quality

   - Increase creativity

   - Recall information

   - Simultaneously process information from multiple sources

   - Develop a broader perspective on a complex and controversial subject

   - Develop a new solution to a complex problem

3. Identify which intellectual capacities, values, traits, and skills would be useful in understanding the complex and controversial issue of undocumented immigrants and justify your choices.

4. How does interdisciplinary studies foster the development of civic responsibility in the world outside of the classroom?

APPLICATIONS AND EXERCISES

1. Concerning the issue, problem, or question that is the focus of the course you are enrolled in or for the independent project you are engaged in, what are your personal biases for or against it? (Note: This question lends itself particularly well to a group conversation.)

2. Select an object, behavior, or controversial issue and identify at least two different disciplinary perspectives on it.

3. From your reading of the intellectual capacities, values, traits, and skills that are fostered by interdisciplinary studies, identify which of these you already possess. Which do you think will be hard for you to develop and why?

4. Construct a sentence that clearly states the intellectual capacities, values, traits, and skills that you are acquiring by engaging in interdisciplinary studies. Then communicate your understanding to another person.

5. As a group, construct a blog post on an issue of the day. Reflect as a group on the different perspectives that were employed and the value of the insights these generated.

Source: ©iStockphoto.com/ xefstock.

Chapter 5 Objectives

The system of higher education in the United States and elsewhere is shaped by the disciplines. Learning occurs in most cases within the context of disciplines, though this is beginning to change. The disciplines are foundational to interdisciplinary studies. Becoming interdisciplinary, therefore, requires being able to differentiate between disciplinary and interdisciplinary approaches to learning and constructing knowledge. The objective of this chapter is to introduce you to the world of academic disciplines and help you understand the concept of disciplinary perspective and its importance to interdisciplinary studies. The chapter also introduces you to the defining elements of disciplines.

Academic Disciplines

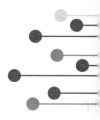

Disciplines and Disciplinarity Defined

There are almost as many definitions of academic discipline as there are disciplines, with each definition emphasizing one or more of its several characteristics. The place to begin is with a dictionary that defines the term "discipline" and includes its etymology or linguistic origin. *The Oxford English Dictionary,* for example, defines an academic discipline as "a branch of knowledge, typically studied in higher education" such as physics, economics, or history. However, the dictionary definition fails to reveal the complexity of the concept and the controversy surrounding it. Acquiring this important information involves examining definitions offered by leading scholars so that you can come to more fully appreciate the term and how it relates to interdisciplinary studies. *The discussion that follows is the interdisciplinary process in action, and the resulting definition is that process applied.*

As you read the following definitions, identify the commonalities that these definitions share in terms of the purpose and content of disciplines.

1. Janet Gail Donald (2002) in *Learning to Think* offers this definition of a discipline, which she bases on the work of earlier scholars:

   A body of knowledge, a specialized vocabulary, an accepted body of theory, a systematic research strategy, and techniques for replication [i.e., duplication] and validation. (p. 7)

Learning Outcomes

By the end of this chapter, you will be able to:

- Define the terms *academic discipline* and *disciplinarity*

- Understand the purpose and content of disciplines

- Understand disciplines as knowledge-producing communities

- Explain disciplines as social communities

- Describe disciplines as organizational units within the university

- Describe the categories of disciplines

- Define "disciplinary perspective" as it applies to academic disciplines

- Explain how perspective taking is used in interdisciplinary studies

- Identify the defining elements of a discipline and how this information is used in interdisciplinary work

- Explain the difference between disciplinary and interdisciplinary approaches to learning and constructing knowledge

2. Veronica Boix Mansilla and Anthony Jackson (2011) in *Educating for Global Competence: Preparing Our Youth to Engage the World* focus on how disciplines shape our perception of reality:

   [Disciplines] or subjects like literature, history . . . provide powerful *lenses through which to interpret the world* [emphasis added]. Students [should] come to view the disciplines as the knowledge and thinking tools that our societies construct and revise to make sense of the world, explain phenomena, solve problems, create products, [and] ask novel questions in informed ways. (p. 13)

3. Lisa Lattuca (2001) in *Creating Interdisciplinarity* emphasizes the powerful but constraining influence of disciplines:

   Disciplines, as conceptual frames . . . delimit the range of research questions that are asked, the kinds of methods that are used to investigate phenomena, and the types of answers that are considered legitimate. . . . Research generally supports this conceptualization, demonstrating close ties among the attitudes, cognitive styles, and behaviors of faculty within disciplines and the character of knowledge domains in which they work. (p. 2)

4. Julie Thompson Klein (1990) in *Interdisciplinarity: History, Theory, Practice* identifies the disciplinary toolkit and how disciplines use these to shape our understanding of reality:

   The term *discipline* signifies the tools, methods, procedures, [phenomena], concepts, and theories that account coherently for a set of objects or subjects. Over time they are shaped and reshaped by external contingencies and internal intellectual demands. In this manner, a discipline comes to organize and concentrate experience into a particular world view. Taken together, related claims within a specific material field put limits on the kinds of questions practitioners ask about their material, the methods and concepts they use, the answers they believe, and their criteria for truth and validity. There is, in short, a certain particularity about the images of reality in a given discipline. (p. 104)

5. Karri A. Holley (2009) in *Understanding Interdisciplinary Challenges and Opportunities in Higher Education* sees disciplines as social and intellectual communities:

   The academic disciplines can be understood in three ways: (1) an identifiable field of study; (2) the body of knowledge associated with the field of study; and (3) a community of scholars who engage in specific fields of knowledge. . . . These definitions suggest that the disciplines serve as a cognitive construct as well as an organizational unit [within the university]. (p. 14)

Reading these definitions superficially might tempt you to conclude that because each definition is so different from the others they have little in common. But reading (or rereading) them closely reveals that they share certain commonalities that can be organized under a few broad headings.

Commonalities Shared by These Definitions

To identify commonalities shared by these definitions, we use the same process used in Chapter 3 to construct an integrated definition of interdisciplinary studies. We begin by listing the key concepts embedded in these definitions:

- "Body of knowledge" (Def. No. 1)
- "Specialized vocabulary" (Def. No. 1)
- "Accepted body of theory" (Def. No. 1)
- "Systematic research strategy" (Def. No. 1)
- "Techniques for replication and validation" (Def. No. 1)
- "Subjects" (Def. No. 2)
- "Provide powerful lenses through which to interpret the world" (Def. No. 2)
- "Powerful but constraining ways of knowing" (Def. No. 3)
- "Conceptual frames" (Def. No. 3)
- "Delimit the range of research questions that are asked, the kinds of methods that are used to investigate phenomena, and the types of answers that are considered legitimate" (Def. No. 3)
- "Set of objects or subjects" (Def No. 4)
- "Shaped and reshaped by external contingencies and internal intellectual demands" (Def. No. 4)
- "Organize and concentrate experience into a particular 'world view'" (Def. No. 4)
- "Put limits on the kinds of questions practitioners ask about their material, the methods and concepts they use, the answers they believe, and their criteria for truth and validity" (Def. No. 4)

- "A certain particularity about the images of reality in a given discipline" (Def. No. 4)

- "An identifiable field of study" (Def. No. 5)

- "Body of knowledge associated with the field of study" (Def. No. 5)

- "A community of scholars who engage in specific fields of knowledge" (Def. No. 5)

- "Serve as a cognitive construct as well as an organizational unit [within the university]" (Def. No. 5)

Having identified the core ideas that form the essential character of disciplines, we can take the next step to categorize these ideas under two broad headings: the purpose of disciplines and the content of disciplines.

The Purpose of Disciplines

- "Provide powerful lenses through which to interpret the world" (Def. No. 2)

- "Serve as a cognitive construct as well as an organizational unit [within the university]" (Def. No. 5)

- "A certain particularity about the images of reality in a given discipline" (Def. No. 4)

- "Put limits on the kinds of questions practitioners ask about their material, the methods and concepts they use, the answers they believe, and their criteria for truth and validity" (Def. No. 4)

- "Organize and concentrate experience into a particular 'world view'" (Def. No. 4)

- "Delimit the range of research questions that are asked, the kinds of methods that are used to investigate phenomena, and the types of answers that are considered legitimate" (Def. No. 3)

- "Powerful but constraining ways of knowing" (Def. No. 3)

The Content of Disciplines

- "Body of knowledge" (Def. No. 1)

- "Specialized vocabulary" (Def. No. 1)

- "Accepted body of theory" (Def. No. 1)
- "Systematic research strategy" (Def. No. 1)
- "Techniques for replication and validation" (Def. No. 1)
- "Subjects" (Def. No. 2)
- "Conceptual frames" (Def. No. 3)
- "Set of objects or subjects" (Def. No. 4)
- "Shaped and reshaped by external contingencies and internal intellectual demands" (Def. No. 4)
- "Body of knowledge associated with the field of study" (Def. No. 5)
- "An identifiable field of study" (Def. No. 5)
- "A community of scholars who engage in specific fields of knowledge" (Def. No. 5)

It is now relatively easy to summarize the key concepts or ideas under each heading. (Note: These commonalities are discussed here only briefly but are examined in greater detail elsewhere in this chapter.)

> The Purpose of Disciplines. Scholars ascribe multiple purposes to disciplines, some of which are pragmatic ("interpret" or "make sense" of the world), some organizational ("an organizational unit" within a university), some operational ("put limits on the kinds of questions practitioners ask about their material, the methods and concepts they use, the answers they believe, and their criteria for truth and validity"), and some political ("powerful but constraining ways of knowing").

> *The purpose of a discipline, then, is to interpret reality according to certain prescribed guidelines and provide its members with organizational support.*

> The Content of Disciplines. Scholars describe the content of disciplines in two ways: academic and social. The academic content of disciplines includes certain "thinking tools" that it uses to study "a set of objects or subjects." These "thinking tools" or "defining elements" (discussed elsewhere in this chapter) constitute the "knowledge domain" of a discipline. The **social content of disciplines** is the community of scholars who engage in the work of the discipline.

The content (academic and social) of a discipline, then, is a body of knowledge *that its members study using a specialized vocabulary, a research method, a body of theory, and techniques.*

An Integrated Definition of Discipline and Disciplinarity

It is now possible to construct a definition of discipline that integrates the key ideas we have identified. Importantly, this integrated definition follows good interdisciplinary practice by drawing on only those definitions under consideration.

> **A discipline** *is an identifiable but evolving domain of knowledge that its members study using certain tools that serve as a way of knowing that is powerful but constraining.*

As used in this book, "discipline" is an umbrella term that also includes **subdisciplines**, which are branches of or specialties within disciplines. For example, political theory is a subdiscipline of political science. A "domain of knowledge" is a defining element of a discipline that is discussed elsewhere in this chapter and in subsequent chapters.

The Epistemic, Social, and Organizational Dimensions of Disciplines

Disciplines as Epistemic Communities

You may have entered the university believing that knowledge is simple, certain, and handed down by authority. As you encounter complex and contrasting information in your course work, you may account for this diversity of opinion by thinking that instructors are not well prepared or are actually using trick exercises to encourage you to find the right answer for yourself. In time, your view may evolve into acknowledging uncertainty while clinging to the hope that this uncertainty will be temporary and that authority will eventually determine what is right and true (Schommer, 1994).

However, human understanding is incomplete, and therefore, scholars often disagree. What you are actually encountering in your classes are different but useful ways of knowing, understanding reality, and determining truth.

Disciplines are epistemic communities, meaning that they share an epistemology, or beliefs about how and how much we can understand about the nature of the world we live in. As a way of knowing, a discipline uses

- distinctive analytical tools, concepts, theories, and methods;

- specialized vocabulary or symbol systems (e.g., musical notation, mathematical equations); and

- different indicators for acceptably demonstrating understanding (a musical score, a lab report, a proof, a legal brief; Boix Mansilla & Jackson, 2011, p. 5).

It should be stressed that these elements are mutually reinforcing. The discipline chooses methods that are particularly good at investigating its favored theories. These are then applied to a set of phenomena to which they are well suited. If, for example, a discipline favors quantitative methods, it will likely insist on a mathematical form of presentation, it will tend to ignore phenomena (such as cultural attitudes) that are hard to quantify, and it will develop a specialized vocabulary for its theories, methods, and phenomena. Moreover, it will have epistemological attitudes, which suggest that very precise and objective understandings of the world are possible.

Disciplines as Social Communities

A discipline is also a social community whose "disciples" practice its techniques and are bound together by shared norms, values, and beliefs (Holley, 2009). Each discipline has its own professional association, one or more leading scholarly journals, and annual conference gatherings. Disciplinary communities located in other countries have their own professional associations. For good reason, critics compare these communities to "academic tribes" (Becher, 1989) or "subcultures of academe" (B. Clark, 1989).

Faculty are members of the university *and* of a disciplinary community within it. The disciplines, though, more than the university, represent the primary source of identity for faculty (Levine, 1993). By the end of the nineteenth century, it was no longer possible for an individual to master all or even several branches of learning (King & Brownell, 1966, p. 55; see Chapter 2). Accordingly, earning a terminal degree in a particular academic discipline became the norm for faculty positions in the United States (Veysey, 1965).

An academic appointment is commonly made to a single department where the individual is recognized as a colleague by other members of the same field. In this mentoring environment that begins with the disciplinary doctorate, new faculty develop fluency in the field's specialized language and familiarity with the norms of their peers. Tenure is conferred when the individual demonstrates proficiency in teaching, research, publication, and service to the university.

In time, the individual develops expertise in a particular segment of the discipline. In these ways, the discipline-as-department system "isolates scholars within a unique—and often segregated—network" and maintains its hegemony over learning and knowledge production (Holley, 2009, p. 15).

These faculty members share common formative experiences—taking certain courses, doing certain kinds of apprentice work (in the field, the lab, or the wider world)—and appreciate a common canon of writings by the "founding fathers" and leading scholars of the disciplines (Boix Mansilla & Jackson, 2011, p. 5).[1] For students of physics, Jerome Friedman's research into the structure of the atomic nucleus (which was awarded the Nobel Prize in 1990) is central to understanding contemporary nuclear science. The work of French anthropologist Claude Levi-Strauss gave birth to the school of structuralism that greatly influenced the disciplines of sociology and anthropology in the twentieth century. The curriculum of each discipline is ultimately representative of the scholars, ideas, and research that distinguish one scholarly community from another and embodies the knowledge that shapes the discipline (Holley, 2009, p. 13).

As social and intellectual communities, the disciplines are interested in transferring knowledge from one generation to the next. They do this in three interconnected ways. The first is to publish their research in the form of books and articles that are peer reviewed (see Box 5.1). This includes textbooks that are intended to introduce students to the discipline and stimulate their interest in it. The second is for departments to offer undergraduate degree programs and majors that serve to recruit students for their graduate programs. They orient their majors in terms of research questions and provide them with the necessary analytical tools and research techniques to engage with these questions. For example, music faculties teach students the skill of deciphering discourse (sheet music) written in unique symbols (music notation). Physics faculties teach the skill of reducing the physical world to complex equations of mathematical symbols and formulas, while history faculties teach students how to analyze written texts so that they can reconstruct the historical context in which they were written. The third is to offer graduate programs leading to master's degrees and doctorates. The discipline recruits new faculty from among their best doctoral students and then guides their careers through the tenure process. Scholars who challenge their discipline's perspective usually find it difficult to progress in their careers.

---

1. Exceptions to this generalization include economists and physicians.

Box 5.1   Peer Review

When a professor writes an article (a process that may take months or even years), they then submit it to an academic journal whose editors will almost always send it off to anonymous "referees" who for disciplinary research are usually scholars from the same discipline. These referees will recommend whether the article should be published or not and make—often extensive—suggestions for how it might be revised. The professor who has not somehow learned which theories, methods, and research questions are favored in their discipline will likely receive very negative referee reports. This will be challenging psychologically and have negative implications for their career because professors at most institutions need to publish in order to advance. Professors want to be accepted and valued within their community. They are thus guided by both practical and social considerations to absorb the preferences of their discipline. Another venue that is critical in this socialization process is the academic conference, where professors present their research to each other: They want their research—and through it, themselves—to be valued by their community. Professors are human, too, and will appreciate a pat on the back during the coffee break or evening reception for a well-received presentation.

Disciplines as Organizational Units

The most basic functions of a university are to teach, conduct research, and award degrees. Universities administer these functions through academic departments that are typically clustered together in separate colleges or schools headed by a dean who administers them, such as the college of natural science, the college of liberal arts (consisting of the social sciences, the humanities, and the fine and performing arts), the college of business, the college of engineering, and the school of education. The cluster of silos in Figure 5.1 is a visual metaphor of these organizational units that constitute a university.

Departments within these organizational units serve several useful functions. Departments hire faculty based on their qualifications in the discipline, offer undergraduate and graduate degrees, and develop curricula and courses to service them. Departments and the colleges to which they belong implement university policies and administer budgets that are funded by the income earned from tuition, endowments, government grants, and other sources.

Figure 5.1   Disciplines Depicted as Silos

Source: ©iStockphoto.com/ P_Wei.

Departments are often physically isolated from other academic units. For example, business majors after completing their general requirements may spend the majority of their academic career in the college of business building with little contact with students in other academic units. Their peers in education are engaged in student teaching at local schools, and those in nursing are involved in internships in area hospitals. Not only is such learning specific to the disciplinary specialty, but the learning occurs in specified institutional spaces. Though this arrangement is designed to further a student's mastery of a specialized content, space can also inhibit learning by physically segregating majors. This is why critics of disciplines often compare disciplinary departments to "silos" and refer to disciplinary learning as the "compartmentalization of knowledge" (see Box 5.2). This compartmentalization of knowledge is commonplace throughout the world.

Janet Gail Donald (2009) offers a less critical perspective on the role that disciplines play in student learning (see Box 5.3).

Box 5.2 Disciplinary Silos

The shadow side of these [dimensions] is the way in which a discipline can often constrain thought—declaring some ways of knowing reasonable and others inadequate or even suspect. According to some sociologists and critical theorists, "disciplining" thought and academic practices (e.g., disciplinary course requirements) represents an exercise of coercive power and a way of reinforcing social and institutional conditions that benefit some groups and perspectives over others. (Boix Mansilla & Jackson, 2011, p. 5)

Box 5.3 Disciplinary Homes

Disciplines provide homes within the larger learning community because they determine the domain of knowledge, the theoretical or conceptual structures and mode of inquiry, and therefore serve as scaffolding for students in the process of exploring different ways of constructing meaning. The trend of students to pursue a series of degrees in various areas of study demonstrates their recognition of the need to acquire different structures and modes of thinking. (Donald, 2009, p. 48)

A Taxonomy of Disciplines, Applied Fields, and Professions

A **taxonomy** groups things according to their common characteristics. Klein (2010) notes that since the late nineteenth and early twentieth centuries, "taxonomies of knowledge in the West have been dominated by the modern system of disciplinarity" (p. 47). Disciplinary departments are organized into broad **disciplinary categories** to form divisions or colleges or schools or "faculties." Typical categories include the natural sciences; the social sciences; the humanities; the fine and performing arts; the applied fields, such as communications and business; and the professions, such as architecture, law, nursing, education, and social work. (Note: The professions typically involve licensure.) In addition to these categories, the contemporary university typically boasts of one or more multidisciplinary and interdisciplinary programs that may stand alone administratively or be administered cooperatively by several disciplinary departments. An environmental science program, for example, may be staffed by faculty from biology, chemistry, and Earth science.

Table 5.1 presents a conventional categorization of many of the traditional disciplines and includes applied fields and professions. A few disciplines may

Table 5.1 A Taxonomy of Disciplines, Applied Fields, and Professions	
Category	**Discipline**
Natural Sciences	Biology
	Chemistry
	Earth Science
	Mathematics
	Physics
Social Sciences	Anthropology
	Economics (Business)[a]
	Political Science
	Psychology
	Sociology
Humanities	Art and Art History
	History[b]
	Literature (English)
	Music Education
	Philosophy
	Religious Studies
Fine and Performing Arts[c]	Art
	Dance
	Music
	Theater

Category	Discipline
Applied Fields[d]	Criminal Justice
	Communications
	Engineering
	Information
	Media Studies
Professions[d]	Education
	Law
	Medicine
	Nursing
	Pharmacy

Source: Repko and Szostak (2016). *Interdisciplinary Research: Process and Theory*, 3rd edition. Thousand Oaks, CA: SAGE Publications, Inc. p. 36.

a. Economics in this taxonomy encompasses the general field of business with its several subfields including business law, finance, human resource management, management, marketing, information systems, and operations management.

b. History can be studied in two broad ways—the social science version that is theory-driven and often quantitative in its scientific testing of hypotheses, and the humanities orientation that is qualitative and narrative, painting mental pictures with words rather than testing formal hypotheses, or with a conceptual and methodological pluralism that draws on both approaches.

c. Some taxonomies of the fine and performing arts include creative writing and film.

d. For the purposes of this taxonomy, we have provided only certain examples of the applied fields and the professions.

be considered part of one category at one university but belong to a different category at another. History, for example, is considered a discipline within the social sciences in some institutions but part of the humanities at others. Though history has elements of both social sciences and humanities, this book follows the traditional taxonomy of including history in the humanities. The fine and performing arts (art, dance, music, and theater) are included with the humanities on some campuses. It is important to note that for administrative reasons, universities pretend that the boundaries between the social sciences and the humanities or between the social sciences and the natural sciences are clear, but in reality they are fuzzy.

The Concept of Disciplinary Perspective

An important step toward developing competence in interdisciplinary studies is to understand the concept of disciplinary perspective and the role of perspective taking.

Perspective Taking in Interdisciplinary Studies

To engage in interdisciplinary perspective taking requires you to develop four specific cognitive capacities:

- *Viewing yourself*—that is, recognizing the influence of culture, politics, religion, and socioeconomic background on your view of a situation, event, issue, or phenomenon

- *Viewing others*—that is, identifying and examining the perspectives of other people, groups, or organizations, and identifying influences on those perspectives (See Box 5.4 for a discussion of role taking)

- *Viewing cultures*—that is, explaining how different access to knowledge, technology, and resources affects cultures (Boix Mansilla & Jackson, 2011, p. 31)

Box 5.4 Role Taking

One type of perspective taking is role taking. This is the art of adopting a set of perspectives associated with a person, a group, or a culture. The literature from social psychology and its research on role taking offers insights that are applicable to interdisciplinary learning and research. The first is that people's judgments are biased in the direction of their own knowledge and values. This was one of the important findings of a series of studies conducted by Susan G. Fussell of Carnegie Mellon University's Human-Computer Interaction Institute and Robert Kraus of Columbia University. Their studies found that judges are prone to "false consensus bias," meaning that they assume that others are more similar to themselves than they actually are (Fussell & Kraus, 1992). There are two implications of Fussell and Kraus's research for interdisciplinary learning: (1) Be aware of your own perspective so that it does not color (consciously or unconsciously) your work; (2) when taking the role of another, you "should be able to perceive the other's perspective in depth and have a full understanding of the other's perspective" (Martin, Thomas, Charles, Epitropaki, & McNamara, 2005, p. 141).

- *Viewing disciplines*—that is, explaining how communities of expertise understand a situation, event, issue, or phenomenon

Interdisciplinary perspective taking, then, is the intellectual capacity to view a complex problem, phenomenon, or behavior from multiple perspectives, including disciplinary ones, in order to develop a more comprehensive understanding of it. Interdisciplinary studies takes on *temporarily* the perspectives of disciplines but treats them as mere viewpoints (see Box 5.3). Importantly, taking on other perspectives often involves temporarily setting aside your own beliefs, opinions, and attitudes. Interdisciplinary studies arrives not at a more comprehensive perspective but at a more comprehensive *understanding*.

Types of Disciplinary Perspective

The term *perspective* is a visual-spatial metaphor that implies two things:

- The knowledge obtained by viewing is subjective
- The knower is situated in some distinctive way in order to see something (Miller & Boix Mansilla, 2004, p. 3)

There are three different senses in which the concept of a perspective is commonly used, as shown in Table 5.2. Miller and Boix Mansilla (2004) explain each of these perspectives:

Table 5.2 Three Senses of Perspective			
	Type of Perspective		
	Individual	**Role**	**Disciplinary**
Description	Based on one's subjective outlook, opinion, beliefs, or knowledge	Based on one's situatedness or enduring role, actor category, or relative position	Based on commitments to a theory system, profession, discipline, or discourse community
Examples	"My perspective"; "this committee's perspective"	The principal's perspective; a board member's perspective (where roles are considered generically)	A psychological perspective; a medical perspective; a statistical perspective; a musical perspective

Source: Miller and Boix Mansilla (2004, p. 4).

- "Perspective in the first sense refers to an individual's viewpoint, belief, or 'take' on something, whether that perspective is short term (e.g., 'my point of view at this moment') or more long term (e.g., 'the way I generally think about things in these situations')."

- Perspective in the second sense "can refer to the concerns, questions, attitudes, and ways of thinking that might be common to a class of individuals in shared situations, roles, or relative positions. In this usage, we generalize about the student by referring to 'the student's perspective,' and similarly, the 'patient's perspective' . . . and so on. While sharing a common role or actor's position does not guarantee adherence to a single world view or set of beliefs, it ordinarily presumes a common set of concerns and a common relationship to other types of actors, roles, and institutions" (p. 4).

- Perspective in the third sense, and the one we focus on in this chapter, "describes seeing the world through the lens of assumptions, concepts, values, and practices of a shared, often 'expert' way of knowing" (p. 4). *It is because these change only slowly for disciplines that we can say that each has an identifiable perspective.*

Disciplinary Perspective Defined Disciplinary perspective is a distinctive form of perspective associated with communities of disciplinary specialties in the natural sciences, the social sciences, the humanities, the fine and performing arts, the applied fields, and the professions. **Disciplinary perspective** is a discipline's unique view of reality that is like a lens through which it views the world (see Figure 5.2). A discipline's perspective embraces, and in turn reflects, the ensemble of its defining elements that include the phenomena it prefers to study, its epistemology, assumptions, concepts, and favored theories and methods.

Each discipline acts like a lens when it filters out certain phenomena so that it can focus exclusively on phenomena that interest it. Disciplines such as Earth science and sociology are not collections of certified facts; rather, they are *lenses* through which they look at the world, interpret it, or ignore certain theories and methods (Boix Mansilla, Miller, & Gardner, 2000, p. 18). In the sciences, for example, disciplines are most easily distinguished by the phenomena they study. A conventional physicist, for example, would not be interested in studying the declining salmon populations in the Columbia and Snake Rivers, but a biologist would. That physicists don't care about salmon is unsurprising; that they ignore some theories and methods *is* surprising and important. A conventional sociologist would not be interested in theological representation in a fifteenth-century oil painting, but an art historian would. Similarly, a conventional historian would likely not be interested in the regulatory hurdles involved in constructing an oil pipeline, but a political scientist would (Repko & Szostak, 2016, p. 31).

As noted above, the defining features of a discipline are mutually reinforcing. The discipline's perspective, then, is coherent: Its epistemological beliefs will encourage the use of certain theories and methods and a focus on certain phenomena. The perspective need not be explicitly taught to students: They will absorb it subconsciously as they are acquainted with the discipline's theories, methods, and guiding questions.

Source: ©iStockphoto.com/Alisa Tsoy.

What Disciplinary Perspective Is Used For *A discipline's perspective is the primary means of distinguishing one discipline from another.* To gain a more comprehensive perspective on any complex problem, you must be able to identify which disciplines are potentially relevant to the problem, and you must understand how each perspective illuminates some aspect of it. This point is illustrated in a poem by American poet John Godfrey Saxe (1816–1887) that is based on an Indian fable about six blind men and an elephant. Each of the men thoroughly investigated a particular part of the massive beast (i.e., the complex problem), and each emphatically concluded that what he had "observed" was very much like a wall (its sides), a spear (its tusk), a snake (its swinging trunk), a tree (its leg), a fan (its ear), and a rope (its tail). The poem ends

> And so these men of Indostan
>
> Disputed loud and long,
>
> Each in his own opinion
>
> Exceeding stiff and strong,
>
> Though each was partly in the right,
>
> And all were in the wrong! (Saxe, 1963)

They were all wrong because each individual's perspective was limited to studying only one part of the problem. Consequently, each was able to offer only a narrow and thus partial understanding of the problem. Similarly, disciplines approach a complex problem by viewing it from their own narrow perspective. This does not mean that their perspectives are necessarily wrong, only incomplete.

Multidisciplinary and interdisciplinary approaches use disciplinary perspectives in different ways. Multidisciplinary approaches typically view the problem through the lenses of a few selected disciplines and consider, in serial fashion, how each perspective illumines some aspect of the subject, much as the men did in the fable of the elephant and blind men. The point of multidisciplinarity is merely to compare perspectives, but it often tacitly prefers one perspective over the other(s).

By contrast, interdisciplinary studies (ideally) is interested in viewing the problem through the lenses of *all* relevant disciplines. *The point of interdisciplinary perspective taking is to gain a more comprehensive perspective on the problem without preferring one perspective over another.* Interdisciplinarity moves beyond merely juxtaposing (i.e., lying side by side) different disciplinary perspectives and their insights to integrating these insights in order to construct a more comprehensive understanding of the problem. As we shall see in Chapter 8, one key element of this process involves critically evaluating disciplinary insights in the context of the discipline's perspective.

Disciplinary Perspective in an Overall Sense Competency in interdisciplinary studies involves developing the capacity to associate disciplines and fields of study with particular perspectives on reality *in an overall sense.* When reading a scholarly publication on the environment, for example, you will be able to recognize the disciplinary perspective that the author is writing from and detect if the author has minimized the importance of other relevant perspectives or omitted them entirely. Table 5.3 describes each discipline's perspective on reality. You should familiarize yourself with these perspectives because you will need to refer to them when working in Chapter 9.

Table 5.3	Perspectives of Natural Sciences, Social Sciences, and Humanities, the Fine and Performing Arts, Criminal Justice, and Education, Stated in General Terms
Discipline	**Perspective on Reality**
Natural Sciences	
Biology	While the other natural sciences focus on the principles that govern the nonliving physical world, biology studies the behavior of the living physical world. When biologists venture into the world of humans, they look for physical, deterministic explanations of behavior (such as genes and evolution) rather than the mental ones (such as the decisions of individuals or groups based on free will or norms) on which the social sciences focus.

Discipline	Perspective on Reality
Chemistry	Chemistry focuses on the distinctive properties of the elements, indivi[dual] compounds, and their interactions. Chemistry sees larger-scale objects [as] well as inorganic, in terms of their constituent elements and compoun[ds.]
Earth Science	Earth science focuses on the large-scale physical processes of planet Earth and is concerned with both the details and functions of four subsystems and their interactions: the lithosphere (the Earth's hard, outermost shell), the atmosphere (the mixture of gases that envelops the Earth), the hydrosphere (the subsystems that contain the Earth's water), and the biosphere (the realm of all living things, including humans).
Mathematics	Mathematics is interested in abstract quantitative worlds mathematicians create with postulates, assumptions, axioms, and premises and then explore by proving theorems.
Physics	Physics studies the basic physical laws connecting objects (atoms and subatomic particles, quanta) and forces (gravitational, electromagnetic, strong, weak) that often cannot be directly observed but that establish the underlying structure of observable reality, and cosmology (the form, content, organization, and evolution of the universe).
Social Sciences	
Anthropology	Cultural anthropology sees individual cultures as organic integrated wholes with their own internal logic and culture as the set of symbols, rituals, and beliefs through which a society gives meaning to daily life. Physical anthropology seeks to understand former cultures through the artifacts it uncovers.
Economics/ Business*	Economics/business emphasizes the study of the production and distribution of goods and services with the individual functioning as an autonomous, rational, and self-interested actor.
Political Science	Political science views the world as a political arena in which individuals and groups make decisions based on the search for or exercise of power. Politics at all levels and in all cultures is viewed as a perpetual struggle over whose values, not just whose interests, will prevail in setting priorities and making collective choices.
Psychology	Psychology sees human behavior as reflecting the cognitive constructs individuals develop to organize their mental activity. Psychologists also study inherent mental mechanisms, both genetic predisposition and individual differences.
Sociology	Sociology views the world as a social reality that includes the range and nature of the relationships that exist between people in any given society. Sociology is particularly interested in voices of various subcultures, analysis of institutions, and how bureaucracies and vested interests shape life.

(Continued)

Table 5.3 (Continued)

Discipline	Perspective on Reality
Humanities	
Art and Art History	Art history views art in all of its forms as reflecting the culture in which it was formed and therefore providing a window into a culture. Art, and thus art history, has a place for universal aesthetic tastes.
History	Historians believe that any historical period cannot be adequately appreciated without understanding the trends and developments leading up to it, that historical events are the result of both societal forces and individual decisions, and that a picture or narrative of the past can be no better than the richness of details drawn from documents and artifacts.
Literature (English)	Literature believes that cultures, past and present, cannot be adequately understood without understanding and appreciating the literature produced by the culture.
Philosophy	Philosophy recognizes a variety of limits to human perceptual and cognitive capabilities. Philosophy views reality as situational and perspectival. Reality is not a collection of imperfect representations that reflect an "absolute reality" that transcends all particular situations. Rather, these representations are the reality that is the world.
Religious Studies	Religious studies views faith and faith traditions as human attempts to understand the significance of reality and cope with its vicissitudes through beliefs in a sacred realm beyond everyday life.
The Fine and Performing Arts	
Art	The study of art as a creative pursuit sees the creative process as a means by which human experience (and therefore the culture in which it exists) can be articulated via a chosen medium (paint, ceramics, clay, stone, etc.). Part of the study of art involves examining the developments in the discipline over time and in different parts of the world.
Dance	The study of dance as a creative art form articulates observations on human experience (and therefore the culture in which it exists) via the movement of the body of one dancer alone or choreographed with two or more individuals, accompanied by sound or silence. Part of the study of dance involves examining developments in the discipline over time and in different parts of the world.
Music	The study of music as a creative pursuit involves the composition and/or performance of music, which is itself produced in response to elements of human experience (and therefore the culture in which it exists). The study of music can include conducting, performing on various instruments, aural training, performing as part of an ensemble or soloist, or composing or arranging. Part of the study of music involves examining developments in the discipline over time and in different parts of the world.

Discipline	Perspective on Reality
Theater	The study of drama as a creative pursuit involves the creation of original dramatic works or acting and/or producing such works. Works of drama express observations about the human experience (and therefore the culture in which it exists). Part of the study of drama involves examining developments in the discipline over time and in different parts of the world.
The Applied Fields**	
Criminal Justice	Criminal justice sees crime and criminal behavior through the lenses of theories on human nature, societal structure, social order, concepts of law, crime and criminals, the logic of crime causation, and the policies and practices that follow from them.
The Professions**	
Education	Education views learning as developmental and governed by a linear and universal model of progress, civilization, democracy, rationality, and science. This modernist view is being challenged by a postmodern recognition of diversity and contextualization that values what is local and different.

Source: Adapted from Repko and Szostak (2016). *Interdisciplinary Research: Process and Theory* (3rd ed.). Thousand Oaks, CA: SAGE Publications, Inc. p. 36.

*Like other professions, business schools are at least multidisciplinary and address sociology as well as economics.

**We have not attempted to survey the wide range of applied fields or professions here. One thing we would stress is that each of these needs to determine which disciplines they will draw upon and how. Medicine has long relied on natural science understandings, but there is increased discussion in the field about integrating social science and humanities understandings, since health professionals regularly confront social problems, and there is considerable evidence that the arts can play a role in healing.

Note: This taxonomy or systematic and orderly classification of selected disciplines and their perspectives raises the question of how students can find perspectives of disciplines, subdisciplines, and interdisciplines not included in this book. Certainly, a good place to obtain leads is this chapter, which has tables that define elements of disciplines (their epistemologies, theories, methods, etc.). Also, the chapter references standard authoritative disciplinary sources. Researchers may also consult content librarians who specialize in certain disciplines. Another strategy is to ask disciplinary experts to recommend sources. This combined approach should produce aids that are authoritative and useful. The issue of finding scholarly research aids is addressed more fully in Chapter 11.

Three Misconceptions About Disciplinary Perspective There are three common misconceptions about the concept of disciplinary perspective:

1. *Each discipline's community of scholars shares a single outlook.* In actuality, "most disciplines are characterized by several competing perspectives and embody often bitterly contested beliefs and values" (Hyland, 2004, p. 11). (See Box 5.5.)

Box 5.5   Disciplinary Subcultures

Disciplines mask an assortment of smaller scholarly communities that bring diverse viewpoints to the production of knowledge. These disciplinary subcultures privilege selected research methodologies, bodies of literature, or research questions. Although individuals may hold membership in the same disciplines, the means by which they engage in those communities may vary. . . . The discipline encompasses a wide margin of practice. . . . Members employ innovative work at the ends of the margins in a manner that changes the disciplinary landscape. Disciplines are the contexts in which disagreements can be debated. (Hyland, 2004, p. 11)

Though disciplines are fractured by disagreements on an assortment of matters that sometimes threaten to tear apart some disciplines (such as art history), they remain intact because an "intellectual center of gravity" enables each discipline to maintain its identity and have a distinctive overall perspective. It is this perspective that is a key component of interdisciplinary studies because it enables you to identify which disciplines *may* be interested in the problem or research question.

(Note: Hiring decisions are generally made by disciplinary departments. Likewise, it is these departments that determine curriculum. There are thus strong institutional reinforcements of a disciplinary-level perspective. A subfield can only survive if the broader discipline will hire its members and offer its courses.)

2. *Disciplinary perspective is similar to, if not identical to, the concept of disciplinary insight.* This is not so. Disciplinary perspective is the discipline's general way of looking at the world. For example, in the fable of the blind men and the elephant, each man represented a different discipline and thus "viewed" the elephant through the lens or perspective of his particular discipline. Part of the disciplinary perspective of economists may be the belief that free capital markets generally produce positive outcomes. Insights are arguments it makes about particular phenomena or the relationships among these. An insight may be an economist's argument as to how a particular market works. Of course, we might then wonder to what degree the insight reflects the discipline's perspective.

3. *Disciplinary perspectives get integrated.* They do not. Only insights into a particular problem get integrated. Two examples from Repko and Szostak (2016) illustrate the point:

- Earth science views planet Earth as a large-scale and highly complex system involving the four subsystems of geosphere, hydrosphere, atmosphere, and biosphere. When this perspective is applied to a particular problem, say damming a river system such as the Columbia, the insight that Earth science may generate (in the form of a scholarly monograph, journal article, or report to a public agency) is that building the system of dams is feasible given the geological characteristics of the Columbia Basin. We can then try to integrate that insight with a biologist's insight regarding the effect of such a dam on fish in the river.

- Sociology views the world as a social reality that includes the range and scope of relationships that exist between people in any given society. When this perspective is applied to a particular problem, say repeated spousal battery, the insight into the problem that sociologists may generate is that it is caused by male unemployment or the desire for patriarchal control. (p. 97)

The Defining Elements of a Discipline

Thus far, we have said that the concept of disciplinary perspective refers to a discipline's view of reality in a general or overall sense. But the concept also refers to those specific elements of a discipline that give it definition and set it apart from other disciplines. A discipline's overall perspective is generated by the interaction among these complementary elements (discussed later). These are called here the **defining elements of a discipline**, which include the phenomena it studies, its epistemology (how one knows what is true and how one validates truth), the assumptions it makes about the natural and human world, its basic concepts, its theories about the causes and behaviors of certain phenomena, its methods (the ways it gathers, applies, and produces new knowledge), and the kind of data it collects. The tendency of disciplinary authors is to privilege a single disciplinary perspective and the elements associated with it (T. Miller et al., 2008, p. 1).

The following discussion provides the most basic information about each of these elements and explains how you will use this information in subsequent chapters. You should know that these elements are typically reflected in the insights that disciplinary authors have published as books or articles in academic journals. Stated differently, the insights produced by a discipline's community of scholars reflects the discipline's defining elements.

Phenomena

Phenomena are the subjects, objects, and behaviors that a discipline considers to fall within its research domain. For example, sociologists are interested in the phenomena of social structure. Second-level phenomena under this broad category include gender, family types, kinship, classes, ethnic/racial divisions, and social ideology. Third-level phenomena include particular family types (i.e., nuclear, extended, single parent, etc.) and occupations (various; Szostak, 2004, p. 29). The disciplines and the phenomena they study are shown in Table 5.4.

Table 5.4 Disciplines and the Phenomena They Study

Category	Discipline	Phenomena
Natural Sciences	Biology	Biological taxonomies of species; the nature, interrelationships, and evolution of living organisms; health; nutrition; disease; fertility
	Chemistry	The periodic table of chemical elements that are the building blocks of matter—their composition, properties, and reactions
	Earth Science	Planet Earth's geologic history, processes, and structures, soil types, topography and land forms, climate patterns, resource availability, water availability, natural disasters
	Mathematics	The logic of numbers, statistics, mathematical modeling, computer simulations, theoretical counterpoint to sensitivity analysis
	Physics	Subatomic particles, the nature of matter and energy and their interactions
Social Sciences	Anthropology	The origins of humanity, the dynamics of cultures worldwide
	Economics/ Business	The economy: total output (price level, unemployment, individual goods and services), income distribution, economic ideology, economic institutions (ownership, production, exchange, trade, finance, labor relations, organizations), the impact of economic policies on individuals

Category	Discipline	Phenomena
	Political Science	The nature and practice of systems of government and of individuals and groups pursuing power within those systems
	Psychology	The nature of human behavior as well as the internal (psychosocial) and external (environmental) factors that affect this behavior
	Sociology	The social nature of societies and of human interactions within them
Humanities	Art and Art History	Nonreproducible art—painting, sculpture, architecture, prose, poetry—and reproducible art—theater, film, photography, music, dance
	History	The people, events, and movements of human civilizations past and present
	Literature (English)	Development and examination (i.e., both traditional literary analysis and theory as well as more contemporary culture-based contextualism and critique) of creative works of the written word
	Music and Music Education	Development, performance, and examination (i.e., both traditional musicological analysis and theory as well as more contemporary culture-based contextualism and critique) of creative works of sound
	Philosophy	The search for wisdom through contemplation and reason using abstract thought
	Religious Studies	The phenomena of humans as religious beings and the manifestations of religious belief such as symbols, institutions, doctrines, and practices
Fine and Performing Arts	Art	Creation and transmission of original nonreproducible and reproducible art. Artifacts reflect on culture, beliefs, values, and ideas.
	Dance	Performance of movement that physicalizes the imagination, drawing on ritual, emotions, and stories (inclusive of theories on choreographic composition)
	Music	Development and production of sound delivered via a particular rate, pattern, and flow (utilizing elements of tone, harmony, rhythm, and melody, artifacts can be either representational or nonrepresentational and can be both formal and informal)

(Continued)

Table 5.4 (Continued)

Category	Discipline	Phenomena
	Theater	Development and examination of creative storytelling via live performance (includes production of both scripted and unscripted events performed for a live audience)
Applied Fields	Criminal Justice	The phenomena of social deviance in all of its manifestations, its causes, costs, and the social, political, and legal systems that deal with it
	Communication	The process of communication whether among individuals or to large numbers of people
Professions	Education	How we learn and internal and external factors that influence learning
	Law	The laws that exist and how these are interpreted; principles of legal systems
	Medicine	The human body, with particular attention to disease and injury, and how these can be ameliorated through medical intervention.

Source: Adapted from Repko and Szostak (2016), *Interdisciplinary Research: Process and Theory* (2nd. ed.). SAGE Publishing, and Szostak, R. (2004). *Classifying science: Phenomena, data, theory, method, practice.* Dordrecht: Springer. pp. 26–29, 45–50.

You will use this information to

- Identify disciplines that may be interested in a particular complex problem (for example, the disciplines potentially relevant to the issue of deviant lifestyles include criminal justice, sociology, psychology, economics, political science, cultural anthropology, history, and education)

- Connect each part of a particular complex problem to the disciplines that typically deal with that part

- Detect in the work of others missed opportunities to develop a more comprehensive understanding of a complex issue because the author consulted only a few disciplines, leaving parts of the issue unexamined

Epistemology

Epistemology is the study of the nature and basis of knowledge. It answers questions such as the following: What is the nature of knowledge? How can

I know what I know? What is truth? How much can we know? (Marsh &
Furlong, 2002, pp. 18–19). Different disciplines embrace different
epistemologies or theories of knowledge. Each discipline has a different
conception of what constitutes knowledge, how it is produced, and how it
should be applied (Rescher, 2003). Each discipline's epistemology is its way
of knowing the part of reality that it considers within its research domain
(Elliott, 2002, p. 85). Understanding the epistemological positions of the
disciplines you are working in and developing your own epistemological
positions (or preferences) are key aspects of what it means to be educated. To
this end, Table 5.5 presents the three overall epistemologies that characterize
disciplinary researchers in the natural sciences, social sciences, and
humanities. These summaries are idealized and debatable and do not include
the more detailed and nuanced descriptions of each discipline's epistemology
presented in Table 5.6. Within any disciplinary approach, there is some scope
for individual deviation.

Epistemologies of the Natural Sciences The epistemologies of the
natural sciences are empiricist (see Table 5.6). **Empiricism** holds that all
knowledge is derived from our perceptions (transmitted by the five senses
of touch, smell, taste, hearing, and sight), experience, and observation.
Empiricism, the "ruling 'ideology' of science," assures us that observation
and experimentation make scientific explanations credible and the predictive
power of its theories ever increasing (Rosenberg, 2000, p. 146). However, the
epistemologies of the natural sciences make scientific approaches inadequate
for addressing *value* issues (Kelly, 1996, p. 95). As noted in Table 5.5,
natural scientists typically embrace the notion that nature and knowledge are
mechanistic, that knowledge is objective and replicable, and that knowledge

Table 5.5 Epistemologies of the Natural Sciences, Social Sciences, and Humanities

Knowledge as Mechanistic	Knowledge as Contingent	Knowledge as Narrative
"Believed to be objective, replicable. Knowledge acquired via the 'scientific method'; is sought to demonstrate causality and allow for predication."	Importance of agent and context. Knowledge seeks causality; relies on behavior, variability, and relation to socially held norms.	Interpretive and critical. Knowledge is inherent to object and represents values that may be shared or individually held.
Nature as mechanistic	Nature as a complex adaptive system	Nature as constructed

Source: Miller, T. R., Baird, T. D., Littlefield, C. M., Kofinas, G., Chapin III, F. S., & Redman, C. L. (2008).
Epistemological pluralism: Reorganizing interdisciplinary research. *Ecology and Society, 13*(2), 1–17.

Table 5.6 Epistemologies of the Natural Sciences

Discipline	Epistemology
Biology	Biology stresses the value of classification and experimental control. The latter is the means of identifying true causes, and which therefore privileges experimental methods (because they are replicable) over all other methods of obtaining information (Magnus, 2000, p. 115).
Chemistry	Chemists use both empirics and theory (especially thermodynamics). Even more than physics, chemistry relies on lab experiments, data collection in the field, and computer simulations. Chemistry involves less fieldwork than Earth science and biology do.
Earth Science	In much of Earth science, the theory of uniformitarianism is used. Since geologists are concerned about the history of the Earth but can't directly observe it, they accept that natural laws and processes have not changed over time (L. Standlee, personal communication, April 2005). Geologists stress the value of field work.
Mathematics	Mathematical truths are numerical abstractions that are discovered through logic and reasoning. These truths exist independently of our ability or lack of ability to find them, and they do not change. These truths or forms of "invariance" enable us to categorize, organize, and give structure to the world. These mathematical structures—"geometric images and spaces, or the linguistic/algebraic expressions"—are "grounded on key regularities of the world or what we 'see' in the world" (Longo, 2002, p. 434).
Physics	Like all the physical sciences, physics is empirical, rational, and experimental. It seeks to discover truths or laws about two related and observable concepts—matter and energy—by acquiring objective and measurable information about them (Taffel, 1992, pp. 1, 5).

Source: Repko & Szostak (2016). *Interdisciplinary Research: Process and Theory* (3rd ed.). Thousand Oaks, CA: SAGE Publications, Inc. p. 47.

is acquired via the "scientific method," which seeks to demonstrate causality and allow for prediction. Truth, then, is that which is scientifically verifiable.

Epistemologies of the Social Sciences The disciplines in the social or human sciences, more so than in the natural sciences, tend to embrace more than one epistemology, as shown in Table 5.7. For example, reflecting the growing postmodernist criticism of empiricism and value neutrality, most social scientists now agree that knowledge in their disciplines is generated by the "continual interplay of personal experience, values, theories, hypotheses, and logical models, as well as empirical evidence generated by a variety of methodological approaches" (Calhoun, 2002, p. 373).

Table 5.7 Epistemologies of the Social Sciences

Discipline	Epistemology
Anthropology	Epistemological pluralism characterizes anthropology. Empiricists hold that people learn their values and that their values are therefore relative to their culture. The rationalist notion is that there are universal truths about right and wrong. Both physical and cultural anthropologists embrace constructivism, which holds that human knowledge is shaped by the social and cultural context in which it is formed and is not solely a reflection of reality (Bernard, 2002, pp. 3–4).
Economics/Business	Economics is the last bastion of logical positivism in the social sciences. Most economists believe in the primacy of empirical evidence and the use of mathematical theories that dominate their models. As empiricists, they stress fixed definitions of words, use a deductive method, and examine a small set of variables (Dow, 2001, p. 63). Even so, postmodernism is making inroads in the discipline with its pluralistic understanding of reality. Postmodernists see reality, and the self, as fragmented. Therefore, human understanding of reality is also fragmented.
Political Science	Political science embraces a rationalist epistemology. However, logical positivists in the discipline are trying to cast the "science" of politics in terms of finding some set of "covering laws" so strong that even a single counterexample would suffice to falsify them. But human beings, according to others in the discipline, while they are undeniably subject to certain external forces, are also in part intentional actors, capable of cognition and of acting on the basis of it. Consequently, these scholars study "belief," "purpose," "intention," and "meaning" as potentially crucial elements in explaining the political actions of humans (Goodin & Klingerman, 1996, pp. 9–10).
Psychology	The epistemology of psychology is that psychological constructs and their interrelationships can be inferred through discussion and observation and applied to treatment (clinical) or a series of experiments with slight variations (experimental). A critical ingredient of a good experiment is experimental control that seeks to eliminate extraneous factors that might affect the outcome of the study (Leary, 2004, p. 208).
Sociology	Modernist (i.e., positivist) sociology shares a rationalist epistemology with the other social sciences, but this epistemology is opposed by critical social theory, a theory cluster that includes Marxism, critical theory, feminist theory, postmodernism, multiculturalism, and cultural studies. What unites these approaches in the most general sense is their assumption that knowledge is socially constructed and that knowledge exists in history that can change the course of history if properly applied (Agger, 1998, pp. 1–13).

Source: Repko & Szostak (2016). *Interdisciplinary Research: Process and Theory* (3rd ed.). Thousand Oaks, CA: SAGE Publications, Inc. p 47.

Epistemologies of the Humanities The humanities, even more so than the social sciences, embrace multiple epistemologies as shown in Table 5.8. This development is explained by the rise of "critical humanities" (e.g., feminism, critical theory, postcolonial studies, cultural studies, gender studies, postmodernism, poststructuralism, deconstructionism, etc.). The humanities prize diversity of perspective, values, and ways of knowing.

Table 5.8 Epistemologies of the Humanities

Discipline	Epistemology
Art and Art History	Modernists determine the value of works of art by comparing them with standards of aesthetics and expertise. But practitioners of the new art history who emerged in the 1960s determine the value of works of art in relation to contestation between values of competing groups. These practitioners understand the value of art in social and cultural contexts (Harris, 2001, pp. 65, 96–97, 130–131, 162–165, 194–196, 228–232, 262–288). Postmodern critics (active from about 1970 to the present) "argue that the supposedly dispassionate old-style art historians are, consciously or not, committed to the false elitist ideas that universal aesthetic criteria exist and that only certain superior things qualify as 'art'" (Barnet, 2008, p. 260).
History	Modernists focus on the authenticity and appropriateness of how an event, person, or period is interpreted by evaluating the work in terms of its faithfulness to appropriate primary and secondary sources. "Truth," they believe, "is one, not perspectival" (Novick, 1998, p. 2). Believing that "structure" is fundamental to understanding the past, social historians focus on structure and infrastructure—on material structure, on the economy, on social and political systems—but do not eliminate the individual. More recently, some social historians have begun to employ "micro-history" or the new cultural history (a blend of social history and intellectual history) as a way of studying ideological structures, mental structures (such as notions of family and community), isolated events, individuals, or actions, borrowing from anthropology the ethnographic method of "thick description," which emphasizes close observation of small details, carefully listening to every voice and every nuance of phrase (Howell & Prevenier, 2001, p. 115).
Literature/ English	In general, modernists focus on the text and employ text-based research techniques. Newer approaches see meaning making as a relational process. The close reading of texts is being informed by background research into the context of the text, such as the circumstances surrounding its production, content, and consumption. Other newer approaches abound. For example, notions of auto/biographic writing have shifted from an idea of presenting "the truth" about someone to presenting "a truth." Oral history is viewed as a means of understanding the workings of "literary and cultural phenomena in and on people's imagination." Critical discourse analysis examines patterns in language use in order to uncover the workings of an ideology to see how it exerted control or how it was resisted. Quantitative researchers are using computers to calculate the frequency with which certain words appear in a text so that they can better interpret its meaning (Griffin, 2005, pp. 5–14).

Discipline	Epistemology
Philosophy	Recently, philosophical questions about perception have become more important. For both empiricist and rationalist positions, one of the major concerns is to ascertain whether the means of getting knowledge are trustworthy. The chief concerns of epistemology in this regard are memory, judgment, introspection, reasoning, "a priori–a posteriori" distinction, and the scientific method (Sturgeon, Martin, & Grayling, 1995, pp. 9–10).
Religious Studies	Religious studies is concerned about the "assumptions and preconceptions that influence the analysis and interpretation of data, that is, the theoretical and analytical framework, even personal feelings, one brings to the task of organizing and analyzing facts" (Stone, 1998, p. 6). Though all humanities disciplines are concerned about the problem of subjectivity, few are as self-critical as religious studies (p. 7).

Source: Repko & Szostak (2016). *Interdisciplinary Research: Process and Theory,* (3rd ed.). Thousand Oaks, CA: SAGE Publications, Inc. p. 49.

You will use this information to

- Develop your own epistemological positions
- Understand the epistemology of interdisciplinary studies (Chapter 6)
- Detect the epistemological beliefs of authors writing on controversial and value-laden issues such as euthanasia. For example, when a humanist writes that we cannot know the answer to a particular question, this may simply reflect an epistemological skepticism rather than an evaluation of the particular question (see Box 5.6).

Box 5.6 The Toolbox Project

The Toolbox Project (funded by the National Science Foundation) met with dozens of interdisciplinary research teams addressing a wide range of topics. They gave these various teams a questionnaire of mostly epistemological and methodological queries. As expected, team members from different disciplines provided different answers. The research team would then discuss their answers. When the questionnaire was given again, there tended to be significant convergence in the answers given. This shows that being self-conscious of disciplinary perspective, and aware of other perspectives, can encourage epistemological flexibility. When surveyed later, team members generally agreed that the epistemological conversation had enabled the team to communicate more effectively. This indicates that a familiarity with disciplinary perspective can indeed allow us to better appreciate disciplinary insights. See Looney et al. (2014).

Assumptions

Assumptions are things that are accepted as true or certain. "All areas of academic study are constructed on assumptions regarding what scholars regard as legitimate knowledge" (Brookfield, 2012, p. 28). Assumptions mostly reflect epistemology but capture elements of ethics, metaphysics, and ideology when these are particularly important. With respect to ethics, disciplines differ in terms of whether they think ethical considerations can or should influence research. You should be wary of supposedly neutral arguments regarding issues such as euthanasia where ethical positions can easily influence research outcomes. Epistemological positions will reflect metaphysical positions. For instance, those who build mathematical models must believe that there is regularity in the interactions they posit. As for ideology, certain disciplines are typically more skeptical of the exercise of governmental power than are others.

Each discipline makes its own assumptions about the natural and human worlds. Grasping the underlying assumptions of categories of disciplines (i.e., the natural sciences, the social sciences, and the humanities) and then of each discipline in each category provides important clues to the assumptions underlying a discipline's insights into a particular problem.

Assumptions of the Natural Sciences There are at least seven basic assumptions of the natural sciences:

1. Nature is orderly.
2. We can know nature.
3. All natural phenomena have natural causes.
4. Knowledge is based on experience.
5. Knowledge is superior to belief unsupported by empirical evidence (Frankfort-Nachmias & Nachmias, 2008, pp. 5–6).
6. Scientists can transcend their cultural experience and make definitive measurements of phenomena (i.e., things).
7. "There are no supernatural or other a priori properties of nature that cannot potentially be measured" (Maurer, 2004, pp. 19–20).

Assumptions of the Social Sciences The social sciences assume that there is some order to society (Frankfort-Nachmias & Nachmias, 2008, p. 5). This assumption surfaces in a popular textbook on behavioral research methods (used in psychology, communications, human development, education, marketing, and social work) when it says, "Data obtained through systematic empiricism allow researchers to draw more confident conclusions than they can draw from casual observation alone" (Leary, 2004, p. 9). Social science assumptions differ from those of the natural sciences because of key differences between the phenomena each studies. The natural sciences study the natural world whose behavior is fixed or governed by instinct or evolution, whereas the social sciences study the world of sentient, willful humans who imagine future and alternative states to the world as it currently is and change their patterns of behavior in light of anticipated or desired futures as well as present realities.

Assumptions of the Humanities Since the humanities also focus on the world of humans, they share many of the assumptions of the social sciences. Table 5.9 contrasts the assumptions of the "new humanities" with older modernist assumptions. The new humanities, says Klein (2010),

Table 5.9	Assumptions of Disciplines in the Humanities
Discipline	**Assumptions**
Art and Art History	Modernists assume that the intrinsic value of the object is primary. Radical art historians—i.e., Marxist, feminist, psychoanalytical, and poststructuralist—"share a broad historical materialism" of outlook: that all social institutions, such as education, politics, and the media, are exploitative and that "exploitation extends to social relations, based, for instance, on factors of gender, race, and sexual preference" (Harris, 2001, p. 264). In general, these critics assume that intrinsic values remain primary, but understanding the social context completes one's grasp of the work (p. 264).[a]
History	Modernist (positivist and historicist) historical scholarship rests on the idea that objectivity in historical research is possible and preferred (Iggers, 1997, p. 9). In general, social history (e.g., Marxian socioeconomic history, the Braudelian method, women's history, African American history, and ethnic history) assumes that those whom traditional history writing had ignored (the poor, the working class, women, homosexuals, minorities, the sick) played an important but unappreciated role in historical change (Howell & Prevenier, 2001, p. 113).
Literature	Literature (broadly defined) or "texts" are assumed to be a lens for understanding life in a culture and an instrument that can be used to understand human experience in all of its complexity. Texts "encompass the continuous substance of all human signifying activities" (Marshall, 1992, p. 162). Another assumption is that these texts are "alien" to the reader, meaning that "something in the text or in our distance from it in time and place makes it obscure." The interpreter's task is to make the text "speak" by "reading" the text using extremely complex skills so as to give the text "meaning." Meaning is "an intricate and historically situated social process" that occurs between the interpreter and audience (i.e., reader) that neither fully controls (pp. 159, 165–166).

(Continued)

Table 5.9 (Continued)

Discipline	Assumptions
Philosophy	There are two schools of thought about how to get knowledge. Rationalists assume that the chief route to knowledge is the exercise of systematic reasoning and "looking at the scaffolding of our thought and doing conceptual engineering" (Blackburn, 1999, p. 4). The model for rationalists is mathematics and logic. Empiricists assume that the chief route to knowledge is perception (i.e., using the five senses of sight, smell, hearing, taste, and touch and the extension of these using technologies such as the microscope and telescope). The model for empiricists is any of the natural sciences where observation and experiment are the principal means of inquiry (Sturgeon et al., 1995, p. 9).
Religious Studies	Religious studies often queries faith, and the history of religions focuses on understanding humans as religious beings. One key assumption of the discipline is that there is something inherently unique about religion and those who study it must do so without reducing its essence to something other than itself, as sociologists and psychologists tend to do. A related assumption is that even though religion is freighted with human emotion, objectivity is possible (Stone, 1998, p. 5).

Source: Repko & Szostak (2016). *Interdisciplinary Research: Process and Theory,* (3rd ed.). Thousand Oaks, CA: SAGE Publications, Inc. p. 57.

a. Marxists assume that class struggle is the primary engine of historical development in capitalist society and that other forms of exploitation are a product of the basic antagonism between classes. Feminists assume connections and causal links between patriarchal dominance within the society as a whole and its art. Psychoanalytic art historians assume that a full understanding of "the subject" requires inquiry into the complex nature of the embodied human psyche and its conscious and unconscious outworkings (Harris, 2001, pp. 262, 264, 195).

"interrogates the dominant structure of knowledge and education with the aim of transforming them" with the "explicit intent of deconstructing disciplinary knowledge and boundaries" (p. 30). This trend, she notes, "is especially apparent in cultural studies, women's and ethnic studies, and literary studies, where 'the epistemological and political are inseparable'" (p. 30).

You will use this information to

- Detect assumptions that support particular disciplinary insights (Chapter 9)
- Contrast disciplinary assumptions on a given issue with interdisciplinary ones

Concepts

Concepts are abstract ideas generalized from particular instances or symbols expressed in language that represent phenomena (Wallace & Wolf, 2006, pp. 4–5; see also Novak, 1998, p. 21). For example, chairs come in various shapes and sizes, but once a child acquires the concept *chair*, that child will refer to anything that has legs and a seat as a chair (p. 21). Examples of concepts favored by each discipline are omitted here because they are too numerous. Most concepts used by disciplines are either phenomena (such as "culture") or involve changes in particular phenomena ("revolution") or relationships between phenomena ("globalization"). Concepts may also represent elements within a particular theory or method (Szostak, 2004, pp. 41–43). In all of these cases, scholarly communication both within and across disciplines will be aided by broadly shared understandings of the meanings attached to concepts. Humanities scholar Mieke Bal (2002) agrees that concepts "need to be explicit, clear, and defined" (pp. 5, 22, 23).

You will use this information to

- Differentiate between concepts and phenomena
- Detect different meanings of the same concept used by different disciplines
- Recognize how interdisciplinarians use concepts to create common ground

Theory

A **theory** is a generalized scholarly explanation about some aspect of the natural or human world, how it works, and why specific facts are related, that is supported by data and research (Bailis, 2001, p. 39; Calhoun 2002, p. 482; Novak, 1998, p. 84). As an interdisciplinary studies student, you need a basic understanding of theory for four practical reasons:

- To work in a discipline successfully, you must know the vocabulary and the *theories* [emphasis added] of the field because "each discipline requires a different mind set" (Donald, 2002, p. 2).
- More than ever before, theory dominates the scholarly discourse (i.e., conversation) within the disciplines and often drives the questions asked, the phenomena investigated, and the insights produced.
- Theories generate many of the disciplinary "insights" into a particular problem, and it is these insights that you will need to integrate as you advance in interdisciplinary studies.

- There is a direct relationship between a discipline's favored theories and its preferred methods of research. Szostak (2004) cautions not to blindly accept the evidence for a theory from the methods preferred by a discipline because disciplines choose methods that make their theories look good (p. 106). This is the sort of synergy that makes disciplinary perspective so powerful.

There are literally thousands of theories in academia, and new ones are created every day. We do not, therefore, attempt a survey here. But Szostak (2004) identifies a handful of questions that can be asked of any theory:

Does it focus on inanimate objects (which may include rules or objects created by humans) or thinking beings? In each case, does it focus on individuals, groups, or relationships between individuals?

Does it focus on actions or attitudes?

How does the theory explain? With inanimate objects, explanation must refer to the innate nature of the object. For thinking beings, we can ask if they acted rationally, followed some decision-rule, were guided by deeply held values, did what other people do, or acted intuitively. For groups, we can analyze group decision-making processes.

What sort of process does the theory envisage: change in a particular direction, cyclicality, stability or movement toward stability, or unpredictable?

Does the theory attempt to explain many events or processes or only one or a few?

If you think that group decision making and attitude formation were important to a problem you are reading about but the theory being applied focuses only on the actions of individuals, you can wonder what sorts of insights a different type of theory might have generated. For example, the rational choice theory favored by economists emphasizes individuals, actions, and rationality (of course), and generally imagines highly generalizable equilibrium outcomes; the theory is powerful in many applications but inevitably downplays groups, attitudes, nonrational decision making, nonequilibrium processes, and the particularities of certain situations.

You will use this information to

- Understand the importance of theory in interdisciplinary studies

- Recognize a theory behind a disciplinary insight

- Recognize how interdisciplinarians create common ground between conflicting theories

- Ask yourself how well the type of theory being applied in a particular situation fits the nature of the problem being addressed

Methods

Methods are particular procedures or processes or techniques used by a discipline's practitioners to conduct, organize, and present research (Repko & Szostak, 2016, p. 159). A discipline's method is the way it gathers, applies, and produces new knowledge (Rosenau, 1992, p. 116). Each discipline tends to devote considerable attention to discussing the method(s) it uses, and it does this by requiring students majoring in the discipline to take a research methods course. The methods a discipline favors correspond to the epistemologies and theories it embraces, as shown in Table 5.10. (Note: Interpretivists assume that there are significant differences among individuals in how they perceive the same phenomenon. Postmodernists, by contrast, argue that using any methodology is rendered impossible by the fragmented nature of discourse-based knowledge; Dow, 2001, p. 66.)

Table 5.10 Disciplines and Fields Correlated to Their Epistemologies and Methods		
Disciplines & Fields	**Epistemology**	**Methods**
Natural Sciences	Positivism	1. Study only that which is observable, such as actions, and not attitudes 2. People are studied independent of their natural environment 3. Quantification of evidence is essential 4. Tends to stress deduction

(Continued)

Table 5.10 (Continued)		
Disciplines & Fields	**Epistemology**	**Methods**
Social Sciences	Positivism	1. Tends to stress deduction
Criminal Justice Education	Interpretivism	1. Since humans are intentional and self-reflective, attitudes rather than actions should be studied 2. People should be studied in their natural environment, seeking to understand rather than to explain 3. Qualitative analysis is emphasized over quantitative analysis 4. Tends to stress induction
Humanities Fine and Performing Arts	Postmodernism	1. On one hand, it denies both the prescriptive and descriptive role of methodology because methodology requires some regularity in techniques for acquiring knowledge (Dow, 2001, p. 66). On the other hand, it uses qualitative methods and methods associated with certain theories.

Sources: Adapted from Repko and Szostak (2016). *Interdisciplinary Research: Process and Theory* (3rd ed.), SAGE Publications, Inc (pp. 69-70); Szostak, R. (2004). *Classifying science: Phenomena, data, theory, method, practice* (pp 62–65, 105). Dordrecht: Springer.

The Scientific Method This cursory discussion of method would be incomplete without commenting briefly on the widely used term "scientific method." The term can be understood in two ways: narrowly as experiments conducted under controlled laboratory conditions or more broadly as a way of knowing that can embrace all methods used in the sciences.

As used in the natural and the "hard" social sciences (e.g., psychology and economics), the term *scientific method* refers to what Remler and Van Ryzin (2011) call "a privileged way of knowing" (i.e., epistemology) because it is "generally transparent, logical, and fact-based." Understood narrowly, the term involves the following actions:

- *Systematic observation*—or measurement of various features or behaviors in the world (including qualitative observation)

- *Logical explanation*—in the form of a theory or model that makes sense according to basic rules of logic and accepted facts

- *Prediction*—in the form of a hypothesis, based on a theory, of what we will observe if the theory is true (this is seen as superior to the after-the-fact, or ex post facto, explanations, which are not falsifiable)

- *Openness*—meaning the methods used to produce evidence are clearly documented and made available for review (this allows for replication, repeating the study to see if the results hold—and in what contexts)

- *Skepticism*—researchers scrutinize and critique each other's work, a process referred to as **peer review**, in search of possible shortcomings or alternative explanations (p. 17)

The second way that the term *scientific method* is used is to refer to a broader way of knowing (compared to biologists and physicists) that is used by researchers in the "soft" social sciences and humanities. Here, phenomena are more complex and varied due to factors such as human personality and culture. So truths in the social sciences and the humanities (e.g., how children learn) are far from the universal truths (e.g., the law of gravity) used in physics (see Box 5.7).

Box 5.7 Subjectivity

How we interpret social phenomena is shaped by language and culturally constructed categories. These categories shape our interpretation and even what we observe, and our constructions vary from time to time, from culture to culture, and from political perspective to political perspective. So even when we try to be objective, our interpretations will be at least somewhat conditioned by our categories of subjective experience and judgment. (Remler & Van Ryzin, 2011, p. 19)

Induction and Deduction There are two basic approaches that researchers use to employ the scientific method to tackle a problem or answer a research question. The **inductive approach**, illustrated in Figure 5.3, begins with making systematic observations, detecting patterns, formulating tentative hypotheses about these patterns, and then formulating a theory that explains the phenomenon in question. In the subdiscipline of cultural anthropology, for example, researchers typically observe people in a community for an extended time before developing an explanatory theory. Qualitative research is often inductive (Remler & Van Ryzin, 2011, p. 17). Szostak (2004) notes that intuition is an invaluable inductive tool because it can suggest hypotheses to researchers that would not have resulted from deductive logic. But, he cautions, intuition can also be misleading because it may cloak bias (Szostak, 2004, pp. 106, 124).

The **deductive approach** calls for the researcher to develop a logical explanation or theory about a phenomenon, formulate a hypothesis that is testable, and then make observations and compile evidence to confirm or deny the hypothesis. This approach is illustrated in Figure 5.4. For example, in criminal justice, researchers might develop a theory that predicts the circumstances in which young teens living in an urban area dominated by gangs are most likely to join a gang. They then use observation and interviews to track a group of young teens to verify if their theory accords with reality. Experiments are best for establishing links between cause and effect. An experiment is primarily a deductive tool because the subject is manipulated in a particular way and results are measured (Szostak, 2004, pp. 106, 119).

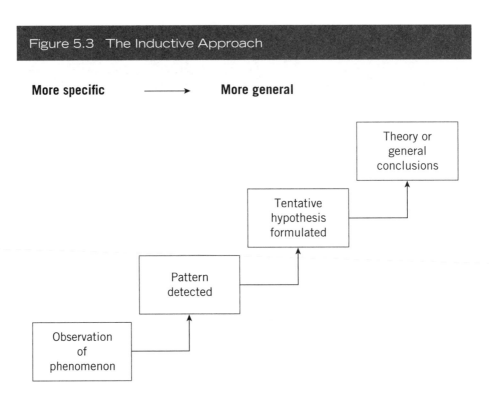

Figure 5.3 The Inductive Approach

More specific ⟶ **More general**

Figure 5.4   The Deductive Approach

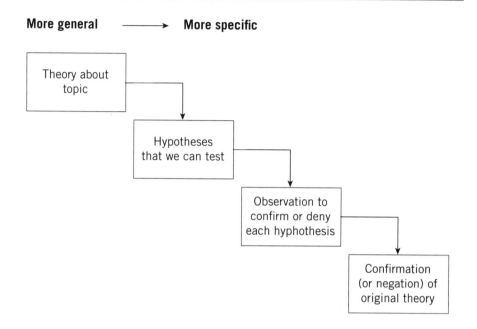

More general ⟶ **More specific**

Theory about topic

Hypotheses that we can test

Observation to confirm or deny each hyphothesis

Confirmation (or negation) of original theory

These approaches can be mutually reinforcing: Induction suggests hypotheses that deduction can test; deduction in turn may guide us to look more closely at certain things. Since methods differ in their potential for induction versus deduction, we thus have another argument for using more than one method to establish truth. Interdisciplinary research will incorporate both approaches depending on the problem under study.

Quantitative and Qualitative Methods Some of the "harder" social sciences (e.g., psychology, economics, and some branches of political science) rely heavily on modernist scientific techniques such as mathematical models and statistical analysis of empirical data. Some of the "softer" social sciences such as sociology and anthropology (e.g., cultural anthropology) use qualitative approaches such as gathering information by making visual observations and interviewing and by using "thick description" to record this information.

The humanities prefer qualitative approaches and rarely insist on quantifying observations.

You will use this information to

- Understand that a complex problem (whose parts are studied by different disciplines using different epistemologies) cannot be studied comprehensively by using a single disciplinary method

- Differentiate between disciplinary methods and interdisciplinary process, the subject of Chapter 7

- Critically analyze disciplinary insights noting their sources of conflict, the subject of Chapter 10

Data

Data are by definition that which is observed (Szostak, 2004, p. 45). Three broad categories of data can be observed: inanimate objects; living things, including people; and events or interactions among people and objects. In our Columbia River dam example, Earth scientists collected information on soil type and the location and type of rock strata below the surface to determine where to locate each dam, whereas biologists collected data on the types of plant and animal life in the river and its tributaries, how much oxygen is dissolved in the river water, and so forth.

Szostak (2004) suggests that interdisciplinarians ask three questions about the data that disciplinary experts use in their work:

1. "Why do authors use particular types of data?" They do so, he explains, to learn about particular phenomena or causal links. The danger is that disciplinary perspective will guide researchers to examine only data that correspond to the phenomena implicated in that discipline's theories. In the case of the Columbia River, no discipline was guided to look in detail for data on how salmon might navigate around the proposed dams.

2. "How do scientists collect and examine data?" There are five broad possibilities for how data can be generated: direct observation by the researcher, direct observation by others, introspection by the researcher, introspection by others, and indirect observation by using instruments. In each case, you can ask whether the method employed is likely to yield data that are representative of the phenomenon in question.

3. "What is the relationship between the data they use and the particular phenomenon or link they are studying?" Scientists are sometimes tempted to downplay or even ignore the necessarily imperfect correspondence between the data and the phenomenon or link they are studying. Disciplinary perspective may guide researchers to assume that their data are a better indicator of the phenomenon in question than they really are. Data exist on almost any topic you can imagine. For example, data exist on frequency of extramarital affairs. These data reflect, among other phenomena, attitudes toward love, marriage, sex, and honesty. Scientists must be careful, Szostak cautions, not to assume that their data are related only to the phenomena they wish to study (p. 49). An increase in extramarital affairs might reflect increased opportunities for them rather than any change in attitudes toward love or marriage. This discussion points up the importance of knowing which part of the subject you wish to study as well as the importance of mapping the subject so as to reveal its parts (pp. 48–49). It is OK to focus on how changing attitudes might lead to an increase in extramarital affairs but not to casually assume that one's data represent only that particular causal linkage.

CRITICAL THINKING QUESTIONS

1. Does the integrated definition of discipline that appears earlier in this chapter adequately reflect the purpose and content of disciplines? Explain.

2. Concerning the two perspectives on disciplines advanced in Box 5.2 and Box 5.3, which do you find more convincing, and why? Is it possible to find common ground between them? Explain.

3. Consult Table 5.4 and identify (and justify) the disciplines that would potentially be interested in the subject of climate change.

4. Identify the critical differences between modern and postmodern approaches to epistemology.

5. What difference does it make if scholars do not separate their epistemological beliefs from their political beliefs? (Note: Review the discussion of assumptions and Table 5.9.)

6. Which research methods would be most applicable to studying a foreign culture? Why?

APPLICATION AND EXERCISES

1. Construct an organizational chart of the disciplines within one of the colleges at your university. If the institution you are attending is not divided into colleges, then construct an organizational chart of the disciplines in the institution. (Note: For the purpose of this exercise, the term *discipline* also refers to the applied fields such as criminal justice and the professions such as education.)

2. Of the specific cognitive capacities associated with the concept of interdisciplinary perspective taking, which one(s) have you already developed and which one(s) are proving the most challenging? Why?

3. From your reading of the book thus far, explain how an interdisciplinarian would approach the object that the "men of Indostan" were attempting to identify?

4. Do you think that those working in the natural sciences can transcend their cultural experience and personal values and make definitive and objective measurements of a controversial phenomenon such as global warming? Why or why not?

5. In a short (250-word) essay, explain whether or not you believe that knowledge is simple, certain, and should be handed down by authorities (e.g., your instructors and/or the text you are using). This is also a very useful question for a group or class conversation.

6. As a class, identify an issue, problem, or object. Formulate your own perspective on it and then compare and contrast your perspective with that of three other class members. Try to account for why your perspective differs from the others.

Source: ©iStockphoto.com/shapecharge.

Chapter 6 Objectives

The objective of this chapter is to make explicit the core elements connecting diverse interdisciplinary fields and programs to each other. These common elements include certain assumptions, theories, epistemology, and perspectives that we call "the DNA" of interdisciplinarity. Combined, they provide interdisciplinary programs with the necessary coherence and rigor. This chapter will also help you understand and recognize these elements as you engage in interdisciplinary work.

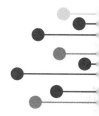

The "DNA" of Interdisciplinary Studies

Interdisciplinarity is a pluralistic idea that is embodied in diverse forms of "studies" programs. Does this mean that there are multiple "interdisciplinarities" just as there are multiple disciplines, each with its own set of assumptions, preferred theories, way of knowing, and thus own perspectives on the world? Not quite. These forms are more like the vast range of dog shapes, colors, and sizes that have their origin in a single ancestral wolflike dog. Digging into the DNA of the diverse forms of interdisciplinarity and looking beneath surface appearances reveals that they share certain assumptions, theories, a commitment to epistemological pluralism, and perspectives on reality. These commonalities, then, constitute the "DNA" of interdisciplinarity as suggested by Figure 6.1, and give coherence to this diverse field. Discordant voices are noted along the way.

Learning Outcomes

By the end of this chapter, you will be able to:

- Identify and explain the assumptions of interdisciplinarity

- Identify and explain the theories supportive of interdisciplinarity

- Understand epistemological pluralism and explain how it integrates critical and instrumental modes of interdisciplinarity

- Identify the perspectives on reality that characterize interdisciplinarity

Figure 6.1   Searching DNA for Commonalities

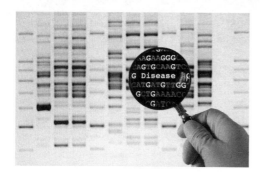

Source: ©iStockphoto.com/Zmeel Photography.

Assumptions of Interdisciplinary Studies

Five assumptions combine to differentiate interdisciplinary approaches to learning and research from disciplinary approaches, though they are contested by some practitioners.

No. 1: The Complex Reality Beyond the University Makes Interdisciplinarity Necessary

Interdisciplinarity assumes that the complex reality beyond the university makes its approach necessary (see Boxes 6.1 and 6.2).

Broadly speaking, there are two categories of problems we face today: those that require a specialized disciplinary approach, and those that require a broader interdisciplinary approach. For example, a specialized disciplinary approach

Box 6.1   Complex Issues

No one can predict the issues that science and society will consider most pressing in the decades to come. But if we look at some high priority issues of today—world hunger, biomedical ethics, sustainable resources, homeland security, and child development and learning—and pressing research questions, such as the evolution of virulence in pathogens and the relationship between biodiversity and ecosystem functions, we can predict that those of the future will be so complex as to require the insights from multiple disciplines. (National Academy of Sciences, 2005, p. 26)

Box 6.2   Complex Systems

The study of complex systems, one of the newest areas of interdisciplinary research, is based on the recognition that different kinds of complex adaptive systems have a common underlying structure despite apparent differences. Methods of analysis can therefore be transferred from one field to another. Ecology, economics, immunology, physics, mathematics, and public policy, cognitive science, political science, biology, and sociology are among the disciplines where the study of complex systems is important. (Casey, 2010, p. 351)

to the subject of freshwater scarcity could focus on depletion rates of freshwater aquifers (Earth science), the destruction of wetlands (biology), or types of pollutants (chemistry). But the same topic of freshwater scarcity would require an interdisciplinary approach if you wanted to learn about it as a complex whole. This would require drawing not only on these disciplines but also on political science (in order to investigate existing or needed legislation), economics (in order to evaluate costs of stiffer environmental regulations), and interdisciplinary fields such as environmental science.

The Association of American Colleges and Universities is the leading association concerned with the quality, vitality, and public standing of undergraduate liberal education and comprises more than 1,250 member institutions of every type and size. Importantly, it recognizes that interdisciplinary approaches to learning and research are uniquely able to "address real-world problems, unscripted and sufficiently broad to require multiple areas of knowledge and multiple modes of inquiry, offering multiple solutions and benefiting from multiple perspectives" (Huber, Taylor, and Hutchins, 2004, p. 13). Its reasoning is this: While disciplinary specialization is appropriate to fill in gaps in knowledge, complex problems necessitate an interdisciplinary approach.

In Chapter 1, we had discussed complex problems as drivers of interdisciplinarity. Here we have extended the argument, noting that these complex problems are likely to become increasingly common in the academy.

No. 2: The Disciplines Are Foundational to Interdisciplinarity

The second assumption of interdisciplinarity is that the disciplines are foundational to its unique purpose, though this notion is vigorously contested by some critical interdisciplinarians. The integrated definition of interdisciplinary studies presented in Chapter 3 makes this connection explicit: "Interdisciplinary studies is a cognitive process by which individuals or groups draw on *disciplinary perspectives* and integrate *their insights and modes of thinking* [emphasis added] to advance their understanding of a complex problem with the goal of applying the understanding to a real-world problem." Interdisciplinarity, particularly in its instrumental form, is not a rejection of the disciplines; it is firmly rooted in them, but offers a corrective to their dominance. We need the specialization, the depth of analysis, and the expertise disciplines provide. But we also need interdisciplinarity to broaden our perspective on a given issue, problem, or question. This "both–and" position is reflected, for example, in the interdisciplinary fields of health sciences and health services. It is also the position of this book and reflects the majority opinion in interdisciplinary literature.

This does not mean that interdisciplinary scholars need to accept the existing structures of disciplines: While the advantages of disciplinary specialization can be appreciated, it might be hoped that disciplines would nevertheless be a bit more open to other theories, methods, and phenomena. And of course, an appreciation of disciplines does not mean that interdisciplinary scholars accept the power that discipline-based departments have wielded since the nineteenth century.

No. 3: The Disciplines Are Inadequate to Address Complexity Comprehensively

A third assumption underlying interdisciplinarity is disciplinary inadequacy. **Disciplinary inadequacy** is the view that the disciplines by themselves are simply not equipped to address complex problems *comprehensively* (i.e., in a way that takes into account the perspectives and insights of other relevant disciplines). Disciplinary inadequacy stems from several factors:

- The disciplines lack breadth of perspective.

- The disciplines are unwilling to assume responsibility for offering broad-based and comprehensive solutions to complex societal problems.

- The disciplines possess an unreasonable certainty that they provide all that is needed to make sense of the modern world.

- The disciplines do not have the cognitive or methodological tools to make sense of reality and provide us with a total picture.

- "The traditional 'reductionist' research approach does not allow for transdisciplinary or problem-based research" (Terpstra, Best, Abrams, & Moor, 2010, p. 509). **Disciplinary reductionism** is the strategy of "dividing a phenomenon into its constituent parts and studying them separately in the expectation that knowledge produced by narrow specialties can be readily combined into the understanding of the phenomenon as a whole" (Newell, 2004, p. 2).

Disciplinary inadequacy as applied to the health sciences is the subject of a study by Terpstra et al. (2010). Their conclusion is summarized in Box 6.3

Box 6.3 Disciplinary Health Science

Over the last century there have been many lessons learned in the health field. A key lesson is that health is a complex phenomenon and the underlying causal pathways for disease and illness are more than just biological. . . . Health is a phenomenon deeply rooted within a social system, and health outcomes result from a dynamic interplay between factors across the lifetime, originating from the cellular level, to the sociopolitical level. . . . As such, efforts to improve health must consider the multifactorial nature of the problem and integrate appropriate knowledge across disciplines and levels of analysis. . . . Health research has implicated a myriad of factors involved in HIV prevention. . . . Unfortunately, incidence rates continue to rise because the knowledge is not being applied in the unified manner necessary to address the complexity of the problem. . . .

Unfortunately, the majority of health research is conducted for the sake of science, and not for the sake of dissemination and implementation. Knowledge created for science's sake tends to be discipline specific and reductionist, producing results that are not easily applied to inform practice and policy decisions. The reality is that health and health service challenges cannot be handled well by any single discipline or social sector, and the traditional reductionist approach to science does not work well for the majority of health service problems. Disciplinary knowledge and levels of analysis are intertwined in health service problems, and, as such, application requires integrative theoretical models and knowledge. As stated by Rosenfeld (1992), "to achieve the level of conceptual and practical progress needed to improve human health, collaborative research must transcend individual disciplinary perspectives and develop a new process of collaboration" (p. 1344). (Terpstra et al., pp. 508–509)

Underlying the assumption of disciplinary inadequacy is the judgment that disciplinary approaches are "partial" and "biased." They are "partial" in that a discipline views a particular problem through the lens of its own unique and narrow perspective. Economists, for instance, are skeptical of research from other disciplines because they value their own theories and methods, and tend to ignore insights generated by alternate theories and methods (Pieters & Baumgartner, 2002). Disciplinary approaches are "biased" in that they are interested in only those concepts, phenomena, theories, and methods that the discipline embraces, while rejecting different concepts, phenomena, theories, and methods preferred by other disciplines. For example, although "power" is a concept relevant to virtually all the social sciences, each discipline has its own definition of power, and each definition is undergirded by certain assumptions, methods, and so forth that are unique to it. To gain a more balanced and comprehensive understanding of "power" as it relates to a problem, we must first understand how each discipline understands the concept of power before attempting to create common ground between these varied and conflicting notions.

No. 4: Interdisciplinarity Is Able to Integrate Insights From Relevant Disciplines

A fourth assumption of interdisciplinarity is that it is able to integrate disciplinary insights into a particular complex problem. This bold assumption is based not on wishful thinking but on a carefully constructed process to achieve integration that instrumental interdisciplinarians have developed in recent years. This process is the subject of Parts II and III of this book. One opposing assumption would be that disciplinary perspectives are mutually incomprehensible. If so, you could not understand the insights of any discipline unless you were in that discipline. But we will show later that it is quite possible to understand and evaluate disciplinary insights.

No. 5: The Disciplines and the Institutional Policies That Reinforce Them Often Present Major Barriers to Interdisciplinarity

A fifth assumption of interdisciplinarity is that the disciplines and the institutional policies that reinforce them often present major barriers to interdisciplinarity. Despite the fact that university presidents now routinely applaud interdisciplinarity, an administrative structure designed in the nineteenth century to serve disciplines is still generally in place. All too often, interdisciplinary studies programs serve as a temporary tool in the wider politics of internal university power struggles and turf wars. University administrators can indulge interdisciplinarity without being committed to its fundamental principles, making it easy to throw it over the side as just so much ballast during economic or political storms (Augsburg & Henry, 2009, p. 2). This is especially easy to do if the professors in interdisciplinary studies programs are cross-appointed into disciplinary departments (though such a strategy may also give interdisciplinary programs support within disciplinary departments). It is not uncommon to hear the "interdisciplinary-mission-fulfilled-by-others" argument advanced by the disciplines, which claims that since "we are now all doing interdisciplinarity" there is no longer need for stand-alone interdisciplinary programs and courses. Such claims rarely involve any familiarity with the definition of interdisciplinarity or how it is practiced. What is needed on campuses that value interdisciplinarity is a storehouse of interdisciplinary expertise and an "intellectual center of gravity." One of the purposes of this book is to provide basic information on what constitutes "strong" and rigorous interdisciplinarity.

Theories Supportive of Interdisciplinary Studies

Theory refers to a generalized scholarly explanation about some aspect of the natural or human world, how it works, and how specific facts are related that is supported by data and research (Bailis, 2001, p. 39; Calhoun, 2002, p. 482; Novak, 1998, p. 84). An example of a theory is "the broken window theory of crime." It communicates the idea that seemingly trivial acts of disorder such as a broken window in a vacant house tend to trigger more serious crime in the neighborhood.

All disciplines embrace certain theories that provide their intellectual core and give them coherence. This is true also of interdisciplinary studies whose theories both provide justification for using an interdisciplinary approach and inform interdisciplinary process. This section examines the theories of complexity, perspective taking, common ground, and integration upon which many of the core concepts of interdisciplinarity are based.

Complexity Theory

Complexity means that there are multiple parts of a system that are connected and interact in sometimes unexpected (e.g., nonlinear) ways with each other. Interdisciplinary complexity theory states that interdisciplinary study is necessitated when a problem or issue is multifaceted and functions as a "system" (see Box 6.4). (Note: As used here, "system" does not imply that the system is stable or that it acts independently of other phenomena because in reality almost all phenomena influence almost all other phenomena somehow.)

This raises the question of why complexity should be a criterion for interdisciplinary studies. The answer involves revisiting the definition of interdisciplinary studies provided in Chapter 3, noting two of its key elements: Interdisciplinary studies "*draw*[s] *on disciplinary perspectives* and *integrate*[s] *their insights.*" The progression of thought, then, is as follows:

- Interdisciplinary studies draws on two or more disciplinary perspectives.
- Complex phenomena and behaviors have facets or parts that cohere.

Box 6.4 Complexity and Interdisciplinarity

What do acid rain, rapid population growth, and the legacy of *The Autobiography of Benjamin Franklin* have in common? Though drawn respectively from the purviews of the natural sciences, social sciences, and humanities, they can be fruitfully understood as behaviors of complex systems, and they all require interdisciplinary study. Thinking of each of them as behavior of a particular complex system can help interdisciplinarians better understand such phenomena; collectively, they can help us better understand the nature and conduct of interdisciplinarity.

The frequent pairing of complexity and interdisciplinarity is no coincidence. It is the contention of this paper that complex systems and phenomena are a necessary condition for interdisciplinary studies. So if a behavior is not produced by a system or the system is not complex, interdisciplinary study is not required. . . . Since the various disciplines have been developed precisely to study the individual facets or sub-systems, interdisciplinary study is a logical candidate for developing specific, whole, complex systems to study such phenomena. By definition, interdisciplinary study draws insights from relevant disciplines and integrates those insights into a more comprehensive understanding.

In order to justify the interdisciplinary approach, its object of study must be multifaceted, yet its facets must cohere. If it is not multifaceted, then a single disciplinary approach will do (since it can be studied adequately from one reductionist perspective). If it is multifaceted but not coherent, then a multi-disciplinary approach will do (since there is no need for integration). To justify both elements of interdisciplinary study—namely that it draws insights from disciplines and that it integrates their insights—its object of study must be represented by a system [that] must be complex. (Newell, 2001, pp. 1–2)

- Each facet is typically the focus of a particular discipline. Some facets are studied by multiple disciplines, which produces conflict in understanding and approach.

- Understanding each facet involves drawing on the insights of the corresponding discipline.

- Understanding the complex phenomenon or behavior *as a whole* involves integrating insights from the relevant disciplines.

Interdisciplinary complexity theory also addresses the special case of the humanities and the arts. These disciplines are more concerned with behavior that is idiosyncratic, unique, and personal. The common practice in these disciplines is to practice **contextualization**. This is the practice of placing "a text, or author, or work of art into context, to understand it in part through an examination of its historical, geographical, intellectual, or artistic location" (Newell, 2001, p. 4). *Since complexity theory is concerned with the behavior of complex phenomena and behaviors, and since contexts are themselves complex, the theory also provides a rationale for the interdisciplinary study of texts, artistic creations, and individuals that are unique and complex.*

Perspective-Taking Theory

Perspective taking is viewing a particular issue, problem, object, behavior, or phenomenon from a particular standpoint other than your own. As applied to interdisciplinary studies, **perspective taking** involves analyzing the problem from the perspective of each interested discipline and identifying the differences and similarities between them.

As developed by cognitive psychologists, perspective-taking theory makes five important claims that are critical to your ability to become interdisciplinary and function successfully in the contemporary world:

1. *Perspective taking reduces the human tendency to negatively stereotype individuals and groups* (Galinsky & Moskowitz, 2000). Assuming the position of the stereotyped individual, either virtually or actually (as John Howard Griffin did in *Black Like Me)*, reverses your perspective. Holding a negative stereotype of an individual or group that is the object of study will certainly skew the interdisciplinary study and fatally compromise the resulting understanding. Stereotyping is inconsistent with good interdisciplinary practice.

2. *Perspective taking helps to move us developmentally from a clear understanding of the differences between disciplines and their perspectives to recognizing distinguishing characteristics of disciplines: the kinds of questions they ask and their rules of evidence* (Baloche, Hynes, & Berger, 1996, p. 3). This cognitive movement is illustrated in Figure 6.2.

3. *Perspective taking facilitates our ability to assemble new sets of potential solutions to a given problem* (Halpern, 1996, pp. 1, 21; see also Galinsky & Moskowitz, 2000). Here the adage "there is wisdom in a multitude of counselors" applies:

UNDERSTANDING DIFFERENCES *BETWEEN* DISCIPLINES → RECOGNIZING DISTINGUISHING CHARACTERISTICS *OF* DISCIPLINES

Examining the insights, even though they conflict, from the perspective of each interested discipline enriches your understanding of the problem and enables you to make creative connections (see Figure 6.3). We should stress the word *creative* here, for perspective taking is often advocated in the literature on creativity.

4. *Perspective taking heightens our awareness that we are biased in the direction of our own knowledge whether it comes from our life experience or prior academic training.* This was one

Figure 6.3 Making Creative Connections

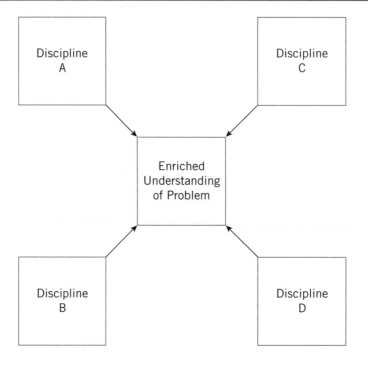

of the important findings of a series of studies conducted by Susan G. Fussell of Carnegie Mellon University's Human-Computer Interaction Institute and Robert Kraus of Columbia University. Their studies found that judges are prone to "false consensus bias," meaning that they assume that others are more similar to themselves than they actually are (Fussell & Kraus, 1991, 1992). The implication of their research for interdisciplinary work is that we need to be aware of our biases, including disciplinary biases, so that these do not prejudice (consciously or unconsciously) our analysis of the problem under study.

5. *Perspective taking invites us to engage in role taking* (Martin, Thomas, Charles, Epitropaki, & McNamara, 2005, p. 141). There are three role-taking aspects of perspective taking, each of which is pertinent to interdisciplinary work:

   - The first is to *accurately perceive how others see and understand the world*. This involves seeing ourselves as role takers, much as those in the theater arts do as they assume the role of a character in play. To engage in interdisciplinary process, we must consciously assume the role, if only briefly, of a disciplinary expert and view the problem through the expert's eyes. This role-taking ability is particularly important for those engaged in non-Western cultural studies, race and ethnic studies, urban studies, women's studies, sexuality studies, and other programs that emphasize difference.

   - The second is to *view a situation broadly from multiple perspectives* (Martin et al., 2005, p. 141). The implications for interdisciplinary process are obvious: We must not limit our inquiries to only those disciplines with which we are familiar or to those expert views with which we agree.

   - The third is to "*perceive the other's perspective in depth and have a full understanding of the other's perspective*" (p. 141). In interdisciplinary work, "depth" and "full understanding" refer to disciplinary depth. This holds special significance for those in the humanities and the fine and performing arts where the ability to understand and even assume or appropriate the identity of another is a critical skill.

Common Ground Theory

Though the concept "common ground" does not appear in the definition of interdisciplinary studies presented in Chapter 3, it is implicit in the concept of integration. The interdisciplinary concept of common ground comes from cognitive psychology's theories of common ground and the emerging field of cognitive interdisciplinarity.

Noted cognitive psychologist Herbert H. Clark (1996) defines common ground in social terms as the knowledge, beliefs, and suppositions that each person must establish with another person in order to interact with that person (pp. 12, 116). That is, certain shared understandings are essential to communication. Central to Clark's theory is the emphasis on the *context* of language. He finds, for example, that all people take as common ground aspects of human nature such as physical senses, communal lexicons (i.e., sets of word conventions in individual communities), and cultural facts, norms, and procedures (pp. 106–108). Figure 6.4 depicts common ground having been established between two people from different cultures.

Clark explains that when it comes to coordinating a joint action, "people cannot rely on just any information they have about each other. They must establish *just the right piece of common ground*, and that depends on them finding a *shared basis for that piece* [emphasis added]" (pp. 93, 99). Accordingly, "two people's common ground is, in effect, the sum of their mutual, common, or joint knowledge, beliefs, and suppositions" (p. 93).

Figure 6.4 Communicating Across Cultures

Source: ©John Warburton_Lee/AWL Images/Getty Images.

Though Clark's definition of common ground is limited to social interaction, his theory has direct application to interdisciplinary work. Trying to create common ground between two persons from different social, cultural, or political backgrounds is similar to trying to create common ground between conflicting insights from different disciplines. Applied to interdisciplinary work, Clark's theory means that the interdisciplinarian has to create the common assumption, concept, theory, value, or principle that can provide the basis for integration.

Cognitive psychologist Rainer Bromme (2000) applies Clark's theory of common ground to communication between academic disciplines. Whether developing a collaborative language for interdisciplinary research teams or integrating conflicting insights, the "theory of cognitive interdisciplinarity" calls for discovering or creating the "common ground integrator" by which conflicting assumptions, theories, concepts, values, or principles can be integrated. In Figure 6.5 the common ground integrator is symbolized by the letter *A* suspended between two conflicting disciplinary insights represented by the two buildings.

Working independently of Clark and Bromme, William H. Newell (2001) was the first interdisciplinarian to define common ground in interdisciplinary terms. Common ground, he says, involves using various *techniques* to modify or reinterpret disciplinary elements (p. 14).

Newell's definition contains three ideas that are consistent with those of Clark and Bromme:

1. Common ground is something that the interdisciplinarian must create.

2. Creating or discovering common ground involves modifying or reinterpreting disciplinary elements (i.e., assumptions, concepts, or theories) that conflict.

3. Modifying these elements to reduce the conflict between them involves using various techniques.

Figure 6.5 Common Ground Between Two Disciplinary Insights

Source: ©Drawn Ideas/Ikon Images/Getty Images.

Newell's particular contribution to understanding common ground is that it is what makes integration of disciplinary insights possible. In effect, Newell has illuminated the mysterious "black box" of interdisciplinary integration so that we can readily perceive how to create common ground and thus achieve integration.

A definition of common ground that integrates Newell's definition with the formulations of Clark and Bromme is as follows: **Common ground** is that which is created between conflicting disciplinary insights, assumptions, concepts, or theories and makes integration possible (Repko & Szostak, 2016, p. 18).

Integration Theory

No aspect of interdisciplinary studies has generated more controversy among practitioners than that of integration. Interdisciplinarians have been divided into two camps: "generalists" and "integrationists."

Generalist interdisciplinarians reject the notion that integration should be *the* defining feature of genuine interdisciplinarity. They understand interdisciplinarity loosely to mean "any form of dialog or interaction between two or more disciplines" while minimizing, obscuring, or rejecting altogether the role of integration (Moran, 2010, p. 14).

The core of the generalist position is that in most cases integration is simply not achievable. They identify at least three factors that complicate, retard, or even prevent integration: (1) epistemological barriers between disciplines, (2) conflicting disciplinary perspectives and modes of thinking, and (3) a variety of possible results. Each of these objections is countered by integrationists.

Integrationist interdisciplinarians regard integration as *the key distinguishing characteristic* of interdisciplinarity and *the goal* of fully interdisciplinary work. They insist that epistemological and other barriers (e.g., conflicting perspectives, insights, and modes of thinking) can be overcome (as we shall see in Parts II and III). What makes integration possible, they argue, is following the interdisciplinary process. As for a variety of possible results materializing from integration, there is always some basis for the choices made, such as choosing one theory over another because of its elegance and compatibility with other theories.

Theories Supportive of Integration The purpose of interdisciplinary studies is not to choose one disciplinary concept, assumption, theory, or method over another but to produce a more complete understanding of the problem by integrating the best elements of competing concepts, assumptions, theories, or methods. The core of the integrationist position is that integration is achievable and that researchers should strive for the greatest degree of integration possible given the problem under study and the disciplinary insights at their disposal. Importantly, integrationists point to recent theories supportive of integration advanced by cognitive psychologists, curriculum specialists, professors of education, and researchers. Moreover, they point to the increasing amount of interdisciplinary work characterized by integration. This book reflects the integrationist position.

We offer support for interdisciplinary integration from education, linguistics, and anthropology. The idea for interdisciplinary integration is grounded in Bloom's classic taxonomy of levels of intellectual behavior that are involved in learning.

Figure 6.6 Updated Bloom's Taxonomy of Levels of Intellectual
Behavior

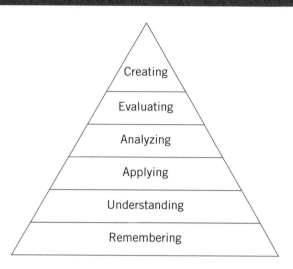

Source: Anderson, Lorin W., Krathwohl, David R., Ajrasian, Peter W., Cruikshank, Kathleen A.,
Mayer, Richard E., Pintrich, Paul R., Raths, James, Wittrock, Merlin C., *Taxonomy for Learning,
Teaching, and Assessing: A Revision of Bloom's Taxonomy of Educational Objectives* (Complete
edition), © 2001, p. 28. Pearson Education, Inc.

Drawing on theories of learning and cognitive development, an interdisciplinary
team of researchers and educators led by Lorin W. Anderson updated Bloom's
taxonomy in 2001. The team identified six levels within the cognitive domain,
with simple recognition or recall of facts at the lowest level through increasingly
more complex and abstract mental levels, leading ultimately to the highest order
ability, creating, as shown in Figure 6.6.

The significance of this taxonomy for interdisciplinary studies is that it
elevates the cognitive abilities of creating and integrating to the highest level of
knowledge. **Interdisciplinary creation** involves putting elements together—
integrating them—to produce something that is new, coherent, and whole.
Integration is central to understanding the nature of interdisciplinary studies and
is a distinguishing feature of this rapidly growing field. Integration is also at the
core of interdisciplinary process.

The idea for interdisciplinary integration finds additional support in the work
of linguists George Lakoff and Gilles Fauconnier, and cultural anthropologist
Mark Turner. Lakoff (1987) introduced the **theory of conceptual integration**

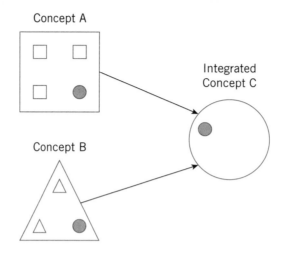

Figure 6.7 Integrating Two Separate Concepts Into a Third Concept

Concept A

Integrated Concept C

Concept B

to explain the innate human ability to create new meaning by blending concepts (p. 335). Fauconnier (1994) deepened our understanding of integration by explaining how our brain takes parts of two separate concepts and integrates them into a third concept that contains some properties (but not all) of both original concepts. For example, the nickname "Iron Lady," referring to former British prime minister Margaret Thatcher, represents a conceptual integration of the concept "iron," a metal used in construction because of its strength, with the concept "lady," a woman who holds political rank. The implicit claim of the metaphor is that Margaret Thatcher acted as *if* she were made of iron (p. xxiii). Conceptual blending is possible because certain commonalities exist in the two original concepts that provide the basis for the new integrated concept. This third concept is different from either of the two original concepts. Figure 6.7 depicts this process.

Anthropologist Turner (2001) extends the theory of conceptual integration still further by arguing that we cannot fully appreciate a concept without understanding its cultural or historical context (p. 17). Accordingly, concepts should be analyzed in the context and theoretical framework of the disciplines from which they come.

The implication of the extended theory of conceptual integration for interdisciplinary work, then, is this: *Integration is an innate human ability that involves taking portions of different perspectives or concepts and creating* an integrated third perspective or concept. This makes sense because in interdisciplinary work we find that the definition of a concept used by different disciplines will vary in its meaning according to each discipline's perspective (Morrison, 2003, p. 3).

Interdisciplinary Integration Defined From this discussion, it is possible to construct an integrated definition of **interdisciplinary integration** as *the cognitive process of critically evaluating disciplinary insights and creating common ground among them to construct a more comprehensive understanding. The new understanding is the product or result of the integrative process.*

> *Interdisciplinary integration is the cognitive process of critically evaluating disciplinary insights and creating common ground among them to construct a more comprehensive understanding. The new understanding is the product or result of the integrative process.*

Epistemology of Interdisciplinary Studies

Another critical part of the "DNA" of interdisciplinarity is its adherence to epistemological pluralism. Of the many ways that disciplinarity contrasts with interdisciplinarity, none is greater than their starkly different approaches regarding epistemology. As we noted in Chapter 2, disciplinarity privileges certain epistemologies over others, which limits our understanding of a complex problem. Part of the attraction of interdisciplinarity is its embrace of **epistemological pluralism**, which rejects notions of absolute truth and embraces the ambiguity that arises out of conflict and difference. In this way, explains James Welch (2011), knowledge emerges from the cross-fertilization of different perspectives. The interdisciplinary approach to knowledge production, he says, involves negotiating within and beyond the epistemological frameworks constructed by the disciplines (p. 32). A theory of epistemological pluralism helps us "to make sense of this fractious, dynamically changing world, and apply that sense to problem solving, decision making, and progress" (p. 32). More particularly, it integrates critical and instrumental modes of interdisciplinarity and it addresses complexity.

Critical and Instrumental Modes of Interdisciplinarity

In Chapter 4 we learned that the idea of interdisciplinarity arose in response to the Enlightenment idea of absolute truth. Science elevated reason over other modes of thought, creating a pervasive method of acquiring knowledge through logic and mathematics and an epistemological standard that tested knowledge through empiricism (Welch, 2011, p. 5). By questioning this utter reliance on reason and empirical evidence as *the* way to know truth, critics of rationalism and disciplinary structure, such as Jacques Derrida and Michel Foucault, gave voice to an emerging critical interdisciplinarity. From its inception, this mode of interdisciplinarity has challenged disciplinary domination and the not-so-subtle order that the disciplines impose upon human thinking, behavior, and social structures (Welch, 2011, pp. 16–17).

Over time, says Welch, "the interdisciplinary idea has evolved from a mere critique of the disciplines to the more sophisticated and pragmatic mission of negotiating within and beyond the epistemological frameworks they project" (Welch, 2011, p. 32). The beginnings of instrumental interdisciplinarity emerged from the idea that truth is not established by authorities but is worked out through the exchange of ideas.

This idea led to another idea: that *progress can result from the interplay of ideas.* This describes the beginnings of the concept of interdisciplinarity, which involves working with multiple perspectives and integrating their insights as these pertain to a particular complex problem. "Here we see the development of core interdisciplinary values, including tolerance for ambiguity, appreciation of diversity, and the utilitarian goal of progress through complex problem solving" (Welch, 2011, p. 21).

Complexity

Complexity has become the cornerstone of interdisciplinarity for good reason. Instead of reducing phenomena to simple structures or idealized models, the theory of epistemological pluralism "approaches knowledge as open-ended and ill-defined, acknowledging its dependence on context, and focusing on relationships between [system] elements" (Welch, 2011, p. 32).

> [Y]et this indicates that interdisciplinarity . . . is working through knowledge systems toward a more integrative creation of new knowledge. . . . Interdisciplinary theory attempts to bring insights from different perspectives into a cohesive understanding of complex phenomena applied toward progress, and in this way fundamentally synthesizes postmodern and pragmatic schools of thought, along with the critical and instrumental modes derived from them. . . . As an epistemology of complexity, interdisciplinary theory established equilibrium between absolutism and nihilism, asserting that knowledge is progressive, while also pragmatic. (Welch, 2011, pp. 32, 34–35)

How Interdisciplinary Studies "Sees"

Since interdisciplinarity assumes many forms, it is problematic to say that interdisciplinarity embraces a particular perspective on reality. It is more accurate to say that interdisciplinary studies, as we have described the field in this book, sees nature and human society through a set of lenses that reflect its assumptions and theories. To be interdisciplinary, then, requires seeing reality in ways that are very different from disciplinary approaches.

It Sees Complexity in the Familiar

Seeing a homeless person pushing a cart filled with plastic bags of what most of us would consider junk is, tragically, a familiar sight in most cities. Disciplinary approaches to the problem of homelessness typically view it through narrow disciplinary lenses. Disciplinary experts set forth theoretical explanations of homelessness that tend to reflect their discipline's narrow perspective on reality. For example, political science typically views homelessness as a public policy issue, and psychology views it primarily as a mental health issue. But interdisciplinarity views homelessness as a complex problem caused by multiple factors that are interconnected and proposes solutions that are more comprehensive than are the narrow disciplinary ones.

It Sees Complex Problems in Context

All complex problems have a particular context or setting. Though disciplines attempt to see problems in context, the context that each discipline typically studies is limited in scope to its perspective. For example, the sociologist might stress that the homeless lack strong personal ties to the wider society, while the economist will note that they have trouble finding jobs. By viewing the homeless person through the lens of only one discipline, the context of the problem will be limited to those factors typically studied by sociologists or economists. But what of other possible causal factors such as the person's education, emotional health, and life experience that are studied by different disciplines? Unlike disciplinary specialists, the interdisciplinarian will place the homeless person in the broadest context possible and (ideally) draw on *all* relevant sources of knowledge to more fully understand the cause of the person's plight.

It Sees Commonality
Amid Difference and Conflict

Disciplinary learning typically stresses difference. Instructors in the social sciences and the humanities often encourage students to argue for or against something, focus on categories, or adopt a particular theoretical or ideological stance. In other words, disciplinary approaches ask students to take sides and thereby become a party to the conflict. They might be asked to judge whether homelessness is the fault of society or of the homeless themselves. By contrast, the interdisciplinarian does not approach a complex societal problem such as homelessness in this way. Rather, the interdisciplinarian is interested in investigating all possible causes of the problem. This is done by drawing on all relevant disciplinary insights, which are scrutinized for conflicts between them, and understanding why they conflict. The interdisciplinarian generally expects that there is some "kernel of truth" in the insights of diverse disciplines. The interdisciplinarian is then able to create common ground among these insights and integrate them in order to create a more comprehensive understanding of the problem.

It Sees Contingency in Certainty

Generally, the result of interdisciplinary study is contingent knowledge, not absolute knowledge. An interdisciplinary study focuses on a complex problem in order to find the best available solution in that particular context, given what insights can currently be drawn from relevant disciplines. In our example of the homeless person, the resulting understanding, though far more comprehensive than what a single discipline is capable of producing, is not definitive. The understanding is the best that can be achieved at that point in time. Interdisciplinary studies makes no claim to come up with general solutions applicable for all times and places. Not only that, the disciplines themselves evolve over time, collecting new information, developing new concepts and theories, and quite possibly generating new insights as a result. Interdisciplinary studies suspends final judgment and is willing to live with ambiguity because it recognizes that understanding any complex problem is an ongoing process. There remains the possibility that new information will require us to modify our understanding.

CRITICAL THINKING QUESTIONS

1. Why are disciplines foundational to interdisciplinarity?

2. Identify (and justify) a complex problem that disciplines *by themselves* are inadequate to address comprehensively.

3. According to Terpstra et al. (Box 6.3), what is the argument for the health sciences and health services to become more interdisciplinary?

4. Why should complexity as defined by Newell (Box 6.4) be considered a criterion for interdisciplinary studies? How does "contextualizing" a problem reinforce Newell's argument that complexity should be a key criterion for interdisciplinary inquiry?

5. What is the relevance of perspective taking to interdisciplinary studies?

6. Why do integrationists view integration as *the* hallmark of interdisciplinarity?

7. How do the theories of conceptual integration developed by Lakoff, Fauconnier, and Turner support the integrationist case?

8. How is Welch's theory of epistemological pluralism relevant to interdisciplinary study?

APPLICATIONS AND EXERCISES

1. Identify an issue, problem, or intellectual question that reflects the complex reality beyond the university but is not referenced in this chapter. How would using an interdisciplinary approach rather than a specialized disciplinary one advance our understanding of it?

2. From your life experience, is Clark correct in saying that "people cannot rely on just any information they have about each other [but] must establish just the right piece of common ground, and that depends on them finding a shared basis for that piece"? Why is common ground often so difficult to achieve between two individuals? In your opinion, what is the single greatest barrier to establishing common ground? (It can be useful here to engage in a conversation in a small group and identify the common ground assumptions that allow the conversation to proceed.)

3. Why is a musical chord a useful metaphor to describe integration? Can you think of another metaphor that would be useful? Explain why.

Thinking Critically About Interdisciplinary Studies

The purpose of Part II is to help you become a critical user of both disciplinary and interdisciplinary work. To do so, you need to think like interdisciplinarians think and understand how they approach complex problems. This theme is explored in three chapters: Chapter 7 explains how to recognize and think critically about disciplinary perspectives; Chapter 8 examines how to recognize and think critically about disciplinary insights; and Chapter 9 focuses on how to recognize and think critically about interdisciplinary integrations and understandings.

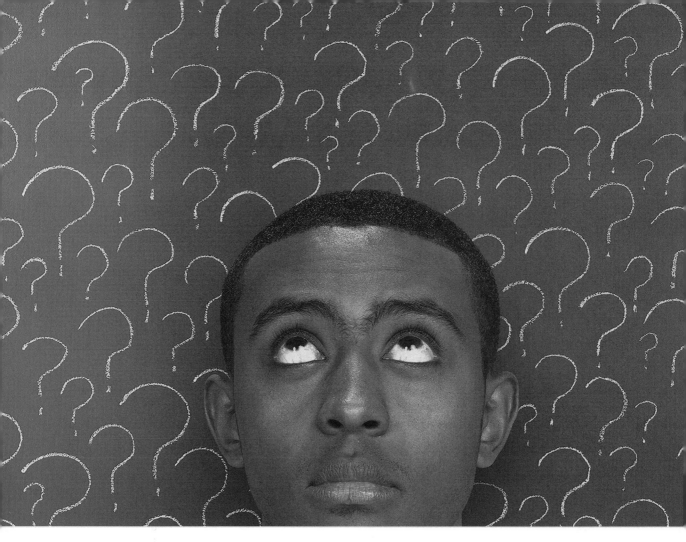

Source: ©iStockphoto.com/ Barcin.

Chapter 7 Objectives

Becoming interdisciplinary involves learning to think critically about disciplinary perspectives on subjects appropriate to interdisciplinary study. The chapter's first objective is to explain why it is essential to develop a sophisticated conception of knowledge to engage productively in interdisciplinary studies. The second objective is to explain why interdisciplinarians interrogate disciplinary perspectives (or practice critical pluralism). The third objective is to explain how to interrogate disciplinary perspectives.

Thinking Critically About Disciplinary Perspectives

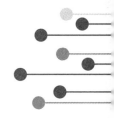

What It Means to Think Critically About Disciplinary Perspectives

In Chapter 5, we learned that each discipline has a perspective that is *partial* when applied to complex multidimensional subjects. Consider the following example based on a real-life situation where multiple and conflicting perspectives arose over the issue of whether to build a sports stadium in a run-down and crime-ridden part of City, USA. From the perspective of the team's owners, their business associates, and professors from the nearby business school, the site made economic sense because it was located next to an interstate highway and the land could be purchased inexpensively. From the perspective of the city, the plan was attractive because it would eliminate a blighted and crime-ridden area, create jobs, and generate new tax revenues. However, from the perspective of sociology, the plan was seriously flawed because it would force hundreds of low-income people to relocate and would destroy the many minority-owned mom-and-pop businesses operating in the area. The professional field of education pointed out the disruptive effect of such massive relocation of the area's children on the city's school system whose budget was already strained. And criminal justice referred to research showing that criminal elements would simply relocate to another part of the city.

Clearly, the issue of whether the sports complex should be built in that location was complex and multifaceted. Each perspective was only partial, and none provided a "big picture" of the issue. Nor was one perspective "wrong" and another "right." To think critically about disciplinary perspectives on an interdisciplinary subject, then, involves (1) developing a sophisticated conception of knowledge and (2) learning how to interrogate disciplinary perspectives.

Learning Outcomes

By the end of this chapter, you will be able to:

- Understand the positions of dualism, relativism, and critical pluralism

- Understand why a critical pluralist position is necessary to engage productively in interdisciplinary study

- Understand why interdisciplinarians interrogate disciplinary perspectives

- Understand how interdisciplinarians interrogate disciplinary perspectives

We should be careful to distinguish "perspectives" from "insights." The perspective of the owners leads them to value the profitability of the team and favor financial calculations as a method; they then derive the insight that the stadium would be a good investment. The perspective of sociologists guides them to stress the communities in which people live and their access to services (which they might evaluate by performing interviews); they then derive an insight that the stadium would be disruptive to a particular community. Both insights are important. In trying to achieve a comprehensive understanding of whether the stadium is a good idea, the student would want to take into account all insights. Then, we shall see in Chapter 8, you would evaluate each insight in the context of disciplinary perspective: It is useful to know why team owners, sociologists, and others think the way that they do.

Developing a Sophisticated Conception of Knowledge

In order to think critically about disciplinary perspectives, it is important to have, or be willing to develop, a more sophisticated conception of knowledge that makes sense of the multiple and often conflicting perspectives and insights that you will encounter. You must, that is, come to accept that there is not always one right answer to complex questions but rather differing insights that reflect differing perspectives, and each contains some "kernel of truth." Arriving at this conception involves (1) reflecting on your present "epistemic position," (2) assessing your tolerance for multiplicity, and (3) moving toward critical pluralism.

Reflect on Your Present Epistemic Position

The term **epistemic position** refers to your understanding of the nature of knowledge and how you determine truth. Research by noted educational psychologist William G. Perry Jr. (1981) finds that many students entering college tend to favor one of the following epistemic positions when confronted with particular controversial and emotionally charged issues: dualism, relativism, or critical pluralism. (Note: This is not to suggest that all students or even most students can appropriately be labeled by how they think or to suggest that all their other traits, abilities, sensibilities, and inclinations pale in comparison to how they think.) These positions are summarized here:

- *Dualism*: Students who are dualistic thinkers believe that knowledge is objective, certain, and absolute. They think in terms of dualistic categories such as right–wrong, true–false, correct–incorrect, or good–bad. So, when confronted with multiple and conflicting pieces of information, they reject as false or mistaken any views that challenge their own (pp. 80–81). Similarly, they tend to reject divergent disciplinary perspectives that are raised in interdisciplinary subjects as being "wrong" while believing their own perspective is "right."

- *Relativism*: Students who are relativist thinkers believe there is no such thing as objective knowledge and view beliefs, theories, and values as inherently relative, contingent, and contextual (pp. 81–82). When confronted with multiple and conflicting perspectives on a subject, they consider conflicting disciplinary insights as mere opinion or personal preference.

- *Critical pluralism*: Students who are critical pluralist thinkers believe that knowledge can be objective but not certain and absolute as dualists assume. Critical pluralists accept the pluralism of relativism without drawing the relativist conclusion that "anything goes." Critical pluralists view multiple and conflicting disciplinary perspectives on a subject as more or less well-reasoned judgments (pp. 81–82). So, when presented with a range of disciplinary perspectives on a subject, critical pluralists view each as partial and none as complete.

Importantly, other cognitive theorists describe a similar progression but use different labels and make some gender distinctions.

Assess Your Tolerance for Multiplicity

Multiplicity refers to when you experience several plausible yet contradictory explanations of the same phenomenon as opposed to one simple, clear-cut, unambiguous explanation (Perry, 1981, pp. 81–82). Such multiplicity is a key feature of interdisciplinary studies when working with conflicting insights coming out of different disciplinary perspectives.

The dualist and relativist positions are **simplistic epistemic positions** because they rest on the assumption you already "know what is true" about a given subject. If you have already taken a simplistic epistemic position concerning what is true about the interdisciplinary subject you are studying, you will be unable to work effectively with the multiple and conflicting disciplinary perspectives and insights concerning it. Even worse, you will misunderstand the aims and expectations of interdisciplinary learning. When faced with a range of plausible expert insights from different disciplinary perspectives where none seem to be simply "right" or "wrong," says Clinton Golding (2009), you will likely react in one of these possible ways: You will experience "intellectual vertigo" and be unable to figure out what is going on, you will stubbornly cling dogmatically to your opinion come what may, or you will retreat to an equally problematic relativist position and think that it's just "all a matter of opinion" (p. 18).

The tragic result of these attitudes will be twofold: (1) You will not understand *why* there is so much disagreement when the experts should just be able to get the "right answer" and move on, and (2) you will see little value in continuing in interdisciplinary studies.

But if you take a **sophisticated epistemic position**, that of critical pluralism, you will see the multiple and conflicting perspectives as *partial understandings of the subject under study.* You will also realize that what is needed is not another partial understanding or uninformed opinion but an understanding that takes into account the subject's complexity and that respects the scholarship of disciplinary experts.

This last point should be stressed: The reward for grappling with multiplicity is the ability to integrate across differing insights in order to achieve a more comprehensive understanding. Though you should be willing to move away from clinging stubbornly to one "right" answer, you need not and should not abandon the hope that we can achieve "better" answers by evaluating and integrating multiple insights.

Move Toward Critical Pluralism

The critical pluralist position is the necessary foundation for interdisciplinary work for two reasons. First, multiple disciplinary perspectives and the insights they produce cannot be simply categorized as true or false or understood as mere opinion. Second, each disciplinary perspective has at least *some* useful insights (though the proportion can vary considerably from discipline to discipline, depending on the problem under study).

Therefore, the dualistic and relativist classification methods cannot support interdisciplinary learning. The reason, explains critical thinking expert Richard Paul (1994), is that these positions have conceptions of "right answers," "wrong answers," or "mere opinion," but they do not have a conception of "reasoned judgment," where ideas are judged "better" or "worse" depending on the appropriateness or quality of reasoning supporting them (pp. 347–348). In particular, we need to be able to recognize both the strengths and limitations of different insights. Without the understanding that only comes with critical pluralism, says Golding (2009), it is impossible to make sense of the complex judgments needed to balance, accommodate, and integrate the perspectives and insights of multiple disciplines (p. 19). In Box 7.1, Repko makes the case for a critical pluralist approach when analyzing the conflicting insights of disciplinary experts.

Part of the task facing interdisciplinarians is to critically evaluate disciplinary perspectives and their insights, *not* to just sort insights into "better" or "worse" categories. Even "worse" insights may have a kernel of truth that the interdisciplinarian needs to identify and use.

Box 7.1 The Fable of the Blind Men and Elephant Redux

A sophisticated epistemic position understands that research conducted by the disciplines is similar to the activity of the blind men trying to make sense of the elephant. We can compare these men to disciplinary experts who are trying to understand a complex phenomenon (i.e., the elephant). They naturally concentrate on that part of the phenomenon that their disciplinary training has taught them to focus on: One disciplinary expert concentrates on the trunk, another focuses on the tusks, and others study the ears, body, legs, or tail. Their disciplinary training has equipped them to approach the problem with a specialized toolkit of assumptions, epistemology, concepts, theories, and methods. This describes disciplinary reductionism in operation. The disciplines are doing exactly what they are supposed to be doing: probing deeply into those parts of the problem (and only those parts) that they are uniquely designed to study and producing narrow, specialized understandings of it. Instead of dismissing conflicting insights as "mere opinion" or "right" or "wrong," it is best to view their work as partial or incomplete.

It is left to the interdisciplinarian to look at the "big picture" and research the whole elephant. We do this, not by duplicating the narrow and specialized work of the disciplinary specialists, but by critically examining their multiple and conflicting insights, integrating them, and producing a more comprehensive understanding which will lead to a workable solution. This, in a nutshell, describes interdisciplinary process. Engaging in it is possible only by exercising "reasoned judgment." (Repko & Szostak, 2016)

Why Some May Find the Transition
to Critical Pluralism Difficult to Make

As you prepare to critically analyze the disciplinary perspectives and insights concerning the problem you are studying, reflect on your epistemic position concerning it and your tolerance for multiplicity. If you find that you are already "entrenched" in a dogmatic position, you may find the transition to critical pluralism difficult to make. As Howard Gardner (1989) explains, epistemic positions tend to be extremely robust and difficult to abandon for two reasons: one internal and the other external. *Internally*, everything people experience and learn is "colored" by their epistemic position. Becoming more flexible epistemically thus challenges their personal identity. *Externally*, social forces such as experiencing discrimination deeply impact and may reinforce their epistemic position. That is, even with good intentions to move toward a sophisticated epistemological position, people who are dualist or relativist thinkers may (1) still interpret the multiple perspectives and conflicting insights from their simplistic epistemic position, (2) reject outright those insights that conflict with their own, (3) categorize insights according to their personal view of the issue, or (4) just lump all the insights together as mere opinion.

How to Move From a Position of
Dualism or Relativism to One of Critical Pluralism

To move from a dualist or relativist position toward a critical pluralist position, consider doing the following:

- Reflect on those past experiences that may have colored your position on the problem you are studying. For example, early memories of the towering stacks of coal-powered electric power plants belching clouds of noxious emissions may be coloring your thinking about whether coal should be used for electric power generation.

- Reflect on social forces (e.g., peer or academic pressures) that may be influencing your position.

- Temporarily set aside your position on the problem so that you can consider the views of others and the possibility that they may be as valid as your own.

- Keep in mind the goal of the interdisciplinary enterprise, which is to develop a more comprehensive understanding of the complex problem.

In Chapter 4, we encouraged students to write an intellectual autobiography. It would be useful here to consult such an autobiography in order to identify experiences that might influence your views of the problem you are studying.

Why Interrogate Disciplinary Perspectives (or Practice Critical Pluralism)

After identifying disciplines relevant to the problem and verifying their relevance by conducting the literature search (we explore these steps in Chapter 11), interdisciplinarians "interrogate" these perspectives (see Chapter 12). To **interrogate in an interdisciplinary sense** means to practice critical pluralism by asking critical and probing questions of each relevant discipline. Fortunately, the interdisciplinarian need not achieve mastery of each discipline to ask such questions.

The Issues of Disciplinary Depth and Interdisciplinary Breadth

The relevant issue is the *minimum* depth that entry-level students need in relevant disciplines. "Minimum depth" refers to knowing the perspective (in an overall sense) of each discipline relevant to the problem as discussed in Chapter 5. Depending on the program, you may also need to know the defining elements of each relevant discipline's perspective (see Chapter 5). Critics of interdisciplinarity argue that in order to work in a discipline, it is necessary to achieve mastery of it by attaining the doctorate or the equivalent degree. Such criticism reflects disciplinary preference for specialization.

But *entry-level interdisciplinary work requires adequacy, not mastery* (see Box 7.2). As an entry-level student, you are taking a major step toward achieving adequacy by engaging the information about the disciplines presented in this book.

Undergraduate interdisciplinarity typically focuses on developing interdisciplinary *breadth* above disciplinary *depth* (although some programs emphasize the latter). **Interdisciplinary breadth** is basic knowledge about each potentially relevant discipline so that you can understand its perspective and access, translate, think critically about, and use its insights. This basic information about disciplines appears in Chapters 2 and 5. The best time to start developing this competency of interdisciplinary breadth is *before* you begin to develop expertise in a particular discipline by majoring in it or decide to pursue a field in interdisciplinary studies.

Box 7.2 Drawing on Disciplines

Much interdisciplinary work does not require disciplinary depth. One example is the interdisciplinarity of a policy analyst, judge, or political decision maker, who uses special interdisciplinary skills to locate information from multiple disciplines and then to understand, balance, and synthesize this information so they can make a final decision. Another possible example is the researcher in an area of study such as education, who does not have a specific disciplinary background, but who has the ability to draw on multiple disciplines when they [are] illuminating, and has general methodological skills for designing and carrying out research.

Expertise in a discipline may be useful for this kind of interdisciplinary work, making it easier to access and understand some disciplinary knowledge, but it is not necessary. . . . The only thing necessary . . . is being able to identify when disciplinary expertise is needed and knowing how to access and use this. (Golding, 2009, p. 5)

Identifying Disciplines Relevant to the Problem

One of the first questions interdisciplinarians ask as they begin studying a complex problem is, "Which disciplines are relevant to the problem?" Answering this question requires connecting the problem to disciplines that study it. To illustrate how this is done, we introduce the issue of human cloning. You can make these connections yourself by consulting Table 5.4 "Disciplines and the Phenomena They Study" in Chapter 5. Concerning human cloning, the *potentially* interested disciplines include biology, psychology, political science, ethics (a subdiscipline of philosophy), religious studies, the applied field of law, and the interdiscipline of bioethics. These disciplines are only *potentially* interested because, at the outset, it is unclear if authors from each of these disciplines have even written on human cloning. If experts from a particular discipline have not yet written on the subject, then that discipline is not relevant, at least to students in an introductory course.

However, it is not enough to connect an interdisciplinary subject as broad and complex as human cloning to a particular discipline such as psychology. Interdisciplinarians must also know the *basis* for making this connection. Table 7.1 identifies disciplines *potentially* relevant to the subject of human cloning because they consider the problem (or some part of it) as falling within their research domain. (Note: We say *potentially* relevant because at this point we do not know if each discipline's community of scholars has published insights on human cloning.)

Table 7.1 Why Each Discipline Is Potentially Relevant to Human Cloning

Disciplines Potentially Relevant to the Issue of Human Cloning	Basis for Relevance
Biology	Analyzes the biological process of human cloning and measures the rates of success or failure
Psychology	Analyzes the psychological impact on the cloned person of a sense of personhood
Political science	Examines the role of the federal government and particular agencies
Philosophy	Probes the ethical implications of cloning a human life
Religious studies	Analyzes the sacred writings of the world's major faith traditions to see if they are consistent with human cloning
Law*	Analyzes the legal rights and relationships of the cloned child and its "parents"
Bioethics**	Examines the ethical implications of the technical procedures required to clone a human, particularly in the event of failure

Source: Repko, A. F. & Szostak, R. (2016). *Interdisciplinary Research: Process and Theory* (3rd ed.). Thousand Oaks, CA: SAGE Publications, Inc. p. 105.

*Law is generally considered a professional program.

**Bioethics is an interdisciplinary field in many taxonomies.

After forming a list of disciplines potentially interested in the problem, and identifying which of these have produced relevant insights, the next question to ask is, "What is the perspective (in a general or overall sense) of each discipline on the problem?" Before discussing how interdisciplinarians go about interrogating disciplinary perspectives, we explain the necessity for performing this critical task.

Why Interdisciplinarians Interrogate Perspectives

Interdisciplinarians are interested in viewing the subject from the perspectives of potentially relevant disciplines for six reasons. Each of these six reasons, as we shall see, is related to the fact that different disciplines will have relevant insights into complex problems, and these insights will reflect the discipline's perspective.

No. 1: Perspective Taking Is a Key Feature of Interdisciplinarity That Is Necessitated by Complexity The very premise of interdisciplinary studies is that each discipline is uniquely able to focus on that part of a subject it considers within its research domain and study that part in depth. But no single discipline is equipped to explain a complex subject comprehensively. This is why studying complex subjects requires tolerance for multiplicity and why the critical pluralist position is the necessary foundation for interdisciplinary work.

Viewing the problem through the lens of each discipline's perspective involves moving from one discipline to another, shifting from one perspective to another. One practitioner describes this process of "moving" and "shifting" in rather colorful terms. The interdisciplinarian, he says, must take off one set of disciplinary lenses and put on another set in their place as each discipline is examined (Newell, 2007, p. 255). Figure 7.1 depicts this process.

The problem, depicted by the multisided figure, is complex, meaning that it has multiple parts or facets. Each disciplinary lens is able to focus on only one facet.

No. 2: Perspective Taking Is a Prerequisite for Turning Multidisciplinary Work Into Interdisciplinary Work We established the critical role that perspective taking plays in interdisciplinary work. Here we add that perspective taking is a prerequisite for turning multidisciplinary work into interdisciplinary work. In multidisciplinary work, we are *not* interested in the discipline's **perceptual apparatus** (i.e., its defining elements) because it is enough to point out that each discipline sees the subject in a certain way but not explain *why* this is so.

The focus of multidisciplinary work is on *comparing insights* rather than integrating them. Hugh Petrie (1976) describes multidisciplinary work this way:

Figure 7.1   Viewing the Problem Through Different Disciplinary Lenses

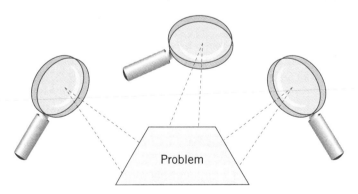

Two disciplines "look at the same thing [but] do not see the same thing" (p. 11). The fable of the blind men and the elephant depicts how disciplinary experts, though looking at the same phenomenon (i.e., the elephant), are compelled by their disciplinary training to quickly zero in on those parts they are trained to study (e.g., ears, tails, legs).

But in interdisciplinary work, interdisciplinarians must understand the significance of each discipline's perspective (i.e., its cognitive map) so that they can think critically about how its insights illumine some part of the problem. Insights from different disciplines often conflict, as in the case of the blind men who described different parts of the elephant. We can only integrate these insights (see Chapter 9) after first evaluating them in the context of disciplinary perspective.[1]

No. 3: Perspective Taking Enables Us to See the Relevance of Other Perspectives Complex problems such as human–environment interactions generally involve interactions among phenomena studied by different disciplines. One practitioner explains why interdisciplinarians cannot ignore the perspectives of other disciplines in these cases:

> [A reason] for this is that . . . the environment is a complex system where the factors addressed by one discipline are affected by factors addressed by other disciplines. The environmental factors studied by a biologist may have effects on the health factors studied by a medical scientist. The culture of a group of people studied by an anthropologist may affect their use of the technology developed by an engineer. In order to solve an engineering problem about the best location of wells in Papua, New Guinea, the engineer . . . had to first use anthropology to help him understand how the local people used water. (Golding, 2009, p. 3)

Only if we can appreciate multiple perspectives will we be able to properly appreciate the insights developed by disciplines that study each relevant phenomenon.

---

1. A detailed discussion of exactly how to create common ground by modifying assumptions, concepts, or theories is the focus of the follow-on text by Repko and Szostak (2016), *Interdisciplinary Research: Process and Theory* (3rd ed.).

No. 4: Perspective Taking Illumines Our Understanding of the Problem as a Whole Perspective taking also illumines our understanding of the problem *as a whole*, as illustrated in this example:

> Implementing an environmental solution from one discipline often requires dealing with factors from other disciplines. For example, to implement new health care or contraceptive methods, we have to understand not only medicine, but also education. To find out what would be the optimal place to dig a well, we have to consult geologists about the hydrogeology and sociologists about how the people currently use water. To build something, architects have to consult engineers, and engineers have to consult mathematicians. Even something as simple as deciding where a bike path will go and how it will be constructed requires the input from multiple disciplines: we may have to consult an engineer about the composition of the pavement, the ergonomist about the design of signs that are noticed by pedaling cyclists, the transport planner about the likely users and their intended trips, the sociologist about the potential impact on neighboring land holders, the licensed surveyor about land titles on the proposed path, the stream ecologist about proposed fords and bridges and their effects on the waterways, and even the animal behaviorist about swooping magpie risks. (Golding, 2009, p. 3)

No. 5: Perspective Taking Reduces the Possibility of Making Poor Decisions Perspective taking reduces the possibility of making poor decisions resulting from failure to take important perspectives into account. When it comes to making decisions and policy recommendations on a host of complex and costly public works projects, bad decisions are likely to result if important perspectives are overlooked:

> Someone might calculate the most efficient energy use for a new community center without considering how people will interact with the center and so they build an efficient center that no one wants to use. Alternatively, someone might argue that, because of sociological factors, fire-destroyed communities should be rebuilt where they are, but because they ignore what planners and architects might say about mitigating fire risk, they rebuild communities that are in imminent danger. (Golding, 2009, p. 4)

No. 6: Perspective Taking Exposes Strengths and Limitations of Disciplines Interdisciplinary subjects bring together multiple disciplinary perspectives. Therefore, one of the responsibilities of the interdisciplinarian is to know the strengths and limitations of each discipline's perspective on the subject. These are more readily apparent when perspectives are juxtaposed, as they are in Table 5.3 from Chapter 5, reproduced here for your convenience.

Table 5.3 (Reproduced From Chapter 5) Perspectives of Natural Sciences, Social Sciences, Humanities, the Fine and Performing Arts, Criminal Justice, and Education, Stated in General Terms	
Discipline	**Perspective on Reality**
Natural Sciences	
Biology/Ecology	While the other natural sciences focus on the principles that govern the nonliving physical world, biology studies the behavior of the living physical world. When biologists venture into the world of humans, they look for physical, deterministic explanations of behavior (such as genes and evolution) rather than the mental ones (such as the decisions of individuals or groups based on free will or norms) on which the social sciences focus. Ecology is an interdisciplinary branch of biology that studies the relations that living organisms have with respect to each other and their natural environment.
Chemistry	Chemistry focuses on the distinctive properties of the elements, individually and in compounds, and their interactions. Chemistry sees larger-scale objects, organic as well as inorganic, in terms of their constituent elements and compounds.
Earth Science/ Geology	Earth science focuses on the large-scale physical processes of planet Earth and is concerned with both the details and functions of the four subsystems and their interactions: the lithosphere (the Earth's hard, outermost shell), the atmosphere (the mixture of gases that envelops the Earth), the hydrosphere (the subsystems that contain the Earth's water), and the biosphere (the realm of all living things, including humans).
Mathematics	Mathematics is interested in abstract quantitative worlds mathematicians create with postulates, assumptions, axioms, and premises and then explore by proving theorems.
Physics	Physics studies the basic physical laws connecting objects (atoms and subatomic particles, quanta) and forces (gravity, electromagnetic, strong, weak) that often cannot be directly observed but that establish the underlying structure of observable reality, and cosmology (the form, content, organization, and evolution of the universe).

(Continued)

Table 5.3 (Continued)

Discipline	Perspective on Reality
Social Sciences	
Anthropology	Cultural anthropology sees individual cultures as organic integrated wholes with their own internal logic and culture as the set of symbols, rituals, and beliefs through which a society gives meaning to daily life. Physical anthropology seeks to understand former cultures through the artifacts it uncovers.
Economics/ Business*	Economics/business emphasizes the study of the production and distribution of goods and services with the individual functioning as a separate, autonomous, and rational entity.
Political Science	Political science views the world as a political arena in which individuals and groups make decisions based on the search for or exercise of power. Politics at all levels and in all cultures is viewed as a perpetual struggle over whose values, not just whose interests, will prevail in setting priorities and making collective choices.
Psychology	Psychology sees human behavior as reflecting the cognitive constructs individuals develop to organize their mental activity. Psychologists also study inherent mental mechanisms, both genetic predisposition and individual differences.
Sociology	Sociology views the world as a social reality that includes the range and nature of the relationships that exist between people in any given society. Sociology is particularly interested in voices of various subcultures, analysis of institutions, and how bureaucracies and vested interests shape life.
Humanities	
Art and Art History	Art history views art in all of its forms as reflecting the culture in which it was formed and therefore providing a window into a culture. Art, and thus art history, has a place for universal aesthetic tastes.
History	Historians believe that any historical period cannot be adequately appreciated without understanding the trends and developments leading up to it, that historical events are the result of both societal forces and individual decisions, and that a picture or narrative of the past can be no better than the richness of its details.
Literature (English)	Literature believes that cultures, past and present, cannot be adequately understood without understanding and appreciating the literature produced by the culture.
Philosophy	Philosophy recognizes a variety of limits to human perceptual and cognitive capabilities. Philosophy views reality as situational and perspectival. Reality is not a collection of imperfect representations that reflect an "absolute reality" that transcends all particular situations. Rather, these representations are the reality that is the world.

Discipline	Perspective on Reality
Religious Studies	Religious studies views faith and faith traditions as human attempts to understand the significance of reality and cope with its vicissitudes through beliefs in a sacred realm beyond everyday life.
The Fine and Performing Arts	
Art	The study of art as a creative pursuit sees the creative process as a means by which human experience (and therefore the culture in which it exists) can be articulated via a chosen medium (paint, ceramics, clay, stone, etc.). Part of the study of art involves examining the developments in the discipline over time and in different parts of the world.
Dance	The study of dance as a creative art form articulates observations on human experience (and therefore the culture in which it exists) via the movement of the body of one dancer alone or choreographed with two or more individuals, accompanied by sound or silence. Part of the study of dance involves examining developments in the discipline over time and in different parts of the world.
Music	The study of music as a creative pursuit involves the composition and/or performance of music, which is itself produced in response to elements of human experience (and therefore the culture in which it exists). The study of music can include conducting, performing on various instruments, aural training, performing as part of an ensemble or soloist, or composing or arranging. Part of the study of music involves examining developments in the discipline over time and in different parts of the world.
Theater	The study of drama as a creative pursuit involves the creation of original dramatic works or acting and/or producing such works. Works of drama express observations about the human experience (and therefore the culture in which it exists). Part of the study of drama involves examining developments in the discipline over time and in different parts of the world.
Applied Fields	
Criminal Justice	Criminal justice sees crime and criminal behavior through the lenses of theories on human nature, societal structure, social order, concepts of law, crime and criminals, the logic of crime causation, and the policies and practices that follow from these.
Professions	
Education	Education views learning as developmental and governed by a linear and universal model of progress, civilization, democracy, rationality, and science. This modernist view is being challenged by a postmodern recognition of diversity and contextualization that values what is local and different.

Source: Adapted from Repko, A. F. & Szostak, R. (2016). *Interdisciplinary Research: Process and Theory* (3rd ed.). Thousand Oaks, CA: SAGE Publications, Inc.

*Like other professions, business schools are at least multidisciplinary and address sociology as well as economics.

How Interdisciplinarians
Interrogate Disciplinary Perspectives

Interdisciplinarians interrogate the perspectives of relevant disciplines by asking three questions.

1. What Is the Discipline's Perspective *on This Particular Subject?*

We have said that a disciplinary perspective concerns a discipline's overall view of reality. As such, it is highly instructive to apply the discipline's perspective to a particular subject that falls within the discipline's research domain, as the following examples of professional work demonstrate. (Note: The examples assume that the authors have done some background reading concerning the subject but have not yet conducted an in-depth literature search.)

***Primarily* From the Natural Sciences:** Dietrich (1995), *Northwest Passage: The Great Columbia River*

In his award-winning study of the causes of the alarming decline of salmon populations in the great Columbia and Snake River systems in the American Northwest, William Dietrich first identified the disciplines that he thought would be relevant to understanding this complex subject holistically. As a journalist, he had no expertise in any of these disciplines. Each discipline's perspective on

Table 7.2 Disciplinary Perspectives on the Causes of Declining Salmon Populations

Disciplines Relevant to the Problem	Perspective on Problem
Biology/Ecology	Views the reduction of salmon populations as an ecological phenomenon
Economics/Business	Views the reduction of salmon populations as having economic/business impacts on local, state, and regional economies
Earth Science (Geology)	Views the reduction of salmon populations as having something to do with the hydrosphere and biosphere
History	Views the reduction of salmon populations as a problem with a historical context
Political Science	Views the reduction of salmon populations as a struggle between competing interests

Source: Adapted from Repko, A. F. & Szostak, R. (2016). *Interdisciplinary Research: Process and Theory* (3rd ed.). Thousand Oaks, CA: SAGE Publications, Inc. p. 118.

Table 7.3 Disciplinary Perspectives on the Causes of Occupational Sex Discrimination (OSD)

Disciplines Relevant to the Problem	Perspective on Problem
Economics	Views OSD as an economic/business problem
History	Views OSD as a historical phenomenon
Sociology	Views OSD as a reflection of a sociological phenomenon
Psychology	Views OSD as a psychological phenomenon
Marxism*	Views OSD as an inevitable consequence of capitalism

Source: Adapted from Repko, A. F. & Szostak, R. (2016). *Interdisciplinary Research: Process and Theory* (3rd ed.). Thousand Oaks, CA: SAGE Publications, Inc. p. 156.

*Marxism is a school of thought that transcends disciplines and offers an all-encompassing explanation of reality.

the problem shown in Table 7.2 is based on its overall perspective on reality as described in Table 5.3.

Primarily **From the Social Sciences:** Fischer (1988), "On the Need for Integrating Occupational Sex Discrimination Theory on the Basis of Causal Variables"

Fischer is grappling with the very complex social problem of the causes of sex discrimination in the workplace. He draws on several disciplines, primarily in the social sciences. His approach is instructive because of the way he simplifies the process for the uninformed reader by briefly describing each perspective in a narrative (not reproduced here) from which we distilled the information that appears in Table 7.3.

Primarily **From the Humanities:** Bal (1999), "Introduction," *The Practice of Cultural Analysis: Exposing Interdisciplinary Interpretation*

Mieke Bal, who helped develop the interdiscipline of cultural analysis, is attempting in this example to decipher the meaning of an enigmatic poem written in yellow paint on a red brick wall in post–World War II Amsterdam, Netherlands:

> Note
>
> I hold you dear
>
> I have not
>
> thought you up

Table 7.4 Disciplinary Perspectives on the Poem	
Disciplines Relevant to the Problem	**Perspective on the Problem**
Anthropology (cultural)	Views the poem as a cultural artifact
Art History	Views the poem as a complex physical object/text
Linguistics (narratology)	Views the poem as a linguistic symbol
Philosophy (epistemology)	Views the poem as an epistemological query
Literature	Views the poem as part of Dutch literature
Psychology	Views the poem as a public expression of deep emotion

Source: Adapted from Repko, A. F. & Szostak, R. (2016). *Interdisciplinary Research: Process and Theory* (3rd ed.). Thousand Oaks, CA: SAGE Publications, Inc. p. 119.

Her study involves drawing on several disciplines and their perspectives (simplified) as depicted in Table 7.4.

2. How Does Each Perspective Illumine Our Understanding of the Subject *as a Whole?*

The next question to ask is how each perspective illumines our understanding of the subject as a whole. The focus here is on the "big picture" and the possible causes (or effects) of the problem.

Primarily **From the Natural Sciences:** Dietrich (1995), *Northwest Passage: The Great Columbia River*

Primarily **From the Social Sciences:** Fischer (1988), "On the Need for Integrating Occupational Sex Discrimination Theory on the Basis of Causal Variables"

By asking this second question, Fischer drills more deeply into each discipline's perspective as shown in Table 7.6. In effect, he asks what, in general terms, does each perspective say is the probable cause of OSD?

Primarily **From the Humanities:** Bal (1999), "Introduction," *The Practice of Cultural Analysis: Exposing Interdisciplinary Interpretation*

Table 7.7 shows that Bal is concerned to probe more deeply into the meaning of the poem from multiple standpoints of the author, those who encountered it when it appeared, and those who grapple with its meaning today.

Table 7.5 How Disciplinary Perspectives Illumine the Problem of Declining Salmon Populations in the Columbia River System as a Whole

Disciplines Relevant to the Problem	How the Perspective Illumines the Problem/Subject as a Whole
Biology/Ecology	The reduction of salmon populations may have something to do with the system of hydroelectric dams that were constructed on the Columbia and Snake Rivers.
Economics/Business	The reduction of salmon populations produced unforeseen economic consequences.
Earth Science (Geology)	The dam system impacted the region's hydrological system.
History	The damming of the Columbia River system tells us something about the nation's confidence in this period of history.
Political Science	The problems arising from the damming of the Columbia River system raise questions about the role of government concerning the future of the system.

Source: Adapted from Repko, A. F. & Szostak, R. (2016). *Interdisciplinary Research: Process and Theory* (3rd ed.). Thousand Oaks, CA: SAGE Publications, Inc. pp. 167–170.

Table 7.6 How Perspectives Illumine the Problem of OSD

Disciplines Relevant to the Problem	How the Perspective Illumines the Problem/Subject as a Whole
Economics	OSD is caused by rational economic/business decision making.
History	OSD is caused and perpetuated by long-standing institutional practices.
Sociology	OSD is caused by a process of socialization that, in turn, is directly reflected in occupational structures.
Psychology	OSD is caused by males perpetuating the traditional male-female division of labor.
Marxism	OSD is a logical extension of attempts to preserve the institutions of capitalism.

Source: Repko, A. F. & Szostak, R. (2016). *Interdisciplinary Research: Process and Theory* (3rd ed.). Thousand Oaks, CA: SAGE Publications, Inc. p. 186.

3. What Are the Strengths and Limitations of Each Perspective?

It is not enough to know the perspective of each discipline on the problem in a general sense or even to know how these perspectives illumine some aspect of the problem. Interdisciplinarians also need to know the strengths and limitations

Table 7.7 How Disciplinary Perspectives Illumine the Meaning of the Poem

Disciplines Relevant to the Problem	How the Perspective Illumines the Problem/Subject as a Whole
Anthropology (cultural)	The poem is an expression of contemporary (i.e., circa 1945) "popular" Dutch culture.
Art History	The poem is a complex artistic creation in its composition and placement.
Linguistics (narratology)	The poem is a symbol.
Philosophy (epistemology)	The poem suggests that love was real or unreal.
Literature	The poem is comparable to other Dutch poetry.
Psychology	The poem is an expression of psychic mourning for a lost love.

Source: Adapted from Repko, A. F. & Szostak, R. (2016). *Interdisciplinary Research: Process and Theory* (3rd ed.). Thousand Oaks, CA: SAGE Publications, Inc. p. 187.

Table 7.8 Strengths and Limitations of Disciplinary Perspectives on the Causes of OSD

Relevant Disciplines	Strengths of Perspective	Limitations of Perspective
Economics	• Economic motivation of employers	• Economists have not decided upon a single explanation of OSD. • Economic motivation fails to account for prejudice, sex-role socialization, and "tastes" adverse to hiring women. • It assumes that individuals are rational and self-interested.
History	• Able to identify historical trends that may have produced the problem • Able to place problem in a broad context	• It is unable to comprehensively analyze behavior of groups. • It is unable to account for psychological motivation of individuals.
Sociology	• Conflict among social groups, institutions • Differences between how men and women are raised	• Its focus on groups fails to account for individual behavior motivated by complex psychological factors or genetic predisposition.

Relevant Disciplines	Strengths of Perspective	Limitations of Perspective
Psychology	• Individual behavior, decision making	• It is unable to study group behavior.
Marxism	• Explains macro trends and developments	• Economic considerations fail to explain behavior of all groups or individuals.

Source: Adapted from Repko, A. F. & Szostak, R. (2016). *Interdisciplinary Research: Process and Theory* (3rd ed.). Thousand Oaks, CA: SAGE Publications, Inc. pp. 197–198.

of each perspective in that particular context, and this information is often revealed only after juxtaposing disciplinary perspectives, as we do in Table 7.8 with Fischer's study.

Fischer's study of the causes of OSD points up the strengths and limitations of each of the disciplines that he identifies as potentially relevant because the subject falls within their research domains. His detailed comments on the limitations of each perspective reflect his expertise in economics and his determination to achieve adequacy in other potentially relevant disciplines.

Simply because a discipline's perspective has limitations does not disqualify it from being used. After all, every perspective has limitations, and these vary depending on the characteristics of the problem and the goal of the study.

Nevertheless, these limitations *do* mean that the insights of the discipline are skewed by the way each author defines the problem, and the interdisciplinarian must acknowledge this as Fischer does.

Critical Thinking Scenario

The following scenario is based on an actual situation in which newly laid-off employees and their union leaders attempted to save their jobs in the supermarket industry in Big City, USA. They planned to pool their resources (e.g., personal savings and 401k retirement plan money) and apply for a large bank loan in order to purchase the bankrupt supermarket where they had worked, and manage it themselves. At the time, a team of academics from a nearby university came together to conduct research on job-saving strategies in areas that were experiencing population loss and economic decline, and decided to focus on this particular experiment in "grassroots capitalism."

1. Identify the disciplinary perspectives that would enable the academic team to develop the most comprehensive understanding of the situation facing the laid-off employees.

2. How would each of these perspectives illumine the situation *as a whole*?

3. What primary strength and limitation would each perspective bring to the subject?

CRITICAL THINKING QUESTIONS

1. Why is it important to understand disciplinary perspectives?

2. In a group, discuss the challenges in progressing toward a critical pluralist outlook.

3. How much does an interdisciplinarian need to know about a discipline in order to draw upon it?

4. Provide your own example of the difference between a perspective and an insight.

APPLICATIONS AND EXERCISES

1. Is it worth looking at the insights generated by a discipline whose perspective faces severe biases in addressing the problem at hand?

2. Identify the issue(s) implicated in the lead story in today's local or national newspaper. Discuss in a group the strengths and limitations of relevant disciplinary perspectives. Be sure to carefully distinguish perspectives from insights.

Chapter 8 Objectives

Students, especially early in their college education, often wonder how they can be expected to critically evaluate books or articles written by experts in a field. Since the author knows so much more about the subject than the student does, how can the student presume to critique? Interdisciplinary students may have an advantage here because disciplinary authors provide an incomplete analysis of any complex problem. Students familiar with the material in earlier chapters will, in other words, know that there is a downside to expertise. Experts may ignore much that is beyond their experience. But this lesson has broader import: No work is perfect, and therefore, all works need to be critically evaluated. The objective of this chapter is to provide practical advice on how you can critically evaluate any text you read, whatever the disciplinary or interdisciplinary orientation of its authors.

Thinking Critically About Disciplinary Insights

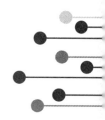

In Chapter 6, we discussed the updated version of Bloom's taxonomy, noting that students often begin their college careers as passive recipients of knowledge, but (hopefully) complete them as critical analysts of knowledge. As an interdisciplinary studies student, you face a far greater challenge than disciplinary students do because you must read and critically analyze works from disciplines with which you have limited familiarity. This chapter will both encourage you to make this transition from passive to active learning and provide practical advice on how to do so. Learning to think critically about disciplinary insights involves approaching the disciplinary work armed with appropriate critical attitudes, critical questions to ask of the work, an understanding of how to critically analyze the work for interdisciplinary use, and a familiarity with mapping the question or problem.

Learning Outcomes

By the end of this chapter, you will be able to:

- Identify and develop attitudes that are conducive to interdisciplinary critical thinking

- Identify four critical questions to ask when reading disciplinary work and distinguish between several types of statements used in the work

- Critically analyze disciplinary work for interdisciplinary purposes

- Map interdisciplinary connections

- Understand how mapping the scholarly enterprise as a whole reveals the critical role played by interdisciplinary studies in the academy

Critical Thinking Attitudes

A key to making the transition from passive to active learning is having certain critical thinking attitudes, some of which were touched upon in Chapter 4. These include awareness of the limitations of expertise, self-awareness, intellectual courage, and respect for different viewpoints.

Awareness of the Limitations of Expertise

The more time you spend in college, the greater will be your awareness of the limitations of expertise. As you read and critically analyze the scores of books and articles that you are assigned, you will realize that these works contain information that is both good and important but that their authors are neither all-knowing nor free from bias. Instead of passively accepting what they say at face value, you can confidently approach their work on the lookout for its strengths and limitations. Awareness of the limitations of expertise will encourage you to read with greater confidence, motivate you to dig deeper into a given subject, and prompt you to develop your own conclusions. The word *confidence* deserves emphasis. By appreciating that no author is perfect, you gain confidence that you can critically read any text. Every individual brings a slightly different set of skills and knowledge and attitudes to any question, and thus it is not only possible but likely that you can spot errors or biases in published works. As an interdisciplinary student, you will be particularly aware of those biases that are rooted in disciplinary perspective. Though the argument made here to justify confidence is straightforward, you will gradually increase your confidence level as you develop your critical reading skills and gain practice in applying them.

Self-Awareness

A second attitude relevant to thinking critically about disciplinary insights is self-awareness. Interdisciplinary students are encouraged to be aware of authorial bias (see the following discussion). But it is even more important for you to become aware of your own biases. It is a common human practice to accept without much examination arguments that you like while seeking the slightest reason to discredit arguments that you dislike. Critical thinking involves treating all arguments with the same degree of informed skepticism. If you allow your biases to determine your opinion of every work that you read, then you are unable to learn, to grow, and to revise your opinions in the face of new information. Only by interrogating your biases can you come to understand who you are and why you believe the things that you do.

Becoming interdisciplinary involves being especially wary of disciplinary bias. As we have seen in Chapter 5, each discipline is characterized by an overarching disciplinary perspective. Likewise, individuals have their own overarching worldview that guides their behavior in general and in particular influences how they react to new situations. For disciplinary scholars, disciplinary perspective will be an important part of their personal worldview. Interdisciplinary students or scholars, however, will not likely be as closely tied to any particular disciplinary perspective. Nevertheless, their personal worldview may incline them to be more receptive to some disciplines than to others. The best antidote to this sort of bias is being aware of your own worldview.

Just as personal growth is stymied by a lack of self-awareness, so also is informed and respectful political debate, or indeed informed and respectful discussion of any question we may face in our lives. Productive conversations take place only if individuals are willing to examine arguments on their merits. There is always a temptation to demonize or disdain those you disagree with rather than reflect both on their perspective and the strengths of their arguments.

In reading, you can enhance self-awareness by asking yourself three key sets of critical questions:

- First, do you like the conclusions reached by a particular work? If you do, ask yourself if as a result you have tended to be too easy in your critical analysis of the work. Are the conclusions in fact justified? You can perform the opposite exercise for conclusions you dislike. Maybe as a result you were overly critical, blowing minor flaws out of proportion.

- You can then usefully ask *why* you like or dislike a particular conclusion. Is it because of closely held religious, ideological, or ethical views? Or is there perhaps something else at work: Do you like a conclusion that foreign aid does not work because it frees you from a sense of guilt and responsibility toward the less fortunate?

- And you can usefully interrogate your attitude toward open-mindedness. Do you want to be a person who never questions who you are or what you believe? Or do you want to be a person who is willing to question your beliefs and worldview and engage in a sometimes challenging process of personal growth? If you opt for the latter, you need to ensure that you act in accord with this goal. An important distinction can be made here between personal growth and personal transformation. Personal growth means that you become more knowledgeable, better at certain behaviors, and more self-aware, whereas personal transformation can be promoted by challenging your overall worldview. While open-mindedness is key to both, the latter requires also a willingness to open yourself to entirely novel experiences and ideas. An interdisciplinary education can promote your personal transformation by opening you up to a variety of ways of looking at the world.

Intellectual Courage

A third attitude relevant to thinking critically about disciplinary insights is intellectual courage. It takes courage both to challenge your own beliefs and worldview and to disagree with your friends and family. In fact, the self-awareness discussed in the preceding section cannot be achieved without the exercise of intellectual courage. Once you start to challenge your own beliefs, you have to be willing to accept a degree of uncertainty: You will often not know what to think about a particular issue, not through ignorance, but through careful examination of opposing arguments. And you will then need to dig deeper, learn more, and pursue further analysis.

Respect for Different Viewpoints

There is a fourth attitude that we discussed in Chapter 4 that is especially relevant to our current subject of thinking critically about disciplinary insights: respect for different viewpoints. If you start out believing that those who agree with you are entirely correct and those who disagree with you are entirely incorrect, then you cannot engage in critical thinking. Interdisciplinarity requires you to recognize that there is likely some kernel of truth in opposing viewpoints. By carefully analyzing competing arguments, you give yourself the chance to identify common ground between apparent opposites. Such common ground is invisible to those who automatically discredit opposing viewpoints in their entirety.

Both critical thinking and interdisciplinarity encourage us to respect not just the arguments but also the motivations of people with whom we disagree. To be sure, there are times when others are guided by extreme selfishness, and you can anticipate at least some degree of self-interest in everyone. In most areas of disagreement in modern society, though, the choice is between competing societal "goods": Almost everyone wants a healthy economy, a healthy environment, and compassion for the unfortunate. We disagree, however, both on the relative weights we attach to different goals and on how and how well we think each can be achieved. Critical thinking and interdisciplinarity guide us to separate our disagreements over goals from our disagreements over means. An argument for decriminalization of marijuana might be grounded in a belief that there is nothing wrong with marijuana use or instead in a view that criminalization has not been an effective policy for reducing marijuana use. Our evaluation of such an argument will proceed quite differently depending on whether it is an argument about goals or means.

Categories of Statements

Developing appropriate attitudes sets the stage for critical evaluation of texts. This involves asking a set of critical thinking questions of every scholarly work that you read. In order to make the transition from being a passive recipient in the learning process to becoming an active participant, you should first ask "Are the conclusions reached justified by the supporting arguments and evidence?" Most of the time, this question is not easily answered. To answer it, you must be able to distinguish among several different categories of statements inherent in any scholarly work. To help you identify the categories, you need to ask these subsidiary questions: "What are the author's conclusions?" "What are the supporting arguments?" "What assumptions does the author make?" and "What evidence does the author marshal?" Only once these elements are identified can you analyze the connections among them. The sequence of thought proceeds as follows: Evidence and assumptions support arguments which support conclusions. We provide examples of this sort of evaluation in what follows.

No. 1: What Are the Author's Conclusions?

Some books and articles, especially in the natural sciences and certain social sciences, will close with a chapter or section titled "Conclusion" or perhaps "Concluding Remarks." Sometimes such sections will contain clear statements of the author's conclusions. Often, though, the reader is expected to carefully read much or all of the work in question in order to discern the author's thinking. It is thus useful for you to develop the habit of asking, "What was the point?" upon finishing any work.

In the humanities, many authors believe that their purpose is not to arrive at a conclusion but to highlight certain facets of a work of art or literature for the reader's deeper reflection. In such cases, you can still usefully try to identify what the author believes is important to communicate.

Interdisciplinary students face two particular challenges. As noted earlier, disciplines differ in both the clarity and positioning of concluding remarks. In order to identify conclusions across many disciplines, you need to appreciate a second challenge: that conclusions may take different forms as well. A conclusion may come in the form of a theoretical argument, a statement about a particular event or process, a mathematical proof, an empirical result, or in various other forms.

No. 2: What Are the Supporting Arguments?

A work in criminology, for example, might conclude that a particular change in the sentences imposed for certain crimes will have a certain impact on crime rates. Such a conclusion could be supported by arguments regarding the likelihood that a prisoner will commit a certain crime again or that other potential criminals will take the penalties into account when deciding whether to commit a crime. There could be more detailed arguments involving the decision-making process of criminals, the efficacy of prison rehabilitation programs, or the chances of criminals being caught.

The first challenge you face here is to distinguish conclusions from supporting arguments. This will be much easier for some works than others. And some works may build slowly toward a conclusion such that the arguments supporting the final conclusion are themselves miniconclusions supported by yet further arguments.

Once again, interdisciplinary students will face a special challenge. Students in a discipline may become accustomed to a particular mode of argumentation. Interdisciplinary students have a greater need to consciously pursue critical thinking strategies, for they will need to identify supporting arguments (and other types of statements) across quite different types of work. When students come to compare the *support* for conclusions from different disciplines, they often find they are comparing apples and oranges.

Earlier chapters in this book spoke of the "insights" generated by a particular work. We can usefully clarify here the precise nature of such insights. *Conclusions*—both main conclusions and supporting arguments—that are supported by a work's arguments and evidence are the work's *insights*.

No. 3: What Assumptions Does the Author Make (*and Are These Justified*)?

Scholarship is an ongoing conversation. No book or article can be entirely self-contained. Authors cannot, in other words, justify every supporting argument that they make. They must necessarily assume certain things to be true. Unfortunately, authors are not always clear about what assumptions they are making or why they are making them: You as the reader must thus often strive to identify hidden assumptions. Whether assumptions are stated or hidden, you can distinguish between three categories of assumptions:

- **Assumptions supported by authors cited in the work.** This book cites many authors: That is, we provide direct quotes or paraphrases of important statements by other authors in the text followed by the author's name, publication date, and page number. You may have wondered why we have done this. Our purpose in citing other authors is to show that our assumption on a given point is supported by one or more other scholars. A scholarly work is necessarily built upon the work of other scholars. In more advanced course work, it is instructive to check an author's citations to probe the subject more deeply. Thinking critically about any work involves asking whether the assumption(s) on which it is based are supported by other scholars. (You could also, then, critically evaluate the justifications provided in other works in support of arguments now being employed as assumptions.)

- **Assumptions that characterize a particular disciplinary perspective.** We have established that disciplinary authors typically write from the perspective of their discipline. They also typically share their discipline's assumptions, which are often not made explicit. In a disciplinary course, students are generally not required to concern themselves with the assumptions of the discipline, though arguably they should be. But in an interdisciplinary course, assumptions become important and they can be challenging to uncover when they are implicit. This is why Chapter 5 is so important. In critically evaluating a disciplinary work, you want to ask to what extent the conclusions are guided by the assumptions associated with disciplinary perspective. The interdisciplinary reader may often appreciate that an author makes an assumption common in his or her discipline but that rules out the appreciation of insights from other disciplines.

- **Assumptions of convenience.** In the real world, almost every phenomenon is influenced by many others. Authors focused on one set of interactions will tend to assume that other interactions are unimportant. (Again, this is often done implicitly and perhaps unconsciously.) You can usefully ask if such an assumption is reasonable in the context of the complex problem being investigated. If an argument is made as to why crime rates have risen or fallen, you can reasonably reflect on what other causes, assumed unimportant by the author, might have been at work.

Authors, it should be noted, do not always carefully distinguish assumptions from conclusions or supporting arguments. But there is a clear distinction between these: Conclusions or supporting arguments are justified by other arguments or evidence in the text, whereas assumptions are not. You as a critical reader should be especially aware of assumptions masquerading as conclusions.

No. 4: What Evidence Does the Author Marshal?

Scholarship involves presenting evidence or data to support the author's arguments. Regarding evidence, you need to focus on two things: the author's research method and the reliability of the data that the method produces. While it may seem presumptuous to suggest that entry-level students can or should question either the method or the data, you can if you use the right approach.

Data and methods are deemed *reliable* if it is likely that similar results would be found if the study were replicated or performed again under similar conditions. Data and methods are considered *valid* if the evidence generated is actually connected to the work's conclusions: A study of sunspots may have no validity for an exploration of criminal behavior, even if the results are reliable. As you will see in the examples below, even entry-level students can critique the evidence by wondering about reliability and validity. Your ability to do so will improve as you learn more about particular disciplinary research methods. We can note for now both that no scholarly method is perfect and that these are often applied imperfectly. (The strengths and limitations of different methods are discussed in detail in Repko & Szostak, 2016, *Interdisciplinary Research: Process and Theory*, 3rd ed.)

Other Types of Statements You Will Encounter

You have already seen that thinking critically about an author's work requires that you distinguish between conclusions, supporting arguments, assumptions, and evidence. In addition to these, a work contains many other types of statements that you must identify:

- **Statements of motivation.** Most works will contain statements as to why the author and/or reader should care about the subject being addressed: "A billion humans lack reliable access to clean water. This book thus investigates strategies for increasing the supply of clean water." You should be careful not to confuse statements of why a work might be important from justified conclusions. A statement of motivation by any one author provides clues about the values of that person and may also provide insight into potential bias. For example, an author whose work is motivated by environmental concerns may draw different conclusions from the same evidence than does an author focused entirely on economic growth. Similarly, statements of motivation by several authors from the same discipline provide clues about the values of the discipline as a whole.

- **Statements of belief.** The same can be said for statements of belief. Authors will sometimes be explicit about what they believe to be true: "We believe that global warming is the greatest threat to humanity." You must be especially wary of interpreting such statements as insights justified by argument and evidence. You should of course be wary of authorial bias whether authors confess their point of view or not. Statements of belief by several authors in a discipline provide clues about the beliefs of that discipline.

- **Guiding questions.** "What was the impact of food shortages on the French Revolution?" You need to distinguish questions from answers and ask whether the conclusions reached in fact respond to the work's guiding questions.

- **Definitions of key concepts** *(such as "revolution" in the previous bullet)*. Again, care must be taken not to confuse a definition with a conclusion. This caveat holds true for all disciplines. Note that authors often do not define the terms they use. You then need to try to figure out the author's understanding of the term and be especially alert to how the term colors the meaning of the text.

- **Statements of evidence or information.** Here is an example: "Twelve of 20 people interviewed agreed that ads regarding the dangers of impaired driving had changed their behavior." This statement may involve evidence developed within the work itself or in other works cited. In either case, you should ask whether the author's evidence is likely an accurate reflection of the phenomenon being studied. In other words, how good is the evidence?

- **Implications.** The author may move beyond conclusions regarding how the world works to make proposals for public policy, business practice, or individual behavior: "We should change the penalties for impaired driving." In this case, the implications of the conclusions are more speculative than the conclusions themselves. The interdisciplinary student should be especially careful of the tendency of disciplinary scholars to assume that only their discipline has important insights into a particular public policy challenge. Inner-city poverty is legitimately the province of (at least) economists, sociologists, political scientists, and psychologists, but scholars from each discipline may make policy suggestions that ignore the insights of the other disciplines.

Summary of This Discussion

An interdisciplinary approach to critical thinking about disciplinary work is fairly straightforward. It identifies statements of conclusions, arguments of support, assumptions, and evidence. And it distinguishes between statements of motivation, belief, guiding questions, key concepts, and implications. But you should be wary of statements of unjustified assertions. Of any assertion, you should ask whether it is justified by the supporting arguments and evidence provided. An unjustified assertion should *not* be treated as an "insight" of the work.

You should be familiar with different types of statements for several reasons. First, it is essential that you not mistake as conclusions statements of belief, motivation, definition, or implications. Second, such statements can reveal authorial as well as disciplinary bias. Third, these statements provide valuable insight into why a particular audience might value the work: It might share the motivations or beliefs that guide the author or applaud the policy implications.

Critically Analyzing Disciplinary Insights

Disciplinarians have long questioned the ability of interdisciplinary scholars to fully understand the disciplinary literatures from which they draw. Certainly the interdisciplinarian cannot be expected to have the same depth of understanding as does the specialized disciplinary scholar. Perhaps the key insight of interdisciplinary scholarship is that this depth of expertise is not essential. The interdisciplinarian need not master an entire discipline in order to understand its perspective and critique its insights. "Mastering" means knowing the discipline well enough to practice it. This is not the goal of the interdisciplinarian in most cases. Rather, the interdisciplinarian wishes to draw upon the discipline for a limited purpose and thus needs only to understand the defining elements of those disciplines relevant to the problem as presented in Chapter 5. These elements are the keys to understanding a discipline's perspective and its insights into the problem you are studying.

A Distinctive Approach to Critically Analyzing Disciplinary Insights

We now address this key question: "Are there differences between disciplinary and interdisciplinary approaches to critical reading and thinking?" The simple answer is "There are." The interdisciplinarian brings a distinctive approach to critically analyzing disciplinary insights.

For one thing, the interdisciplinary reader can compare and contrast insights generated by different disciplines. You can then use the insights of one discipline to critique the insights of another. For instance, economists may not find it odd that another economist assumes that criminals rationally evaluate whether to commit a crime (and will thus take into account penalties and the objective probability of being caught), whereas if you have also read a work by a psychologist talking about how certain criminals act on impulse, you are guided to question the economist's assumption.

Second, the interdisciplinary reader can ask to what extent the discipline's insights reflect the discipline's perspective. The disciplinarian who is not self-conscious of disciplinary perspective cannot ask such a question. Even as an entry-level student, you can usefully apply the brief sketches of disciplinary perspective provided in Chapter 5 when reading a work from any one of the disciplines covered in that chapter. Note that in so doing interdisciplinary students are encouraged to view as problematic the same disciplinary expertise that most disciplinary students are taught to respect. That is, you come to see disciplinary specialization as a two-edged sword: It is at once the source of an author's strength but also a source of limitations.

Third, while the disciplinarian may have more detailed knowledge of a particular theory or method, the interdisciplinary reader can bring an understanding of the relative strengths and limitations of different theories and methods. This may allow you to identify problems missed by the disciplinarian (because each discipline tends to downplay the limitations of its favored theories and methods). It also facilitates your identifying alternative theories and methods that might generate different conclusions. This sort of approach will become easier as you progress in your education and learn more about different theories and methods.

Fourth, by mapping the complex problem or system to reveal its disciplinary parts, the interdisciplinary reader can place any disciplinary insight in broad context. (Mapping is discussed later.) All too often, disciplinary researchers will examine a particular relationship—how B influences C—in detail, then draw a conclusion about how A influences D by simply assuming that A affects B and C affects D in a particular way. Often these assumptions are not made explicit. But by mapping the problem, the interdisciplinary reader may be able to draw on other disciplines that actually study these other relationships. Through mapping, you may find that these relationships do not always operate as the first discipline has casually assumed.

Fifth, the interdisciplinary reader can ask whether the disciplinary analysis has ignored critical variables studied by other disciplines and analyze how the discipline's conclusions would change if these were included (see examples that follow).

Finally, the evaluation provided by the interdisciplinary reader is *complementary* to the evaluation that would be provided by a disciplinary reader. Interdisciplinary readers should thus always want to know how a work has been received by experts in that discipline's theories and methods. By reading scholarly reviews of the work (especially books) in disciplinary journals, you can explore whether a work has been cited and, if so, whether it has been cited positively. (Note: Reviews of scholarly books that appear on many Internet sites, including Amazon.com, are not peer reviewed and are often unreliable.) This does not mean that a discipline's judgment should be accepted without question, for it might reflect the biases inherent in disciplinary perspective. On the other hand, you should be careful of celebrating a work that is disdained in its discipline of origin.

How to Find What You Need in Disciplinary Insights

The challenge facing students new to interdisciplinary studies is how to find what they need to find in disciplinary insights and not settle for a superficial understanding of what they are reading. It is thus useful to have some standards by which you can evaluate the quality of the texts you are reading.

Clarity The most important standard is *clarity*. If an author's statements are not clear, then the task of critical analysis is difficult, if not impossible. You should not demand perfection here, for philosophers of language have long noted that some degree of ambiguity is inevitable in human communication. Indeed, there are occasions when the author's lack of clarity is deliberate for artistic reasons, as in a poem when the author is speaking metaphorically or using other linguistic devices to elicit various emotions or images. A rule of thumb is whenever you confront lack of clarity in a work, ask why it is so.

There are several possible reasons why an author's work lacks clarity. One is the author's poor communication skills. Another may be the author's deliberate attempt to mislead. Indeed, political speeches are often filled with ambiguities in the hope that audiences will hear what they want to hear. A promise to "give everyone what they deserve" without any detail on how this will be done may be heard by everyone as "more for me." Whether the ambiguity is deliberate or not, you should be skeptical of lines of argument that lack clarity. You should ask whether the argument can be made clearer and, if so, whether the more clear argument makes sense.

Perhaps the most common reason for lack of clarity is the author's use of technical jargon, which is familiar to experts in the field but not to outsiders. All fields define certain concepts in particular ways. Doing so makes it easier for people within the field to communicate with each other. Yet while some fields define core concepts fairly clearly (such as "mass" and "force" in physics), other key concepts are much more ambiguous ("globalization" and "culture" are defined in many different ways). You have two tasks here. First, you need to make sure that you understand what is meant by these concepts when they are used. You should ask if the author—or the author's field—is clear about what is meant. An article about globalization that is not clear about what is meant by the term should be carefully evaluated: Precisely what arguments is the author making? Second, you need to ask if in using these concepts the author is making assumptions that are questionable. If an author uses "globalization" in a way that implies there is an international conspiracy of some sort, you can ask what evidence is provided for this.

One common mistake is to assume that a familiar concept in everyday speech necessarily has the same meaning inside a discipline. You need also to be aware that the same technical term will typically have different meanings in different disciplines. Instead of looking up key terms in the dictionary, you should look them up in key reference works of that discipline.

Depth and Breadth Two other guidelines for critically analyzing a disciplinary work are its *depth* and *breadth*. These terms capture the essential tension between disciplinarity and interdisciplinarity. Disciplinarians emphasize the need to have a deep understanding of a particular subject matter, which we have called "disciplinary reductionism." Interdisciplinarians, by contrast, stress the importance of breadth of vision, broad context, and systemic thinking. Interdisciplinarians resolve this tension by seeing disciplinarity and interdisciplinarity as complementary enterprises. Interdisciplinarians propose a solution whereby the deep explorations and insights of disciplinary scholars are evaluated and integrated into a more comprehensive understanding. While interdisciplinary readers may naturally focus on breadth, they should not neglect depth: As noted earlier, if you know that a work is viewed skeptically in its home discipline, you should ask if this is merely because it runs against the discipline's prevailing perspective or instead because it involves inappropriate application of the discipline's theory or methods.

With regard to breadth, you need to ask yourself what has been left out in a disciplinary analysis of the subject: What phenomena (or theories or methods) studied by other disciplines should have been included in the analysis, and how might the results have changed if they had been included? When looking at an interdisciplinary analysis of a particular subject, a key question is whether the analysis has drawn from all relevant disciplines and evaluated disciplinary insights within the context of each disciplinary perspective. An interdisciplinary analysis of global warming that ignores the insights of natural sciences should be seen as incomplete. So should an interdisciplinary analysis of crime that cites only one sociologist whose insights seem at odds with the disciplinary perspective of sociology.

Logic The most obvious standard for critically analyzing a disciplinary work is perhaps its logical integrity. Do arguments flow logically from the evidence, and do subsidiary arguments build to the overall conclusion? It is very useful to list the steps in an argument, and ask whether each flows from the previous argument. It is very easy for an argument to seem stronger than it is by simply omitting certain steps. For example, one can move easily from a lengthy list of abuses of the welfare system to a compelling conclusion that it should be scrapped if one does not also seek some measurement of the benefits of the system and some attempt to compare costs and benefits. In this hypothetical case, the author has moved directly from a statement that "welfare is abused" to a conclusion that "the system should be scrapped." You can recognize that such a conclusion requires a judgment that "the costs of the system outweigh the benefits." Although the author has implicitly assumed this to be true, he or she has not established this. Note that the interdisciplinary reader should be particularly adept at spotting missing arguments, for these will often be arguments that are made in other disciplines.

Examples of Applying an Interdisciplinary Approach to Critically Analyzing Disciplinary Insights

We present three hypothetical examples of applying an interdisciplinary approach to critically analyzing disciplinary insights. These examples assume that the interdisciplinary reader has already distinguished conclusions and supporting arguments from other types of statements and thus answered the first two of the critical questions described earlier: "What are the conclusions?" and "What are the arguments supporting the conclusions?" As you read each example, notice the focus on the other two critical questions:

- What assumptions does the author make? (Note that these may be explicit—that is, stated by the author—or implicit.)

- What evidence does the author marshal? (Note: The primary issue regarding evidence for interdisciplinarians is *relevance* of evidence. Relevance will in turn depend on both the *reliability* and *validity* of the evidence [see the previous discussion]. Evidence that is relevant to the part of the problem of interest to that discipline is likely to be less compelling when applied to other parts [and thus to the complex problem as a whole]. Again, the interdisciplinarian can use insights from other disciplines to assess the relevance of evidence.)

In effect, these questions provide a handy checklist of questions you should ask of any disciplinary insight, starting with the following examples of hypothetical insights.

In the following examples we focus on how to critically read a disciplinary insight by itself. In a later section we show how critical thinking is further enhanced when insights from different disciplines or authors are compared and contrasted.

Example 1: An Analysis of Crime by an Economist An economist calculates the potential burglar's costs and benefits. The benefits are the money the burglar can receive by selling what he steals. The costs are the probability of being caught multiplied by the penalty imposed for burglary. The economist calculates the penalty that needs to be imposed in order for the costs to exceed the benefits and thus crime to be deterred.

There are several useful ways to approach critical reading of this work, all of which start from first summarizing the author's main arguments.

Readers, especially those not trained in economics, may be so dazzled by the mathematical equations or overwhelmed by the jargon employed that they do not follow the argument. Carefully reading the work's introduction and conclusion, however, should allow you to identify the author's main arguments.

With the main arguments identified, you might next look for assumptions. Ask, "What assumptions is the economist making about the problem?" There are at least two important assumptions: Potential burglars make rational calculations, and the only things they care about are the economic costs and benefits. Both assumptions bear further scrutiny.

What if the burglar acts on impulse? He sees an empty house or store and suddenly decides to break in. The calculation the economist imagines may not be performed at all. Certainly, the potential burglar will lack the time to make accurate calculations. He may be particularly prone to underestimating the chances of being caught.

You might ask many other questions. What if the crime was an initiation? What if it was revenge? What if the item stolen was not to be sold but kept as a symbol or pragmatically used by the burglar?

Do only economic considerations matter? There is a social stigma attached to crime in most but not all social groups. And most but not all members of society think of burglary as ethically wrong. These cultural and ethical considerations may be far more important than are narrow economic calculations, causing most but not all people to turn away from crime.

You might ask about missing variables. This question too might alert you to the cultural and ethical considerations noted earlier. A host of other omitted variables—personality characteristics, local policing practices, and so on—might be identified.

Note that you would have been aided in appreciating these assumptions by being familiar with the disciplinary perspective of economics (available in Chapter 5). Economists commonly assume rational decision making and stress economic variables. You would also have been aided by reading insights on crime in other disciplines.

You should also critique the evidence. Given that selling stolen goods is a crime, how trustworthy is the estimate of the financial benefits of crime? Given that many crimes go unreported, how trustworthy is the estimate of the chances of being caught? These questions address *validity*: They explore whether reported statistics reflect the real phenomena under investigation. Scientists will often pretend that their estimates are more accurate and precise than it is possible to be. It is a useful practice to ask, "How can they know that?" Depending on the actual data reported, you might also query *reliability*.

Analysis of this hypothetical work has pointed to several limitations. However, it has not shown the work to be *wrong* but rather *incomplete*. While it is likely true that criminal decisions are not entirely rational, it is also likely true that they are not completely irrational. And while noneconomic influences may abound, who can doubt that burglars care about economic variables? Interdisciplinarity, like critical thinking, tries to move us away from the simplistic idea that a work is either entirely right or entirely wrong. *It is a common finding in interdisciplinary research that while a disciplinary study tells us something useful, it leaves out much that is important.* In this example, you could accept the insight that some criminals will attempt some sort of calculation, and that economic variables will loom large in this, while remaining skeptical of the precise calculations performed.

Example 2: A Newspaper Article on Global Warming An article in your local newspaper reports that average summer temperatures were higher in your locality by two degrees than they were the previous summer. The author worries that global warming will destroy local agriculture within two decades.

Again, you can identify troublesome assumptions. Most obviously, the article assumes that this 1-year rise reflects global warming and can be extrapolated into the future. You do not need to be deeply familiar with the global warming literature to question this assumption. Temperatures fluctuate from year to year for a variety of reasons. Nobody imagines that global warming is occurring this fast.

You can look at missing variables. Temperature is not the only influence on agricultural output. Rainfall may be more important (and trends in rainfall are much harder to predict). It could be that rainfall will increase and your locality can grow more profitable crops. More narrowly, you can critique the 2-decade time frame: On what basis does the author focus on the future 2 decades hence?

And, of course, you can query the evidence. Local temperature readings are problematic. Urbanization causes temperatures in city centers to rise faster than in the surrounding countryside. You can thus wonder about both the *reliability* and the *validity* of the one data point provided.

It is notable that this newspaper article fails the test of logic. The conclusion regarding the future of agriculture simply does not flow from the evidence provided. Several intermediate arguments are simply missing.

The author of the newspaper article may be biased: Perhaps the author wants to see stricter environmental policies and wants therefore to encourage readers to think that disaster is imminent. Note in this regard that disciplines are not the only source of authorial bias and that an interdisciplinary approach to critical reading is valuable even when confronting nonacademic publications.

Though the newspaper article in this example is much weaker than the study addressed in the previous example, you should not totally discount the possibility that there are worrisome trends in local weather patterns, that these need to be understood, and that there may be serious implications.

Example 3: An Article by a Literary Theorist on a Nineteenth-Century Latin American Novelist A literary theorist describes at length how a particular Latin American novelist of the early nineteenth century had critiqued practices of free trade and free enterprise. This conclusion involved close reading of the novelist's works, for the novelist had never issued a political manifesto. Nor were the novels explicitly economic in focus but, rather, followed the intertwined lives of several families. But at various points in these novels, the characters experience severe difficulties that can be traced to free trade or free enterprise. The theorist suggests that this result is important for much more than literary understanding.

You can reflect here on what the theorist is suggesting. Is it suggested that the novelist had some keen insight into the workings of the economy and that the critique implied by the novels is thus valid? Or perhaps it is suggested that the novelist's critique reflected how particular social groups perceived the economy at that point in time. In either case, you can ask if arguments and evidence are supplied in support of these suggestions (that is, you can interrogate *validity*). Or does the literary theorist assume these things to be true? You may have cause to critique the logic and/or clarity of the argument.

You can also critique the *reliability* of the evidence provided. Are you confident that there are not also many examples in the novelist's writing where characters benefited from free trade and enterprise?

As with the other examples, *your critical analysis that explores limitations should guide you not to reject the work in its entirety but to see it as incomplete.*

Mapping Interdisciplinary Connections

Thinking critically about disciplinary insights is aided considerably by deconstructing a complex problem to reveal its disciplinary parts, each of which is studied by a different discipline. Since the interdisciplinary reader often grapples with relationships among several variables, it is generally useful to visually map these relationships. Knowing how to map a problem is an important skill for interdisciplinary students to develop when reading about a problem or when they are going to conduct research themselves.

Figure 8.1 provides a map of the question, "What causes economic growth?" It reflects the analysis performed by Szostak (2009), which showed that each arrow in the figure was likely of some importance. This figure forcefully establishes that no one discipline has all the answers to that question. And it guides researchers and students alike to be wary of any simplistic prescription for encouraging economic growth. Students will generally draw maps with only a handful of key variables (as in the examples that follow) and should thus not be overwhelmed by this figure.

Understanding how to map relationships among phenomena (that is, variables) serves several purposes. First, it helps to identify relevant phenomena. You can then usefully ask which relationships have been studied by which disciplines. Second, it clarifies which relationships among phenomena may be most

Figure 8.1 The Causes of Economic Growth

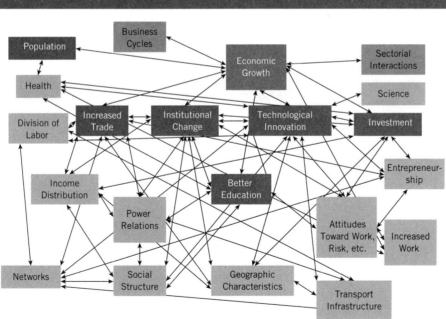

Source: Adapted from information in Szostak, R. (2009). *The Causes of Economic Growth: Interdisciplinary Perspectives.* Berlin: Springer.

important. Third, it allows you to identify which set of relationships a particular work addresses. Note that different disciplines will tend to address different sets of relationships and may reach different conclusions because of this. Fourth, it helps you to identify situations where disciplines, seeming to be disagreeing, are actually focusing on different relationships within a larger system. Fifth, mapping reveals when disciplines are disagreeing about the same relationship. You can then seek to identify why they do so. And sixth, mapping may identify positive or negative "feedback loops" that may encourage the system of relationships toward either stability or change. (Note that disciplinary researchers may not fully appreciate feedback loops that involve phenomena studied by other disciplines.)

Returning to Example 1: An Analysis of Crime

In the first hypothetical example presented earlier, an economic study of crime was critically analyzed. Now suppose that you have also read a book by a sociologist who studies peer pressure and recommends after-school programs for at-risk teens as the best policy for reducing crime. And then you read an article by a psychologist that identifies certain personality traits associated with criminal activity, and proposes a counseling strategy to reduce crime. (You can usefully reflect on how you would critically analyze these other works.)

You must avoid becoming frustrated at this point. Three experts study the causes of crime and reach three distinct conclusions. What are you to think? Suppose you map these arguments as shown in Figure 8.2.

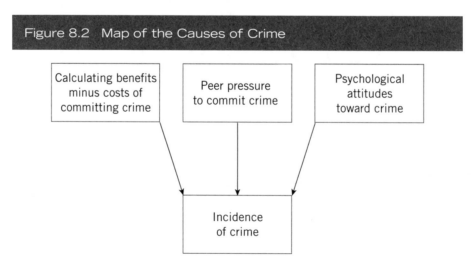

Figure 8.2 Map of the Causes of Crime

Source: Adapted from information in Szostak, R. (2009) *The Causes of Economic Growth: Interdisciplinary Perspectives.* Berlin: Springer.

You can begin by placing the three arguments on the same map. Even this simple task illustrates the possibility that the different arguments may be *complementary*. If so, then economic, social, and psychological strategies may all be able to reduce crime. There is a strong tendency for all disciplines to assume that the things they study are most important. If your critical evaluation of each text has concluded that each has useful insights, then you should not be too perturbed by the fact that each disciplinary expert has assumed that "only my stuff matters."

There is a more interesting—and more likely—outcome than that the causal factors identified by each discipline operate independently. We have already suggested that economic calculations could be shaped by cultural values. If so, you might imagine an arrow from the second box above to the first, as well as other arrows as shown in Figure 8.3. (You can reflect on how personality traits might also influence these first two boxes.)

You might also remove arrows from the original diagram. Perhaps peer pressure, while important, exerts its influence only indirectly by affecting economic calculations (perhaps only of people with certain personality characteristics).

Such a map shows how each specialized analysis could be tied into a more comprehensive understanding. There are, of course, still other influences on crime that could be included in a more comprehensive map. However, recognizing that interdisciplinary analysis is an ongoing process, you should not insist that your maps include every possible variable.

Figure 8.3 Mapping the Influences on Criminal Behavior

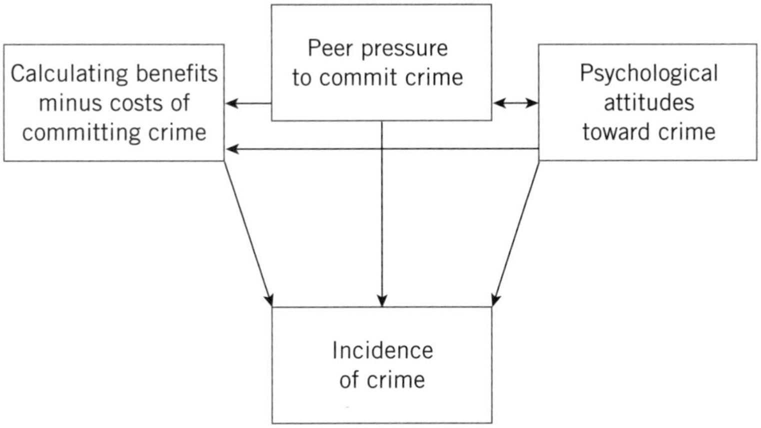

Source: Adapted from information in Szostak, R. (2009) *The Causes of Economic Growth: Interdisciplinary Perspectives.* Berlin: Springer.

So far, your mapping exercise has not uncovered any conflicts. Authors reached different conclusions only because they studied different relationships. But what if the economist had explicitly denied that economic calculations were influenced by culture, while the sociologist had argued that all decisions are determined culturally? Then you would have identified an explicit conflict regarding the strength of the arrow from the second box to the first. While solving such conflicts is beyond the scope of this chapter (see Chapter 9), you could conclude that neither the economist nor the sociologist was entirely correct.

What Mapping the Scholarly Enterprise Reveals

As noted in Chapter 1, one thing that students should gain during their college education (yet rarely do) is a sense of how the academy as a whole is organized. Thus, it is useful to digress from our focus on mapping particular questions or problems to mapping scholarship as a whole. In so doing, we make a point that should not be forgotten in any mapping effort: Every map we make of any question or problem necessarily abstracts away from the far more complex map of *all* the interactions that scholars do and should study. In other words, each of the phenomena on earlier our maps undoubtedly interacts with countless phenomena not mapped. And we must always be ready to ask how important those omitted phenomena are.

Many colleges and universities are huge, with tens of thousands of students strewn across many acres in multiple buildings. Such institutions are almost inevitably "organized" around a set of colleges (or faculties), departments, programs, and schools. This array can seem bewildering not only to students but to professors, administrators, and boards of governors as well.

Our discussion of disciplinary perspective in Chapters 5 and 6 allows us to potentially make some sense of the modern university. Every discipline— indeed every program—will address certain questions. These could each be mapped in terms of a set of relationships among phenomena, as described in the preceding section.

Now imagine for a moment that someone had developed a list of all of the phenomena studied by all scholars. This is a more feasible project than you might imagine, for there are only a couple dozen broad categories of the things that scholars study, though there are multiple subclasses within these broad divisions (especially in the natural sciences where there are countless species and chemical compounds). And indeed our library catalogues have necessarily striven for an exhaustive summary of the things we study, though unfortunately not in a manner that allows users to readily understand the organizing structure (in large part because these catalogues have been developed in an ad hoc fashion that confuses phenomena and the relationships among these). For now, we need not produce this list, only imagine it.

You could then map each discipline or program onto this grand list. Chemistry would be found to look at reactions among chemicals. Pharmacology would study how certain of these compounds affect the functioning of certain organs. Art history would look at the influences on and of art.

This grand map would be messy. There would be inevitable overlaps, as when chemists and pharmacologists study chemical compounds in different ways. And there might be gaps, where relationships or even phenomena are ignored by all disciplines. The mess evolves through time, as disciplines take on new questions and shed old, and as new fields arise to address relationships that were previously understudied. And then there are interdisciplinarians, who both play a major role in the evolution of new fields and draw connections that no discipline or field is capable of tackling.

Though messy and evolving, this exercise in placing every field of study on our grand list of the things we collectively study might just give us hope that the academy is studying most (though not all) of the relationships of interest, and that collectively we should be advancing our understanding of how the natural and social worlds work in their full complexity. This mapping exercise should also reinforce your sense of the importance of interdisciplinarity: Each discipline will occupy a small place on your "map," and it must seem that these islands of disciplinary insight need to be connected. The many overlaps that would appear on your map raise a further need for interdisciplinarity, for different disciplines studying the same thing often reach different conclusions because they fail to communicate.

You should appreciate that this imperfect sense of order has not been ordained from the top. University presidents have not sat at their desks and attempted a logical division of the scholarly enterprise. Disciplines, as you learned in Chapter 2, have evolved through time, taking on new questions of interest. New disciplines and fields have emerged to tackle questions that seemed underappreciated by others. This evolutionary process has been imperfect: It has left gaps and unnecessary overlaps that an omniscient planner would not have permitted. It has allowed scholars to follow their curiosity into new areas of study. Interdisciplinarity has arisen both to deal with the conflicts that emerge in overlaps and to draw connections that no discipline or field is studying.

You could expand your mapping enterprise by introducing other dimensions of disciplinary perspective. Each discipline not only studies a subset of the phenomena and relationships that scholars as a whole study but does so by employing a subset of possible theories, methods, assumptions, and epistemological approaches. By adding these other dimensions, you would introduce an expanded set of overlaps and omissions. While many disciplines may use the same theory or method, most will utilize only a minority of the theories and methods that might be thought relevant to the questions they study.

Mapping the scholarly enterprise, even in this cursory manner, highlights certain key facts about interdisciplinarity:

- That interdisciplinarians make connections between otherwise isolated disciplines

- That interdisciplinarians address conflicts where disciplines overlap

- That interdisciplinarians may identify relationships or even phenomena that deserve to be studied in greater detail than they are by disciplines

- That interdisciplinarity can bring a greater sense of order to a scholarly enterprise that evolves in a complex fashion

- That interdisciplinarians have a role to play in ensuring that useful theories and methods are not ignored simply through disciplinary bias

- That any interdisciplinary analysis of any particular problem or question should always ask whether there are relationships with other phenomena that need to be accounted for in the analysis (see Szostak, 2003)

CRITICAL THINKING QUESTIONS

1. What attitudes are necessary for interdisciplinary critical thinking? Explain why.

2. What four critical questions should interdisciplinarians ask of any disciplinary work?

3. What are the key differences between disciplinary and interdisciplinary approaches to thinking critically?

4. Why is it useful to map the problem or subject under study?

5. What purpose would be served by mapping the scholarly enterprise at your institution?

APPLICATIONS AND EXERCISES

1. What decisions have you made in the last 48 hours? (These could be major life decisions or more mundane decisions such as what to eat for lunch.) For each decision, examine what your purpose was, what assumptions you made, how you justified your decision, and what biases might have affected your interpretation of relevant evidence.

2. What are the major decisions you see yourself making in the near future? Again, examine the assumptions, information, and especially the purposes that are involved in these decisions. Does being explicit to yourself about goals, assumptions, and information guide you to better decisions? Have you been favoring some goals over others? Is there additional information you should seek? Are there assumptions that deserve to be questioned?

3. Draw a map of a complex problem of interest to you. (This is a particularly useful group exercise, for different group members will usually suggest different phenomena and relationships.)

4. Earlier in the text, we mapped Example 1 with added insights from other disciplines. Do the same for Example 2 or 3. Explain where you would look for alternative insights. (This is another very useful group exercise.)

5. List seven beliefs that you hold. For each of these, ask what sort of new information would be required for you to change your belief.

6. Critically analyze a text that you or your instructor chooses. Reflect on which critical thinking questions were most useful to you.

Source: ©iStockphoto.com/tang90246.

Chapter 9 Objectives

Becoming interdisciplinary involves developing an understanding of interdisciplinary integration and its results. One objective of this chapter is to introduce you to the most commonly used approaches to achieve integration and critically evaluate their strengths and limitations. A second objective is to describe the possibilities that integration opens up for understanding complex problems and formulating solutions to them.

Thinking Critically About Integration and Its Results

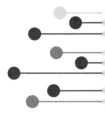

We have said that the idea of interdisciplinarity is embodied in varied and multifaceted "studies" and programs. Yet depending on the subject and disciplines involved, these often hold very different conceptions of interdisciplinarity, approach integration differently, and produce a wide range of results. Chapter 6 introduced the concept of interdisciplinary integration, examined the controversy between generalists and integrationists, and identified the theories supportive of the integrationist position that informs this book. This chapter builds on that discussion by introducing four commonly used approaches to integration. It concludes by examining the result of integration, which is a "more comprehensive understanding" of the subject under study.

Learning Outcomes

By the end of this chapter, you will be able to:

- Understand the meaning of interdisciplinary integration

- Understand four commonly used approaches to achieve integration

- Explain the strengths and limitations of each approach

- Recognize examples of creating common ground and performing integration using assumptions and concepts

- Understand the meaning of the term *more comprehensive understanding*

- Explain the core premises underlying the term *more comprehensive understanding*

Approaches to Interdisciplinary Integration

In contrast to many of the multiple definitions of interdisciplinarity noted in Chapter 3, only a few authors define "interdisciplinary integration." For example, Yassin, Rahman, and Yamat (2010) define it as "how the facts, concepts and generalizations in the various disciplines are held in common," implying that some undefined process is at work (p. 377). Repko and Szostak (2016) offer a more detailed definition that focuses on process: Interdisciplinary integration is "the cognitive *process* [emphasis added] of critically evaluating disciplinary insights and creating common ground among them to construct a more comprehensive understanding" (p. 221). In this definition, "process" refers to what goes on in interdisciplinary thinking. These definitions, though different, agree on two points: (1) The disciplines are foundational to interdisciplinary study, and (2) integration is an integral part of interdisciplinary studies.

Interdisciplinarians have developed four approaches to integration. The first three, *contextualization*, *conceptualization*, and *problem centering*, reflect, respectively, the nature and structure of knowledge primarily in (1) the humanities and fine and performing arts, (2) the sciences, and (3) the applied fields. *These are not well-developed approaches. Nor is much written on how these ad hoc approaches should be performed.* Our purpose in presenting brief overviews of these approaches is to acknowledge that some practitioners use them. However, there is a more concrete approach that we call the Broad Model that subsumes and supersedes these three more partial approaches. That is, the Broad Model integrates the best elements of these other approaches to interdisciplinary integration. This model is our primary focus.

Integrative Approach 1: Contextualization

Contextualization is an approach used by humanists and those in the fine and performing arts to embed the object of study in the fabric of time, culture, and personal experience. Under this approach, the process of integration is not standardized and varies from context to context. There are multiple ways to contextualize knowledge, and we touch upon three of these here: history, metaphysics, and epistemology (Nikitina, 2006, p. 257).

History as Integrative Context Using history as the integrative context involves connecting different disciplinary insights and pieces of knowledge to a moment or event in time. For example, answering the question "Why did the American Civil War break out in 1861?" involves integrating insights from science and technology (to explain the significance of the invention of the cotton gin), economics (to explain the slave-owning South's dependence on cotton production and the plantation system), religion (to explain the splits within the major Christian denominations over the issue of slavery that provided theological underpinnings for abolitionist and pro-slavery stances), literature (to explain the profound impact of Harriet Beecher Stowe's *Uncle Tom's Cabin* on the North), psychology (to explain the emotional impacts of increasing incidents of violence such as John Brown's raid on Harper's Ferry), and politics (to explain the rise of the Republican Party and the election of Abraham Lincoln).

Metaphysics as Integrative Context A second way humanist and fine and performing arts interdisciplinarians approach integration is to pose philosophical or broad metaphysical questions (e.g., Who am I? What is the purpose of my existence? What do I believe?) as vehicles for connecting and integrating multiple disciplinary insights. The question of the meaning of life can be addressed by viewing the paintings by Édouard Manet and Jean Courbet (art history), reading the philosophical theories of Karl Marx and Soren Kierkegaard (philosophy), examining representative texts from various faith traditions (religious studies), studying the text of Katherine Mansfield's story "Garden Party" (1988) or Samuel Beckett's play *Waiting for Godot* (1949) (literature), and then integrating one's reflections (that is, the disciplinary insights one draws from each) on these (Nikitina, 2006, p. 258).

Epistemology as Integrative Context A third approach is to use epistemology as the integrative context. An epistemological approach to understanding the human condition is distinctive (as compared to a historical or metaphysical approach) because of its specific focus on the act of knowing. Here "disciplinary perspectives are connected, not by historical events or ethical or philosophical questions, but through belonging to a particular mode of reasoning and meaning-making" (Nikitina, 2006, p. 259). For example, poetry and mathematics take different paths toward knowing what is true and define "knowing" in different ways. For poetry, knowing comes from subjective experience and our five senses. Poetry awakens our senses, connects us with ourselves and others, and leads us to think in synthesizing ways by using the language of analogy and metaphor (Hughes, 2007, p. 1). For mathematics, knowing is based on objective reality (truths exist independently of our ability or lack of ability to find them, and they do not change). However, mathematics, like poetry, also uses analogy to extend the boundaries of what is known and unknown and to create new forms of expression (Birken & Coon, 2001). Growney (2008) thus argues that mathematics and poetry require similar kinds of creativity and that mathematics provides "precise and vivid imagery" for poems. In turn, physicists exploring subatomic reality rely heavily on mathematical models but often also pursue analogy or poetry in order to visualize this reality (Lederman & Hill, 2011). It is thus both possible and useful to integrate these two different ways of knowing.

Using an epistemological approach to achieve integration of disciplinary insights often involves focusing on disciplinary assumptions. Every discipline is based on certain assumptions (discussed in Chapter 5) that limit understanding of the subject matter and force us to look at it in a certain way. By uncovering each discipline's assumptions about reality (and more narrowly about the specific subject under study), we see not only how disciplinary systems of knowing differ but also how they are complementary or connected as they seek to make meaning of the world around us. For example, historian of science Zajonic (1993) in *Catching the Light: The Entwined History of Light and Mind* captures the crossing of scientific and philosophical ways of knowing into the nature and meaning of light, claiming that the integration of physical and psychological perspectives is the only way to go. He writes,

> Light . . . has been treated scientifically by physics, symbolically by religious thinkers, and practically by artists and technicians. Each gives voice to part of our experience of light. When heard together, all speak of one thing whose nature and meaning has been the object of human attention for millennia. During the last three centuries, the artistic and religious dimensions of light have been kept severely apart from its scientific study. . . . The time has come to welcome them back, and to craft a fuller image of light than any one discipline can offer. (Zajonic, 1993, p. 8)

Example of a Contextual Integration Interdisciplinarians working primarily in the humanities and the fine and performing arts engage in interdisciplinary integration in ways that are quite different from those used by interdisciplinarians working in the sciences and the applied fields. For one thing, they often resist the drive for a single best integration of disciplinary insights. Instead, they prefer to lay out the range of possibilities for integration because they wish to respect the deliberate ambiguity inherent in the art object or text they critically examine. For another, these authors do not seek to integrate on behalf of others, as interdisciplinarians in the sciences and the applied fields do, by presenting their integration as a finished product. Instead, humanists and those in the fine and performing arts seek to draw others (audiences, viewers, readers) into the integrative process and encourage them to participate in a *shared* integrative experience. In other words, these scholars set up integration (usually implicitly) by offering prompts that suggest some starting points for viewers to engage in integration themselves (Newell, 2012, p. 301).

This approach is exemplified by Mieke Bal, who comes out of the humanities and the fine and performing arts (hereafter the humanities). In this excerpt, she explains how and why those in the humanities approach interdisciplinary integration differently than those in the sciences and the applied fields:

> The objects of study in much of the humanities are generally works of art and their historical, philosophical and theoretical contexts. [These works are] traditionally "high art" but also more widely circulating cultural objects, often referred to as "popular culture." This simple fact prescribes a research agenda a bit different from that in other fields. First, the artworks—literary, theatrical, cinematic, visual, musical—demand to be treated with due respect as complex artifacts made by people, for

people, to intervene in the cultural life of communities. Second, the examination of their cultural role also demands a critical perspective, which frequently leads to evaluative assessments. Most importantly and thirdly, their genre affiliations have dictated the formation of disciplines and their methods. With the advent of artifacts that can no longer be confined to such labels as "painting," "sculpture," or "film," the awareness has grown that . . . many artworks fit uneasily in the disciplinary categories designed for their study. Just think of opera. Finally, the fact that these objects are made by people for people gives them a historical position as well as a social function. The need to understand that position and that function is a fourth reason why research in the humanities tends to exceed the disciplinary frameworks designed to understand these objects. . . .

[M]odels of interdisciplinarity that work well for other domains may not be the most productive to address the specific research questions humanists develop. In particular, both the respect due to the objects and the need to analyze critically if and how they serve the people they address in the most adequate way are two requirements potentially in tension with each other. Tension, therefore, is indispensable, and sometimes overrules the wished-for integration. Here lies in my view the specific contribution of the humanities for our reflection of how to do interdisciplinary research. (Bal, 2012, pp. 91–92)

The object of Bal's study is an anonymous love poem (introduced in Chapter 7) written in yellow paint on a red brick wall of a bombed-out building in post–World War II Amsterdam:

Note

I hold you dear

I have not

Thought you up

Bal's goal is to present possible integrated meanings of the poem based on insights from literature, linguistics, art, and philosophy. From a literature perspective, the poem is a particular form of discourse intended to publicize someone's views. From linguistics, the poem seems to say, "Look!"—often implying, "That's how it is." From the perspective of art, the "Look!" aspect is reinforced by the visual contrast of the bright yellow handwriting on the red bricks of the wall. From epistemic philosophy, the "I have not thought you up" or "That's how it is" aspect involves the authority of the author, who knows from personal experience the heartbreak of loss and is willing, for some reason, to make this emotion public. Bal (1996) creates common ground between these disciplinary insights by focusing on their one commonality: They are all gestures intended to *expose* something about the writer, the beloved, and those viewing the poem (then and now) and pondering its meaning (p. 2). Having made these disciplinary connections and presented these prompts, Bal leaves it to the reader (or viewer) to engage in the actual process of integration, thereby making it personal, creative, and subjective.

Strengths and Limitations of Approaches to Contextual Integration Contextualization approaches to interdisciplinary integration allow humanists to enable readers and viewers to make highly creative and far-reaching connections among disciplinary insights. This includes the sciences *when* the goal is to place science in the cultural and historical fabric of time and bring out its social responsibility (see Box 9.1). A limitation of the contextualization approach is that it leaves out other critical elements of the contributing disciplines such as their specific assumptions, concepts, theories, and methods. Nor can contextualization substitute for other integrative strategies (Nikitina, 2006, p. 260).

Box 9.1   Scientific Wisdom

[Scientists in the twenty-first century] do not lack technical expertise; they lack wisdom. We live in a world where biology enables our ability to manipulate the human genome . . . [which] is far ahead of our legal or philosophical ability to regulate how to use this knowledge in fruitful ways. . . . How do we help scientists think in an ethical context? How do we help scientists decide whether or not certain questions should be pursued? (Nikitina, 2006, p. 260)

Integrative Approach 2: Conceptualization

Conceptual integration seeks "to make meaning from different concepts that, on the surface, have no apparent connection or commonality" (Morrison, 2003, p. 1). The approach is based on a general theory of cognition that describes how elements from different contexts are "blended" in a subconscious process known as "conceptual blending" thought to be common in everyday thought and language. As James L. Morrison (2003) explains,

> Two concepts are integrated into a third concept that contains some properties of both original concepts, but not all of the properties of the two original concepts. Commonalities of the two original concepts provide the basis for an emerging concept that is different from either of the two original concepts. The literature refers to the concepts as mental spaces, and the conceptual integration as the blending of the spaces. (p. 1)

Nikitina (2006) reports that conceptualizing is an integrative strategy used widely in the sciences and is designed to take scientific and mathematical thinking beyond the facts to the level of the underlying concepts. Such core concepts as *linearity, change,* and *scale*, she says, can effectively tie together algebra and geometry, physics, and biology, illuminating a hidden pattern of relationships. Conceptualization, she adds, provides a strong model for integrative work because it proceeds from factual and technical information to the level of conceptual abstraction from which generalization becomes possible (Nikitina, 2006, p. 261.)

Strengths and Limitations of the Conceptual Approach to Integration A major strength of this integrative approach is its rigorous correlation of related (i.e., not too epistemologically distant) knowledge and rich exchange in discipline-specific content (i.e., facts, theories, methods; Nikitina, 2006, p. 262). However, the conceptualization approach is limited in three respects. First, it limits the breadth of disciplinary connections to disciplines and their insights that are epistemologically close. Second, it obscures the process by which integration occurs. And third, though it properly emphasizes achieving integration at the start of the project, it neglects to identify points along the way where taking additional integrative actions or reflecting on earlier steps is likewise essential.

Integrative Approach 3: Problem Centering

The **problem-centering** or instrumental approach to integration uses issues of public debate, product development, or policy intervention as focal points for making connections between disciplines and integrating their insights. For example, the Center for Bioethics at the University of Pennsylvania brings together all the disciplinary tools it can to bear on such complex and vital issues as human cloning, stem cell research, and organ transplantation. Unlike contextualization and conceptualization, which focus on promoting self-understanding or building coherence among concepts, problem centering is aimed at generating tangible outcomes and change. This approach is attractive to the applied sciences, business, technology, and the fields of applied social science that aim to create new products, improve on existing conditions, or develop policies for social change. Other users of this approach include such interdisciplinary fields as bioethics, public health, and environmental studies (Nikitina, 2006, p. 263).

The epistemological goal of this model is not so much to make knowledge personally meaningful (as in contextualization), or to advance fundamental knowledge (as in conceptualization), but to attack a pressing problem by drawing on *all* available disciplinary tools in order to resolve it.

Ruth Beilin (2012) presents a case study illustrating how integration by problem centering works. The problem facing the researchers was how to help farmers in the highly eroded and steep hill country of Victoria, Australia, change their farming practices in the face of deteriorating climate conditions. Beilin describes what she and her fellow researchers faced:

> The contested values between conservation and production associated with the landscape meant there were sensitivities regarding how much land could be "taken out of production" for "tree planting"; and because of the strong need to remain financially viable, local farmers were suspicious of someone asking the question in that way. (p. 98)

The challenge was to integrate the apparently conflicting needs for production *and* conservation. The researchers succeeded in helping the farmers, suspicious of outside "experts" from the city, view the problem of declining productivity from a system perspective. By placing their farms in the broad context of the region as a whole, they were able to conceive of the landscape as the place where social and ecological systems are intertwined. This integrated understanding was aided by a model of how water moved through the farming landscape with eight suggestions for improving recharge (i.e., capturing and retaining rainfall) and minimizing erosion. As a result, the farmers' concept of land stewardship changed as they engaged with the practical outcomes of changing their approach to managing their farms (Beilin, 2012, p. 109).

Strengths and Limitations of the Problem-Centering Approach In its focus on the human predicament, the problem-centering approach may seem similar to the humanities-based contextualization approach. However, the two approaches engage human concerns in different ways. In contextualization work, the goal is to attain a deeper understanding of the human condition, whereas in problem-centering work, "the fundamental metaphysical questions of 'who we are' and 'why are we here' are distinctly secondary to the primary goal of finding causes and cures for human calamities" (Nikitina, 2006, pp. 265–266).

A major strength of the problem-centering approach is its emphasis on the development of a solid understanding of the relevant disciplines with an activist view of how to put the disciplines at the service of the problem. The approach does not hesitate to draw on disciplines that are epistemologically distant as long as these are relevant to the problem. Practitioners are willing to borrow theories and methods that seem like they may be useful.

However, the problem-centering approach suffers from four limitations. First, the disciplinary "tools" that it uses are primarily methodological (i.e., quantitative or qualitative) and tend to exclude other tools that may be equally relevant to the problem, such as each contributing discipline's perspectives, assumptions, concepts, and favored theories. Second, there is no systematic process for choosing the best theories, methods, or disciplines, or for placing disciplinary insights in context. The approach may thus borrow without much question from works that are viewed with suspicion in their home discipline. Third, the problem is seldom mapped to reveal its complexity and causal links. This omission tends to obscure difference or conflict between disciplinary perspectives on the problem (see the following discussion). Fourth, the process of how integration actually occurs tends to be obscured by the primary focus of the approach, which is on blending viewpoints (in an additive way), articulating the author's personal stand on the issue, and formulating a policy or recommending legal action (Nikitina, 2006, p. 264).

The Broad Model Approach to Integration

The Broad Model that we introduce here reflects the instrumentalist focus on problem solving (Chapter 3) and subsumes the approaches of contextualization, conceptualization, and problem centering addressed earlier. The model defines "problem" broadly to include almost any line of inquiry that requires an interdisciplinary approach. The model is "broad" because it

(a) draws on *all* disciplines for insights whether they are epistemologically distant or close;

(b) uses *all* "disciplinary tools" including assumptions, concepts, theories, and methods to study a problem;

(c) maps complex problems to reveal their complexity and causal links;

(d) critically evaluates disciplinary insights as well as stakeholder views (provided that these reflect disciplinary thinking);

(e) makes the process of integration explicit and transparent by breaking it down into discrete STEPS that require reflecting on earlier STEPS; and

(f) creates common ground among disciplinary insights on the basis of one or more key assumptions, concepts, or theoretical explanations, thereby melding conflicting insights until the contribution of each becomes inseparable. Importantly, what the model integrates are *not disciplines or their perspectives* but the insights they generate. Table 9.1 compares the Broad Model to the other approaches.

Examples of How the Broad Model Integrates

In the following sections, we present two examples of how the Broad Model integrates, each preceded by a brief discussion of whether this is achieved by focusing on assumptions or concepts.

Working With Assumptions A possible source of conflict between insights is the assumptions that underlie each discipline, and thus the insights that they produce. An assumption is something taken for granted, a supposition. These assumptions are accepted as the truths upon which the discipline is based. Stated another way, a discipline's defining elements—its theories, concepts, and methods—are simply the practical manifestations of its assumptions. Grasping the underlying assumptions of a discipline as a whole provides important clues to the assumptions underlying the writings of its experts on a particular problem and often proves useful in creating common ground (Repko, 2008, p. 89).

Consider Allen Repko's (2012) study of the causes of suicide terrorism where each author advances a particular theory, based on research, to explain the cause of this horrific behavior. He begins by probing the assumptions of each prominent theory and notes that some assumptions are shared by more than one theory.

Table 9.1 Comparison of Approaches to Integration

Approach	Category	Goal	Method	Integration
Contextualization	Humanities and the fine and performing arts	Deeper understanding of the human condition	Contextualization and other methods (see Tables 5.9 and 5.10)	Prompts provided but integration is left to the reader or viewer. In the performing arts, the product (the performance or art installation) is itself an example of integration.
Conceptualization	Sciences	Extend scientific knowledge	Scientific methods (see Tables 5.9 and 5.10)	Integration is typically limited to developing a common language
Problem Centering	Social sciences and applied fields	Solution to practical problems	Methods limited to quantitative and qualitative approaches	Additive: "blending" of views
Broad Model*	All categories	All goals	Uses *all* defining elements of disciplines, including assumptions, concepts, and theories	Makes process of integration explicit and transparent by using STEPS

*The cognitive process involved in performing integration is both compelling and elusive. It is compelling because the idea of integration is heavily supported by theory; it is elusive because, other than the Broad Model, none of the specialized approaches delineates explicit actions, operations, or steps that make it possible (but not inevitable in every case) to achieve integration in a wide range of contexts.

For example, the psychology theories of terrorist psycho-logic (Post), self-sanction (Bandura), and martyrdom (Merari) share the assumption typical of psychology: understanding the behavior and motivation of suicide terrorists requires studying the mental life and psychological constructs of individual terrorists. The [political science] theories of strategic rational choice (Crenshaw), sacred terror (Rapoport), and identity (Monroe and Kreidie) share the assumption that suicide terrorists follow logical processes that can be discovered and explained. These theories also assume

that the primary focus of study should be the behavior
of terrorist groups rather than the behavior of individual
terrorists. But only sacred terror theory and identity theory
assume that a terrorist's religious affiliation is an effective way
to explain the "political" phenomenon of suicide terrorism.
Fictive kin theory (Atran) assumes that the determining
factor in shaping the development of a suicide terrorist is the
terrorist's loyalty to an intimate cohort of peers, all of whom
share an intense devotion to religious dogma. This theory
shares with identity theory the assumption that religion is an
important factor in understanding the development of a suicide
terrorist. Finally, modernization theory (Lewis) rests on the
assumption that suicide terrorism is the result of Islam's failure
to embrace Western institutions and values. (pp. 139–140)

At first glance, these different disciplinary theories and their conflicting
assumptions appear unbridgeable. However, the Broad Model emphasizes
the critical importance of discovering or creating common ground between
conflicting insights by focusing on the assumptions, concepts, and theories
underlying them. Once this commonality is identified, integration can proceed.
In the present case, Repko (2012) discovered that these theories shared a deeper
assumption that provides the basis for their integration:

A key assumption of self-sanction theory (Bandura) is that
understanding the behavior and motivation of suicide
terrorists requires studying *primarily* the mental life and the
psychological constructs of *individual* terrorists. By contrast, the
key assumption of identity theory (Monroe and Kreidie) is that
understanding the behavior and motivation of suicide terrorists
requires studying their cultural as well as their religious identity,
but not at the expense of taking into account personality
traits (inherent and acquired). However, a deeper probing
of the assumptions of both theories reveals a commonality
that both share, namely the *goals* of suicide terrorists. These
are not defined in terms of self-interest, as rational choice
advocates (e.g., Crenshaw and Rapoport) would have it, but
rather as "moral imperatives" or "sacred duties." This deeper
assumption is also shared by the theories of fictive kin (Atran),
strategic rational choice (Crenshaw), "sacred terror" (Rapoport),
martyrdom (Merari), terrorist psycho-logic (Post), and
modernization (Lewis). *The common ground assumption shared*

by all of the theory-based insights to varying degrees, then, is that the goals of suicide terrorists are "moral" and "sacred"—and thus, rational as defined by Islamic fundamentalism [emphasis added]. (p. 145)

Clearly, using assumptions to explain a complex behavior such as suicide terrorism does not erase all differences between the various conflicting insights and theories. Instead, it focuses on the fundamental commonality of almost all the theories, namely, the goals that these terrorists share.

Working With Concepts When working with concepts, interdisciplinarians pay close attention to how the *same concept* may have different meanings when used by different disciplines within the context of the *same* problem. For example, the concept "efficiency" has quite different meanings for economists (money out/money in), biologists (energy out/energy in), and political scientists (influence exerted/political capital expended) (Newell, 2001, p. 19).

Interdisciplinarians are also alert to how experts from different disciplines use *different concepts* in their discussion of the same problem. And they are able to distinguish between cases in which these different concepts refer to *quite different things* and cases where different concepts have *overlapping meanings*. Both are common occurrences. From these, it is often possible to identify one concept that can be modified by redefining it. This interdisciplinary move brings out its common meaning, making it applicable to different disciplinary texts and contexts.

When redefining a concept, interdisciplinarians avoid using terminology that tacitly favors one disciplinary approach at the expense of another. Using the technique of redefinition can reveal commonalities in concepts that may be obscured by discipline-specific language. Once this language is stripped away, the concept can be redefined, enabling it to become the basis for creating common ground between the conflicting insights. Sometimes this occurs in conjunction with other integrative techniques, as shown in the following example of student work.

Janet Delph (2005) demonstrates the usefulness of the Broad Model when working with concepts to achieve integration. She questions whether advances in criminal investigatory techniques are able to eliminate the possibility of the "perfect crime." She defines a "perfect crime" as one that goes unnoticed and/ or for which the criminal will never be caught. Of the several disciplines and subdisciplines that are relevant to crime investigation, Delph finds three most relevant: criminal justice, forensic science, and forensic psychology. She identifies the current theories embraced by these rapidly evolving subdisciplines and finds that the source of conflict between them is their preference for two different investigatory methods and reliance on two kinds of evidence. Forensic science analyzes *physical* evidence, whereas forensic psychology analyzes *behavioral* evidence. Each approach constructs a "profile" of the criminal, with forensic science using physical evidence and forensic psychology using a combination of intuition informed by years of experience and information collected from interviews and other sources.

Delph (2005) creates common ground between the conflicting approaches by redefining the concept of profiling to include both forensic science, with its emphasis on physical evidence, and forensic psychology, with its emphasis on "intuition" born of extensive experience and insights derived from crime scene analysis. This redefinition of criminal profiling enables her to bridge the physical (i.e., forensic science) and behavioral (i.e., forensic psychology and criminal investigation) sciences. Forensic scientists do not need to use profiling as long as they have adequate evidence to analyze. But in the absence of such evidence, profiling can move the investigation forward by using a combination of "intuition" born of extensive experience and insights derived from crime scene analysis (p. 29). In this way, the redefined concept of profiling serves as common ground between the specialized knowledge that criminal investigation, forensic science, and forensic psychology offer (Repko & Szostak, 2016, p. 281).

"Partial" and "Full" Integration

The four approaches to integration raise these questions: What does integration change, and does integration change only the contribution of each discipline or are the disciplines themselves somehow changed? The answer to these questions is that it depends on which approach is used. Contextualization, conceptualization, and problem-centering approaches focus on *which* of several contributing disciplinary elements—that is, assumptions, concepts, theories, and methods—to use in performing integration. The chosen element remains unchanged and acts like a magnet around which other elements gather or are "integrated." Under these approaches, the integration may be considered "partial" because the contributing elements are not changed. However, users of the Broad Model maintain that these contributing elements must change for common ground to be created and "full" integration achieved. The important point is not so much whether integration is "partial" or "full" (though the latter is preferable to the former) but that integration is actually taking place.

As important as integration is, it is not the end of the interdisciplinary enterprise. Integration is the process used to achieve the ultimate goal and purpose of interdisciplinary work, which is to produce an interdisciplinary result.

Strategies for Integration

Four useful strategies have been identified for integrating insights that appear to disagree. These are briefly described here; more detail and many examples of their application are provided in Repko and Szostak (2016).

Redefinition involves carefully analyzing the way that key concepts are used within different insights. It will often be found that scholars only appear to be disagreeing because they are employing words in different ways. We have illustrated earlier how redefinition can be employed in practice. Van der Lecq (2012) was able to achieve an integrated understanding of the evolution of human language capability by reconciling different usages of the word "evolution" by different authors. In some cases it may be necessary to identify different meanings of a term (Bergmann et al., 2012).

Organization involves mapping the different arguments made by different authors. We have already seen in Chapter 8 how the act of mapping can identify how the insights of different authors might be seen as complements rather than substitutes. Authors may be disagreeing simply because each stresses the importance of the phenomena they study and ignores the phenomena studied by others.

Extension involves extending the analysis of one discipline (or an interdisciplinary field) so that it includes insights from other fields. A theory, for example, can be extended to include variables suggested by other disciplines. Such an approach flows naturally from a suggestion in Chapter 8: We should ask of every disciplinary insight what is missing. Repko (2012) was able in his study of suicide terrorism to extend one theory to embrace concerns raised by alternative theories once he had identified a common assumption across theories.

Transformation involves placing seeming opposites along a continuum. We discussed in Chapter 8 a hypothetical analysis by an economist of rational calculations by a potential criminal. A sociologist might suggest instead various nonrational influences on behavior. As noted in Chapter 8, the potential criminal is likely neither perfectly rational nor completely nonrational. Rather, we can imagine a continuum from perfect rationality to perfect nonrationality. Then we can consider where along that continuum a particular person might fall in a particular situation. Rather than choosing between the economist's and sociologist's insights, we can weight these appropriately in developing a more comprehensive understanding of criminal behavior.

The Result of Integration

We come now to the possibilities that are opened up as a result of creating common ground and performing integration. These possibilities are summed up in the term "more comprehensive understanding" of the subject, problem, or question.

A More Comprehensive Understanding

We define **more comprehensive understanding** as a cognitive advancement that results from integrating insights that produces a new whole that would not be possible using single disciplinary means. Authors use a variety of other terms that have similar meanings, such as *holistic understanding, interdisciplinary understanding, integrative understanding,* and *interdisciplinary product;* what one calls the understanding that results from integration is a matter of preference.

Unpacking the definition of "more comprehensive understanding" deepens our understanding of it:

- "More comprehensive" means that the interdisciplinary result "combines more elements than does any disciplinary understanding or theory" (Repko & Szostak, 2016, p. 323).

- "Cognitive advancement" refers to a variety of possible outcomes such as explaining a process, solving a problem, creating a product, or raising a new research question in ways that would have been unlikely through single disciplinary means (Boix Mansilla, 2005, p. 16).

- "New" refers to the improbability of any one discipline or mode of thinking (e.g., Marxism, postmodernism) producing a similar result, and that "no one (other than the interdisciplinarian) takes responsibility for studying the complex problem, object, text, or system that falls between the disciplines or that transcends them" (Repko & Szostak, 2016, p. 324).

- "Whole" refers to the comprehensiveness of the research result: "It cannot be reduced to the disciplinary insights from which it emerged" (Repko & Szostak, 2016, p. 238).

Core Premises That Underlie the Concept

Boix Mansilla (2005) identifies four core premises that underlie the concept of more comprehensive understanding:

1. "It builds on a performance view of understanding—one that privileges the capacity to *use* knowledge over that of *having* or *accumulating* it [emphasis added]" (pp. 16–17). This is consistent with both the critical and instrumental approaches to interdisciplinarity discussed in Chapter 3. For example,

   > We understand the psychological construct "theory of mind" (that is, an individual's recognition of others' mental state, beliefs, and intentions) when we can use the concept to explain why a given child might be unusually empathetic, or how a political campaign manager makes strategic decisions. From this vantage point, understanding the concept of "theory of mind" is a high order cognitive endeavor that goes beyond simply having an accurate definition of the term. (p. 17)

2. It "is 'disciplined'—i.e., deeply informed by disciplinary expertise."

   > An interdisciplinary explanation of a phenomenon like autism, for instance, differs from a naïve or "commonsense" explanation in that it builds on insights that have survived the scrutiny of expert communities such as neurology or psychology using commonly agreed upon methods and validation standards. And while such disciplinary insights are clearly open to further revision, they embody the most reliable and up-to-date accounts of the natural and social world available. (p. 17)

3. "It involves the integration of disciplinary views." In interdisciplinary work, disciplinary insights are not merely compared to each other or added together but actively inform one another, thereby leveraging understanding. For instance,

   > In exploring the phenomenon of autism, the psychological concept of "theory of mind" (a missing construct among

autistic individuals) enables us to characterize expected patterns of behavior in a child. In turn, such patterns provide adequate categories with which to study the autistic brain and begin to explain behavior at a neurological level. It is in epistemic exchanges of this kind, in this instance between psychology and biology, that an interdisciplinary "whole" stands as more than the sum of its disciplinary parts. (p. 17)

4. It "is purposeful." Integrating disciplinary insights and modes of thinking are not ends in themselves but a means to achieve a cognitive advancement such as a new insight, a solution, an account, or an explanation.

    In interdisciplinary work, many integrations are possible and viable. Autism, for example, can be explored at the crossroads of psychology and sociology by examining the unique forms of social discrimination associated with autistic children. Or it could be investigated at the crossroads of neurology and medical ethics if one intended to experiment with novel medical procedures. (p. 17)

The interdisciplinary understanding is the product of, but distinct from, the various contributing disciplinary insights into the problem. The resultant "interdisciplinary 'whole,'" Boix Mansilla (2005) says, "stands as more than the sum of its disciplinary 'parts'" (p. 17). The metaphor, model, narrative, new question or avenue of research, new physical product, new policy, plan, program, or schema each expresses the integration between the parts and whole of the problem.

Reflecting on What Was Achieved

This chapter concludes Part II of the book, which explains how you can become a critical user of both disciplinary and interdisciplinary work. By now, you should be beginning to think like an interdisciplinarian and understand how to approach complex problems. Specifically, you have learned to recognize and think critically about disciplinary perspectives. You have also learned how to recognize and think critically about disciplinary insights and the importance of mapping them. Finally, you have learned to recognize and think critically about interdisciplinary integrations and understandings.

For some readers, the journey to becoming interdisciplinary ends here. For those of you who are expected to do interdisciplinary work of your own, your journey continues into Part III. These next chapters provide practical advice on how to engage in the interdisciplinary research process yourself and evaluate your work as you go.

Critical Thinking Scenario

You have been called on to evaluate whether a student project is interdisciplinary. Based on your understanding of this chapter, what questions or criteria would you use to evaluate the student's project? Justify each criterion.

CRITICAL THINKING QUESTIONS

1. Describe the key elements of the four approaches to integration and how the Broad Model subsumes the first three.

2. Why is the Broad Model broad?

3. Why do we value "more comprehensive understanding"?

APPLICATIONS AND EXERCISES

1. Discuss in what situations the four strategies for integration are best employed.

2. Politicians often give opposing arguments on key issues of public policy. Identify one such disagreement and discuss in a group how (and how well) strategies of integration might be employed.

3. Could the Broad Model also be employed in the pursuit of *critical* interdisciplinarity?

Interdisciplinary Research and Writing

The purpose of Part III is to provide an easy-to-follow road map for writing an interdisciplinary paper that demonstrates your ability to think like an interdisciplinarian and apply the concepts covered in earlier chapters. Chapters 10, 11, and 12 explain how to apply the STEPS approach of the Broad Model of the interdisciplinary process and evaluate your work as you go.

Source: ©iStockphoto.com/Lemiuex.

Chapter 10 Objectives

Part of what it means to be educated is to understand the power of research and how you can use it to achieve your academic and professional goals. This chapter compares disciplinary and interdisciplinary approaches to research. Second, it introduces the Broad Model of the interdisciplinary research process and unpacks the meaning of its beginning STEPS. Third, the chapter presents the Broad Model Rubric to evaluate critical aspects of interdisciplinary work discussed in earlier chapters.

CHAPTER 10

An Interdisciplinary Research "Road Map"

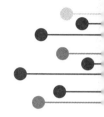

If you are studying to become a researcher or analyst, then you already understand how important research is to your future career (see Figure 10.1). But if you are planning to administer a program, deliver a service, lead an organization, or start your own business, you may not fully appreciate the importance of research. **Research** is the process of gathering information to understand how some aspect of the natural or human world functions.

Learning Outcomes

By the end of this chapter, you will be able to:

- Understand the importance of research and why it is part of what it means to be educated

- Compare disciplinary and interdisciplinary approaches to research

- Understand the Broad Model of interdisciplinary process

- Apply STEPS 1 and 2 of the Broad Model in writing

- Evaluate examples of professional and student interdisciplinary work using the Broad Model Rubric

Figure 10.1   Laboratory Work With Genetically Modified Potato

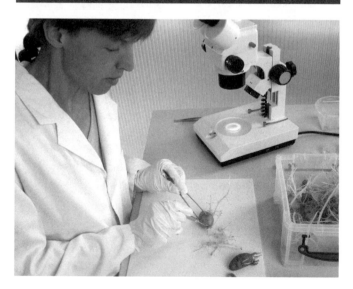

Source: ©iStockphoto.com/Andreas Reh.

The Power and Usefulness of Research

Regardless of your academic or professional goals, there are several reasons why you should understand the power and usefulness of research:

- It provides critical information for making important decisions.
- It enhances your understanding of a particular subject, problem, or question.
- It provides evidence about how things really are.
- It reveals options available to you.
- It provides advance warning if you are heading in the wrong direction.
- It provides evidence for convincing others.
- It provides guidance on how to make things better.

In short, the ability to conduct, evaluate, and apply research is empowering (see Box 10.1).

Box 10.1 Research and Employment

We live and work in an "information age" in which the ability to find, understand, and make use of complex sources of information—such as research—represents an important skill. An explosion of data of all kinds—from governments and other institutions as well as data generated by programs and organizations—means that those who know how to handle, analyze, and interpret data have great value to organizations and employers. Agencies and organizations regularly commission research, and so their top leaders or managers must know how to make sense of and apply research findings to improve policies and programs. Funding agencies and legislative bodies demand "evidence-based"—meaning research-based—programs and management reforms. To win grants or funding for your program or agency, you need the ability to demonstrate an understanding of research in your field of policy or practice.

So, without a grasp of research methods, you will be at a disadvantage in applying for jobs, advancing into leadership positions, and attracting financial and political support for your program or cause. With a good understanding of research methods, you can do more and go further in your career. (Remler & Van Ryzin, 2011, p. 5)

Disciplinary and Interdisciplinary Approaches to Research

We can divide research into two broad categories: disciplinary and interdisciplinary. They differ in their approach to creating new knowledge and in the outcomes they seek.

In general, the approach of **disciplinary research** is to choose from upward of a dozen or so specialized methods to study a particular phenomenon. As explained in Chapter 5, each discipline has its own preferred or methods of conducting research that are consistent with its epistemology and favored theories. Though the disciplinary approach has been spectacularly successful in expanding our knowledge, it suffers from several shortcomings that limit its ability to address a whole new class of problems that confront nature and human society. These limitations, some of which we discussed in earlier chapters, are listed here:

- No disciplinary method is able to incorporate other methods within it.

- Disciplinary methods are unable to address complexity *fully* in terms of explaining those parts of the problem that fall outside of the discipline's research domain.

- No disciplinary method is able to create common ground between insights that conflict.

- No disciplinary method is able to integrate insights from different disciplines.

- Quantitative as well as qualitative methods can be biased.

- The disciplines are characterized by "disciplinary ethnocentrism," which is the tendency of members of one discipline to look across the disciplinary divide at another discipline and see what the other discipline is "getting wrong." They rarely see what the other discipline is "getting right" (Lewis, 2003, p. 74).

The approach of **interdisciplinary research** is to study a topic or question that is inherently complex and whose parts are the focus of two or more disciplines, integrate their insights, and construct a more comprehensive understanding of the problem or question. Table 10.1 compares disciplinary and interdisciplinary approaches to research.

Table 10.1 Comparison of Disciplinary and Interdisciplinary Approaches to Research

Disciplinary Approach	Interdisciplinary Approach
1. The problem in its entirety must fall within the discipline's research domain to be considered researchable by the discipline.	1. The problem must be complex (i.e., have parts requiring insights from two or more disciplines).
2. Limited to a single disciplinary perspective	2. Inclusive of all relevant disciplinary perspectives
3. Uses the discipline's favored method	3. Uses an overarching process
4. Does not critically analyze insights from other disciplines	4. Critically analyzes insights from relevant disciplines
5. Does not integrate insights from other disciplines	5. Integrates insights from relevant disciplines
6. Product of research is an understanding or conclusion that is limited to the contributions of a single discipline	6. Product of process is an understanding that is more comprehensive than the contribution of any single discipline

The interdisciplinary approach also differs from the disciplinary approach in terms of learning outcomes and motivation. In terms of learning outcomes, engaging in interdisciplinary research enables students to demonstrate higher-order thinking skills of creativity and integration, strong-sense critical thinking, balanced thinking or judgment, tolerance of ambiguity and diversity, ability to demystify expertise and challenge power structures, and ability to address complex real-world problems. In terms of motivation, students see real-world relevance to their education, get to think about the "big picture" context of the problem, and with their more comprehensive understanding are enabled to move from talk to informed action.

The Broad Model of the Interdisciplinary Research Process

As discussed in Chapter 9, interdisciplinarians use several approaches to research, including contextualization, conceptualization, and problem centering, as well as the Broad Model. We said that the Broad Model has the advantage over these other approaches of being able to subsume them, as shown in Figure 10.2.

The Broad Model brings another advantage. It enables researchers in any interdisciplinary field or program to draw on disciplines from across the natural sciences, the social sciences, the humanities, the fine and performing arts, and the applied fields *regardless of their epistemological distance from each other* (see Figure 10.3).

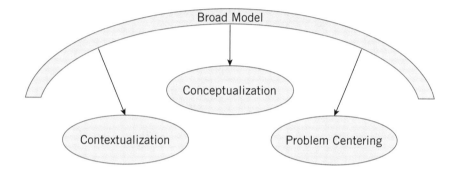

Figure 10.2   The Broad Model as It Relates to Other Integrative Approaches

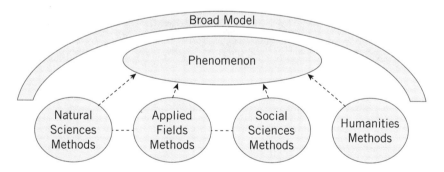

Figure 10.3   The Broad Model Draws on Disciplines From All Categories

Source: Repko, A. (2012). *Interdisciplinary Research: Process and Theory* (2nd ed.). Thousand Oaks, CA: SAGE Publications, Inc. p. 72.

Note: The dotted lines connecting the Applied Fields to the Natural Sciences and the Social Sciences show that the Applied Fields (such as education, criminal justice, communication, law, and business) use research methods drawn from the Natural Sciences and the Social Sciences.

A third advantage of the Broad Model is that it portrays interdisciplinary research as a cognitive process that proceeds developmentally from problem to understanding, as shown in Figure 10.4.

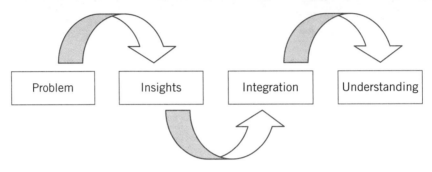

Figure 10.4   The Broad Model's Cognitive Movement From Problem to Understanding

| Problem | Insights | Integration | Understanding |

Source: Repko, A. (2012). *Interdisciplinary Research: Process and Theory* (2nd ed.). Thousand Oaks, CA: SAGE Publications, Inc. p. 73.

A further advantage of the Broad Model is that it provides an easy-to-follow road map of the interdisciplinary process consisting of step-like decision points (see Figure 10.5). Following the Broad Model is *not* a linear exercise similar to moving in a straight line from Point A to Point B without interruption

Figure 10.5   The Broad Model of Interdisciplinary Process (Entry-Level Version)

STEP 1: Define the problem or state the research question.

STEP 2: Justify using an interdisciplinary approach.

STEP 3: Identify relevant disciplines.

STEP 4: Conduct a literature search.

STEP 5: Critically analyze the disciplinary insights into the problem and locate their sources of conflict.

STEP 6: Reflect on how the interdisciplinary process has enlarged your understanding of the problem.

(though this may be possible in some cases). Rather, following the Broad Model commonly involves reflecting on each STEP or decision point before moving on to the next STEP and may require that you revisit earlier STEPS to revise or complete your work.

By breaking down the research process into discrete STEPS, the Broad Model enables you to confidently perform each part while keeping the "big picture" in mind.

In this and the following chapters, our focus is to help you perform each of these STEPS yourself. We begin with STEPS 1 and 2.

STEP 1: Define the Problem or State the Research Question

What Is a Good Research Question?

A good interdisciplinary problem or research question must have these two qualities, each of which is discussed in the following:

- It must be complex.
- It must be researchable in an interdisciplinary sense.

A problem or topic is ripe for interdisciplinary study if it is complex. This means that it has multiple parts and that each part is studied by a different discipline. For example, the topic of terrorism is certainly complex and assumes many forms (e.g., domestic terrorism, suicide terrorism). Skimming the literature on one form of terrorism reveals its many aspects—historical, cultural, political, and religious—each of which is typically studied by a different discipline.

A subject is **researchable in an interdisciplinary sense** if experts from two or more disciplines have written about it. Conducting a preliminary search of academic databases will quickly confirm whether the subject is researchable. There are many problems that, at first glance, appear to be admirably suited to interdisciplinary study but that, upon closer examination, are not. A topic may be "in the news" and the subject of heated public debate, but if scholars have not published research on it, then it is not appropriate for interdisciplinary study at the introductory level. Such was the case, for instance, when students wanted to investigate "the effects of physician shortages on rural communities." The topic is complex and is certainly one that is important to society. But for whatever reason, it had failed to attract scholarly interest outside the field of medicine.

In an introductory interdisciplinary course, therefore, the topic was not appropriate for study and had to be abandoned. On matters of public controversy, there is usually a "lag time" of several months or even years from when the issue surfaces to when scholars begin publishing their research on it.

How Do You Develop a Good Research Question?

A research question identifies the subject, problem, or behavior to be studied. It is generally stated in the form of a question, though sometimes declarative sentences are used to describe the problem to be investigated. One of the advantages for students of stating the research question as a question is that the question guides them to seek an answer rather than to simply describe the problem at hand. A well-thought-out interdisciplinary research question provides critical information to readers about your project and has these characteristics:

- It identifies the focus of the study in an easy to understand sentence or two.

- It defines the *scope* or boundaries of the study (i.e., "frames" the topic), and characterizes the study as an interdisciplinary one.

- It avoids three tendencies that run counter to interdisciplinary process (see below).

- It answers the "so what?" question.

The Research Question Identifies the Focus of the Study The research question should state the focus of the study clearly and concisely. The following statement, for example, demonstrates lack of focus: "The majority of complaints registered by the Childcare Licensing Agency (CLA) concern unsafe childcare facilities." It is unclear what the focus of the study is: the complaints (whether or not they are valid), the lack of enforcement of safety regulations by the CLA, the lack of funding of the CLA by the federal government, or the lack of legislation that establishes strict enforcement procedures. Assuming that the focus of the study is on unsafe childcare facilities, the sentence could be rewritten like this: "What are the causes of unsafe childcare facilities?"

The Research Question Defines the Scope of the Study
Scope refers to the parameters of what is included or excluded from the study. In other words, how much of this topic will be studied? What are the boundaries of the investigation? (Szostak, 2002, p. 105; Wolfe & Haynes, 2003, p. 140).

For example, the subject of terrorism is very broad and the literature on it is vast, making it essential to narrow the scope of inquiry to something more manageable, such as the cause of some specific form of terrorism. The scope can be narrowed still further by limiting the study to a particular historical period or to some region of the world or to a specific country.

Though both disciplinarians and interdisciplinarians are concerned with the scope of the problems they study, they differ in how they think about scope. Interdisciplinarians are interested in conducting studies that reach beyond the confines of a single discipline, so they think of "scope" broadly. Disciplinarians, on the other hand, are concerned that the study stays within the confines of their discipline, so they think of "scope" narrowly. For example, if the problem under study is repeat spousal battery, how will this be approached? Disciplinarians will likely approach it from the narrow perspective of their discipline such that they will see it as a sociological problem or a psychological problem but not both. By contrast, interdisciplinarians will approach the same problem from multiple disciplinary perspectives and seek to integrate the relevant and conflicting disciplinary insights. Interdisciplinarians are concerned about making the "scope" of any study they undertake manageable, perhaps (in this example) by *narrowing* its focus to either the *causes* or *effects* of the behavior. It is common to narrow the focus of a study in this way when confronted with an unmanageable number of insights.

The Research Question Avoids Three Tendencies In stating the research question, practitioners need to avoid three tendencies that run counter to interdisciplinary process: **disciplinary jargon**, **disciplinary bias**, and **personal bias**.

The research question should be free of *disciplinary jargon*. This refers to using technical terms and concepts that are not generally understood outside the discipline. If a technical term must be used, best practice calls for redefining the term or concept more broadly or generally so it is meaningful to each discipline. Here is an example of a statement that includes disciplinary jargon: "The recidivism of domestic battery is a significant problem in the United States because of its psychological effects on the victim." This statement contains two technical terms that require definition: *recidivism* and *domestic battery*. These terms are commonly used in social work, sociology, criminal justice, political science, and law but will likely be unfamiliar to those outside these fields.

The research question should be free of *disciplinary bias*. This refers to using language that connects the problem to a particular discipline. For example, the problem of freshwater scarcity in Arizona is connected to the discipline of political science in this statement of the problem: "Partisan politics in the state legislature has prevented the passage of needed water conservation legislation."

Returning to our hypothetical study of domestic battery, note that its focus is on the "psychological" effects on the victim of domestic battery. The reference to "psychological" suggests that the study is reliant on psychology, implying that information from other disciplines is unlikely to be included. If the student limits the study to the psychological effects of these behaviors, then a simple disciplinary (i.e., psychology) approach will do. But if the student intends the study to be interdisciplinary, then the reference to "psychological" should be dropped, or the statement should be broadened to include other effects on the victim beyond psychological ones.

There is a practical reason why the research question should be free of disciplinary bias. Connecting the problem to a particular discipline privileges that discipline over other relevant disciplines. This runs counter to the purpose of interdisciplinary work, which is to produce a more comprehensive understanding. The understanding cannot be comprehensive if one discipline and its perspective (including the discipline's favored research method) dominate the study. In these circumstances, the interdisciplinary enterprise cannot succeed. Recall that the role of the interdisciplinarian is similar to that of a marriage counselor whose job is not to take sides but to impartially weigh the evidence submitted by both parties to the conflict.

Finally, the research question or statement of the problem should be free of *personal bias* or personal point of view of the problem as discussed in Chapter 4. While arguing a personal point of view is common in many disciplinary contexts, it runs counter to best practice in interdisciplinary contexts. The reason for avoiding personal bias is straightforward: The purpose of interdisciplinary work is to produce a more comprehensive understanding of the problem. Arguing a point of view at the outset of the study suggests to the reader that relevant insights that conflict with this viewpoint may be excluded, thereby rendering the study of little interdisciplinary value.

Note the author's personal bias in this statement of the problem concerning the high failure rate among young NBA players: "Young NBA stars are not prepared to cope with the pressures of success." The author obviously believes this and would prefer to write a paper advancing this point of view. However, the role of the interdisciplinarian is not to play either prosecuting attorney or defense counsel for the accused. The role of the interdisciplinarian is to achieve a more comprehensive understanding of the problem. Injecting personal bias at the outset of the study is normal in many disciplinary contexts but is inappropriate in interdisciplinary work. The simple reason is that the interdisciplinarian should be approaching the problem with a frame of mind that is decidedly different from that of the disciplinarian. That frame of mind is one of neutrality (or at least suspended judgment) until all the evidence is gathered and analyzed. This means being open not only to different disciplinary perspectives but also to their insights, even if these insights happen to conflict with your personal views on the topic.

Challenge question: How might this question about young NBA stars be stated?

The Research Question Answers the "So What?" Question A fourth quality of a good interdisciplinary research question or problem statement is for it to answer the "so what?" question. This means explaining why we should care about the problem. To begin, write down multiple possible research questions or statements of the problem before selecting one or two to focus on. Here are some possible questions (not "so what?" questions) that can be asked about the course theme of global citizenship:

- What does the term *global citizenship* mean?
- What assumptions (or theories) underlie the concept of global citizenship?
- What values are associated with being a global citizen?
- How does becoming a global citizen affect my being a citizen of my country?
- What abilities must I develop to become a global citizen?

In applied social or policy research, the problem is often a practical one for which a solution is needed. So in your writing, be sure to complete this sentence: "I am seeking to answer this question *in order that* (or *so that*) . . ." (adapted from Remler & Van Ryzin, 2011, p. 499). You thus need to add a sentence or two of *motivation* to the sentence or two in which you articulate your research question.

By putting the suggestions for STEP 1 together, you have the following progression of thought, as shown in Figure 10.6, beginning with the course theme and ending with an answer to the "so what?" question.

Figure 10.6   Progressing From Course Theme to Research Question

Course theme or subject: global citizenship

Specific topic: the knowledge involved in becoming a global citizen

Focused research question: What knowledge is critical to becoming a global citizen?

Significance of question: to develop a more comprehensive understanding of the knowledge needed to become a global citizen

Source: Adapted from Booth, Columb, and Williams (2008).

The Broad Model Rubric Applied to STEP 1 Evaluating research questions involves using a **rubric**, which is an explicit set of criteria for evaluating a particular type of work or activity. We introduce a rubric in Figure 10.7 that we call the Broad Model Rubric (Appendix D). It is so named because it is based on the Broad Model of the interdisciplinary research process introduced earlier. The rubric was developed by Repko and used by the faculty of the interdisciplinary studies program at the University of Texas at Arlington for many years with great success. Its purpose is threefold: (1) to evaluate students' ability to follow a *process,* (2) to evaluate the *quality* of student work, and (3) to enable students to evaluate their own work before submitting their project for a grade. The rubric can be used to evaluate a variety of student projects including papers, posters, and performances. Experience has shown that the rubric greatly reduces student anxiety over how their project is going to be evaluated. Instructors can easily modify the rubric: In place of the "yes," "no," or "incomplete information" responses, instructors can substitute point values for each criterion. (Note to instructors: Experience has shown that points based on a continuum of compliance with each criterion creates more confusion than clarity in the minds of entry-level students.) The rubric is also useful to students working in small groups tasked with evaluating examples of practitioner or student work. Using a common rubric ensures that everyone is evaluating the same thing in the same way.

Note that the rubric's center column specifies criteria in bold face for each STEP called for in the Broad Model and that each criterion is broken down to more detailed criteria that are shown here as 1.1, 1.2, 1.3, and 1.4. This feature makes it easy for you to fully perform STEP 1 and for your instructor to evaluate your work. The possible responses to each criterion are "yes," "no," or "incomplete information." We suggest that you use this (or a similar rubric provided by your instructor) to guide you as you develop your project.

Figure 10.7   The Broad Model Rubric (STEP 1)

THE BROAD MODEL RUBRIC (STEP 1)		
ID PROCESS	CRITERIA	Y/N/I
STEP 1		
Define the problem or state the research question.	Introduces the problem or research question that is the subject of study and states the purpose or objective of the study	
	1.1. The author defines the problem or states the research question in a way that is appropriate to interdisciplinary study.	
	1.2. The author clearly defines the scope of the study.	
	1.3. The author avoids the three tendencies that run counter to interdisciplinary process: disciplinary bias, jargon, and personal bias.	
	1.4. The author answers the "so what?" question.	

We begin with two examples of professional work and one of student work. Example No. 1 concerns the subject of sex discrimination in the workplace (which is as relevant today as it was when Fischer, an economist, studied the problem years ago). Example No. 2 concerns how building the series of dams on the Columbia and Snake River systems in the American northwest has impacted the salmon populations and the communities and industries that depend on them. Example No. 3 is from an entry-level student project on globalization. These examples are excerpted from the introduction to each author's work.

Example No. 1

Title: "On the Need for Integrating Occupational Sex Discrimination Theory on the Basis of Causal Variables" (1988)

Author: Charles C. Fischer

The majority of complaints filed with the Equal Employment Opportunity Commission under Title VII of the Civil Rights Act involve sex discrimination. Complaints of sex discrimination

(Continued)

(Continued)

pertain mainly to pay discrimination, promotion (and transfer) discrimination, and occupation discrimination. Occupational sex discrimination (OSD) is particularly serious since other forms of sex discrimination are, to a large degree, symptomatic of a lack of female access to "male" occupations—those occupations that pay good wages, that are connected to long job ladders (that provide opportunities for vertical mobility via job promotion), and that offer positions of responsibility (p. 22).

Evaluation

1.1: Does the author define the problem or state the research question clearly and concisely?

The author clearly identifies the problem of sex discrimination but does not state the problem in the form of a research question. One or the other is all that criterion 1.1 requires.

1.2: Does the author clearly define the scope of the study?

The author narrows the scope of the study to "lack of female access to 'male' occupations."

1.3: Does the author avoid the three tendencies that run counter to interdisciplinary process (disciplinary jargon, disciplinary bias, and personal bias)?

Yes, though admittedly it is difficult to draw a definitive conclusion based on this small excerpt.

1.4: Does the author answer the "so what?" question?

Yes. The very fact that Fischer chose to study this issue implies that this widespread practice concerned him and that he wanted to develop a deeper understanding of its possible causes. The excerpt establishes that the problem is widespread.

Example No. 2
Title: *Northwest Passage: The Great Columbia River* (1995)
Author: William Dietrich

Historically, the Columbia River in the Pacific Northwest was the most prolific salmon-producing river in the world. In the nineteenth century, runs of all five salmon species occurring in the Pacific Northwest resulted in 10–35 million spawners each year! However, since the construction of dams on the Columbia River, there has been a loss of more than 80%

of the total run. Today, even with the existence of special hatcheries and fish ladders, only 2.5 million fish survive. Although dams in the Columbia/Snake River basin have interrupted many of the salmon's river runs, they have also brought economic success to the area. The dams provide hydroelectricity to millions of people as well as allow navigation from the Pacific Ocean. *Currently there is a [growing] debate about whether four federally owned dams should be removed from the Snake and Columbia Rivers* [emphasis added]. (Pacific Salmon vs. Hydropower Dams, 1999, p. 2)

Evaluation

1.1: Does the author define the problem or state the research question clearly and concisely?

The author clearly identifies the general topic that concerns the dams on the Columbia/Snake River basin.

1.2: Does the author clearly define the scope of the study?

The author narrows the scope of the study to the debate about whether four federally owned dams should be removed from the Snake and Columbia Rivers.

1.3: Does the author avoid the three tendencies that run counter to interdisciplinary process (disciplinary jargon, disciplinary bias, and personal bias)?

Yes.

1.4: Does the author answer the "so what?" question?

Yes. He does so by providing data on the scope of the problem and its far-reaching effects.

Example No. 3

Title: "The Chaos of Financial Order: An Interdisciplinary Perspective" (2012)

Author: James Harman

The importance of a relatively stable financial system is almost impossible to overstate. It is the founding paradigm on which all activity in a modern capitalist market economy is based. If the waves and shocks of the financial sector are not harmonized with the business cycle,

(Continued)

(Continued)

the distribution of vital products and services is endangered. Traditionally, it has fallen to governments to walk that most fine of lines, balancing the excesses of the market with the needs of society by way of finely tuned regulation. In this new age of globalized activity spanning across national borders every second of every day, the question of how globalization affects the nation states' ability to regulate financial markets is a complex one.

Evaluation

1.1: *Does the author define the problem or state the research question clearly and concisely?*

The student identifies the general topic of globalization, and of financial markets, and suggests an examination of the effects of one on the other.

1.2: *Does the author clearly define the scope of the study?*

The student narrows the scope of the course topic study to the more particular topic of the ability of nations to regulate financial markets.

1.3: *Does the author avoid the three tendencies that run counter to interdisciplinary process (disciplinary bias, disciplinary jargon, and personal bias)?*

The student's reference to "financial markets" *runs the risk* of privileging the discipline of economics.

1.4: *Does the author answer the "so what?" question?*

Yes. The importance of financial markets to the wider economy is stressed.

STEP 2: Justify Using an Interdisciplinary Approach

STEP 2 is to justify using an interdisciplinary approach. Though it is straightforward and closely related to STEP 1, it should be considered a separate STEP for undergraduate projects. This STEP requires the student to devote another sentence or two to explaining why a particular research project should take an interdisciplinary approach. As we have noted in previous chapters, there are many research questions for which a single disciplinary approach is adequate. The student needs to indicate why the particular project requires interdisciplinary analysis.

Commonly Used Justifications

Practitioners frequently include a statement in their introductory remarks justifying an interdisciplinary approach. There are just a handful of reasons that are usually provided; authors often point to more than one of these:

- The problem or research question is complex.
- Important insights into the problem are offered by two or more disciplines.
- No single discipline has been able to address the problem *comprehensively.*
- The problem is an unresolved issue or unmet societal need.

The Problem or Research Question Is Complex Complexity, as we have often noted, is a key criterion that justifies interdisciplinarity and is frequently cited by practitioners as a primary justification for using an interdisciplinary approach. There are two reasons for this:

- Complexity means that the topic or problem has parts that fall within the research domains of two or more disciplines.
- Complexity means that the topic or problem needs to be studied using *both* interdisciplinary process *and* disciplinary methods.

Recall that interdisciplinary process is an overarching approach for dealing with complexity *and is open to using multiple disciplinary methods for studying the problem.* This criterion is important because in some work that claims to be interdisciplinary, the author privileges one of the participating disciplines by using its preferred research method to study the problem while rejecting or subordinating other disciplinary methods. The result is a study that is more disciplinary (because of its reliance on a particular disciplinary method) than it is interdisciplinary. *In work that is truly interdisciplinary, interdisciplinary process is creatively applied to the problem and no one disciplinary method dominates.*

Important Insights Into the Problem Are Offered by Two or More Disciplines A second criterion that practitioners use to justify an interdisciplinary approach is that two or more disciplines have produced insights into the problem. These insights typically reflect the perspectives (i.e., assumptions, epistemologies, concepts, theories, and research methods) of the disciplines that produce them. This means that the insights typically conflict in multiple ways:

- In their understanding of the problem (e.g., is it primarily a sociological problem or an economic problem?)

- In the methods they use to study the problem (e.g., quantitative or qualitative)

- In the language or discourse they use (e.g., using, perhaps, the same concepts but with different meanings)

The point is this: *Only interdisciplinary process is able to work with conflicting insights in a way that is evenhanded and that does not privilege any one discipline or its perspective.*

No Single Discipline Has Been Able to Address the Problem Comprehensively The key word in this criterion is *comprehensively*. A comprehensive study takes into consideration all relevant insights regardless of the disciplines that have produced them. It should come as no surprise that a complex issue such as terrorism is the subject of intense study by many disciplines including religious studies, cultural anthropology, criminal justice, economics, history, law, political science, psychology, and sociology. Yet despite these efforts and with rare exception, each community of experts has failed (a) to consider the research of experts from other communities and (b) to produce an explanation that is inclusive of all insights. The unfortunate result is the creation of multiple "islands of specialized insights" in a sea of information on the subject of terrorism. *Only the interdisciplinarian using the interdisciplinary process is able to address the problem comprehensively. And only the interdisciplinarian "sees" the particular constraints imposed by individual disciplines on understanding the problem as a whole* (Boix Mansilla, Dillon, & Middlebrooks, n.d., p. 60).

The Problem Is an Unresolved Issue or Unmet Societal Need The fourth criterion is that the problem is an unresolved issue or unmet societal need. One possible reason for a problem to remain unresolved is that it may have been the object of biased treatment (e.g., disciplinary, personal, or ideological) that left all sides unsatisfied and even more entrenched in their respective positions. What the interdisciplinarian offers is an approach that is balanced, inclusive, and more comprehensive than what narrow disciplinary and ideological advocates are capable of offering. This criterion also speaks to the significance of the problem and answers the ubiquitous "so what?" question that readers and audiences demand of research.

Instrumental interdisciplinarity, as noted earlier, is concerned with what interdisciplinarians call **problem-focused research**. This type of research draws upon basic research (e.g., laboratory experiments or surveys) or pure theoretical research in order to address societal needs and practical problem solving. Examples include how to *evaluate* the feasibility of a new residential development on prime agricultural land, how to *manage* a valuable natural resource such as a forest in a sustainable yet economically beneficial way, and how to *design* a community space that is ecologically friendly, architecturally beautiful, and able to meet the needs of the community's residents. These types of problems often generate an abundance of disciplinary or specialized research. But what is often lacking is an overall approach that integrates the specialized insights and constructs a more comprehensive understanding of the problem. In the absence of such understanding, satisfying solutions to the problem may not be achievable.

(Note: While the initial justification of an interdisciplinary approach may only take a sentence or two, the student should ensure that evidence for these arguments is provided in the body of the paper. If students speak of complexity, they should discuss which parts of the problem are studied by different disciplines. If students have asserted that the problem is addressed in multiple disciplines, they must clearly identify insights from more than one discipline. If students argue that no discipline has comprehensively addressed the problem, they must show the limitations of each insight discussed. If students have claimed that the problem is unresolved, they must identify remaining challenges.)

The Broad Model Rubric Applied to STEP 2

We expand the Broad Model Rubric (see Figure 10.8) to include the criteria for STEP 2 to help you recognize and evaluate practitioner and student justifications for using an interdisciplinary approach.

Figure 10.8   The Broad Model Rubric (STEPS 1 and 2)

THE BROAD MODEL RUBRIC (STEPS 1 AND 2)		
ID PROCESS	**CRITERIA**	**Y/N/I**
STEP 1		
Define the problem or state the research question.	Introduces the problem or research question that is the subject of study and states the purpose or objective of the study	

(Continued)

Figure 10.8 (Continued)

THE BROAD MODEL RUBRIC (STEPS 1 AND 2)		
ID PROCESS	**CRITERIA**	**Y/N/I**
	1.1. The author defines the problem or states the research question in a way that is appropriate to interdisciplinary study.	
	1.2. The author clearly defines the scope of the study.	
	1.3. The author avoids the three tendencies that run counter to interdisciplinary process: disciplinary bias, jargon, and personal bias.	
	1.4. The author answers the "so what?" question.	
STEP 2		
Justify using an interdisciplinary approach.	Explains why the problem or research question requires using an interdisciplinary approach	
	2.1. The author states that the problem or research question is complex and explains what this means.	
	2.2. The author states or implies that there are important insights into the problem offered by two or more disciplines.	
	2.3. The author states or implies that no single discipline has been able to address the problem comprehensively.	
	2.4. The author states that the study addresses an important and as yet unresolved issue concerning nature or society.	

Evaluating Practitioner and Student Justifications

We introduce two examples of practitioner work that illustrate this STEP. Example No. 1 concerns the complex problem of grizzly bear management in the Greater Yellowstone Ecosystem. Example No. 2 concerns the very controversial issue of the conflicted role that the institution of Jewish marriage plays in Israel. We also introduce in Example No. 3 student work on globalization that focuses on how it is facilitating the spread of Western culture throughout the world. These examples are excerpted from the authors' introductions to their works.

Example No. 1

Title of Bulletin: *Interdisciplinary Problem Solving in Species and Ecosystem Conservation* (2001)

Author: Tim W. Clark

Grizzly bear (*Ursus arctos*) management in the Greater Yellowstone Ecosystem (GYE) is one particularly high-profile case. Threats to grizzly bears may be defined in terms of habitat and population fragmentation and the biological measures needed to maintain or restore populations (e.g., Knight et al., 1999). However, they may also be understood as an interdisciplinary management problem, realizing that the conservation of grizzly bears and their ecosystem are only partly a technical problem and largely an outcome of complex human social dynamics—a policy process. Understanding this policy process and making it more effective is the key to achieving effective grizzly bear and ecosystem conservation. This paper first offers a brief overview of the policy process. Second, it examines three basic interdisciplinary problem-solving elements or perspectives that can be applied to species and ecosystem conservation.

Evaluation of Step 2

2.1: *Does the author state that the problem or research question is complex and explain what this means?*

The author notes that "the conservation of grizzly bears and their ecosystem are only partly a technical problem and largely an outcome of *complex* [emphasis added] human social dynamics."

2.2: *Does the author state or imply that important insights into the problem are offered by two or more disciplines?*

The author suggests this by referring to needed "biological measures" and "a policy process," which suggests the need for insights from political science.

2.3: *Does the author state or imply that no single discipline has been able to address the problem comprehensively?*

Yes, by implication. The author views the problem of grizzly bear conservation as "an interdisciplinary management problem" part of which is "a technical problem and largely an outcome of complex human social dynamics—a policy process."

2.4: *Does the author state that the problem addresses an important and as yet unresolved issue concerning nature or society?*

The author sees the problem of grizzly bear populations as an important issue that is part of the larger "human social dynamic."

A study of the institution of Jewish marriage and its place in Israel's conflicted identity may generate insights that can be applied to broader issues of inequality such as the situation of Israeli Arabs, a sizable minority who face issues in some ways analogous to those of non-Orthodox Jews and other non-Jews in Israel. An interdisciplinary approach to the institution of Jewish marriage is necessary because no single discipline is able to provide a comprehensive understanding of its complex and emblematic role in Israeli democracy. The interdisciplinary research process offers the most effective way to consider each contributing discipline's perspective, find common ground between conflicting insights, integrate these insights, and apply the resulting understanding to broader issues in Israel as a Jewish and democratic state.

Evaluation of Step 2

2.1: *Does the author state that the problem or research question is complex and explain what this means?*

The author states that the institution of Jewish marriage plays a "complex and emblematic role in Israeli democracy."

2.2: *Does the author state or imply that important insights into the problem are offered by two or more disciplines?*

The author acknowledges this indirectly, stating that "the interdisciplinary research process offers the most effective way to consider *each contributing discipline's perspective* [emphasis added]," which clearly implies that the study will involve drawing on multiple disciplinary insights.

2.3: *Does the author state or imply that no single discipline has been able to address the problem comprehensively?*

The author states that an interdisciplinary approach is necessary "because no single discipline is able to provide a comprehensive understanding of its complex and emblematic role in Israeli democracy."

2.4: *Does the author state that the problem addresses an important and as yet unresolved issue concerning nature or society?*

Yes, the author believes that studying the issue of Jewish marriage will help us understand "broader issues in Israel as a Jewish and democratic state."

Example No. 3

Title of Paper: "Globalization: An Interdisciplinary Approach to Explain How Western Culture Spreads Around the World" (n.d.)

Author: Kathryn D. Funchess

Globalization is spreading Western culture throughout the world and overwhelming or replacing more traditional cultures. To understand how this is happening, it is necessary to use an interdisciplinary approach [because] no single discipline can explain this complex process.

Evaluation of Step 2

2.1: *Does the author state that the problem or research question is complex and explain what this means?*

The author states that the spread of Western culture throughout the world through globalization is a "complex process."

2.2: *Does the author state or imply that important insights into the problem are offered by two or more disciplines?*

No.

2.3: *Does the author state or imply that no single discipline has been able to address the problem comprehensively?*

The author states that "no single discipline can explain this complex process."

2.4: *Does the author state that the problem addresses an important and as yet unresolved issue concerning nature or society?*

The author believes that this is an important societal issue.

CRITICAL THINKING QUESTIONS[1]

1. For each of the three introductory paragraphs on the topics of grizzly bears, Jewish marriage, and culture we **provided in Examples 1 through 3**, rewrite them so that clearly positive answers are given to each of the four questions asked.

2. Do these three authors address the "So what?" question? If not, how might they do so?

3. Do these three authors display disciplinary jargon, disciplinary bias, or personal bias? How so?

APPLICATIONS AND EXERCISES

1. Describe the role research is likely to play in the profession or job that you plan to enter after graduation.

2. From your reading of this chapter, do the following excerpts from the essay by Alba and Nee (2005) appear to be disciplinary or interdisciplinary? Justify your answer.

Title: "Rethinking Assimilation Theory for a New Era of Immigration" (2005)

Authors: Richard Alba and Victor Nee

Assimilation theory [i.e., a theory of the process by which peoples of diverse racial origins and different cultural heritages are brought into the mainstream of American life] has been subject to extensive critique for decades. Yet no other framework has provided the social science community with as deep a corpus of cumulative findings concerning the incorporation of immigrants and their descendants. We argue that assimilation theory has not lost its utility for the study of contemporary immigration to the United States. . . . Though the record is clearly mixed, we find evidence consistent with the view that assimilation is taking place, albeit unevenly. . . .

---

1. Note to instructors: Answers to Critical Thinking Questions, Applications and Exercises, and Peer Evaluation Activities are in Appendix E.

Yet whatever the deficiencies of earlier formulations and applications of assimilation, we hold that this social science concept offers the best way to understand and describe the integration into the mainstream experienced across generations by many individuals and ethnic groups. . . . In this essay, we attempt to redefine assimilation in order to render it useful to the study of the new immigration. . . . Our reformulation of assimilation emphasizes its utility for understanding the social dynamics of ethnicity in American society, as opposed to its past normative or ideological applications. As a state-imposed normative program aimed at eradicating minority cultures, assimilation has been justifiably repudiated. But as a social process that occurs spontaneously and often unintended in the course of interaction between majority and minority groups, assimilation remains a key concept for the study of intergroup relations. In what follows, we review the sociological literature on assimilation, with an eye to assessing its strengths and weaknesses; assay the validity of arguments for rejecting assimilation in understanding the new immigration; and sift through recent studies for clues concerning assimilation's course among the new immigrant groups. (pp. 35–36)

Conclusion

Assimilation as a concept and as a theory has been subject to withering criticism in recent decades. Much of this criticism rejects assimilation out of hand as hopelessly burdened with ethnocentric, ideological biases and as out of touch with contemporary multicultural realities. It has been common in this critique to portray assimilation as reliant upon simplistic conceptions of a static homogeneous American culture and to target the normative or ideological expression of assimilation: Anglo-conformity. While we think this criticism is frequently unfair in that it fails to consider, and properly discount, the intellectual and social context in which the canonical statements of assimilation were written, we recognize that it often enough hits the mark. But there is danger in the view of many critics that they have provided a strong rationale for rejecting assimilation, rather than for amending it. We believe that the latter is the appropriate course, for assimilation still has great power for the understanding of the contemporary ethnic scene in the United States. It must, in our view, remain part of the theoretical tool kit of students of ethnicity and race, especially those who are concerned with the new immigration. . . . (p. 60)

Peer Evaluation Activity

Evaluate the following problem statement using the expanded Broad Model Rubric (Figure 10.8) and identify specific language that supports each criterion. Note that in some instances, there may be insufficient information to answer the question. Select one of the possible responses in the right-hand column next to each criterion.

- "Yes" means that you are able to identify wording in the introduction that clearly meets the criterion.

- "No" means that the author makes no attempt to meet the criterion.

- "Incomplete information" means that explicit language is missing.

Title: *Nurse Burnout: An Integrative Approach to a Multidimensional Problem* (n.d.)

Author: Kathleen A. McKay

Nurse burnout is a problem that continues to plague the medical community. While it has always been an issue in the nursing profession, it has become profoundly difficult for researchers to find any real solutions. . . . Burnout is an extremely complex issue, with varying levels of degree. Also, the type of burnout a nurse experiences may differ within a particular clinical environment, such as an emergency room, psych unit or oncology/hospice unit. . . . To address the problem effectively, it is necessary to understand what burnout is and the reasons why it is so prevalent in this profession. Using an interdisciplinary approach to study why nursing burnout happens is important for medical professionals and administrators in order to understand the problem and propose a more comprehensive solution to it.

The importance of researching and addressing the issue of nurse burnout is vital to the future of our country's health care system. According to the Journal of the American Medical Association (2002), "Forty percent of hospital nurses have burnout levels that exceed the norms for health care workers." This is an alarming statistic! Ignoring this issue can have devastating consequences, not only on the macro-level (the health care system itself), but on an individual level as well. Nurses who are experiencing burnout may suffer tremendously both psychologically and physiologically. But it is not just the nurses that are suffering; it's the patients who are under the care of these nurses who ultimately pay the price. Nobody wants their loved one to be cared for by a nurse who isn't performing at peak level.

Nursing shortages are on the rise and are only predicted to worsen. The American Association of the College of Nursing (2011) reports that "despite the current easing of the nursing shortage due to the recession, the U.S. nursing shortage is projected to grow to 260,000 registered nurses by 2025." Multiple polls and research affirm that nursing shortages in the workplace influence the delivery of health care in the United States and negatively impact patient outcomes while increasing medical mistakes. As importantly, nursing shortages lead to added stress in the workplace. While it's easy to blame nurse burnout on shortages, and it is a legitimate factor, it is not the only reason. . . .

Using an interdisciplinary approach to study this problem is appropriate because the problem is multifaceted. This approach allows for a comprehensive perspective and provides a broader framework, without strict boundaries.

Source: ©iStockphoto.com/mediaphotos.

Chapter 11 Objectives

Interdisciplinary studies is rooted in the disciplines and draws on their perspectives and insights. One objective of this chapter is to present strategies for identifying disciplines and their insights that are relevant to the problem you are studying. A second objective is to provide basic information on how to gather, organize, and manage information about the problem. A third objective is to demonstrate how to use the Broad Model Rubric to evaluate professional and student work in preparation for evaluating the quality of your own work as you perform STEPS 3 and 4 of the interdisciplinary research process.

Identifying Relevant Disciplines and Gathering Information About the Problem

In the previous chapter, you began applying the Broad Model to researching and writing an interdisciplinary paper. By recognizing and assessing statements describing the problem (STEP 1) and justifying an interdisciplinary approach (STEP 2), you are beginning to think like an interdisciplinarian. This chapter focuses on the next STEPS of the Broad Model, which are shown in Figure 11.1 in italics: Identify relevant disciplines (STEP 3), and conduct a literature search (STEP 4).

Learning Outcomes

By the end of this chapter, you will be able to:

- Take four actions to identify disciplines that are relevant to the problem

- Gather information about the problem and avoid three mistakes

- Apply the Broad Model Rubric to practitioner and student work in preparation for self-evaluating your own work

STEP 3: Identify Relevant Disciplines

After completing and reflecting on STEPS 1 and 2, the next task is to identify relevant disciplines. STEP 3 begins with identifying disciplines that are *potentially* relevant to the problem and ends with identifying a few disciplines that are the *most* relevant. A discipline is **potentially relevant** if the problem falls within its research domain but it is not known whether the discipline's experts have written about the problem. If they have not (and the literature search will reveal this), then the discipline is *not* relevant (although more advanced researchers might still consider such a discipline). If the discipline's experts have produced one or more insights into the problem, then the discipline is **relevant**. Performing STEP 3, then, involves taking four actions. As with the STEPS in the Broad Model themselves, these four actions are interrelated: You may find in practice that you blend actions and revisit earlier actions while performing later actions.

STEP 1: Define the problem or state the research question.

STEP 2: Justify using an interdisciplinary approach.

STEP 3: Identify relevant disciplines.

STEP 4: Conduct a literature search.

Action No. 1: Connect the Problem *as a Whole* to Phenomena Typically Studied by Disciplines and Interdisciplinary Fields

We begin by viewing the problem *as a whole* and connecting it to the phenomena typically studied by disciplines listed in the right-hand column of Table 5.4 (introduced in Chapter 5 and reproduced here). By making these connections, we end up with a list of disciplines that are *potentially* relevant to the problem. The interdisciplinary fields will follow.

Table 5.4   (Reproduced From Chapter 5) Disciplines and the Phenomena
            They Study

Category	Discipline	Phenomena
Natural Sciences	Biology	Biological taxonomies of species; the nature, interrelationships, and evolution of living organisms; health; nutrition; disease; fertility
	Chemistry	The periodic table of chemical elements that are the building blocks of matter—their composition, properties, and reactions
	Earth Science	Planet Earth's geologic history, processes, and structures, soil types, topography and land forms, climate patterns, resource availability, water availability, natural disasters
	Mathematics	The logic of numbers, statistics, mathematical modeling, computer simulations, theoretical counterpoint to sensitivity analysis
	Physics	Subatomic particles, the nature of matter and energy and their interactions

Category	Discipline	Phenomena
Social Sciences	Anthropology	The origins of humanity, the dynamics of cultures worldwide
	Economics/ Business	The economy: total output (price level, unemployment, individual goods and services), income distribution, economic ideology, economic institutions (ownership, production, exchange, trade, finance, labor relations, organizations), the impact of economic policies on individuals
	Political Science	The nature and practice of systems of government and of individuals and groups pursuing power within those systems
	Psychology	The nature of human behavior as well as the internal (psychosociological) and external (environmental) factors that affect this behavior
	Sociology	The social nature of societies and of human interactions within them
Humanities	Art and Art History	Nonreproducible art—painting, sculpture, architecture, prose, poetry—and reproducible art—theater, film, photography, music, dance
	History	The people, events, and movements of human civilizations past and present
	Literature (English)	Development and examination (i.e., both traditional literary analysis and theory as well as more contemporary culture-based contextualism and critique) of creative works of the written word
	Music and Music Education	Development, performance, and examination (i.e., both traditional musicological analysis and theory as well as more contemporary culture-based contextualism and critique) of creative works of sound
	Philosophy	The search for wisdom through contemplation and reason using abstract thought
	Religious Studies	The phenomena of humans as religious beings and the manifestations of religious belief such as symbols, institutions, doctrines, and practices
Fine and Performing Arts	Art	Creation and transmission of original nonreproducible and reproducible art; artifacts reflect on culture, beliefs, values, and ideas

(Continued)

Table 5.4 (Continued)

Category	Discipline	Phenomena
	Dance	Performance of movement that physicalizes the imagination, drawing on ritual, emotions, and stories (inclusive of theories on choreographic composition)
	Music	Development and production of sound delivered via a particular rate, pattern, and flow (utilizing elements of tone, harmony, rhythm, and melody, artifacts can be either representational or nonrepresentational and can be both formal and informal)
	Theater	Development and examination of creative storytelling via live performance (includes production of both scripted and unscripted events performed for a live audience)
Applied Fields	Criminal Justice	The phenomena of social deviance in all of its manifestations, its causes, costs, and the social, political, and legal systems that deal with it
Professions	Education	How we learn, and internal and external factors that influence learning

Source: Adapted from Repko, *Interdisciplinary Research: Process and Theory* (2nd ed.) 2012. SAGE Publications, pp. 106–107, and Szostak, R. (2004). *Classifying science: Phenomena, data, theory, method, practice.* Dordrecht: Springer. pp. 26–29, 45–50.

In the following examples, students were asked to connect each problem or research question to at least two disciplines that are *potentially relevant* because it falls within their research domain.

Problem/Research Question No. 1: What is the cause of teen apathy toward learning? Students saw this question as falling within the research domains of education and psychology. They reasoned that learning is a component of *education* and feelings of apathy are a state of mind studied by *psychology*.

Problem/Research Question No. 2: Should natural gas replace coal as a fuel source for electricity production? Students saw this subject as an environmental and public policy issue and connected it to the disciplines of *Earth science* and *biology* because they focus on the environment and *political science* because it focuses on the process of passing environmental legislation and enforcing regulations.

Problem/Research Question No. 3: What is the meaning of the growing popularity of action super heroes in media? Students saw the growing popularity of action super heroes in film and video games as a cultural phenomenon that was connected in some way to the public's anxiety about the future and the need for heroic intervention. Using Table 5.4, they connected the question to *philosophy*, *anthropology* (particularly the subdiscipline of *cultural anthropology*), and *history*.

Notice that in these examples, the research questions are connected to one or more *interdisciplinary fields*. This is common in interdisciplinary research, meaning that you need to be aware that interdisciplinary fields draw on particular disciplines for their information. Table 11.1 identifies the major interdisciplinary fields (left column) and the disciplines from which each field typically draws its information (right column). Importantly, these fields have their own journals (in some cases, multiple journals), which means that you will have to consult not only disciplinary sources but also interdisciplinary sources. Since interdisciplinary fields have their own journals and scholarly organizations, and sometimes even their own PhD programs, they may come to behave more like disciplines over time (see the characteristics of disciplines in Chapter 5), preferring a subset of the theories and methods that they might borrow from their parent disciplines (Fuchsman 2012).

Challenge question: On what basis did these students connect the question to these particular disciplines?

By consulting Table 11.1, students in each example were able to verify their original selection of potentially relevant disciplines and in some cases add one or more interdisciplines as shown in Table 11.2.

Table 11.1	Interdisciplinary Fields and the Disciplines From Which They Typically Draw Their Information
Interdisciplinary Field	**Disciplines From Which the Field Typically Draws Its Information**
Non-Western Cultural Studies Asian area studies Latin American area studies African area studies Middle Eastern studies	History, religion, anthropology (cultural), sociology, economics, political science, literature

(Continued)

Table 11.1 (Continued)	
Interdisciplinary Field	**Disciplines From Which the Field Typically Draws Its Information**
Race and Ethnic Studies African American studies Ethnic and race studies Chicano, Hispanic studies American Indian studies Asian American studies	History, religion, anthropology (cultural), sociology, economics, linguistics, political science, literature
Western Studies European, North American studies Western period history studies European origin studies Western studies Canadian studies	History, religion, anthropology (cultural), sociology, economics, linguistics, political science, literature
Environmental Studies	Biology, Earth science, political science
International and Global Studies International relations, global studies Peace, conflict studies Political economy	History, political science, economics, law
Civic and Government Studies Urban studies Public affairs, public policy Legal studies	Political science, history, law, sociology, economics, education, literature
Women's Studies	History, sociology, psychology, religious studies, literature
American Studies American culture or studies U.S. regional studies	History, sociology, anthropology, education, literature, art history

Interdisciplinary Field	Disciplines From Which the Field Typically Draws Its Information
Brain and Biomedical Science	Biology, chemistry, psychology, communications
Cognitive neuroscience	
Biological psychology	
Biomedical, biotechnology	
Medical technology	
Media Studies	Psychology, philosophy, literature, political science, sociology
Communication	Psychology, philosophy, sociology, political science
Other	All disciplines
Interdisciplinary studies	Art history, history, sociology, literature
Film studies	Social science disciplines primarily
Liberal studies	Sociology, biology, psychology
Gerontology	Biology, sociology, psychology
Health studies, public health	Religion, religious studies, history, literature
Judaic studies	Natural sciences, history, philosophy
Science and society	Theater, dance, art, music, business
Arts management	Anthropology, history
Folk studies	Philosophy, literature, history, sociology, psychology
Ethics, values	Biology, literature, sociology, history, psychology
Sexuality studies	

Source: Data on interdisciplinary fields (left column) primarily compiled from College Catalog Study Database by Brint, S. G., Turk-Bicakci, L., Proctor, K., & Murphy, S. P. (2009). Expanding the Social Frame of Knowledge: Interdisciplinary, Degree-Granting Fields in American Colleges and Universities, 1975–2000. *Review of Higher Education, 32*(2), 155–183. The data in the right column were compiled by A. F. Repko.

Action No. 2: "Decompose" the Problem

Breaking down a problem into its component parts is called **decomposing the problem**. Decomposing a complex problem is the essence of analysis and serves several practical purposes:

Table 11.2 Example of Connecting Problem to Disciplines and Interdisciplinary Fields

Problem or Research Question	Disciplines (From Table 5.4)	Interdisciplinary Fields (From Table 11.1)
What is the cause of teenage apathy toward learning?	Education, psychology	Cognitive neuroscience, biological psychology
Should natural gas replace coal as a fuel source for electricity production?	Earth science, political science	Environmental studies
What is the meaning of the growing popularity of action super heroes in media?	Philosophy, anthropology, history	Film studies, cultural studies, American studies

- It helps to identify potentially relevant disciplines that we may have overlooked in Action No. 1.

- It may reveal a gap in our understanding of the problem.

- It may reveal an overemphasis on one part of the problem or on a particular discipline.

- It reveals the true nature of the problem: whether it concerns a *concept* or a *system* (thus requiring that we use systems thinking described in Chapter 8).

- It may indicate that we need to modify our statement of the problem by expanding or narrowing its focus.

Decomposing the problem is almost always aided by *externalizing the problem* to reveal its disciplinary parts, as demonstrated in Chapter 8. Another effective decomposition strategy is to critically analyze the wording of the problem statement or research question. Specifically, Action No. 2 involves looking for key concepts (i.e., phenomena) that can be connected to disciplines that typically study them. For example, analysis of research question No. 1 reveals that it references two phenomena: attitude and learning, as shown in Table 11.3.

This example demonstrates the value of decomposing a complex problem because it reveals another potentially relevant discipline, namely, sociology, which had been overlooked in Action No. 1. It also reveals a gap in our understanding of the problem by expanding our focus from studying primarily *internal* psychological factors to investigating *external* social influences such as

Table 11.3 Decomposing a Research Question		
Research Question	**Phenomena**	**Disciplines**
What is the cause of teen apathy toward learning?	Attitude	Psychology, education
	Learning	Education, psychology, sociology

pressures from family and peers. In other words, the action of decomposing the problem reveals missing or overlooked parts of the problem and in this example prevents us from overemphasizing internal factors at the expense of external ones. The action of decomposing the problem also provides us with a more accurate picture of the problem in that the subject of teen apathy toward learning is more complex than first thought. However, there does not seem to be a need, at this point in the research process, to modify the research question.

Action No. 3: Externalize the Problem

A good follow-on strategy for identifying potentially relevant disciplines is to "externalize" the problem *after* decomposing it. **Externalizing the problem** means getting the problem out of your head and down on paper or your iPad or computer screen in some simplified form to show its main variables, parameters, or elements and how these relate to each other. In effect, externalizing the problem involves drawing a picture of it.

When it comes to working with complex problems, we find it difficult to keep all the relevant factors at the forefront of our consciousness at the same time. Fortunately, anything that has parts also has structure that relates the parts to each other. It is important to visualize how the problem is structured so that you can identify its component parts and connect each part to the discipline that studies that part. This action also serves to verify that the disciplines identified in Action No. 2 as potentially relevant are indeed so (Heuer, 2008).

There are tools commonly used to depict the structures of complex problems (see mapping in Chapter 8). Two of the most commonly used are "nodes" and "links," which are the primary components of drawing a picture or map of the problem. **Nodes** are the important concepts or the phenomena under study. Nodes are usually depicted as circles around the concepts or phenomena but may also be depicted as ovals, squares, or rectangles. The two important aspects of nodes are their visual appearance and their verbal content. **Links** are the directional arrows that connect the nodes and indicate the relationships of nodes to each other. Links are labeled with a standard set of symbols (e.g., P = Part; L = Leads to). The labeled links provide the relationship information that is typically conveyed in a sentence (Danserau & Newbern, 1997, pp. 133–134). Using nodes and links, we decompose our hypothetical question concerning teen apathy toward learning, as shown in Figure 11.2.

Figure 11.2   Diagram of the Causes of Teen Apathy Toward Learning

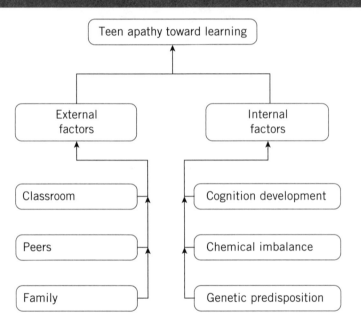

Challenge questions: Do these external and internal factors interact? Why or why not? If so, what are the implications of this interaction?

Drawing a diagram can raise questions about the problem that were not previously apparent. In this example, the diagram implies that "classroom" leads to "external factors." But "classroom" may well be a component of internal factors.

The point of externalizing the problem is to reveal its component parts (or factors or variables) to help you visualize the problem, see it as a complex whole, and decide which part(s) you really want to focus on. If drawn properly, the structure of the problem should reflect all the information gathered from earlier actions. In our example, the structure begins with the research question that is broken down into two broad categories of causal factors labeled "external" and "internal." "External" factors that affect teen learning may include the classroom environment (e.g., quality of instruction and quality of physical space), peer behavior, home environment, and so forth. "Internal" factors may include students' cognitive development, chemical imbalances, genetic predispositions, and so forth.

Note that picturing the problem may cause you to revisit the first two actions. As you draw the picture, you may identify additional phenomena, and thus disciplines, that had not occurred to you at first. And in so doing, you further the process of decomposition. We might also note here that the act of drawing a picture aids the creative process of identifying a novel solution to the problem under examination: Our subconscious minds play a critical role in creative processes and tend to operate visually rather than lingually (Buzan, 2010).

Challenge question: Connect each of these external and internal nodes (or factors or phenomena) to disciplines that study each phenomenon. To what extent does this action verify our earlier selection of potentially relevant disciplines?

Action No. 4: Reflect on the Problem

Interdisciplinary process is not linear but rather involves reflecting on and possibly revising earlier decisions as new information comes to light. We now need to decide if Action No. 3 shows that the research question is too broad and needs to be narrowed to only external *or* internal factors.

This decision involves taking STEP 4, which calls for gathering information about the problem. Actually, we have been gathering information about the research question all along, but now we must *skim* insights produced by the disciplines we have listed as potentially relevant (see Box 11.1 for an explanation of "skimming"). Taking STEP 4 at this point will achieve two practical purposes: It will reveal if there is too much or too little information on the original research question and will help us decide if we are more interested in investigating external factors rather than internal factors. Again, these early STEPS of the research process are more fluid than Figure 11.1 depicting the Broad Model suggests.

Skimming the disciplinary literature may guide you to narrow the focus of your research question. You might limit yourself as in the example below to only the internal or external forces at work (as long as you can still draw upon multiple disciplines). You might limit the geographical coverage or temporal coverage of a particular problem: perhaps only in your town and over the last year. Of course, you will not wish to so narrow your question that it ceases to be interdisciplinary. In any case, the purpose of refocusing the research question is to ensure that you are able to embrace a manageable set of insights from different disciplines.

Box 11.1 The Meaning of "Skimming"

Skimming means reading the publication (book, journal article, or online paper) cursorily, not with the intent to fully comprehend the author's argument and findings. Skimming or cursory reading enables you to identify relevant disciplines and insights. It entails flipping through a volume in the library to see if it contains needed information. The action of skimming printed materials involves looking for key components beginning with the abstract (if it is a journal article), preface or introduction (if it is a book), or table of contents (if it is a book), then moving to section or chapter headings, lists, summary statements or conclusions, definitions, and illustrations. . . . This process is applicable to digital documents where search features (such as the "Look Inside" function offered by Amazon.com for books) make it easier to pinpoint keywords, theories, and so on. . . . Researchers are making increased use of journal abstracts in full-text databases. . . . However, students are cautioned not to substitute skimming for eventually reading the full publication. Scholars often begin with skimming the preliminary parts of a document such as the table of contents and introduction before printing it for later reading. (Repko & Szostak, 2016, p. 136)

Here is an example of how to narrow the original question on teen apathy toward learning:

Original statement of the problem or research question: "What is the cause of teen apathy toward learning?"

Possible modification or narrowing of the question: What *external* factors contribute to teen apathy toward learning?

Challenge question: If we narrowed the research question to external or internal factors, would it still be interdisciplinary?

"Rules of Thumb" to Help You Perform STEP 3

Interdisciplinary work involves drawing on insights from two or more disciplines. Regardless of the problem or research question, following these "rules of thumb" will help you perform STEP 3 and identify disciplines that you can then mine for insights:

- *Think through the research question yourself and attempt to identify its main parts.* Some problems are more complex than others. In any case, you should decompose the problem to identify its main parts, understand how they interact with each other, and then consider whether you need to modify your research question.

- *Develop familiarity with the phenomena that disciplines typically study.* Experienced practitioners who regularly work with a set of disciplines and interdisciplinary fields have developed familiarity with the phenomena they typically study. This explains why Bal, for instance, is able to identify the several disciplines, subdisciplines, and interdisciplinary fields that are relevant to her subject. But because you are new to crossing disciplinary boundaries, you should draw on the information in Table 5.4 "The Disciplines and the Phenomena They Study," which is an invaluable tool for quickly connecting the complex problem or issue you want to study to particular disciplines.

- *Be inclusive as you perform STEP 3.* This means you should err on the side of identifying as many potentially relevant disciplines as possible before narrowing these to a few. Interdisciplinarians know that relevant information sometimes comes from unexpected sources. Indeed, major breakthroughs in scholarly understanding often involve drawing connections across insights that nobody had previously thought to connect (Root-Bernstein, 1989). If the literature search (STEP 4) reveals that a discipline has little of use to say about your research question, or if it offers insights that overlap too much with those of another discipline, the discipline can always be removed from the study.

STEP 4: Conduct a Literature Search

Those new to interdisciplinary research often make four mistakes when searching for insights from different disciplines. These mistakes can greatly complicate their work, waste time later on, and result in a flawed product. To avoid these mistakes, follow the four practices described next.

Remember That Different Disciplines Employ Terminology Differently

One mistake is to give up too quickly on a particular discipline that you have chosen to address your research question. If you are not finding relevant publications from that discipline, it may be because it employs different terminology to discuss the question than you are employing in your search. One strategy in "Keyword" searching, where you simply input the terms from your research question into your library's search interface, is to identify synonyms for your search terms. That is, your research question may not be as unbiased as it appears.

A second strategy is to use "Subject" searching: All books in a library are identified according to a set of Subject Headings. Once you have found one relevant publication, you search for the Subject Heading(s) associated with this publication. In any case, you should be aware that in some disciplines (especially economics and the natural sciences) insights may appear in journal articles that are hard to find in books: Journal articles are searchable within a set of disciplinary and interdisciplinary databases but are not usually searchable in the library's online catalog. Most universities and colleges employ librarians who give advice to students on how to search the library's resources—though some institutions have moved away from doing so in the face of budgetary challenges and online searching.

Categorize Publications According to Their Disciplinary Source

A second mistake is to fail to pay attention to the disciplinary source of insights. Keeping track of which insights are produced by which discipline is important when it comes to critically analyzing the insights. If a publication's disciplinary source is not immediately evident, conduct a Google search of the author's name, which should reveal the author's institutional and disciplinary affiliation. In some cases, the author may have an interdisciplinary affiliation.

Focus on Quality Rather Than Quantity

A third mistake is to be unduly influenced by the *quantity* of insights a discipline has produced. For example, if psychology has produced only a few articles on the problem but sociology has produced many, it would be wrong to assume that sociology is more relevant than psychology. *The criterion for disciplinary relevance is not the quantity of publications a discipline has produced but their quality.* It may be that the one article produced by psychology on the problem contains information of such significance that an interdisciplinary understanding of the problem that is truly comprehensive would not be possible without it.

Develop a Data Management System

A fourth mistake is to fail to develop a system that permits easy retrieval of critical information from the insights you are analyzing. Granted, the number of insights in an entry-level course is probably limited. But when you closely read each insight for specific content, as you will in STEP 5, the amount of data can quickly mushroom. A rule of thumb is this: If you invest more time here on the front end of the project, you will save a lot of time on the back end.

Creating a data table (Table 11.4) is a demonstrated and effective way to capture and organize information. It helps track the overall progress of your research,

Table 11.4 Example Data Table			
Disciplines Consulted	**Author(s) of Publication/Insight**	**Focus of Insight**	**Evaluation of Insight**
History	Smith	Presents early history of globalization	Information dated: stops in 1998
Political Science	Jones	Focuses on the effect of globalization in general terms on Middle Eastern societies	Very useful
Anthropology (Cultural)	Harvey	Provides overview of how globalization impacts traditional cultures and folkways	Very useful
	Nickels & Dimes	Explains the rise of religious fundamentalism in societies that are being threatened by materialist and godless Western culture	Very useful
Economics	Wheeler	Describes how building factories in underdeveloped societies accelerates their economic modernization	Somewhat useful but does not focus on how economic development affects culture
Music	Oats	Describes how Western music and its lyrics are transforming the music of developing countries	Very useful

connects authors to their discipline, states concisely the focus of the insight, and evaluates the relevance of each insight. This table is expandable (if created in Word or Excel) so that you can easily add additional columns to capture other critical information.

In this example, the table contains data gathered from insights from five disciplines on the subject of globalization and its impact on developing countries. The research question is, "How is globalization impacting the cultures of developing countries?"

The column labeled "Focus of Insight" helps you keep the research question clearly in mind while conducting the literature search. As a result, you will be able to easily identify the three most relevant disciplines (the number required in our hypothetical assignment) and their most important insights into the question of how globalization affects the cultures of developing countries. More examples of data management tables can be found in Repko and Szostak (2016) and Menken and Keestra (2016).

The Broad Model Rubric Applied to STEPS 3 and 4

In Chapter 10 we introduced the Broad Model Rubric to evaluate STEPS 1 and 2. Here we use the rubric (minus the earlier steps) to evaluate STEPS 3 and 4.

Figure 11.3 The Broad Model Rubric (STEPS 3 and 4)

THE BROAD MODEL RUBRIC (STEPS 3 AND 4)		
ID PROCESS	**CRITERIA**	**Y/N/I**
STEP 3		
Identify relevant disciplines.	**Identifies the disciplines potentially relevant to the problem or research question and then reduces these to those that are most relevant**	
	3.1. The author identifies the disciplines *potentially* relevant to the problem.	
	3.2. The author narrows these to those that are *most* relevant and explains the basis for doing so.	

THE BROAD MODEL RUBRIC (STEPS 3 AND 4)		
ID PROCESS	*CRITERIA*	*Y/N/I*
STEP 4		
Conduct a literature search.	Identifies insights from two or more disciplines, confirming that they are most relevant to the problem	
	4.1. The author reports that the literature search confirms the identity of the disciplines and their insights that are most relevant to the problem.	

Examples

Applying this rubric to practitioner and student examples of STEPS 3 and 4 will further develop your thinking as an interdisciplinarian and prepare you to self-evaluate your work. Examples No. 1, No. 2, and No. 3 are of practitioner work; examples No. 4 and No. 5 are of student work.

Example No. 1 From the Natural Sciences (Primarily)

Title: "Why We Talk: An Interdisciplinary Approach to the Evolutionary Origin of Language" (2012)

Author: Ria van der Lecq

Van der Lecq works with several disciplines, including linguistics, as well as with various subdisciplines and an interdisciplinary field. In this excerpt, she explains to readers how each of these is relevant to the problem she is studying.

Potentially relevant disciplines are linguistics, (evolutionary) biology (with its sub-disciplines: primatology, ethology and anatomy), psychology, cognitive science, philosophy, anthropology, and archeology. They were identified before the full-scale literature search was conducted. An analysis of them shows that disciplinary boundary crossing occurs in various ways. Psycholinguistics and biolinguistics, for example, are subdisciplines of linguistics. Psycholinguistics links psychology and linguistics when it studies language and the mind. Biolinguistics links biology and linguistics in the study of the biological foundations of language. Evolutionary biology is a special branch of biology that tries to explain psychological traits such as language as evolved adaptations. Other potentially relevant subdisciplines of biology are ethology (the study of animal behavior) and primatology (the study of primates), but anthropologists also study animal communications. Neuroscience is sometimes referred to as neurobiology, but it also has a subfield called cognitive neuroscience.

(Continued)

(Continued)

Cognitive science, in its turn, is an interdisciplinary field embracing philosophy, psychology, artificial intelligence, neuroscience, linguistics, and anthropology. (p. 193)

Van der Lecq then explains how she narrows these disciplines to those that are most relevant:

The *most relevant* disciplines are those that have generated direct insights on the question of the primary (original) function of language and its sub-questions mentioned above. The in-depth literature search reveals that biology (including the study of primates), anthropology, and cognitive science have generated such insights. . . . The developments in evolutionary biology have had far-reaching implications for our understanding of human (linguistic) behavior. These developments made an end to the claim of social scientists that language, being an aspect of human behavior, is a social phenomenon that lies beyond the pale of biological explanations (Dunbar, 1996). Evolutionary biologists make use of anthropological and archaeological evidence to support their claims. Cultural anthropologists study language in its cultural context, and some of them appear to be interested in the origin of communication in social networks. Cognitive science studies language in relation to knowledge, which leads to distinct insights regarding the original function of language. The insights of cognitive scientists are especially helpful when it comes to addressing the problem of language complexity. (Repko, A. F., Newell, W. H., and Szostak, R. (Eds.). *Case Studies in Interdisciplinary Research*, SAGE Publications, Inc. Thousand Oaks, CA; p. 194)

THE BROAD MODEL RUBRIC (STEPS 3 AND 4)		
ID PROCESS	**CRITERIA**	**Y/N/I**
STEP 3		
Identify relevant disciplines.	**Identifies the disciplines potentially relevant to the problem or research question and then reduces these to those that are most relevant**	
	3.1. The author identifies the disciplines *potentially* relevant to the problem.	Yes
	3.2. The author narrows these to those that are *most* relevant and explains the basis for doing so.	Yes
STEP 4		
Conduct a literature search.	**Identifies insights from two or more disciplines, confirming that they are most relevant to the problem**	
	4.1. The author reports that the literature search confirms the identity of the disciplines and their insights that are most relevant to the problem.	Yes

Example No. 2 From the Social Sciences (Primarily)

Title: "Jewish Marriage as an Expression of Israel's Conflicted Identity" (2012)

Author: Marilyn R. Tayler

[Each discipline] is characterized by its own perspective or world view. . . . The potentially relevant fields for this study include religion, religious studies, political science, law, history, sociology and cultural studies. . . . In the present study, several disciplines are eliminated through the literature search. Cultural studies, an interdiscipline, is eliminated because its insights are encompassed within some of its constituent disciplines, which are among the other disciplines selected. Sociology is eliminated because its contribution through research on Israeli society would de-focus the research question through an emphasis upon groups within the society rather than governing structures. History is eliminated because it essentially provides background to contextualize other disciplines' perspectives. To be included as a discipline, history would have to be considered in terms of patterns, contexts, and causal links, which are not the primary focus of the present study. Religious studies is eliminated because it is the academic study of religion from external perspectives. In contrast, religion, which is one of the essential disciplines for this study, refers to the theological belief system internal to Judaism; in Israel, this is generally equated with the Orthodox denomination of Judaism. The essential disciplines for this study, then, are religion, political science, and law. (Repko, A. F., Newell, W. H., and Szostak, R. (Eds.). *Case Studies in Interdisciplinary Research*, SAGE Publications, Thousand Oaks, CA; pp. 26–27)

In this example, *you* are to supply the missing evaluation of each STEP in the right-hand column. Tayler (2014) discusses how she employs this case study to illustrate the interdisciplinary research process.

THE BROAD MODEL RUBRIC (STEPS 3 AND 4)		
ID PROCESS	**CRITERIA**	**Y/N/I**
STEP 3		
Identify relevant disciplines.	**Identifies the disciplines potentially relevant to the problem or research question and then reduces these to those that are most relevant**	
	3.1. The author identifies the disciplines *potentially* relevant to the problem.	
	3.2. The author narrows these to those that are *most* relevant and explains the basis for doing so.	

(Continued)

(Continued)

THE BROAD MODEL RUBRIC (STEPS 3 AND 4)		
ID PROCESS	**CRITERIA**	**Y/N/I**
STEP 4		
Conduct a literature search.	**Identifies insights from two or more disciplines, confirming that they are most relevant to the problem**	
	4.1. The author reports that the literature search confirms the identity of the disciplines and their insights that are most relevant to the problem.	

Note to Instructor: Evaluations of this and subsequent examples are in Appendix E.

Example No. 3 From the Humanities
Title: *"Mektoub:* When Art Meets History, Philosophy, and Linguistics" (2012)
Author: Mieke Bal

The art work Bal is studying is Finnish artist Ahtila's large-format video installations showing a mixture of documentary footage of the Algerian war and fiction, set in both Algeria and Finland.

Here are the terms the work sets for us. A Finnish artist brings her work to France; she engages with French history at one of its most painful moments. If I may highlight the terms that refer to disciplines: this work raises questions of *history* and of *politics*, triggering international cultural sensibilities. Her work is *cinematic* and *theatrical*—thus soliciting responses from two disciplines simply by its own medium. Moreover, it uses *language*, in *literary* forms, and raises profound *philosophical* questions. According to this brief summary, to understand, interpret, and review this work critically, one must responsibly call upon at least seven different disciplines, plus the interdisciplinary domain of cultural sensibility in international relations. . . . [J]ust as this interdisciplinarity is inevitable, it is equally impossible to make full use of the entire paradigms and methodological packages of these disciplines. Nor is it possible for any individual to be knowledgeable in the canonical texts whose importance these disciplines tend to take for granted. This leaves us confronted with the primary challenge interdisciplinarity poses. (Repko, A. F., Newell, W. H., and Szostak, R. (Eds.). *Case Studies in Interdisciplinary Research*, SAGE Publications, Thousand Oaks, CA; p. 93)

In this example, *you* are to supply the missing evaluation of each STEP in the right-hand column.

THE BROAD MODEL RUBRIC (STEPS 3 AND 4)		
ID PROCESS	**CRITERIA**	**Y/N/I**
STEP 3		
Identify relevant disciplines.	**Identifies the disciplines potentially relevant to the problem or research question and then reduces these to those that are most relevant**	
	3.1. The author identifies the disciplines *potentially* relevant to the problem.	
	3.2. The author narrows these to those that are *most* relevant and explains the basis for doing so.	
STEP 4		
Conduct a literature search.	**Identifies insights from two or more disciplines, confirming that they are most relevant to the problem**	
	4.1. The author reports that the literature search confirms the identity of the disciplines and their insights that are most relevant to the problem.	

Importantly, van der Lecq was able to identify the most relevant disciplines only after completing an in-depth literature search, which revealed the disciplines that produce the most important insights on the question.

Example No. 4 Student Paper
Title: *Globalization and Its Effects on the Environment* (n.d.)
Author: A. Dhole

Three disciplines help us to understand the relationship between globalization and [its] effects on the environment. The first . . . is economics [which] is . . . concerned with the production, consumption, and transfer of wealth. A company expands globally to maximize profits by lowering the cost of production. . . . The second discipline . . . is environmental science [which draws on] physics, chemistry and biology in order to explain the effects of several elements that are generated and released into the atmosphere. [It helps us] understand how the environment is affected

(Continued)

(Continued)

> when manufacturing plants emit toxic waste elements into the atmosphere. The third discipline . . . is sociology [which] is defined as the study of structure, development, and functioning of human society. Corporations have not limited themselves to a certain country or group of countries. Because of this, whenever a corporation decides to outsource its production plants overseas, there are several effects on the population of that particular country. (Dhole, A. (n.d.). *Globalization and its effects on the environment.* Unpublished paper.

In this example, *you* are to supply the missing evaluation of each STEP in the right-hand column.

RUBRIC FOR THE BROAD MODEL (STEPS 3 AND 4)		
ID PROCESS	**CRITERIA**	**Y/N/I**
STEP 3		
Identify relevant disciplines.	Identifies the disciplines potentially relevant to the problem or research question and then reduces these to those that are most relevant	
	3.1. The author identifies the disciplines *potentially* relevant to the problem.	
	3.2. The author narrows these to those that are *most* relevant and explains the basis for doing so.	
STEP 4		
Conduct a literature search.	Identifies insights from two or more disciplines, confirming that they are most relevant to the problem	
	4.1. The author reports that the literature search confirms the identity of the disciplines and their insights that are most relevant to the problem.	

Bal does not distinguish between disciplines that are potentially relevant and those that are most relevant because her mastery of the literatures of these disciplines enables her to proceed directly to identifying the disciplines that she is going to use. For Bal, the literature search is not something that she engages in when taking on a new project but is an ongoing activity that transcends a particular research project.

Searching through scholarly databases for the causes of nurse burnout [reveals] a multitude of factors that cause burnout: Nursing shortages caused by budgetary restraint, work overload, role conflict, lack of social/emotional support, lack of autonomy, dependency on physicians, and eroding of professional values.

For the interdisciplinary research process to begin, it is important to select the appropriate disciplines. . . . Typical research on nurse burnout comes from the sociological perspective only and blames mainly environment issues such as nursing shortages. But . . . nurse burnout should also be viewed [from the perspectives of] psychology and ethics. Nurses must make ethical decisions every day when treating patients. . . .

From a psychological perspective, in order to perform their job, nurses must be able to understand their patients' behavior and emotional state. An optimistic nurse who brings comfort to patients has the ability to encourage positive thinking, which is important for the healing process to take place. But what if nurses are suffering from job stress? Are they going to be optimistic in their approach? A key component in psychology is the inner conflicts that motivate a person's behavior. If a nurse is struggling emotionally, the desire to perform at peak potential is negatively impacted (Janssen, De Jonge, & Bakker, 1999).

Approaching nursing burnout from a sociological perspective is relevant for many reasons. First, there are many environmental factors that can cause stress, leading to burnout. These factors may include less than ideal working conditions, such as staffing shortages, poor management, lack of support, and the actual type of nursing environment such as trauma, hospice, and critical care. One important sociological theoretical perspective is the critical social theory, which includes "conflict, competition, change and constraint within a society.". . . When taking care of a patient, nurses must constantly adapt to rapid changes in a patient's condition, which can bring about conflicting ideas of how to treat them, all the while working within the constraints of managed care.

Ethics . . . is integral to the medical field. Nursing is a profession whose "ethic of care" is vital to its claim for professionalism "and in which the ability to effectively manageone's

(Continued)

(Continued)

own and others' emotions is critical to the provision of excellent patient care" (Erickson &
Grove, 2008). Making ethical decisions is an everyday occurrence when treating a patient,
and there is always a possibility that a mistake will be made. Nurses must be able to
ethically assess a situation using their personal values and morals, while still keeping the
patients' best interest at heart. This process may be further complicated by constraining
factors, such as hierarchical systems, leaving less autonomy, resulting in moral distress
(McKay, K. A. (n.d.). *Nurse burnout: An integrative approach to a multidimensional problem.*
Unpublished paper.)

In this example, *you* are to supply the missing evaluation of each STEP in the right-hand column.

THE BROAD MODEL RUBRIC (STEPS 3 AND 4)		
ID PROCESS	**CRITERIA**	**Y/N/I**
STEP 3		
Identify relevant disciplines.	**Identifies the disciplines potentially relevant to the problem or research question and then reduces these to those that are most relevant**	
	3.1. The author identifies the disciplines *potentially* relevant to the problem.	
	3.2. The author narrows these to those that are *most* relevant and explains the basis for doing so.	
STEP 4		
Conduct a literature search.	**Identifies insights from two or more disciplines, confirming that they are most relevant to the problem**	
	4.1. The author reports that the literature search confirms the identity of the disciplines and their insights that are most relevant to the problem.	

As in the previous example, students were not asked to first identify disciplines
potentially relevant to the problem by decomposing the problem and then
connecting its parts to disciplines that typically study those parts. Instead, the
instructor required students to explain the basis for selecting the disciplines to be
mined for insights, which this student does.

Analysis of Examples

In the preceding examples, practitioners and students connected the research question and its component parts to disciplines (including subdisciplines and interdisciplinary fields) that study those parts. Practitioners are generally able to decompose complex problems without having to externalize their structures. Two of these (van der Lecq and Tayler) say that they identified the potentially relevant disciplines *before* conducting the literature search. Nonetheless, a rule of thumb is to allow the results of the literature search to help you decide each discipline's relevancy.

The examples of student work are more uneven in their performance of these STEPS. In Example No. 4, the student did not meet Criteria 3.1 and 4.1 because the course did not require students to identify a list of potentially relevant disciplines and then narrow these to the most relevant ones. Instead, the instructor provided a course pack of articles produced by several disciplines from which students were to draw information on the course theme of globalization. Students had to formulate research questions based on the course theme and then search for additional information from academic databases. The instructor also gave students the flexibility to draw on information from multidisciplinary and interdisciplinary fields such as environmental science, which the student did.

In Example No. 5, the student was *not* instructed to first identify disciplines potentially relevant to the problem by decomposing the problem and then connecting its parts to disciplines that typically study those parts. This would have helped the student visualize the problem as a whole and then connect its component parts to disciplines that study those parts. However, the course did require students to explain the basis for selecting the disciplines to be mined for insights, which this student does.

Having performed STEPS 3 and 4, we are now ready to critically analyze these insights, which is the next phase of the research process and the subject of Chapter 12.

CRITICAL THINKING QUESTIONS

1. Perform the four actions in STEP 3 for one of the following contemporary public policy challenges: suicide terrorism; the refugee crisis; and tracking and storing personal information by governments.

2. How would you go about searching for relevant insights on these issues?

CRITICAL THINKING SCENARIO

Professor Blatz, who teaches at a university located in the American Southwest, is very concerned about declining annual rainfall, shrinking reservoirs on which cities rely for their supply of water, aquifers that are being depleted by farmers who use them to irrigate their crops, and the continuing rapid pace of urban sprawl that is literally "paving over" valuable farmland and watershed. He is also concerned about the rising cost of food caused, in large part, by the rising cost of growing it (irrigating land) and transporting it (rising fuel prices). After sharing his concerns with his students, he asks them to divide themselves into groups and do the following (which you are to do also):

1. Develop a research question relating to the course theme of water that would address one of Professor Blatz's concerns and involve *primarily* (but not be limited to) the natural sciences, the social sciences, *or* the humanities.

2. For each research question, apply STEPS 3 and 4 of interdisciplinary process and end up with two disciplines that are most relevant to the question.

3. Decompose the problem and then externalize it.

PEER EVALUATION AND EDIT ACTIVITY_____

After writing or developing posters on the STEPS performed in the critical thinking scenario, assess and suggest ways to improve the work of the other group members applying STEPS 3 and 4 using the Broad Model Rubric.

Source: ©iStockphoto.com/ PamelaJoeMcFarlane.

Chapter 12 Objectives

The approach of the Broad Model to interdisciplinary research involves making a series of step-like decisions and reflecting on them as you go. It also involves applying the Broad Model Rubric to assess the quality of work at each STEP. One objective of this chapter is to explain how to perform the remaining STEPS of the Broad Model: STEP 5 calls for critically analyzing disciplinary insights and locating their sources of conflict, and STEP 6 calls for reflecting on how interdisciplinary research process has enlarged your understanding of the problem. A second objective is to prepare you to evaluate your own work by applying the Broad Model Rubric to work by both practitioners and students like yourself.

CHAPTER

12

Analyzing Insights and Reflecting on Process

Having completed the first four STEPS of the Broad Model, you are now ready to perform the two remaining STEPS. STEP 5 calls for critically analyzing disciplinary insights and locating sources of conflict between them. STEP 6 involves reflecting on how using an interdisciplinary approach (as reflected in the Broad Model) has enlarged your understanding of the problem. These remaining STEPS are italicized in Figure 12.1.

The applicability of this rubric extends beyond the classroom since many real-world complex problems benefit from this kind of careful, systematic, and holistic analysis. Developing an effective research strategy for addressing complex problems and identifying deficiencies in expert work are vital skills for life in contemporary complex societies. These analytical skills will serve you long after graduation.

Learning Outcomes

By the end of this chapter you will be able to:

- Apply strategies to analyze disciplinary insights and expose their sources of conflict

- Apply the Broad Model Rubric to assess examples of practitioner and student performance of STEP 5

- Reflect on how the interdisciplinary research process has enlarged your understanding of the problem

- Evaluate your own performance of STEP 6 using the Broad Model Rubric

STEP 5: Critically Analyze the Disciplinary Insights Into the Problem

This discussion has two objectives: (1) to provide proven strategies for analyzing the disciplinary insights you have gathered and locate sources of conflict between them and (2) to demonstrate how the Broad Model Rubric is used to assess examples of practitioner and student performance of STEP 5, to prepare you to evaluate your own performance of this STEP. We discuss how entry-level students can critically analyze the insights of unfamiliar disciplines in Box 12.1 at the end of this section.

Figure 12.1 The Broad Model of Interdisciplinary Process
(STEPS 5 and 6)

STEP 1: Define the problem or state the research question.

STEP 2: Justify using an interdisciplinary approach.

STEP 3: Identify relevant disciplines.

STEP 4: Conduct a literature search.

STEP 5: Critically analyze the disciplinary insights into the problem and locate their sources of conflict.

STEP 6: Reflect on how using an interdisciplinary approach has enlarged your understanding of the problem.

Strategies for Critically Analyzing Disciplinary Insights

There are three proven strategies for critically analyzing disciplinary insights and locating their sources of conflict: identifying the key elements of each insight, organizing this information, and critically analyzing it. In Chapter 8 you were introduced to the basic principles of critical reading. Here, you will build on those insights with an eye to comparing and contrasting the insights produced by different disciplines.

Strategy No. 1: Identify the Key Elements of Each Insight In critically analyzing insights, we are interested in identifying the key elements of each insight so that we can locate points of conflict between them. As you read each insight closely, look for the elements that follow. Depending on the author, some of this information will be easy to spot while other information will require more effort. For instance, it is common for authors to make their theories and methods of research and data collection explicit, but it is not common for them to make their assumptions and epistemologies explicit. In addition to the usual bibliographic information (author's name, publication date, and title), these are the key elements that you should be looking for as you read each insight:

- The author's disciplinary affiliation. This provides important clues about the author's perspective and assumptions concerning the problem. For instance, if the author is writing from the perspective of economics (which we have said includes most areas of business), then it is likely that the author will assume the participants are making rational choices motivated by economic self-interest.

- The author's insights, thesis, or argument (that is, the author's conclusions and justified supporting arguments)
- The author's assumption(s) concerning the problem
- The author's epistemological position (which usually reflects the epistemology of the author's discipline)
- Key concepts and their meanings
- The theory advanced by the author and grounded in research that explains the data collected
- The author's research method (which reflects the method favored by the author's discipline)
- The phenomena addressed and the relationship of parts to whole (information invaluable for mapping the problem)
- The author's bias (ethical or ideological)

Strategy No. 2: Organize This Information A useful way to organize this information is to create a table in Word or Excel as we advised earlier. In Table 12.1, students were asked to provide information about each author's insight into the subject of suicide terrorism. Note in this example that the author's thesis is a direct quote rather than a paraphrase. This eliminates the possibility of skewing the writer's meaning as may occur when paraphrasing. If you are reading insights produced by an interdisciplinary field such as gender studies or global studies, you should treat it in the same way as you would a traditional discipline.

As you read each insight, keep adding information on the key elements of each one. The extra effort you make on this "front end" activity will be rewarded when you come to the "back end" of the research process and Strategy No. 3.

Strategy No. 3: Critically Analyze This Information In Chapter 8, we advised asking whether the author's conclusions actually followed from their evidence and supporting arguments, or they were instead driven by disciplinary perspective or personal biases. To "critically analyze" requires being critical of expert evidence and to look for points of conflict and their sources.

Table 12.1 Checklist of Things to Look for When Reading

Author	Disciplinary Perspective	Thesis	Assumption	Theory Name	Key Concept(s)	Method	Phenomena Addressed	Author's Bias
Post	Psychology (cognitive)	"Political violence is not instrumental but an end in itself. The cause becomes the rationale for acts of terrorism the terrorist is compelled to commit" (Post, 1998, p. 35).	Humans organize their mental life through psychological constructs.	Terrorist Psycho-logic	Special Logic (Post, 1998, p. 25)	Case study	Individual human agents	Suicide terrorists are irrational.

Source: Adapted from Repko & Szostak (2016), and Repko, A. F., Newell, W. H., & Szostak, R. (2012) (Eds.). *Case Studies in interdisciplinary Research.* Thousand Oaks, CA: SAGE Publications, Inc.

Note: If constructed using Excel, the table can be easily expanded horizontally to include additional information about any one insight as well as vertically by adding as many insights as necessary. The utility of this table for interdisciplinary work on the undergraduate level will be increasingly evident as the interdisciplinary research process unfolds.

Be Critical of Expert Evidence. Being critical of expert evidence means being keenly aware that the factual information presented by the author may be "skewed" and understanding the implications of this bias. The term **skewed** refers to "the degree to which an insight reflects the biases inherent in the discipline's perspective and thus the way an author understands the problem resulting from the author's deliberate decision or unconscious predisposition to omit certain information that pertains to the problem" (Repko & Szostak, 2016, p. 190). We learned in Chapter 5 that each discipline has an epistemology or way of knowing, and that it collects, organizes, and presents data in a certain way that is natural to it. By saying that the factual information presented by disciplines may be "skewed" is not to allege that the data are falsified or sloppily gathered or presented in a biased way (though the latter is sometimes the case). Rather, it is to say that disciplines are notorious for omitting certain kinds of facts and data. This is because disciplines are interested in certain kinds of questions and amass data to answer these questions without consciously realizing that they may be excluding other data that would, if included, modify or even contradict the study's findings.

In reading and thinking about each insight, you should ask, "What counts as evidence in this author's discipline?" and "What kind of evidence is this author omitting that would shed additional light on the problem?" These questions deal with issues of the depth and breadth addressed in Chapter 8. We illustrate the close connection between an author's disciplinary perspective (which includes assumptions, epistemology, and research method) and the kind of supportive evidence the discipline considers reliable by examining two essays by experts from psychology and education on the question, "Should schools adopt computer-assisted education for young children?" Their findings are summarized here:

> *Psychology (Learning Theory).* The National Research Council (NRC) is the research arm of the National Academy of Sciences, a private, nonprofit scholarly society that advises the federal government in scientific and technical matters. Its study *How People Learn: Brain, Mind, Experience, and School* argues that computer-assisted education can enhance learning (Bradsford, Brown, & Cocking, 1999). The supportive evidence used by the NRC includes references to state-of-the-art learning software and several experimental projects such as GLOBE, which gathered data from students in over 2,000 schools in 34 countries (Bradsford et al., 1999).

> *Education.* In 1999, The Alliance for Childhood, a partnership of individuals and organizations, issued a report, *Fool's Gold: A Critical Look at Computers in Childhood,* that subsequently appeared in a leading education journal. The report argues that computer-assisted education does not benefit young children. This view, a matter of heated debate within the profession, was nevertheless included in the Education Department's own 1999 study of nine troubled schools in high poverty areas, as well as extensive references to studies by leading education experts, including Stanford Professor (Education) Larry Cuban, theorist John Dewey, Austrian innovator Rudolf Steiner, and MIT Professor Sherry Turkel (Alliance for Childhood, 1999).

Challenge question: Why do these insights conflict?

These insights demonstrate how each discipline or profession amasses and presents evidence that reflects its preferred research methodology and the kind of evidence that it considers reliable. However, in all these cases, experts omit evidence that they consider outside the scope of their discipline or profession. "Facts," then, are not always what they appear to be. They reflect only what the discipline and its community of experts are interested in.

It is easy to be seduced by the data that an author presents on the subject, mistakenly concluding that the data must surely mean that the insight of the author who collected the data is "correct." But Newell (2007) warns that interdisciplinarians need to be attuned to the subliminal message of facts, and keep track of the complex problem that interests an author without being sidetracked by the narrower, value-laden interests of the discipline on which the author draws (pp. 254–255). It is also easy to be seduced by the data when you happen to agree with the author's position on the issue. The lesson here is that you must be aware of an author's discipline, analyze carefully *the kind of evidence* the author privileges, and know *how the author uses that evidence*.

Look for Points of Conflict and Their Sources. Critical analysis of disciplinary insights also involves identifying conflicts between insights and locating their sources. When comparing insights from different disciplines, commonalities seldom surface between any of their defining elements (i.e., perspectives, assumptions, epistemologies, theories, methods, and data). This is because an author's insight typically reflects the author's disciplinary affiliation and training. When concepts appear to be the same or similar, they too will have different meanings to reflect each discipline's understanding of the concept. For example, the concept of "sustainability" will have an economic orientation when an economist uses it but an environmental orientation when a biologist uses it. It is important to keep track of the concepts that each writer uses to see how their meaning may vary when used by authors in different disciplines.

What is almost certain when comparing different disciplinary insights on the same subject is that they will conflict at one or more points. You will see these points of conflict more readily when these key elements are juxtaposed as in Table 12.1. The mapping exercise outlined in Chapter 8 is another useful technique for identifying—and understanding the sources of—conflicts in disciplinary insights.

Box 12.1 Disciplinary Adequacy

As noted in Chapter 2, disciplinary scholars worry about how interdisciplinary scholars can develop enough expertise in different disciplines in order to draw on these knowledgeably. Entry-level students likewise wonder how they can be expected to draw on multiple disciplines with which they have limited or no familiarity. Yet we saw in Chapter 8 that entry-level students are quite capable of critically analyzing texts from **unfamiliar** disciplines. One of the key insights of interdisciplinary scholarship is that interdisciplinarians need not have the same depth of knowledge in disciplines as disciplinary specialists have in order to draw on these.

- Here is what you need to know (**i.e., develop adequacy**) about an **unfamiliar** discipline in order to draw upon its insights and critically analyze them: (Note: The level of familiarity required will vary with the requirements of a particular course.)
- First, understand the perspective of each relevant discipline. This perspective will shape the insights produced by scholars in the discipline. It is important to evaluate a discipline's insights in the context of its perspective.
- Second, read the insights (i.e., books and articles) of each relevant discipline on the problem. Though disciplinary perspective shapes insights, scholarly disagreements are commonplace within disciplines. Strive to ascertain whether a particular insight is widely shared in a discipline or viewed with suspicion. You can do this not by reading just a single article but by reading other works on the problem that may cite the article (check footnotes and the sources cited).
- Third, identify the theory on which the insight is based.
- Fourth, identify the appropriateness of the method the author uses.

In Chapter 5, we discussed **how to** approach different theory types and methods. The example above of computer-assisted learning **shows** that even entry-level students can reasonably critique the method employed in a research study. **Since no** theory or method is perfect, you can always ask whether a particular theory or method likely biases the insight in a particular direction. (The evaluation of theories and methods is addressed in greater detail in Repko and Szostak, 2016.)

Figure 12.2 The Broad Model Rubric (STEP 5)

THE BROAD MODEL RUBRIC (STEP 5)		
ID PROCESS	*CRITERIA*	*Y/N/I*
STEP 5		
Critically analyze the disciplinary insights into the problem and locate their sources of conflict.	**Identifies the key elements of insights and locates their sources of conflict**	
	5.1. The author identifies the key elements of the most important disciplinary insights into the problem.	
	5.2. The author identifies both the sources of conflict and/or agreement between insights.	
	5.3. The author maps or compiles a table that sets out how the insights from contributing disciplines are interconnected or fit together.	

The Broad Model Rubric Applied to STEP 5[1]

Applying the Broad Model Rubric to assess examples of practitioner and student performance of STEP 5 will prepare you to evaluate your own performance of this important STEP. Examples No. 1 and No. 2 are of practitioner work and Example No. 3 is of student work.

Example No. 1 From the Sciences
Title: "Why We Talk: An Interdisciplinary Approach to the Evolutionary Origin of Language" (2012)
Author: Ria van der Lecq

Van der Lecq introduces her discussion of this STEP, explaining why conflicts between insights are of interest to interdisciplinarians.

Conflicts typically occur between insights in a discipline and between disciplines, but also between insights resulting from interdisciplinary theories, especially in the study of language where so many disciplines are involved. It is only natural that insights resulting

---

1 Note to instructors: Answers to the Broad Model Rubric Applied to STEPS 5 and 6 are in Appendix E.

from different disciplinary perspectives conflict, because disciplines focus on different aspects of a problem. Interdisciplinary theories, as they appear in this study, may already have solved some of the conflicts between disciplinary insights, but even then each theory represents a different view of the problem, so that new conflicts arise between the insights based on those theories. It is necessary, therefore, to identify the conflicts between the theory-based insights, *because these stand in the way of achieving integration* [emphasis added]. (pp. 212–213)

Then she locates the sources of conflict between insights in their concepts and assumptions:

Conflicting Concepts

One of the most important sources of conflict is the concepts used by the various writers. In this study it is of utmost importance to see if the concepts *evolution* and *communication* have the same meaning in all relevant theories.

Evolution, as noted earlier, is not the same as natural selection. Evolution can have many causes and natural selection is one of those causes. Our focus question asks for an account of the adaptive significance of language, i.e., an explanation in terms of natural selection. GG [grooming and gossip theory] and RSt [the relevance for status theory] use the term *evolution* in this sense: with modification by natural selection. NCt [niche construction theory] does the same, but extends the theory of evolution by natural selection in order to explain the interaction between natural and cultural events. Ct [complexity theory] compares the evolution of linguistic complexity with the evolution of societies and cultural institutions. This kind of evolution is not likely to be the result of natural selection, because selection occurs culturally rather than genetically. Thus, we have to conclude that Ct uses the concept of *evolution* in a broader sense than the other three theories [do].

Communication is also a central concept in this discussion. The theories under review see language as a form of communication, but GG and NCt consider communication as a social activity (the cooperative sharing of information), whereas for RSt and Ct (both rooted in cognitive science) communication is primarily a cognitive activity (producing knowledge in the minds of hearers). For GG, perceptual processing (i.e., cognitive) skills are byproducts of the fact that the (primate) brain evolved to handle day-to-day social problems.

(Continued)

(Continued)

Conflicting Assumptions

Since the most important insights in this study are interdisciplinary, it is not necessary to identify disciplinary assumptions. Identifying the assumptions that are made within a theory, however, is particularly important. Table 1 [not shown] shows that the assumptions in this debate are several and conflicting. Dunbar (GG) and Odling-Smee and Laland (NCt) share the sociality assumption ("man is a *social* animal"). This may not surprise us because they all have some affiliation with anthropology, a social science. Dessalles (RSt) sees man as a *political* animal. At first sight, this is just another way of saying the same thing. After all, most people see politics as a social activity. But for Dessalles, politics is a consequence of the biological function of language: the coalition game. The social function of language is, for him, only a consequence of its primary function: communication of salient features. As a cognitive scientist, he sees communication as a cognitive activity, i.e., producing knowledge in the minds of hearers. Although Dessalles and Sampson share an affiliation with cognitive science, they could not differ more in their assumptions: for Sampson, languages are wholly cultural constructs with no biological origins whatsoever. He would, presumably, share the assumption of NCt that human language is socially learned and rapidly changing (and growing more complex).

RUBRIC FOR THE BROAD MODEL (STEP 5)		
ID PROCESS	**CRITERIA**	**Y/N/I**
STEP 5		
Critically analyze the disciplinary insights into the problem and locate their sources of conflict.	**Identifies the key elements of insights and locates their sources of conflict**	
	5.1. The author identifies the key elements of the most important disciplinary insights into the problem.	Y
	5.2. The author identifies both the sources of conflict and/or agreement between insights.	Y
	5.3. The author maps or compiles a table that sets out how the insights from contributing disciplines are interconnected or fit together.	N

Tayler prefaces her analysis with a brief explanation of the interdisciplinary process to readers who are possibly unfamiliar with it:

> Conflicts occur between insights within a discipline and between disciplines. Possible sources of conflict are the underlying assumptions, constituent concepts and theories that are expressed as disciplinary insights. . . . Since each discipline has its own worldview, insights of different disciplines may not simply be combined but must rather be evaluated first in the context of the specific question (Newell, 1998, p. 110). The differences in disciplinary assumptions provide greater likelihood for conflicts between rather than within disciplines. The scholarly insights of religion, political science, and law, as described earlier, are explored in [this] Step . . . to highlight conflicts [between] each discipline.
>
> One source of conflict between disciplines involves insights in support of the primacy of religion, religious politics, and laws favoring religion. These are termed *religious-based insights*. The other source of conflict involves insights that arise because of the effects of "religious-based insights" upon the civil rights of those affected by decisions made on a religious basis. These are termed *civil rights violation insights*. Once these sources of conflict are identified and clarified, the process of creating or discovering common ground can proceed.

She proceeds with explaining why the insights conflict. The term *halakhah* denotes Jewish law as derived from the Torah and ancient scholarly works as interpreted by modern Orthodox Jewish rabbinical authorities (Tayler, 2012, p. 30).

Religious-Based Insights

A contrastive study of "religious-based insights" reveals conflicts between groups of insights across disciplines. The "halakhah governing human conduct" insight is viewed from the standpoint of Orthodox Judaism as the role of divine revelation in human affairs. The legal application of the religious insight is the "halakhic pre-law

(Continued)

(Continued)

legal antecedents" insight, which represents the efforts of halakhic scholars in the pre-state era to develop halakhic law as the national law for the future state of Israel.

These insights conflict with the political reality of the creation of the pluralistic yet Jewish state of Israel. The "secular Zionist religious-political accommodation" insight demonstrates compromises to retain the status quo of the Orthodox Jewish pre-state monopoly in matters of Jewish marriage. In other words, a secular Zionist government adopted a purely religious solution to Jewish marriage for reasons of political accommodation. At the same time, the Orthodox Rabbinate joined with the secular Zionists to play "halakhic politics" in order to maximize the role of the Orthodox in the nonhalakhic state of Israel.

Civil Rights Violation Insights

From the legal perspective, the "interrelationship of religion and state" insight demonstrates the embedded role of religion within the legal system. Yet, it is not the interrelationship itself that causes problems but the violations of civil rights that result from the impermissible imposition of religion.

Each of the disciplines deals with individuals and groups whose civil rights are denied due to the monopoly of the Orthodox Rabbinate in the matter of Jewish marriage. Some of the insights are theory-based, while others are not. Religion's Orthodox hegemony theory attributes the motivations of the Orthodox to the preservation of power rather than to a desire for doctrinal purity. Political science's "religious-political coercion" insight recognizes that the Zionist accommodation of the Orthodox monopoly in matters of Jewish marriage results in religious coercion exercised against secular Jews, among others. Law's "freedom of and from religion" insight recognizes that the status quo results in a lack of equal protection for the majority which must function under the religious dictates of a majority. While most Israelis recognize the legitimate interest of maintaining a Jewish majority in Israel, they acknowledge that the present approach to Jewish marriage imperils the civil rights of citizens.

In this example, *you* are to supply the missing evaluation of each criterion in the right-hand column.

RUBRIC FOR THE BROAD MODEL (STEP 5)		
ID PROCESS	CRITERIA	Y/N/I
STEP 5		
Critically analyze the disciplinary insights into the problem and locate their sources of conflict.	**Identifies the key elements of insights and locates their sources of conflict**	
	5.1. The author identifies the key elements of the most important disciplinary insights into the problem.	
	5.2. The author identifies both the sources of conflict and/or agreement between insights.	
	5.3. The author maps or compiles a table that sets out how the insights from contributing disciplines are interconnected or fit together.	

Example No. 3 Student Paper

Title: *Nurse Burnout: An Integrative Approach to a Multidimensional Problem* (n.d.)

Author: K. A. McKay

After describing the perspectives of the various disciplinary insights, McKay compares and contrasts the insights under review:

> Two of the three disciplines selected, sociology and psychology, are both social sciences. While methodologically different, the epistemological basis for both is similar in perspective. . . . As discussed earlier, there is a certain amount of crossover in the research methods associated within the social sciences. In some psychological research methods, the effects of social or institutional programs are relevant to gaining interdisciplinary perspectives.

> While the third discipline of philosophy, or the sub-discipline of ethics, is from the humanities perspective, its elements such as values, morals and the greater good can be closely related to psychological well-being. Compromising of one's moral/ethical beliefs can have a negative psychological impact, leading to stress, lack of motivation, and ultimately job burnout (McKay, K. A. (n.d.). *Nurse burnout: An integrative approach to a multidimensional problem*. Unpublished paper.)

In this example, *you* are to supply the missing evaluation of each criterion in the right-hand column.

RUBRIC FOR THE BROAD MODEL (STEP 5)		
ID PROCESS	**CRITERIA**	**Y/N/I**
STEP 5		
Critically analyze the disciplinary insights into the problem and locate their sources of conflict.	Identifies the key elements of insights and locates their sources of conflict	
	5.1. The author identifies the key elements of the most important disciplinary insights into the problem.	
	5.2. The author identifies both the sources of conflict and/or agreement between insights.	
	5.3. The author maps or compiles a table that sets out how the insights from contributing disciplines are interconnected or fit together.	

Notably, the two practitioners use tables similar to the ones in this book to aid readers in making comparisons and contrasts between the key elements of insights. These practitioners agree that using tables helped them to locate points of conflict between insights. They also agree that juxtaposing key elements of insights is an effective strategy for quickly identifying *all* sources of conflict.

STEP 5 is critical to preparing for the integrative phase of interdisciplinary research. Integration consists not of adding different or similar things together but of reducing difference and conflict by creating common ground between insights. Though creating common ground and performing integration are not the focus of this book, it is important to learn how to *prepare to integrate* if you intend to advance in interdisciplinary studies. Exactly how to integrate is the subject of the follow-on book to this one, *Interdisciplinary Research: Process and Theory* (3rd ed.).

STEP 6: Reflect on How an Interdisciplinary Approach Has Enlarged Your Understanding of the Problem

This book stops short of actually showing you how to integrate insights and thus to create a comprehensive understanding—though we did provide a brief survey of techniques for integration in Chapter 9. These tasks are pursued in detail in Repko and Szostak (2016) and are typically reserved for more advanced courses focusing on interdisciplinary research and senior capstone projects. Yet you have gained much already, including an understanding of the nature of interdisciplinarity and disciplinarity, an ability to critically evaluate both disciplinary and interdisciplinary works, and an understanding of the first STEPS in the interdisciplinary research process.

One key element of interdisciplinary research is reflection. So far, we have urged you to reflect on bias in the work of others and your own. STEP 6 asks you to reflect on something new: how an interdisciplinary approach has enlarged your understanding of the problem. To assist you, we break this action down into four questions:

- How has the project challenged your bias toward the problem?

- How has the research process influenced your perception of disciplinary perspective and expertise?

- How has an interdisciplinary approach enlarged your understanding of the problem *as a whole*?

- How is an interdisciplinary approach applicable beyond the classroom?

Acting on STEP 6 should characterize your final course project (which might be a paper, presentation, exhibit, or performance). You might in such an exercise even speculate on how you would attempt to actually integrate insights (but this should not be expected of you in an introductory course). If you do, you might refer to the updated Bloom's taxonomy in Chapter 6. Acting on STEP 6 will establish that you have advanced to (at least) the capacity to understand and engage in high-level critical thinking.

How Has the Project
Challenged Your *Bias* Toward the Problem?

Interdisciplinary reflection begins by considering what bias you may have consciously or unconsciously brought to the subject. Szostak (2009) makes a compelling case for why reflecting on our biases is necessary and should be mandatory in interdisciplinary work:

> A key guiding principle of interdisciplinary analysis is that no piece of scholarly research is perfect. If we accept that no scholarly method can guide a researcher flawlessly towards insight, then it follows that scholarly results may reflect researcher biases. This does not mean that results reflect only such biases, as some in the field of science studies have claimed.

But it does mean that one way of evaluating the insights
generated by research is to interrogate researcher bias. (p. 331)

Szostak makes two points. First, no scholarly research is perfect because
it is skewed by predispositions and biases. However, you should not
conclude from this statement that research is a matter of mere opinion or
flawed approach. Rather, this statement calls for researchers, including
interdisciplinary researchers, to be transparent in their biases. (Note:
Postmodernists encourage this practice as well, and more authors are starting
to make such disclosures.) Second, researcher bias should be included in the
criteria we use to evaluate our own work, as well as the work of others.

How Has the Research Process
Influenced Your *Perception* of
Disciplinary Perspective and Expertise?

Second, interdisciplinary reflection involves considering how the research
process has influenced your perception of disciplinary perspective and expertise.
A premise of interdisciplinary studies is that viewing a complex problem
from multiple disciplinary perspectives is essential in order to develop a more
comprehensive understanding of it. Interdisciplinary research draws on and
leverages disciplinary research, which is produced by humans with limited
perceptual and cognitive capabilities. It is appropriate, therefore, to state how
you may at first have overestimated, or underestimated, the ability of particular
disciplines and their experts to know enough about the problem under study.
In other words, *interdisciplinary reflection involves articulating your awareness
of the limitations and benefits of the contributing disciplines and how the disciplines
intertwine.* Interdisciplinary work, say Boix Mansilla, Duraisingh, Wolfe, and
Haynes (2009), requires a "careful evaluation of disciplinary insights for their
potential contributions and limitations" (p. 345).

How Has an Interdisciplinary
Approach Enlarged Your Understanding
of the Problem *as a Whole*?

Third, interdisciplinary reflection asks you to consider how an interdisciplinary
approach has enlarged your understanding of the problem *as a whole*. Granted,
we did not create common ground or perform integration and thus produce a
more comprehensive understanding called for in the more advanced conception
of the Broad Model (the focus of Repko and Szostak's, 2016, *Interdisciplinary*

Research: Process and Theory, 3rd ed.). Nevertheless, performing the STEPS of the Broad Model has advanced our knowledge of the problem in significant ways: by comparing disciplinary perspectives on it, by critically analyzing disciplinary insights relevant to it, and by identifying how these insights conflict. This analysis is something disciplinarians do not do but which interdisciplinarians must do because it is basic to interdisciplinary research.

This preparatory work constitutes a cognitive advancement for four reasons. First, it reveals the essential disciplinary *components* of the problem. Second, it introduces the research *process* used (e.g., the STEP approach of the Broad Model). Third, it informs us about the power of *perspective taking* (both disciplinary and interdisciplinary). Fourth, it amounts to consciously taking concrete steps that move us toward creating common ground and performing integration. Together, these aspects of the interdisciplinary research process and the cognitive activity involved in performing the STEPS of the Broad Model enable us to see the problem as a complex whole and open a pathway to a more comprehensive understanding of it.

How Is an Interdisciplinary Approach Applicable Beyond the Classroom?

Finally, interdisciplinary reflection involves considering how an interdisciplinary approach is applicable to the world beyond the classroom. This brings us back to Chapter 1, which connects interdisciplinary learning and research to the real world, and to Chapter 4, which connects interdisciplinarity to the development and application of certain abilities, values, traits, and skills. Evidence is mounting that traditional ways of knowing, of generating knowledge, and of framing public discourse about the great issues of our time are no longer adequate. Interdisciplinarity is an idea whose time has come.

The Broad Model Rubric Applied to STEP 6

Applying the Broad Model Rubric (see Figure 12.3) will further develop your ability to think like an interdisciplinarian as you apply it to reflective statements written by practitioners and students, preparing you to evaluate the quality of your own work. Examples No. 1 and No. 2 are of practitioner work, and Example No. 3 is of student work.

Van der Lecq reveals no prior bias concerning her subject. However, she appreciates the "rich diversity of [disciplinary] perspectives regarding all aspects of language" and explains in the first two paragraphs how an interdisciplinary approach has enlarged her understanding of the complex problem of human language. Finally, van der Lecq explains how an interdisciplinary approach is applicable beyond her work: "Interdisciplinarians interested in language can use their integrative skills to create more comprehensive understandings on all [its] aspects" (pp. 221–222).

Figure 12.3 The Broad Model Rubric (STEP 6)

THE BROAD MODEL RUBRIC (STEP 6)		
ID PROCESS	CRITERIA	Y/N/I
STEP 6		
Reflect on how using an interdisciplinary approach has enlarged your understanding of the problem.	**Reflects on how interdisciplinary process has enlarged your understanding of the problem**	
	6.1. The author explains how an interdisciplinary approach challenged his or her bias on the problem.	
	6.2. The author explains how an interdisciplinary approach has influenced his or her perception of disciplinary expertise.	
	6.3. The author explains how an interdisciplinary approach has enlarged his or her understanding of the problem as a whole.	
	6.4 The author explains how an interdisciplinary approach is applicable beyond the classroom.	

Example No. 1 From the Sciences
Title: "Why We Talk: An Interdisciplinary Approach to the Evolutionary Origin of Language" (2012)
Author: Ria van der Lecq

Van der Lecq reflects on how using an interdisciplinary approach has enlarged her understanding of why humans talk.

In this interdisciplinary study we have developed a comprehensive theory explaining the primary function of language in an evolutionary framework. The original aim of this project was to integrate insights on the origin and development of language, but a preliminary literature search revealed that this would be overly ambitious.

Many scientists have studied language for many years, with the result that the literature is enormous. The focus on the question *why* we talk made the task manageable. . . .

According to our new theory, the most likely function for which language emerged is social bonding, but, once the possibility of linguistic communication had emerged, its primary function may have differed for different individuals, as it does today. Language is used for the exchange of very complicated thoughts, but it also serves as a "bonding" instrument in various contexts, social as well as political. Further study might fruitfullyexamine the role of reciprocal altruism in the emergence of speech.

The focus of this study was on one aspect of the origin of language, the question of *why* we talk. There is, however, a rich diversity of perspectives regarding all aspects of language, its nature, its origin (how and when) and its development. Interdisciplinarians interested in language can use their integrative skills to create more comprehensive understandings on all [its] aspects.

THE BROAD MODEL RUBRIC (STEP 6)		
ID PROCESS	**CRITERIA**	**Y/N/I**
STEP 6		
Reflect on how using an interdisciplinary approach has enlarged your understanding of the problem.	**Reflects on how interdisciplinary process has enlarged your understanding of the problem**	
	6.1. The author explains how an interdisciplinary approach challenged his or her bias on the problem.	N
	6.2. The author explains how an interdisciplinary approach has influenced his or her perception of disciplinary expertise.	Y
	6.3. The author explains how an interdisciplinary approach has enlarged his or her understanding of the problem as a whole.	Y
	6.4 The author explains how an interdisciplinary approach is applicable beyond the classroom.	Y

Example No. 2 From the Social Sciences, the Humanities, and the Applied Fields

Title: "Jewish Marriage as an Expression of Israel's Conflicted Identity" (2012)
Author: Marilyn R. Tayler

The integrative process provides a paradigm for producing an interdisciplinary understanding of the institution of Jewish marriage reflecting Israel's conflicted identity as a Jewish and democratic state. The problem is complex and cannot be comprehended without taking into account the perspectives and insights of different disciplines. The unique contribution of the interdisciplinary approach is found in the second part of the process, through the achievement of integration. Here, conflicts were found between "religious-based insights" and "civil rights violation insights." Since Israel does not have separation of religion and state, the situation is complex. Creating common ground bridges the perspectives of religion, politics, and law, to achieve an understanding that no one discipline could produce. Integration builds upon the secular nature of the state, the need to ensure the civil liberties of all citizens, and the deference to be paid to religion in certain aspects of Israeli life. The possibility of fruitful compromise through the introduction of civil marriage does not impede religious marriage but it does provide an alternative. The present study lays the foundation for the application of its process and findings to another great problem of civic inequality, the situation of Israeli Arabs. Thus, the institution of Jewish marriage provides a model for an interdisciplinary approach to other aspects of Israel's conflicted identity as a Jewish and democratic state.

In this example, *you* are to complete the missing evaluation of each criterion in the right-hand column. Tayler reveals no prior bias concerning her subject.

THE BROAD MODEL RUBRIC (STEP 6)		
ID PROCESS	**CRITERIA**	**Y/N/I**
STEP 6		
Reflect on how using an interdisciplinary approach has enlarged your understanding of the problem.	**Reflects on how interdisciplinary process has enlarged your understanding of the problem**	
	6.1. The author explains how an interdisciplinary approach challenged his or her bias on the problem.	N

THE BROAD MODEL RUBRIC (STEP 6)		
ID PROCESS	CRITERIA	Y/N/I
	6.2. The author explains how an interdisciplinary approach has influenced her perception of disciplinary expertise.	
	6.3. The author explains how an interdisciplinary approach has enlarged her understanding of the problem as a whole.	
	6.4. The author explains how an interdisciplinary approach is applicable beyond the classroom.	

Example No. 3 Student Paper

Title: *Nurse Burnout: An Integrative Approach to a Multidimensional Problem* (n.d.)

Author: K. A. McKay

To approach the problem of nurse burnout from just a single discipline would unjustly limit the research findings to a one-dimensional perspective. The purpose of integrating the different disciplinary approaches is to come to a new understanding, and therefore, a new perspective in which to formulate solid solutions. Hospital administrators and nursing supervisors must be able to understand that sociologically, the nursing environment plays a big part in the negative psychological effects it can create. This includes understanding the day-to-day critical decision-making process nurses endure and the impact of the personal responsibility involved in making ethical choices.

Because the problem of nurse burnout is viewed from different disciplines, the various perspectives have allowed for a more comprehensive and integrative approach to understanding the causes, without the constraints of disciplinary boundaries. By first examining and then integrating the sociological, psychological and ethical implications behind burnout, the big picture becomes much clearer, allowing for a comprehensive understanding of how and why burnout occurs.

In this example, *you* are to supply the missing evaluation of each criterion in the right-hand column.

THE BROAD MODEL RUBRIC (STEP 6)		
ID PROCESS	**CRITERIA**	**Y/N/I**
STEP 6		
Reflect on how using an interdisciplinary approach has enlarged your understanding of the problem.	**Reflects on how interdisciplinary process has enlarged your understanding of the problem**	
	6.1. The author explains how an interdisciplinary approach challenged his or her bias on the problem.	
	6.2. The author explains how an interdisciplinary approach has influenced his or her perception of disciplinary expertise.	
	6.3. The author explains how an interdisciplinary approach has enlarged his or her understanding of the problem as a whole.	
	6.4 The author explains how an interdisciplinary approach is applicable beyond the classroom.	

Conclusion

By now you will agree that interdisciplinary learning and research is unlike any disciplinary learning and research you may have experienced. Though a challenging enterprise, the interdisciplinary research process is manageable and easy to understand if it is broken down into discrete actions we call STEPS. The Broad Model Rubric is particularly helpful because it references the criteria associated with each STEP. Additionally, by referring back to the comprehensive descriptions of each STEP detailed in Chapters 10 through 12, you will be able to reflect on your work after you complete each STEP to make sure you have not overlooked a criterion or addressed it with insufficient detail. Hopefully, your experience of reading this book and applying its principles has made you a more discerning and self-aware reader. You may not have considered the applicability of such an academic exercise beyond the classroom. Increasingly, however, it is just this kind of scrutiny and self-conscious examination of all aspects of a complex problem that is necessary if you are to approach such problems in a way that will yield new understandings and comprehensive solutions.

CRITICAL THINKING QUESTIONS

1. For any one of the three examples (language, Jewish marriage, nurse burnout) provided above of identifying conflicts in disciplinary insights, try to map the identified conflicts as recommended in Chapter 8.

2. Reflect on how insights regarding computer-assisted education may have evolved since the stark disagreement we identified earlier.

3. Reflect on how your understanding of the Broad Model might aid you in your future career.

4. In a group, sketch how you might pursue a Broad Model approach to a public policy challenge of the group's choosing.

APPENDIXES

APPENDIX A

INTELLECTUAL AUTOBIOGRAPHY

This appendix includes the following:

> Content and Format Guidelines
>
> Sample A: Grading Rubric
>
> Sample B: Sample Student Intellectual Autobiography With Grading Rubric Applied

(Note to instructors: The points assigned to each aspect in the model grading rubric will vary from instructor to instructor. Some instructors may wish to modify the rubric as well as the points assigned to each aspect. The content of the intellectual autobiography assumes that the student is enrolled in an interdisciplinary studies program which allows students to personalize their program of study.)

Content and Format Guidelines

Your instructor will provide guidelines for the intellectual autobiography and will likely ask that it include the following elements:

- Your place and date of birth
- Key events in your life
- Influential people and ideas
- Your current worldview (ideas about politics, religion, the environment, social issues, etc., and how they evolved)
- Your intellectual journey prior to interdisciplinary studies
- Why you chose interdisciplinary studies, how it has changed your view of yourself, of others, and of the world
- How you plan to use the course work in your program of study

It is useful to read other people's intellectual autobiographies before writing your own. Here are two examples that are well worth reading: Sternberg, G.

"From Intelligence to Leadership: A Brief Intellectual Autobiography," *Gifted Child Quarterly*, Volume 55, issue 4 (October 2011), 309–312; Lin, M. (2000). *Boundaries.* New York, NY: Simon & Schuster Paperbacks.

As an alternative to writing the traditional prose narrative autobiography, you might choose to construct a *visual* intellectual autobiography. A visual intellectual autobiography contains all the elements required in a prose narrative response (including critical thinking, self-reflection, and metacognition). But rather than being entirely dependent upon prose narrative, it uses your choice of visual media, accompanied, if necessary, by explanatory notes. For example, you could create a cognitive map or mind map using one of a host of free mind mapping software products to illustrate your intellectual journey in words and pictures. Figure A.1 is the beginning of a mind map that would be accompanied by explanatory notes or embedded audio information, which expands upon the images and text provided.

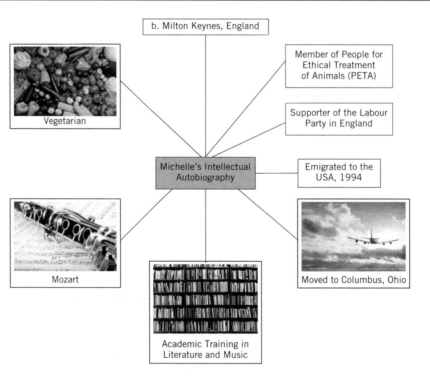

Figure A.1   Intellectual Autobiography as Cognitive or Mind Map

Sources: (Clockwise from bottom): ©iStockphoto.com/luoman; ©iStockphoto.com/filipfoto; ©iStockphoto.com/mediaphotos; ©iStockphoto.com/anyaberkut.

Alternatively, you could create a video documentary where you narrate your intellectual journey with appropriate accompanying visual images. You could combine formats by embedding links to videos in your cognitive/mind map or even in your prose narrative. The format of the intellectual autobiography is less important than the thought processes that underpin it. Choose a format that allows you to be authentic and demonstrate your development as an interdisciplinarian.

SAMPLE A: Grading Rubric

INTELLECTUAL AUTOBIOGRAPHY
SAMPLE GRADING RUBRIC

Section: _____
Student Name: _____

VALUE: 25 Points (25% total value of course)

INTELLECTUAL AUTOBIOGRAPHY		
ASPECT	**CRITERIA**	**POINTS**
Introduction		**(2 pts)**
Work is prefaced or contexualized so that the audience is aware of its purpose and is sufficiently engaged to proceed.	Audience is able to determine the purpose of work via written introduction or other appropriate cues. Written or visual introductory cues are engaging and creative.	
Learning Outcomes		**(20 pts)**
Create an engaging and comprehensive intellectual autobiography.	All major elements of Intellectual Autobiography (i.e., elements that have bearing on the author's worldview or affinity with interdisciplinary studies) are present, which may include but is not limited to • Place and date of birth • Upbringing and early education • Academic interests • Influential ideas • Hobbies, pursuits • Worldview (religion, politics, social concerns, etc.) • Interest in particular "big idea" • Traits and skills of an interdisciplinarian already identified • Interdisciplinary traits and skills that are interesting (you look forward to developing these skills and traits), and why they are of interest/importance to you • Concentrations chosen for interdisciplinary study (if appropriate) • How these concentrations might be applied in an interdisciplinary project **(6 pts)**	

INTELLECTUAL AUTOBIOGRAPHY		
ASPECT	**CRITERIA**	**POINTS**
Describe the traits and skills that interdisciplinary learning fosters, and identify where you see an affinity between these skills and your own particular characteristics.	Successfully identifies the traits and skills that interdisciplinary learning fosters. Reflects on where there is an affinity with these characteristics. **(2 pts)**	
Demonstrate the following higher order thinking skills: • Strong-sense critical thinking • Self-reflection • Metacognition	Successfully identifies own biases and values and articulates why this is important to interdisciplinary work. Successfully reflects on own attitudes and worldview. Is able to identify why this self-reflection is relevant to interdisciplinary work. Successfully identifies and describes attitudes/worldview and thought processes in a detached way, perhaps tracing them to their origins and/or predicting how these attitudes/worldview may affect interdisciplinary work. Is able to explain why metacognition is relevant to effective interdisciplinary research. **(12 pts)**	
Conventions and Presentation		**(3 pts)**
Conventions for **prose narrative** intellectual autobiography **(1.5 pts)**	Complies with APA guidelines concerning quotations and citations **(.5 pt)** Acknowledges all sources and cites them properly **(.5 pt)** Formats paper according to APA guidelines **(.5 pt)**	
Writing—for **prose narrative** response **(1.5 pts)**	Uses clear, precise language—strong verbs, nouns, and adjectives **(.5 pt)** Demonstrates a consistent command of spelling, punctuation, capitalization, grammar, word usage, and sentence structure **(1 pt)**	
Conventions for **visual** intellectual autobiography **(1.5 pts)**	Complies with APA guidelines concerning quotations and citations **(.5 pt)** Acknowledges all sources and cites them properly **(.5 pt)** Professional presentation reflecting relevant best practices for chosen medium **(.5 pt)**	
Presentation—for **visual** intellectual autobiography **(1.5 pts)**	Clear and creative depiction of information using chosen medium **(.5 pt)** Accurate writing, where present **(1 pt)**	
	TOTAL POINTS	

SAMPLE B: Sample Student Intellectual Autobiography With Grading Rubric Applied

Assignment 2-4: Intellectual Autobiography
Maria Dunham
IDST300-F1WW Introduction to Interdisciplinary Studies
Prof. Jean Parker
July 24, 2011

Where Am I From?

"I was born in the Philippines."

These six words reveal so much and, at the same time, so little. They answer the inevitable question of "Where are you from?" when meeting someone new. "Oh," most would reply, drawing their conclusions and filling in the rest.

Yes, I was born in the Philippines; a beautiful archipelago in the west Pacific was indeed my birthplace. This statement explains my physical appearance, my Asian features. It gives me a geographical location, a *hometown*. It confers on me an "exotic" cultural background, a different worldview, a firsthand perspective on important global issues such as poverty and overpopulation. In short, it gives me an identity, a neat life story.

Yet on a deeper level, I cannot truthfully say that I am *from* the Philippines. I am a child of not one, but of several diverse cultures. I had left the country when I was 8 years old. I became a global nomad, living the life of an adventurer and always anticipating change at the turn of each year. From Honduras to California, to Hawaii then back to the Philippines, then on to Thailand and eventually to Ohio. . . . I have travelled many miles and called all of these places my home. It is this collection of places that can truly help answer where I am from.

What Is Important to Me?

Our childhood experiences have helped shape who we are as people today. My experiences are not an exception. The cultures I had been immersed in have greatly influenced my personality and values. Each has left its own strong, indelible impression. They have also helped me be more sensitive to differences in people and societies, be appreciative of the diversity found in the United States, and value flexibility and adaptability. These are interdisciplinary characteristics that I have had to learn by necessity, but have come to greatly appreciate over time (Augsburg, 2006).

According to the Character Strengths results from the University of Pennsylvania's Authentic Happiness website, my greatest character strength is "love." I agree. It is not actually the places I have been to that have had the greatest impact on me. It is the memories of the people whom I have cared for and who have shared part of their lives with me that I treasure the most. It is this close relationship with others, rather than spirituality and religiousness, that gives me purpose and provides meaning.

One such meaningful part of my life is family. In part, this attachment may be the result of the close familial ties fostered by Asian culture. I place high value on affection, love, and loyalty—qualities my parents have displayed in abundance. I recognize the many sacrifices they went through to provide for me a good education, a place to call home, and a healthy diet. Changing countries and schools every two years was stressful while growing up, but with their care and guidance, I was able to live a stable and happy life.

I tried to emulate my parents' kindness by moving to Ohio and providing similar support to my grandfather. I consider it my duty and a privilege to be able to look after him and provide him some companionship. To my family and relatives, I am someone whom they can trust, a person they can lean on for comfort. I relish this role, and am grateful to be of service to my loved ones.

My decision to stay in Ohio proved to be life-changing—not just personally, but professionally as well. It helped push me to pursue a more creative career and to help turn my attention back to academics.

Interdisciplinary Studies

When I was first introduced to Interdisciplinary Studies as a program of study, I did not seriously consider it. I was committed to pursuing an education in business administration. It had been my choice of study at my previous college in Thailand, and I wanted to finish what I had started.

However, after much contemplation, I took a step back and reassessed my future. I had been out of school for several years, and it felt foolish to box myself in simply because of the past. I wanted to learn new things, to dedicate my efforts to subjects that were really what I wanted to study. Education would be my new adventure, and the interdisciplinary studies focus areas being offered afforded me the flexibility to set my own path.

I took a risk, and set my heart on global business and web design. More than the other subjects, these two focus areas interested me the most. And I could see the potential applications both could have in the future. In an increasingly globalized world, I wanted to study the effects of technology, design, as well as culture and business in everyone's lives. I recognized the need for an interdisciplinary approach to addressing global communication problems online.

I had actually begun freelancing as a web designer several years before. The design projects I took on played well to my strengths: appreciation for beauty and excellence, as well as creativity, ingenuity, and originality. But having been largely self-taught, I wanted to formally learn the design principles that would help me gain greater competency in the field. It was not enough to simply know best design practices. I needed to understand why certain colors evoked particular moods and how copyright law affects my work. And with clients from countries as far away as Australia and as near as Canada, I also found it necessary to be able to communicate and conduct business on a global scale.

Some of the real-world interdisciplinary problems I most want to address, however, are not directly related to my work. Large global issues such as poverty and greater autonomy for women, particularly mothers, have always interested me. There are numerous organizations, some local, conducting charity work that directly benefit poverty-stricken areas and women. They work beyond and across national borders, but have no presence on the web. I want to be able to provide them a gateway to new opportunities and to provide them a way to communicate their mission and vision to the world.

Conclusion

My path to interdisciplinarity has not been straightforward, but looking at my life so far, it seems natural. Having been blessed with a rich and diverse background at a young age, I took an interest in the environments around me and grew to love seeing situations and issues from multiple perspectives simultaneously. The world showed me seemingly endless possibilities and cultivated my mind to seek broad interests. I'm convinced that choosing to pursue my studies and learn about subjects I was truly interested in was the right decision. I look forward to using the graphic design skills I have been practicing, acquiring greater understanding of global issues, and applying the concepts from marketing and finance in my future career as a web designer, entrepreneur, and volunteer.

APPENDIX B

STUDENT PORTFOLIOS AND BLOGGING

This appendix includes the following:

- Sample A: Portfolio Grading Rubric
- Sample B: Extracts From a Student e-Portfolio
- Sample C: Extract from a Sample Blog Site
- Portfolio Types, Guidelines, and Content
- E-Portfolios, Blogging, and Thinking About Security

(Note to instructors: The points assigned to each aspect in the Portfolio Grading Rubric will vary from instructor to instructor. Some instructors may wish to modify the rubric as well as points assigned to each aspect.)

SAMPLE A: Portfolio Grading Rubric

IDS____
PORTFOLIO GRADING RUBRIC

Section: ____
Student Name: _____

VALUE: 25 Points (25% total value of course)

PORTFOLIO		
ASPECT	**CRITERIA**	**POINTS**
Introduction		(1 pt)
Work is prefaced or contexualized so that the audience is aware of its purpose and is sufficiently engaged to proceed.	• Audience is able to determine the purpose of work via written introduction or other appropriate cues. • Written or visual introductory cues are engaging and creative.	
Learning Outcomes		(19 pts)
Created an engaging and comprehensive portfolio designed for a specific audience. (Note: depending on the intended use for the portfolio, the learning outcomes and criteria will change. The sample provided is for a portfolio used for internal program assessment purposes.)	All major elements of portfolio are present, which may include but is not limited to • Landing page—provides context and purpose for portfolio (e.g., electronic resume, application for graduate school, capstone requirement, etc.) (**1pt**) • List of courses taken for focus areas/concentrations and goal for capstone integration of these areas (**1pt**) IDST PROGRAM OUTCOMES: • Communicate effectively • Think critically • Demonstrate ethical decision making • Apply interdisciplinary thinking • Integrate knowledge from different disciplines • Solve or respond to a complex problem • Conduct effective academic research • All program outcomes addressed (at least one artifact uploaded, narrative reflection provided, where possible an example of an early and later piece of work provided for each outcome—narrative compares work and identifies specific areas of improvement) (**8 pts**)	

PORTFOLIO		
ASPECT	**CRITERIA**	**POINTS**
	• Program reflection (includes reflection on internship/service learning/capstone project where appropriate) (**2 pts**)	
	• Honors, certificates, and testimonials (**1 pt**)	
	(**13 pts**)	
Demonstrate the following higher order thinking skills: • Self-reflection • Critical thinking • Metacognition	• Artifacts intentionally chosen to provide comprehensive picture of abilities (**2 pts**)	
	• Demonstrated ability to analyze requirements of portfolio for given audience and evaluate best artifacts for selection (**2 pts**)	
	• Awareness of learning process. Thoughtful comments on what has been learned and what might be improved (**2 pts**)	
	(**6 pts**)	
Conventions and Presentation		(**5 pts**)
Conventions for **best practice in web design**	• Effective use of white space and layout—avoidance of scrolling, effective chunking of text for web viewing (**.5 pt**)	
	• Consistent naming convention for linked documents (**.25 pt**)	
	• Effective and relevant use of images (**.25 pt**)	
	• All links functional (**.25 pt**)	
	• Clear navigation (**.25 pt**)	
	• Appropriate font (readability) for audience and destination device (**.5 pt**)	
	(**2 pts**)	
Writing	• Uses clear, precise language—strong verbs, nouns, and adjectives (**.5 pt**)	
	• Demonstrates a consistent command of spelling, punctuation, capitalization, grammar, word usage, and sentence structure (**1 pt**)	
	• Complies with APA* guidelines concerning quotations and citations (**1 pt**)	
	• Acknowledges all sources and cites them properly (**.5 pt**)	
	(**3 pts**)	
	TOTAL POINTS	

*We recognize that some instructors will have other preferences.

For additional information on **grading rubrics** for portfolios, see Stefani, Mason, and Pegler's (2008) excellent chapter on "E-portfolios and assessment of student learning," which includes a comprehensive four-point scale rubric (p. 82).

SAMPLE B: Extracts From a Student e-Portfolio

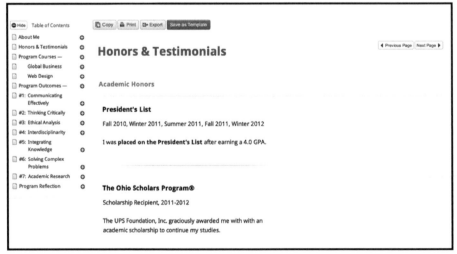

Source: Created by Maria Dunham on http://www.livetext.com.

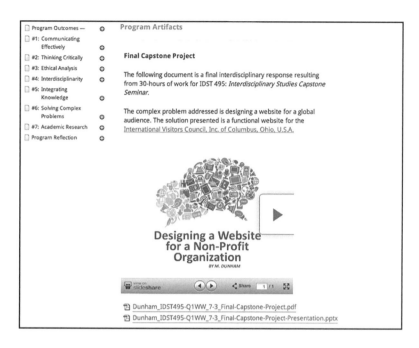

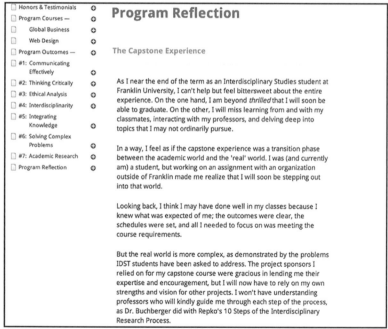

Source: Created by Maria Dunham on http://www.livetext.com. Image of speech bubbles (top) from http://www.istockphoto.com/vector/conversation-speech-bubbles-gm481967741-15086443.

Portfolio Types, Guidelines, and Content

Stefani et al. (2008) identify six different kinds of portfolio:

1. Assessment—used to demonstrate achievement against some criteria

2. Presentation—used to evidence learning in a persuasive way, often related to professional qualifications

3. Learning—used to document, guide, and advance learning over time

4. Personal development—related to professional development and employment

5. Multiple owner—allow more than one person to participate in development of content

6. Working—combine previous types, with one or more e-portfolios and also a wider archive to provide evidence of learning at work (pp. 13–14)

Your professor will provide you guidelines for your portfolio, which may be a combination of several of the portfolio types listed earlier, but as with all projects, its purpose and proposed audience will affect the way in which you organize and structure your work. For example, a portfolio designed as an electronic résumé will be a showcase of your best work, skills, and aptitudes. It is less likely, therefore, to include works in progress, complete with feedback and comments, and it may be less dependent on program outcomes and assessment rubrics that are more relevant and recognizable to an academic audience.

Certain elements are common to many interdisciplinary studies program portfolios:

- An "about me" or "about this portfolio" page, where the portfolio is given context for the audience, including its purpose

- An explanation of interdisciplinary studies captured in a 30-second explanation called an "elevator speech" (named after the short duration of a typical elevator ride during which you may have an opportunity to pitch your "big idea" to a decision maker)

- Courses completed in the major, concentrations, or focus areas

- A sample of work from each course that demonstrates mastery of the course's learning outcomes and a narrative that explains how these samples are relevant to the program as a whole

- Interdisciplinary research or capstone project illustrating how the concentrations or focus areas were integrated to address a complex problem and/or illustrating the interdisciplinary research process

- Samples of work from early in the student's academic career compared with work from the senior year with a narrative identifying how the work has evolved

- Letters of recommendation, certificates, or important documents such as transcripts, military documents (DD214), etc.

- Evidence from a service-learning project or internship

- Reflections on the program

E-Portfolios, Blogging, and Thinking About Security

E-portfolios

The emergence of the e-portfolio has revolutionized the way portfolios are used in teaching and learning. Like their paper-based predecessors, e-portfolios can reflect work from an individual course or the learning outcomes of an entire program. Competencies that had previously eluded capture in a paper or on a test may now be incorporated in the form of multimedia, links to videos of presentations, speeches, performance art (recorded and uploaded to YouTube or TeacherTube, etc.), documents and slideshows with audio narration, as well as photographs and recorded musical compositions. The ability to design the look and feel of the portfolio also provides another avenue for students who want to personalize their "e-presence," to shape the way they present themselves to internal and external audiences, and to link to the ever-proliferating possibilities of social networks.

Some e-portfolio products include commenting tools, peer review access, and sharing capabilities that facilitate team collaboration. E-portfolios also relieve many of the logistical challenges and stressors associated with the transportation and storage of their unwieldy, paper-based predecessors.

However, along with these almost limitless possibilities for expression, mobility, and enhanced opportunities for student–professor and student–student collaboration comes the challenge of security, an issue raised by numerous authors and summarized succinctly by Tanya Augsburg (2003, p. 116) in "Becoming Interdisciplinary. The Student Portfolio in the Bachelor of Interdisciplinary Studies Program at Arizona State University."

While security concerns have certainly not disappeared in the subsequent decade, a vibrant emergent market in e-portfolio software and web hosting products has provided many choices to students and professors who wish to incorporate e-portfolios into their programs without compromising security for sensitive student information.

The sample e-portfolio provided in this Appendix was composed using a purchased product called "LiveText,"[1] a web-based e-portfolio solution where students may provide external viewers with a "visitor pass," which can be revoked at any time at the student's request using his or her user ID and password from any computer with Internet access.

Although students should always be cautioned that once shared, an e-portfolio's content cannot be completely safeguarded, products like LiveText do provide a greater level of security than do the many free e-portfolio-authoring tools currently available. Additionally, the technical support provided by such purchased products can mitigate the potential disasters inherent in technology when it is used to house irreplaceable student work samples. It also puts the responsibility for resolving many of the time-consuming problems with such technology (forgotten passwords, compatibility with individual PCs, Macs, and ever-proliferating mobile devices) into the hands of product customer support instead of those of the teaching faculty.

E-portfolios certainly provide exciting opportunities for teaching and learning, but as with all new technological advances, it is best to choose software with caution and implement the solution that best suits the purpose and audience for which they are intended.

---

1. There are numerous membership-type e-portfolio products currently on the market. LiveText and Task Stream are two such products. In 2015–2016, the student cost to purchase a 5-year membership of LiveText or TaskStream was approximately $130. This membership can be renewed or the portfolios exported before the membership expires.

Blogging

Blogging (web logging) became increasingly popular in the early 2000s, with interest peaking in a readership that exceeded 57 million American adults and over 12 million authors (Lenhart & Fox, 2006, p. i). Despite that number declining with the advent of social media, this is a known and thriving technology; students either have their own blogs or have created them in other classes. This often makes the creation of a blog page more attractive for students than purchasing an e-portfolio product for three reasons: First, it is a familiar technology; second, it is used extensively in the workplace,[2] so creating and updating blog pages is often considered a transferrable and marketable skill; and, third, unlike the e-portfolio software described earlier, it is free.

One of the most popular blogging software products is WordPress, which can be accessed at www.wordpress.com (not to be confused with wordpress.org, which does not provide web hosting services). Other blogging products such as Wix .com and Google's Blogger.com are also free and easy to use. Since many blogging software products are web based, there is no software to purchase or download. However, students must create their own accounts with no administrative access possible for the faculty member, so password and account maintenance is entirely in the hands of the student.

---

2. Large corporations and organizations have used WordPress to create their web presence. These include BBC America and *The New Yorker Magazine*, Best Buy, and Reuters Blog site among many others. (Source: http://www.wpbeginner.com/showcase/40-most-notable-big-name-brands-that-are-using-wordpress/ [last accessed 5/27/2016]).

SAMPLE C: Extract From a Sample Blog Site

Figure B.1: Class website created using WordPress.com. Class blogs can then be linked to this page so that students may view and discuss each other's work. A digital résumé page may be shared by copying the URL of the page and e-mailing it to prospective employers.

Welcome to BIS201

DECEMBER 21, 2014 / 1 COMMENT / EDIT

BLOGS I FOLLOW

You are not yet following any blogs. Try finding your fr... or check out our

Source: https://wordpress.com/.

I have found the WordPress software easy to learn, and a page can be created and customized in about 10 minutes. There are numerous free tutorials available to assist students, although they are rarely required. Using this software, students may upload pictures and assignments and participate in discussions of their work with others.

Thinking about Security

With increasing advances in blogging software, it is now possible to limit the degree to which uninvited viewers may view student work. A setting is available on WordPress to limit page viewing. However, as with all web pages, it is almost impossible to control exactly what may be viewed and by whom. Purchased packages like LiveText do offer more stringent safeguards for privacy, but students should always proceed with caution when posting any personal information online.

Figure B.2: Privacy settings are also available in WordPress that make it more difficult for students' work to be viewed by unintended audiences.

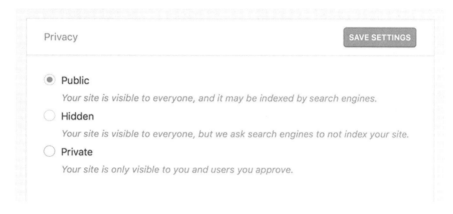

WordPress.com   Features

→ *Configuration*

Settings » Privacy Settings

The Privacy setting controls who can view your site, allowing you to make the site private or public. To access this setting, go to **My Site** → **Settings** and look for **Privacy**.

Privacy	SAVE SETTINGS

⦿ **Public**
  Your site is visible to everyone, and it may be indexed by search engines.

◯ **Hidden**
  Your site is visible to everyone, but we ask search engines to not index your site.

◯ **Private**
  Your site is only visible to you and users you approve.

Source: https://wordpress.com/.

APPENDIX C

SERVICE LEARNING, INTERNSHIPS, AND ALTERNATIVE PROJECTS FOR NONTRADITIONAL STUDENTS

This Appendix includes the following:

> Part I: Service learning
>
> Part II: Internships
>
> Part III: Alternative Projects for Nontraditional Students

This Appendix includes documents, guidelines, and information for students and other stakeholders in service-learning or internship projects as well as grading rubrics and sample projects. The samples may be adapted for use by faculty, but they are provided to inform students about the internship and service-learning process. Because the definition of what constitutes service learning or an internship experience may vary from one institution to another, you should consult with your university to ensure that any proposed service-learning or internship project meets the requirements for that institution and that the project itself meets university or graduation requirements.

In light of the growing number of nontraditional students who also seek to benefit from service-learning and internship opportunities, Part III of this Appendix contains examples of a project proposal, a sample project sponsor letter, sample projects, and a grading rubric and how that grading rubric might be applied to projects that accommodate the needs of nontraditional students.

PART I—SERVICE LEARNING

The following sample documents are provided in this section:

- SAMPLE A: INFORMATION FOR STUDENTS ABOUT SERVICE LEARNING

- SAMPLE B: SERVICE-LEARNING APPLICATION FORM AND PROPOSAL

- SAMPLE C: SERVICE-LEARNING FAQs
- SAMPLE D: INFORMATION FOR SERVICE-LEARNING SPONSORS
- SAMPLE E: GRADING RUBRIC FOR SERVICE-LEARNING PROJECT

SAMPLE A: INFORMATION
FOR STUDENTS ABOUT SERVICE LEARNING

(Note to instructors: SAMPLE A reflects information to students in a particular program and will vary according to the criteria established by different programs.)

Purpose:

The purpose of the service-learning course is to provide you with an opportunity to apply and further develop the capacities, values, traits, and skills fostered by interdisciplinary studies; enhance your competitive advantage in the job market and/or when applying for graduate study; and provide a meaningful and lasting product or service for the community or organization whom you are serving.

Qualifying for the service-learning course involves the following:

- Prior completion of at least ___ of upper level course work

- Current enrollment in, or prior completion of, IDS ___ or IDS ___

- Current enrollment at the university during the service-learning semester

- A minimum overall GPA of ____ and/or a minimum GPA of ___ in the upper level courses in the program of study

- Completion of the application process during the semester *prior to* the semester of enrolling in the service-learning course

Projects that can be used for service learning:

- Projects appropriate for service learning will be determined by the instructor and meet program and university requirements.

- The project requires a minimum of 140 hours of supervised work for 3 credits, involving about 10 hours per week. **The student must keep a time log**.

- The project must allow the student to apply the intellectual capacities already acquired.

Procedure for applying for IDS 4395:

- Complete the service-learning proposal.
- The service-learning proposal must be completed and approved by the service-learning instructor <u>prior to</u> the student enrolling in the course.

Receiving credit for the service-learning project involves the following:

- A completed service-learning project that counts for 75% of the student's grade for the course
- An essay that counts 25% of the student's grade for the course

SAMPLE B: SERVICE-LEARNING APPLICATION FORM AND PROPOSAL

APPLICATION FORM AND PROPOSAL FOR SERVICE LEARNING

1. STUDENT NAME: _____ DATE: ___/___/____

2. DESCRIPTION OF PROPOSED SERVICE-LEARNING ACTIVITY (USE SINGLE SPACING AND TRY TO INCLUDE ON A SINGLE SHEET):

3. NAME OF ORGANIZATION: _____

4. SPONSOR NAME AND TITLE: _____

    PHONE: _____-_____-_____E-MAIL: _____

5. PROJECT START DATE: _____ PROJECTED COMPLETION DATE: _____

7. STUDENT SIGNATURE: _____ DATE: _____

8. SPONSOR SIGNATURE: _____ DATE: _____

9. INSTRUCTOR APPROVAL: _____ DATE: _____

SAMPLE C: SERVICE-LEARNING FAQs

Q: *What is the interdisciplinary studies service-learning project?*

A: A service-learning project involves receiving academic credit for a particular project that is appropriate to your personal, professional, and/or academic goals.

Q: *Who secures placement in a service-learning activity?*

A: In most cases, you have to secure the service-learning opportunity. You may have a particular organization in mind with which you wish to work or your instructor or the university may have a network of organizations who have presented possible projects from which you may choose.

Q: *What are the qualifications and prerequisites for the service-learning course?*

A: Successful completion of IDS _____ ("B" or better), a 3.0 GPA in program course work, and approval of the service-learning instructor.

Q: *When do I apply?*

A: You must apply for the service-learning course *the semester before the semester of the service-learning course.* This involves (a) securing the service-learning agreement (see Information for Prospective Service-learning Sponsors) and (b) submitting the completed signature page of the <u>Application Form</u> to the service-learning instructor.

Q: *How will my grade for the course be assessed?*

A: Seventy-five percent (75%) of your grade for the course will be based on the service-learning project. Twenty-five percent (25%) of your grade will be based on a 6- to 8-page essay explaining how the service-learning experience has helped to prepare you for your professional or academic goal.

Q: *What if I am unable to complete everything by the end of the semester when grades are due?*

A: Requests for an incomplete must conform to the IDS program's policy as stated in the course syllabus. You must complete all remaining work by the end of the following semester.

Q: *How is this course different from other courses I have taken?*

A: This course is conducted primarily as a distance learning course. The class meets the first day of classes and the final week of classes. The instructor communicates with students primarily through the class electronic mailing list but also through e-mails, phone calls, and occasional personal meetings with students during the semester.

SAMPLE D: INFORMATION
FOR SERVICE-LEARNING SPONSORS

Background: A growing number of the nation's nonprofit and community organizations have service-learning programs for qualified students. The reason is simple: Students possess skill sets that can be applied to complete projects that serve an organization or community and that bring about a long-term improvement in the well-being of that community.

Objective: The Interdisciplinary Studies program at _____ offers qualified students the course IDS ____: SERVICE LEARNING that allows them to receive academic credit for working on a project that is mutually agreed upon by the sponsoring organization or community representative, the student, and the IDS program represented by the service-learning instructor. Student qualifications include a 3.0 GPA in the student's major at the time of application.

Service-Learning Sponsor Responsibilities:

1. The service-learning sponsor is the individual in the service organization who is responsible for developing the service-learning project for the student in consultation with the program instructor. Ideally, the service-learning project should be consistent with the student's program focus and career goal. For example, the student could be asked to develop a fund-raising plan, organize the construction of a safe new playground for a day-care center, and so on. The sponsor must sign the service-learning application form. However, it is the student's responsibility to submit the completed and signed form to the instructor of the service-learning course.

2. The sponsor will use a grading rubric supplied by the service-learning instructor to evaluate the student's progress during the semester and the final project. The sponsor may wish to add criteria to the grading rubric if this is deemed necessary.

3. The sponsor provides a **midterm progress report** either using the grading rubric or summarizing the student's progress in an e-mail to the service-learning instructor. At the end of semester, the sponsor grades the service-learning project using the grading rubric and e-mails it or faxes (FAX #: _____) it to the service-learning instructor. Performance on this project constitutes 75% of the student's grade for the course.

SAMPLE E: Grading Rubric for Service-Learning Project

Grading Scale
Interdisciplinary Service-Learning Project

STUDENT NAME: _____ SEMESTER: _____

ORGANIZATION: _____

PROJECT DESCRIPTION: _____

SPONSOR NAME and TITLE: _____

SPONSOR CONTACT INFORMATION: _____

Sponsor: Please grade student on a scale from 1 to 10 for each Grading Criteria section. The student can earn a total of 100 points. The Final Grade for the project will be based on the total points earned out of 100.

FINAL GRADE

Grading Criteria	Points
The student developed the factual and procedural knowledge required by the project.	
The student decomposed the project into its constituent parts and connected these to relevant disciplinary perspectives.	
The student used perspective taking in working with others on the project.	
The student used critical thinking in approaching the project.	
The student used metacognitive skills to monitor and improve progress on the project.	
The student demonstrated the ability to integrate information and knowledge with on-the-job experience.	
The student proposed one or more solutions to the project.	
The student communicated effectively with the sponsor and others.	
The student complied with the deadlines and standards established by the sponsor.	
The student met the needs of the organization by his or her contribution to the project.	
Total Points: _____ Grade: ____	

<u>Grading Scale:</u>

90–100 points = A; 80–89 points = B; 70–79 points = C; 60–69 points = D; Below 60 points = F

_____   _____
SPONSOR'S Signature   Date

PART II—INTERNSHIPS

(Note to instructors: Samples A–E can be easily modified in most cases by substituting "internship" for "service learning" and so are not reproduced here.)

PART III—ALTERNATIVES FOR NONTRADITIONAL STUDENTS

The following sample documents are provided in this section:

- SAMPLE A: SAMPLE LETTER TO SERVICE-LEARNINGP ROJECT SPONSOR
- SAMPLE B: PROJECT PROPOSAL TEMPLATE
- SAMPLE C: EXAMPLES OF FOCUS AREAS AND PROJECTS USING SPONSORS
- SAMPLE D: SAMPLE GRADING RUBRIC FOR PROJECT

These documents are used in an online interdisciplinary project (a 12-week, 4 credit-hour course) for nontraditional students.

A: SAMPLE LETTER TO SERVICE-LEARNING PROJECT SPONSOR

Date

Dear Project Sponsor,

Thank you for agreeing to lend your knowledge and guidance to a Franklin University Interdisciplinary Studies Major student as he or she completes this project.

Interdisciplinary Studies Major students combine course work from two areas of academic focus to create a highly customized bachelor's degree program. Near the conclusion of their studies, students take this course, which requires them to utilize the knowledge and skills acquired during their focus area studies in the completion of an interdisciplinary project.

The role of the Project Sponsor is an informal one that is largely defined by the student and sponsor. Customarily, project sponsors assist students with identification of project objectives and provide support and guidance during the course of project completion. Sponsors should be able to provide at least 10 to 15 minutes of consultation time to the student each week and discuss the student's progress with me (the instructor) at least once during the 12-week course.

At the beginning of the project, the sponsor communicates his or her approval of the project proposal by sending an e-mail or letter to my attention indicating that the proposal's scope and content is appropriate and feasible within the time restraints of the course. Upon the project's completion, project sponsors also provide students with **a signed letter**, directed to my attention, composed on official letterhead. The letter indicates that the project was completed as proposed, offers observations on the student's performance, and is included in the student's final SAMPLE project. The student will inform you of the due dates for these communications.

Again, thank you for agreeing to be of assistance as this student completes this course requirement for his or her baccalaureate degree. Please contact me with any questions.

Complementary Close
Instructor's Name/Signature
Return address and e-mail

SAMPLE B: PROJECT PROPOSAL TEMPLATE

Miami University
INTERDISCIPLINARY STUDIES: INTERDISCIPLINARY PROJECT PROPOSAL

Guidelines for the Project Proposal

This course involves your planning and implementing a 30 clock-hour project over the course of the next 12 weeks. The intent of the project is for you to demonstrate your ability to think in an interdisciplinary way about a specific complex problem or phenomenon by leveraging your two focus areas as you formulate a solution or response. Your response/research/solution must be supervised by two sponsors (one for each focus area), identified by you, who will validate that the scope and content of your work is appropriate, accurate, and worthwhile.

The project proposal will be captured using this template, which includes a cover page format and six sections as outlined in the following. The actual completed project will be submitted in a separate document.

Note: If you plan to submit a project that refers to or includes any aspect of work proprietary to your place of employment, you must gain permission to do so before you embark on your project plan.

A Project Proposal
for

Miami University

Interdisciplinary Studies: Project

by

Full Name

Term 20xx

SECTION 1

INTRODUCTION

Offer a brief description of the proposed project. The project may propose and/or develop a solution to a problem. Your response should include an explanation of these three things:

- why the topic requires an interdisciplinary response,
- how your two focus areas are relevant in this interdisciplinary response, and
- *briefly* how you predict key theories and approaches or methods within each of your focus areas will be leveraged in your interdisciplinary response.

OBJECTIVES

Provide background information concerning the context and nature of the need or problem to be addressed. Also, clearly and convincingly explain the intended outcomes and benefits.

Clearly identify how courses from your focus areas will be leveraged in the completion of this project.

SECTION 2

SPECIAL CONSIDERATIONS

Describe any anticipated conflicts, difficulties, or extenuating circumstances and explain how these will be addressed.

PERSONAL QUALIFICATIONS

Explain why you are personally qualified to fulfill the requirements of the proposal (e.g., your access to qualified project sponsors, your success/interest in this topic area, your opportunities to apply response or solution in "real-world" environment). Consider current or future opportunities to apply this information. Also consider the instruments you took as part of IDST300 (even perhaps your Intellectual Autobiography)—is there anything you learned from these instruments or assignment that makes it likely that this is a good choice of topic for you?

SECTION 3

PROJECT SPONSORS IDENTIFICATION

Identify the names and qualifications of the two sponsors who will provide oversight and insights for your project. Explain how each sponsor is appropriate to provide such oversight and insight for each focus area.
Focus Area 1

Sponsor name and contact information for Focus Area 1 (i.e., mailing address, telephone number, regularly checked e-mail address):

Qualifications or experience that make this a good choice of sponsor:

List Courses completed within Focus Area 1 (include syllabi—course description and outcomes—for each course):

Focus Area 2

Sponsor name and contact information for Focus Area 2 (i.e., mailing address, telephone number, regularly checked e-mail address):

Qualifications or experience that makes this a good choice of sponsor:

List Courses completed within Focus Area 2 (include syllabi–course description and outcomes—for each course):

SECTION 4

PROJECT SCHEDULE

Date and list the successive tasks and time allocation involved in your proposed project through to completion (30 hours total). The 30 hours may also include the initial planning and research that occur in weeks 1 through 6 of the course. Indicate the resources and equipment necessary for each phase.

Projects must be completed by the date determined between the student and the instructor. If you wish, you may construct a project plan using appropriate software, but the data must be inserted into this document. For example, you could plan out your project as shown.

Purpose of project:
To review the programmer/analyst job description at Acme Corporation, and to develop effective performance criteria to ensure equity in the developmental process.

Focus Areas: Human Resources (HR) and Information Technology (IT)

Week	Task	Detail (Resources/Equipment)	Time Allocated
3	Discussion with HR to discuss the ISS department's needs in relation to my project	Access to HR director (sponsor 1)	1 hour
4	Completion of skills inventory to accurately assess programmer/analyst job description	Old textbooks to acquire information necessary. Use this to help formulate literature review.	3
5	Proposal draft	Finalize literature review.	5
6	Proposal submission	Sponsor sign off complete	5
7	Meet with ISS director to review job description to ensure accuracy and to get feedback on how to design the project checklist.	Access to ISS director (sponsor 2)	3
8	Review Career Architect tool to assign competencies to the project checklist and performance evaluation criteria.	Access to Career Architect tool	4
9	Attend ISS managers' meeting to receive input on project. Begin draft.	Access to ISS managers' meeting	2
10	Finalize feedback on project — make amendments.		5
11	Complete write up of first draft. Gain approval from sponsors.		5
12	Complete final draft for submission and prepare presentation.		2
			Total: 35 hours

All projects are different. Some will take more or less time than the indicated 30 hours. The project plan is designed to help you ensure you have sufficient time to implement your ideas. Your sponsors will be a great help in making this determination. Some of the 30 hours may be allocated to the research and planning process itself, but the allocation of hours for the project does not officially begin until Week 7, which is why this sample project exceeds the 30 hours. Use your best judgment and be realistic.

SECTION 5

LITERATURE SEARCH

List all references you find in your initial literature review, adhering to APA citation guidelines. A complete reference page must be provided with your completed project.

A literature review is meant to provide you with an idea of what is current in the field you are about to study in some depth. For the purposes of your project, it will be useful for you to see who else (if anyone) has examined your topic, or aspects of it, from particular disciplinary perspectives, and how your project might leverage, expand, or even contradict these insights:

- Organize your review by focus area as it relates to your chosen research topic. For example, if your research problem is on American involvement in the Middle East from the focus areas of Social/Behavioral Sciences and Communication Arts, you may want to start with looking at the problem from a sociological, psychological, and then anthropological perspective. Then you could look at journalistic writings on the issue, perhaps looking for elements of bias. Remember, you want to harness the information from your focus areas (and hence the courses you have taken within them) and then decide how you will tackle the research.

- Aim for at least 15 resources in your list. You may include books, journal articles, and websites. All should be current (published within the last 5 years), reliable, and appropriately cited.

- Beneath each source, provide a paragraph summarizing the main content or central theme of the source. Remember, one of the uses of a literature review is a resource to which you can return should you want to revisit a particular source when you are writing up your final project. Take careful, accurate notes of your sources.

SECTION 6

....

PROJECT SPONSOR
ENDORSEMENT OF PROJECT PLAN

Verify that sponsors have approved the project plan.

SAMPLE C: EXAMPLES OF
FOCUS AREAS AND PROJECTS USING SPONSORS

- Web Design and Global Business "Redesigning the Website for an International Nonprofit"
  - Student indentified a client (local nonprofit) and worked with two sponsors: a web design professional and a global business faculty member who was also a volunteer with the nonprofit organization. The client decided to implement the suggested website after its completion.

- Business Administration and Marketing "Amazing Photography: Gaining New Clients Through Interdisciplinary Actions"
  - Student had her own small business but wanted to pursue the venture as her sole method of income. She worked with two sponsors, a successful professional photographer with an MBA, and the owner of Velvet Ice Cream, who provided insights from both marketing and business administration. The student noticed a marked improvement in the number of clients she had even by the end of the 12-week course.

- Sociology and Communication Arts "How Can We Create a Positive Impact on Bullying in Ninth Grade?"
  - Student wants to be a high school teacher and intends to apply for graduate school. She enlisted a communication arts high school teacher and a sociology faculty member to serve as her sponsors and designed a teaching module to identify some of the sociological causes of bullying, using effective communication strategies to teach a module on bullying.

- Public Relations and Psychology "Improving Employee Engagement at XYZ Bank"
  - Working with her supervisor at the bank, this student consulted with a PR professional and psychology PhD student to apply insights to her revision of the annual employee engagement survey. She developed an implementation plan to design questions and draw data from this survey and predicted plans of action that might be used to address these findings and ultimately improve the "engagement score" at the branch.

- Web Design and Communication Arts "Returning to College and to Creativity"
  - Applying insights from these two focus areas, the student designed a web-delivered teaching module to assist working adults as they transitioned to college. The student consulted with a web design professional and a communications faculty member to develop the response.

SAMPLE D: GRADING RUBRIC
FOR SERVICE-LEARNING PROJECT

Grading Rubric—Service-Learning Project

STUDENT NAME: _____ TERM: _____

SPONSOR NAMES: (1) _____ (2) _____

SPONSOR(S) CONTACT INFORMATION: (1) _____
(2) _____

PROJECT TITLE OR DESCRIPTION: _____

GRADING RUBRIC FOR SERVICE-LEARNING PROJECT		
LEARNING OUTCOMES	**CRITERIA**	**POINTS**
Describe the project.	**Introduces the project and states its purpose or objective.**	
	1.1. The student introduces the project and describes its scope.	
	1.2. The student clearly describes his or her role in the project.	
Justify using an interdisciplinary approach.	**Explains how using an interdisciplinary approach helps to understand the project.**	
	2.1. The student establishes that the problem or research question is complex.	
	2.2. The student states or implies that no single discipline is able to address the project *comprehensively*.	
Identify relevant disciplines.	**Identifies the disciplines potentially relevant to the project and then reduces these to those that are most relevant.**	
	3.1. The student identifies the disciplines *potentially* relevant to the problem.	
	3.2. The student narrows these to those that are *most* relevant and explains the basis for doing so.	

GRADING RUBRIC FOR SERVICE-LEARNING PROJECT		
LEARNING OUTCOMES	**CRITERIA**	**POINTS**
Engage in interdisciplinary perspective taking.	**Engages in interdisciplinary perspective taking and comprehensive understanding of the project.**	
	4.1. The student explains interdisciplinary perspective taking and how it helps to understand the project as a whole.	
	4.2. The student applies perspective taking to the task assigned, identifying any limitations of narrow disciplinary approaches to a complex problem that exist or may arise.	
Critically analyze the project.	**Demonstrates the ability to engage in thinking critically about the project.**	
	5.1. The student identifies the disciplinary key elements of the project.	
	5.2. The student maps the project that sets out its disciplinary parts and how these are interconnected or fit together.	
	5.3 The student identifies sources of conflict arising from different disciplinary approaches to the project.	
Reflect on how using an interdisciplinary approach has enlarged your understanding of the project.	**Reflects on how using an interdisciplinary approach has enlarged your understanding of the project.**	
	6.1. The student reflects on his or her bias or the bias of others and how this affected the project.	
	6.2. The student reflects on how an interdisciplinary approach has influenced his or her perception of disciplinary expertise.	
	6.3. The student explains how an interdisciplinary approach has enlarged his or her understanding of the project as a whole.	
	6.4 The student explains how an interdisciplinary approach is applicable beyond the classroom.	

APPENDIX D

THE BROAD MODEL RUBRIC: INSTRUCTOR VERSION AND SAMPLE STUDENT OUTLINE

Legend: Y = Yes; N = No; I = Incomplete information

THE BROAD MODEL RUBRIC (STEPS 1–6)		
ID PROCESS	**CRITERIA**	**Y/N/I**
STEP 1		
Define the problem or state the research question.	**Introduces the problem or research question that is the subject of study and states the purpose or objective of the study**	
	1.1. The student defines the problem or states the research question in a way that is appropriate to interdisciplinary study.	
	1.2. The student clearly defines the scope of the study.	
	1.3. The student avoids the three tendencies that run counter to interdisciplinary process: disciplinary jargon, disciplinary bias, and personal bias.	
	1.4. The student answers the "so what?" question.	
STEP 2		
Justify using an interdisciplinary approach.	**Explains why the problem or research question requires using an interdisciplinary approach**	
	2.1. The student states that the problem or research question is complex and explains what this means.	
	2.2. The student states or implies that there are important insights into the problem offered by two or more disciplines.	
	2.3. The student states or implies that no single discipline has been able to address the problem *comprehensively.*	
	2.4. The student states that the problem addresses an important and as yet unresolved issue concerning nature or society.	

(Continued)

(Continued)

THE BROAD MODEL RUBRIC (STEPS 1–6)		
ID PROCESS	**CRITERIA**	**Y/N/I**
STEP 3		
Identify relevant disciplines.	**Identifies the disciplines potentially relevant to the problem or research question and then reduces these to those that are most relevant**	
	3.1. The student identifies the disciplines *potentially* relevant to the problem.	
	3.2. The student narrows these to those that are *most* relevant and explains the basis for doing so.	
STEP 4		
Conduct a literature search.	**Identifies insights from two or more disciplines, confirming that they are most relevant to the problem**	
	4.1. The student reports that the literature search confirms the identity of the disciplines and their insights that are most relevant to the problem.	
STEP 5		
Critically analyze the disciplinary insights into the problem and locate their sources of conflict.	**Identifies the key elements of insights and locates their sources of conflict**	
	5.1. The student identifies the key elements of the most important disciplinary insights into the problem.	
	5.2. The student identifies both the sources of conflict and/or agreement between insights.	
	5.3. The student maps or compiles a table that sets out how the insights from contributing disciplines are interconnected or fit together.	
STEP 6		
Reflect on how using an interdisciplinary approach has enlarged your understanding of the problem.	**Reflects on how interdisciplinary process has enlarged your understanding of the problem**	
	6.1. The student explains how an interdisciplinary approach challenged his or her bias on the problem.	
	6.2. The student explains how an interdisciplinary approach has influenced his or her perception of disciplinary expertise.	

THE BROAD MODEL RUBRIC (STEPS 1–6)		
ID PROCESS	**CRITERIA**	**Y/N/I**
	6.3. The student explains how an interdisciplinary approach has enlarged his or her understanding of the problem as a whole.	
	6.4 The student explains how an interdisciplinary approach is applicable beyond the classroom.	

Interdisciplinary Research Project:

Factory Farms in the United States
Maria Fox

Step 1: Define the Problem

The research question I decided to pursue is:
Why does the agricultural industry in the United States, particularly factory farms, treat farm animals so poorly and what are the ramifications of such treatment?

Step 2: Justify an Interdisciplinary Response

This topic addresses an important and unresolved issue concerning nature *and* society. This topic also justifies an interdisciplinary approach because there is no single discipline that can answer my question comprehensively. It is very much a complex issue that must be investigated through multiple lenses. I have chosen to examine the philosophical, biological, and political aspects of factory farming. An interdisciplinary response is the most effective way to find common ground and to understand the individual complexities that make up the issue. Without using an interdisciplinary approach, one is exposed to a very limited, narrow scope on the subject.

Step 3: Identify Disciplines

There were many disciplines that I thought would be potentially relevant to factory farming, including economics (profit); Political Science/Criminal Justice (law & legislation); Biology (sentient beings); Anthropology (culture); and History (farming: then & now). As I conducted my research, I discovered that each aforementioned perspective had published articles, but the most relevant seemed to be published under Political, Biological, Economical, and Philosophical perspectives. The common thread of economics surprised me throughout my research; no matter the article or disciplinary perspective, economics almost always played a role and was mentioned and/or discussed. I was also surprised by the many articles that discussed the negative impact factory farms have on people's lives and health, from infectious diseases to antibiotic resistance, for example; I never even considered the medical perspective in relation to factory farming.

Step 4: Conduct a Literature Review

The research I have attached below confirms my findings:

Discipline(s) consulted	Title of Article	Author of Article/ Insight	Focus of Insight	Evaluation of Insight
From which disciplinary perspective do the insights come?	Full name of article. Use the same name for the file when you save it.	Author of article/ insight	What is the important point(s) (insight[s]) you may use from the article?	How useful is this insight?
Political Science, Law, Criminal Justice	#1. Don't Be Cruel Anymore: A Look at the Animal Cruelty Regimes of the United States and Brazil with a Call for a New Animal Welfare Agency	Cassuto & Eckhardt	• Focuses on the contradictory laws regarding factory farming animal welfare, shows how it benefits humans more than animals • Discusses the economic factors in factory farming • proposes AWA—an animal welfare agency that would protect agricultural animals	Very Useful
Biology	#2. Interaction of the role of Concentrated Animal Feeding Operations (CAFOs) in Emerging Infectious Diseases (EIDS)	James E. Hollenbeck Insights: Engering, A., & Gregor, M.	• Considers the role CAFOs play in relation to emerging infectious diseases • Suggests ways to prevent EIDS through better quality employee standards	Useful
Philosophy	#3. Clarifying the Concept of Cruelty: What Makes Cruelty to Animals Cruel	Julia Tanner • Cites many sources throughout article	• Concepts & definitions of cruelty are examined • Farm animals & cruelty	Partially Useful

(Continued)

(Continued)

Discipline(s) consulted	Title of Article	Author of Article/ Insight	Focus of Insight	Evaluation of Insight
Political Science, Law, Criminal Justice	#4. "Won't You Be My Neighbor?" Living with Concentrated Animal Feeding Operations	Emily A. Kilbe	• Discusses CAFOs in Iowa and their relation to personal health, the environment, and animal welfare	Useful— Connected to article #2 with CAFOs
Philosophy	#5. Could animal production become a profession?	David Fraser	• Provides history of animal welfare— emphasis on Industrial Revolution • Distinguishes between profession and industry—can animal production become a profession • Suggests a professional model for factory farms to adopt	Useful— shows how deeply rooted animal welfare is in society
Political Science, Law, Philosophy	#6. A Return to Descartes: Property, Profit, and the Corporate Ownership of Animals	Darian M. Ibrahim	• Descartes's theory on animals being machines: automata • Corporate ownership of animals • Consumer demand for cheap products • Being socially responsible	Only useful because of theory?

Step 5: Analyze Insights

Article #	Author	Disciplinary Perspective	Thesis	Assumption	Theory Name	Key Concept	Method	Phenomena Addressed	Author's bias	Connection to other insights (#)
1. Don't Be Cruel Anymore: A Look at the Animal Cruelty Regimes of the United States and Brazil with a Call for a New Animal Welfare Agency	David N. Cassuto & Cayleigh Eckhardt	Political Science	Agricultural animals are exempted from the ineffective and rarely enforced animal welfare and anticruelty regulations that exist today.	Empirical and quantitative, rather than normative and qualitative, analysis is the most effective way of knowing political reality. There is some order to society.	N/A	The laws that are set up to protect/ regulate animal welfare are more beneficial to humans and their economic gain than to the actual animals.	Describes legal governments, examines ideas and laws on the federal and state level - examines statistics and current laws and a proposal for social action	Laws and legislation in relation to farm animals on factory farms	No— considers own perspective (Law) along with economics and environment	Relates to Article #4 and partially #6
2. Interaction of the role of Concentrated Animal Feeding Operations (CAFOs) in Emerging Infectious Diseases (EIDS)	James E. Hollenbeck, Insights from Engering and Gregor	Biology	With the development of CAFOs around the world, the need for training of animal caretakers to observe, identify, treat, vaccinate, and cull is important to safeguard public health.	Nature is orderly and understandable. Deductive reasoning is superior to inductive reasoning.	N/A	CAFOs play a role in negatively impacting human health through emerging infections diseases (EIDS).	Extensive medical research on health and disease, and citations	Infectious disease in relation to farm animals	Yes—only considers the medical perspective	Relates to Article #4, dealing with medical issues

(Continued)

(Continued)

Article #	Author	Disciplinary Perspective	Thesis	Assumption	Theory Name	Key Concept	Method	Phenomena Addressed	Author's bias	Connection to other insights (#)
3. Clarifying the Concept of Cruelty: What Makes Cruelty to Animals Cruel	Julia Tanner Insights from many sources	Philosophy	Farming practices have changed and our understanding of the concept of cruelty needs to change with them. Our application of the concept of cruelty is inconsistent.	The chief route to knowledge is perception (using the five senses and an extension of them). Observation and experiment are the principal means of inquiry.	Persons and Nonpersons Theory • Moral Theory	Examines the various definitions of cruelty and investigates what constitutes animal cruelty	Distinguishes between concepts of cruelty through contemplation, linguistic analysis, abstract thought, and debate	The meaning of cruelty—Ethics	No— considers both sides of cruelty	Relates to Article #5 and Article #6
4. "Won't You Be My Neighbor?" Living with Concentrated Animal Feeding Operations	Emily A. Kilbe	Political Science	Iowans should look for a variety of ways to address the negative health impacts CAFOs are having on personal health and environmental well-being.	There is some order to society. Empirical and quantitative, rather than normative and qualitative, analysis is the most effective way of knowing political reality. Political science can be capable of prediction and explanation.	N/A	CAFOs in Iowa and their relation to negative impacts on personal health and the environment	Examination & research of many court cases, bills, and/or laws/ legislation	Feeding lots and their effects on human and environmental health	No— considers not only law but economics, chemistry, environment, and personal health	Relates to article #1 with laws Relates to Article #2, dealing with medical/ health

Article #	Author	Disciplinary Perspective	Thesis	Assumption	Theory Name	Key Concept	Method	Phenomena Addressed	Author's bias	Connection to other insights (#)
5. Could animal production become a profession?	David Fraser	Philosophy	A professional model of animal production could help to achieve good animal welfare and other socially important goals, and could provide an alternative means for animal producers to establish public trust.	The chief route to knowledge is the exercise of systematic reasoning and conceptual engineering, or mathematics and logic.	N/A	Distinguishes between factory farming as an industry vs. profession	Discusses the history of welfare and distinguishes between then (Industrial Revolution) and now. Much research and citations added from outside sources. Use of tables. Contemplation and argument	Animal production and animal welfare. Standards and professionalism	No—considers history and sociology as well	Relates to Article #3, cruelty vs. industry/profession
6. A Return to Descartes: Property, Profit, and the Corporate Ownership of Animals	Darian M. Ibrahim	Political Science & Philosophy	The efficiencies of factory farms enable both rich and poor consumers to afford meat and corporations to profit from selling more of it. We need to redefine socially responsible corporations as those that abstain from animal use altogether.	Empirical and quantitative, rather than normative and qualitative, analysis is the most effective way of knowing political reality. The chief route to knowledge is the exercise of systematic reasoning and conceptual engineering, or mathematics and logic.	• Animals as machines theory "automata"	Descartes's theory on animals being machines—corporate ownership of animals. Consumer desire for affordable means. Social Responsibility	Conducted a history search. Use of statistics and data from outside research. Use of argument and debate	Animals as property	No—Balance of the pros and cons of factory farming and corporate ownership. Multiple perspectives considered	Relates to Article #3. Theory/concept of cruelty

Step 6: Reflect on the Interdisciplinary Response

No matter the disciplinary perspective an article was written from, my research seems to acknowledge and agree that the conditions and treatment of animals on factory farms are harsh, severe, and often cruel. Where my research tends to disagree is in regards to ethics; whether or not it is considered right or wrong. For example, some people view animals as machines, producers for human; others view animals as sentient beings who deserve respectable rights and humane treatment. Some argue that the animals experience unnecessary pain and suffering, while others argue that pain and suffering is necessary in order for humans to consume meat.

One key insight that I learned from my research study is that laws are often worded in ways that seem beneficial to animals but in reality they are more beneficial for humans. For instance, a law might state that an animal in confinement must have access to the outdoors and fresh air. An animal could live its entire life inside of a cage; so long as the animal has a window to look out of, no law has been broken. Another key insight I learned from my research study is that economics play an entirely centralized role in factory farming. There is absolutely no way to separate the two. Almost every disciplinary perspective I read about considered economics in their findings and writing.

I did not have much of a bias as I began my research project because I didn't know too much about factory farming. After reading many articles, I discovered there was bias in the rhetoric surrounding factory farming. Some articles seemed to be black or white, right or wrong. The interdisciplinary process enlarged my understanding of factory farming as a whole by providing and educating me with factual, scholarly information, which leads to a deeper understanding of the issue. I am now able to see how different elements like philosophy, biology, and political science, for example, intersect and interact with each other.

I relied heavily on the experts to answer my question but realized there were too many insights to sift through, in such a short amount of time, to gain a complete understanding. I realized that disciplinary perspectives/experts could determine the "attitude" of a text, and therefore the attitude of the person reading the text.

The interdisciplinary approach and the Broad Model are applicable beyond the classroom in almost all arenas of life. Considering where to send my son to school is an example of how I could utilize the Broad Model outside of this course. When searching for the right school, I will pick the school apart and look at its individual parts. For instance, I will consider the economic factor:

what kinds of resources will the school be able to provide for my son? I will also consider religious aspects by choosing whether to send my son to a private or public school. I will consider the history of the school: Is the school known for its Academics? Its Arts? Sports? Has it won any prestigious awards? And, finally, I will look at the educational aspect. By dissecting the school into its constituent parts, I will be able to come to a better understanding of what I feel would be most appropriate or suitable for my son.

If I could have done something differently, I would have investigated the psychological aspects of factory farms on animals and humans. There are obvious psychological effects on the animals in factory farms, I would be more interested in the psychological effects on workers at factory farms. One thing that I learned about my topic that I did not know prior to this project is just how misleading animal welfare laws are. The laws are set up to benefit human economic gain more than the animal. The most difficult step in this process was conducting the literature search. Having to read and sort through a large number of scholarly articles and determine their usefulness is no easy task. What I took away from this process is learning the importance of being aware of the disciplinary perspective a text is written in or an opinion/information is coming from. Know the credentials and credibility of the source because this can drastically influence and shape your understanding of a problem or issue.

I would recommend that anyone learn the six steps of the Broad Model because it is highly beneficial and helpful when conducting research. The Broad Model helps you pick out the most important information and organize it in a way that is helpful and easy to refer back to. This is beneficial in countless aspects of life, including the personal, educational, and professional realms. Regardless of the kind of decision that is to be made, the Broad Model is a road map to making a decision based off quality research and understanding.

APPENDIX E

ANSWER KEY

CHAPTER 10

Critical Thinking Questions

1. For each of the three introductory paragraphs (on grizzly bears, Jewish marriage, and culture) provided in Examples 1 through 3, rewrite them so that clearly positive answers are given to each of the four questions asked:

---

a. Does the author state that the problem or research question is complex and explain what this means?

b. Does the author state that important insights into the problem are offered by two or more disciplines?

c. Does the author state or imply that no single discipline has been able to address the problem comprehensively?

d. Does the author state that the problem addresses an important and as yet unresolved issue concerning nature or society?

A: Title of Bulletin: *Interdisciplinary Problem Solving in Species and Ecosystem Conservation* (2001)

Grizzly bear (*Ursus arctos*) management in the Greater Yellowstone Ecosystem (GYE) is one particularly high-profile case. Threats to grizzly bears may be defined in terms of habitat and population fragmentation and the biological measures needed to maintain or restore populations (e.g., Knight et al., 1999). The problem of threats to grizzly bears is complex because it transverses numerous disciplinary domains, including the threats to habitats and their ecosystems (environmental science and ecology) and fragmentation of the population, which is largely dependent on *complex* human social dynamics. Attempts to address this situation therefore also demand effective and appropriate policy decisions (environmental science, political science). Since no single discipline has been able to effectively address and resolve this ongoing and pressing complex problem, it is appropriate for interdisciplinary inquiry.

B: Title of Book Chapter: "Jewish Marriage as an Expression of Israel's Conflicted Identity" (2012)

A study of the institution of Jewish marriage and its place in Israel's conflicted identity may generate insights that can be applied to broader issues of inequality such as the situation of Israeli Arabs, a sizable minority who face issues in some ways analogous to those of non-Orthodox Jews and other non-Jews in Israel. An interdisciplinary approach to the institution of Jewish marriage is necessary because no single discipline is able to provide a comprehensive understanding of its complex and emblematic role in Israeli democracy. Insights into this complex problem might be offered by considering the disciplines of religious studies, sociology, history, and political science. Since no one discipline is able to encapsulate the complexity and breadth of this complex and continuing problem, the interdisciplinary research process offers the most effective way to consider each contributing discipline's perspective, find common ground between conflicting insights, integrate these insights, and apply the resulting understanding to broader issues in Israel as a Jewish and democratic state.

C: Title of Paper: "Globalization: An Interdisciplinary Approach to Explain How Western Culture Spreads Around the World" (n.d.)

Globalization is spreading Western culture throughout the world and replacing more traditional cultures. The topic of globalization and its effects on other cultures is complex because it demands an examination of many relevant aspects of the topic. These include the causes of globalization (which draws on both economics and political science), the affected cultures themselves and how they are being changed (anthropology), and a consideration of how these changes have come about over time to allow for informed future projections (history). Since no single discipline can explain this complex process, an interdisciplinary approach is necessary. Being able to recognize and describe the effects of globalization on these cultures will allow for a more holistic understanding of this complex issue.

2. Do these three authors address the "So what?" question? If not, how might they do so?

A: Title of Bulletin: *Interdisciplinary Problem Solving in Species and Ecosystem Conservation* (2001)

There is little emphasis on why we should care about this problem, although we may infer that without careful management, populations of the grizzly bear are under threat. This might be addressed by a consideration of what might happen to grizzly bear numbers without careful population management (population trend statistics, for example) and examples of what has happened to the species in areas other than the GYE, both with and without the implementation of interdisciplinary population management strategies.

> **B: Title of Book Chapter: "Jewish Marriage as an Expression of Israel's Conflicted Identity" (2012)**
>
> The author does imply that this question has wider impact than the examination of the topic of Jewish marriage alone because its investigation might provide a more holistic understanding of the "broader issues in Israel as a Jewish and democratic state," which continues to be a source of political strife in the region.

> **C: Title of Paper: "Globalization: An Interdisciplinary Approach to Explain How Western Culture Spreads Around the World" (n.d.)**
>
> The author's title suggests that the paper will examine how Western culture spreads around the world, but the opening paragraph implies that it will focus on the results of this expansion. If the author wishes to engage us with why we should care about this expansion, she might want to include an example of how such expansion has affected traditional cultures. Perhaps she could include an example of such a threatened culture and how its loss is a detriment to diversity, or she could show how a traditional culture has a relationship with natural resources that are more aligned with conservation and how such knowledge is of use to the world.

3. Do these three authors display disciplinary jargon, disciplinary bias, or personal bias? How so?

> **A: Title of Bulletin: *Interdisciplinary Problem Solving in Species and Ecosystem Conservation* (2001)**
>
> The author of this article has a PhD in zoology, so the inclusion of *disciplinary jargon* such as the Latin species name for the grizzly bear is not surprising. This jargon could be omitted since the author also includes the common name. *Disciplinary bias*, the focus on zoology or the biological sciences, generally is not apparent in the article, as the author implies that other disciplines are necessary to provide a holistic understanding of the complex problem. There is no evidence of *personal bias*.

B: Title of Book Chapter: "Jewish Marriage as an Expression of Israel's Conflicted Identity" (2012)

The author of this article has a PhD in Spanish and a JD; however, there is no *disciplinary jargon* drawn from either of these disciplines nor *disciplinary bias* of any other kind. There is also no *personal bias* evident in this introduction.

C: Title of Paper: "Globalization: An Interdisciplinary Approach to Explain How Western Culture Spreads Around the World" (n.d.)

Although there does not appear to be *disciplinary jargon* nor *disciplinary bias* in this introduction, there is *personal bias*. The author implies that the forces of globalization are negative before providing any evidence or contextual discussion of this term. Using words like "overwhelming" to describe the effect on traditional cultures suggests that globalization is a powerful and negative force. Rewriting this sentence to remove this loaded language would remove this bias: "Globalization is spreading Western culture throughout the world and replacing more traditional cultures."

Applications and Exercises

2. From your reading of this chapter, does the following essay by Alba and Nee (2005) appear to be disciplinary or interdisciplinary? Justify your answer.

ANS: The essay is disciplinary, is written from a sociological perspective, and employs a sociological methodology.

Peer Evaluation Activity

Title: *Nurse Burnout: An Integrative Approach to a Multidimensional Problem* (n.d.)
Author: K. A. McKay

Evaluate the following problem statement using the expanded Broad Model Rubric, and identify specific language that supports each criterion. Note that in some instances, there may be insufficient information to answer the question. Select one of these possible responses in the right-hand column next to each criterion.

- "Yes" means that you are able to identify wording in the introduction that clearly meets the criterion.

- "No" means that the author makes no attempt to meet the criterion.

- "Implied" means that the criterion is met though explicit language is missing.

Peer Evaluation: *Nurse Burnout: An Integrative Approach to a Multidimensional Problem*

Figure 10.8 The Broad Model Rubric (STEPS 1 and 2)

THE BROAD MODEL RUBRIC (STEPS 1 AND 2)

ID PROCESS	CRITERIA	Y/N/I
STEP 1		
Define the problem or state the research question.	Introduces the problem or research question that is the subject of study and states the purpose or objective of the study	
	1.1. The author defines the problem or states the research question in a way that is appropriate to interdisciplinary study.	Yes
	1.2. The author carefully defines the scope of the study.	Yes
	1.3. The author avoids the three tendencies that run counter to interdisciplinary process: disciplinary jargon, disciplinary bias, and personal bias.	Yes
	1.4. The author answers the "so what?" question.	Yes

STEP 2		
Justify using an interdisciplinary approach.	**Explains why the problem or research question requires using an interdisciplinary approach**	
	2.1. The author states that the problem or research question is complex and explains what this means.	Yes
	2.2. The author states or implies that there are important insights into the problem offered by two or more disciplines.	Implied
	2.3. The author states or implies that no single discipline has been able to address the problem *comprehensively*.	No
	2.4. The author states that the study addresses an important and as yet unresolved issue concerning nature or society.	Yes

CHAPTER 11

Example No. 2 From the Social Sciences (Primarily)

Title: "Jewish Marriage as an Expression of
Israel's Conflicted Identity" (2012)

Author: Marilyn R. Tayler

ID PROCESS	CRITERIA	Y/N/I
STEP 3		
Identify relevant disciplines.	**Identifies the disciplines potentially relevant to the problem or research question and then reduces these to those that are most relevant**	
	3.1. The author identifies the disciplines *potentially* relevant to the problem.	Yes
	3.2. The author narrows these to those that are *most* relevant and explains the basis for doing so.	Yes
STEP 4		
Conduct a literature search.	**Identifies insights from two or more disciplines, confirming that they are most relevant to the problem**	
	4.1. The author reports that the literature search confirms the identity of the disciplines and their insights that are most relevant to the problem.	Insufficient information

Example No. 3 From the Humanities

Title: *Mektoub*: **When Art Meets History, Philosophy, and Linguistics" (2012)**

Author: Mieke Bal

ID PROCESS	CRITERIA	Y/N/I
STEP 3		
Identify relevant disciplines.	**Identifies the disciplines potentially relevant to the problem or research question and then reduces these to those that are most relevant**	
	3.1. The author identifies the disciplines *potentially* relevant to the problem.	Yes
	3.2. The author narrows these to those that are *most* relevant and explains the basis for doing so.	Yes
STEP 4		
Conduct a literature search.	**Identifies insights from two or more disciplines, confirming that they are most relevant to the problem**	
	4.1. The author reports that the literature search confirms the identity of the disciplines and their insights that are most relevant to the problem.	Yes

Example No. 4 From Student Work

Title: *Globalization and Its Effects on the Environment* (n.d.)

Author: A. Dhole

ID PROCESS	CRITERIA	Y/N/I
STEP 3		
Identify relevant disciplines.	Identifies the disciplines potentially relevant to the problem or research question and then reduces these to those that are most relevant	
	3.1. The author identifies the disciplines *potentially* relevant to the problem.	No
	3.2. The author narrows these to those that are *most* relevant and explains the basis for doing so.	Yes
STEP 4		
Conduct a literature search.	Identifies insights from two or more disciplines, confirming that that they are most relevant to the problem	
	4.1. The author reports that the literature search confirms the identity of the disciplines and their insights that are most relevant to the problem.	No

ID PROCESS	CRITERIA	Y/N/I
STEP 3		
Identify relevant disciplines.	**Identifies the disciplines potentially relevant to the problem or research question and then reduces these to those that are most relevant**	
	3.1. The author identifies the disciplines *potentially* relevant to the problem.	No
	3.2. The author narrows these to those that are *most* relevant and explains the basis for doing so.	Yes
STEP 4		
Conduct a literature search.	**Identifies insights from two or more disciplines, confirming that they are most relevant to the problem**	
	4.1. The author reports that the literature search confirms the identity of the disciplines and their insights that are most relevant to the problem.	Yes

Critical Thinking Questions

1. Perform the four actions in STEP 3 for one of the following contemporary public policy challenges: suicide terrorism; the refugee crisis; tracking and storing personal information by governments.

   i. Action No. 1: Connect the Problem as a Whole to Phenomena Typically Studied by Disciplines and Interdisciplinary Fields

   ii. Action No. 2: "Decompose" the Problem

   iii. Action No. 3: Externalize the Problem

   iv. Action No. 4: Reflect on the Problem

Suicide Terrorism:

i. ## Action No. 1: Connect the Problem as a Whole to Phenomena Typically Studied by Disciplines and Interdisciplinary Fields

Discipline or Interdiscipline	Phenomena Studied	Relevance to Topic
Psychology	The nature of human behavior as well as the internal (psychosociological) and external (environmental) factors that affect this behavior	Suicide terrorism is a human behavior.
Political Science	The nature and practice of systems of government and of individuals and groups pursuing power within those systems	Suicide terrorism is generally used as a tactic to stimulate change or challenge existing power structures.
Sociology	The social nature of societies and of human interactions within them	Human interactions in societies where suicide terrorism occurs will be important to this study.
Criminal Justice	The phenomena of social deviance in all of its manifestations, its causes, costs, and the social, political, and legal systems that deal with it	Suicide terrorism is treated as a problem of social deviance.

ii. ## Action No. 2: "Decompose" the Problem

Research Question	Phenomena	Disciplines
What is the cause of suicide terrorism?	Political	Political science
	Religious	Religion studies, psychology, sociology
	Psychosis	Psychology
	Poverty	Economics
	Encroachment of other cultures	Religion studies, political science, anthropology, geography, history, sociology

iii. Action No. 3: Externalize the Problem

Figure E.1   Diagram of the Causes of Suicide Terrorism

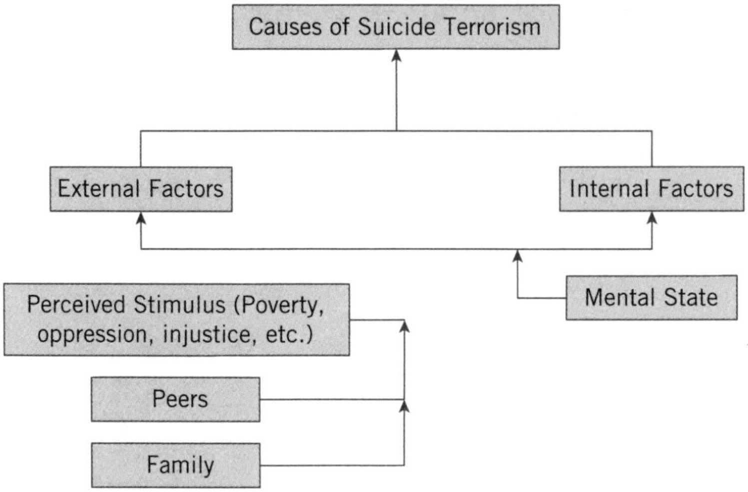

iv. Action No. 4: Reflect on the Problem

Interdisciplinary process is not linear but rather involves reflecting on and possibly revising earlier decisions as new information comes to light. We now must decide if Action No. 3 shows that the research question is too broad and needs to be narrowed to only external *or* internal factors.

Research Question	Phenomena	Disciplines
What is the cause of suicide terrorism?	Political	Political science
	Religion	Religion studies, psychology, sociology
	Psychosis	Psychology
	Poverty	Economics
	Encroachment of other cultures	Religion studies, political science, anthropology, geography, history
	Peers and Family	Sociology, anthropology

2. How would you go about searching for relevant insights on these issues?

Using library searches, it would be possible to find articles that examine the topic of suicide terrorism from the perspective of these disciplines. For example, to find a discussion from the perspective of sociology, a search of library articles could be initiated using the key terms "suicide bombing" and "sociology" as a Boolean phrase.

Figure E.2 Search for Articles on Suicide Terrorism From the Perspective of Sociology

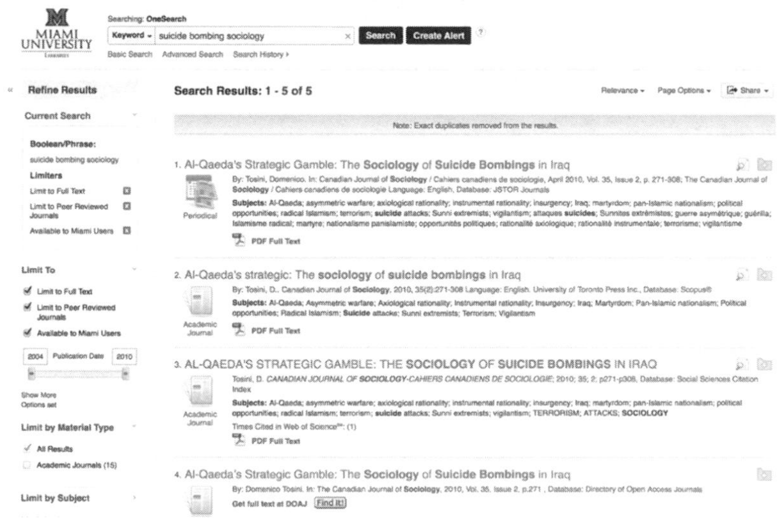

CHAPTER 12

The Broad Model Rubric Applied to STEP 5

Example No. 2 From the Social Sciences, the Humanities, and the Applied Field of Law

Title: "Jewish Marriage as an Expression of Israel's Conflicted Identity" (2012)

Author: Marilyn R. Tayler

ID PROCESS	CRITERIA	Y/N/I
STEP 5		
Critically analyze the disciplinary insights into the problem and locate their sources of conflict.	**Identifies the key elements of insights and locates their sources of conflict**	
	5.1. The author identifies the key elements of the most important disciplinary insights into the problem.	Yes
	5.2. The author identifies both the sources of conflict and/or agreement between insights.	Yes
	5.3. The author maps or compiles a table that sets out how the insights from contributing disciplines are interconnected or fit together.	No

Example No. 3 From Student Work

Title: *Nurse Burnout: An Integrative Approach to a Multidimensional Problem* (n.d.)

Author: K. A. McKay

ID PROCESS	CRITERIA	Y/N/I
STEP 5		
Critically analyze the disciplinary insights into the problem and locate their sources of conflict.	**Identifies the key elements of insights and locates their sources of conflict**	
	5.1. The author identifies the key elements of the most important disciplinary insights into the problem.	Not completely
	5.2. The author identifies both the sources of conflict and/or agreement between insights.	Not completely
	5.3. The author maps or compiles a table that sets out how the insights from contributing disciplines are interconnected or fit together.	No

The Broad Model Rubric Applied to STEP 6

Example No. 2 From the Social Sciences, the Humanities, and the Applied Field of Law

Title: "Jewish Marriage as an Expression of Israel's Conflicted Identity" (2012)

Author: Marilyn R. Tayler

ID PROCESS	CRITERIA	Y/N/I
STEP 6		
Reflect on how using an interdisciplinary approach has enlarged your understanding of the problem.	**Reflects on how interdisciplinary process has enlarged your understanding of the problem**	
	6.1. The author explains how an interdisciplinary approach challenged his or her bias on the problem.	No*
	6.2. The author explains how an interdisciplinary approach has influenced his or her perception of disciplinary expertise.	No**
	6.3. The author explains how an interdisciplinary approach has enlarged his or her understanding of the problem as a whole.	Yes
	6.4. The author explains how an interdisciplinary approach is applicable beyond the classroom.	Yes, by implication

*Interdisciplinarians typically do not comment on their bias.

**Interdisciplinary scholars are well aware of the limitations of disciplinary expertise and therefore do not address this in their work.

Example No. 3 Student Paper

Title: *Nurse Burnout: An Integrative Approach to a Multidimensional Problem* (n.d.)

Author: K. A. McKay

ID PROCESS	CRITERIA	Y/N/I
STEP 6		
Reflect on how using an interdisciplinary process has enlarged your understanding of the problem.	**Reflects on how interdisciplinary process has enlarged your understanding of the problem**	
	6.1. The author explains how an interdisciplinary approach challenged his or her bias on the problem.	No
	6.2. The author explains how an interdisciplinary approach has influenced his or her perception of disciplinary expertise.	Yes
	6.3. The author explains how an interdisciplinary approach has enlarged his or her understanding of the problem as a whole.	Yes
	6.4 The author explains how an interdisciplinary approach is applicable beyond the classroom.	Yes

GLOSSARY OF KEY TERMS

Analytical intelligence: The ability to break a problem down into its component parts, solve problems, and evaluate the quality of ideas. [1]

Assumptions: Things that are accepted as true or certain. [5]

Capacity: The "cognitive" or "intellectual" ability to think, perceive, analyze, create, and solve problems. [3]

Close reading: Careful analysis of a text that begins with attending to individual words, sentence structure, and the order in which sentences and ideas unfold. [3]

Common ground: That which is created between conflicting disciplinary insights, assumptions, concepts, or theories and makes integration possible. [6]

Complexity: Having multiple parts that are connected and interact in sometimes unexpected (e.g., nonlinear) ways with each other. [6]

Concepts: Abstract ideas generalized from particular instances or symbols expressed in language that represent phenomena. [5]

Context: The circumstances or setting in which the problem, event, statement, or idea exists. [2]

Contextual thinking: The ability to view a subject from a broad perspective by placing it in the fabric of time, culture, or personal experience. [1]

Contextualization: The practice of placing "a text, or author, or work of art into context, to understand it in part through an examination of its historical, geographical, intellectual, or artistic location" (Newell, 2001, p. 4). [6]

Creative breakthroughs: Often occur when different disciplinary perspectives and unrelated ideas are brought together. [2]

Creative intelligence: The ability to formulate ideas and make connections. [1]

Critical interdisciplinarity: Questions disciplinary assumptions and ideological underpinnings. In some cases, it aims to replace the existing structure of knowledge (i.e., the disciplines) and the system of education based upon it. [3]

Critical pluralism: Belief that knowledge can be objective, but not certain and absolute as dualism assumes. [7]

Critical reflection: The process of analyzing, questioning, and reconsidering the activity (cognitive or physical) that you are engaged in. [3]

Critical thinking: The capacity to analyze, critique, and assess. [4]

Decomposing the problem: Breaking a problem down into its component parts. [11]

Deductive approach: Calls for the researcher to develop a logical explanation or theory about a phenomenon, formulate a hypothesis that is testable, and then make observations and compile evidence to confirm or deny the hypothesis. [5]

Defining elements of a discipline: These include the phenomena it studies, its epistemology (i.e., how one knows what is true), and how one validates truth, the assumptions it makes about the natural and human world, its basic concepts, its theories about the causes and behaviors of certain phenomena, its methods (the ways it gathers, applies, and produces new knowledge), and the kind of data it collects. [5]

Disciplinarity: The system of knowledge specialties called disciplines. [3]

Disciplinary bias: Favoring one discipline's understanding of the problem at the expense of competing understandings of the same problem offered by other disciplines. [4]

Disciplinary categories: Divisions or colleges or schools or "faculties" including the natural sciences; the social sciences; the humanities; the fine and performing arts; the applied fields, such as communications and business; and the professions, such as architecture, engineering, law, nursing, education, and social work. [5]

Disciplinary inadequacy: The view that the disciplines by themselves are simply not equipped to address complex problems *comprehensively* (i.e., in a way that takes into account the perspectives and insights of other relevant disciplines). [6]

Disciplinary jargon: Using technical terms and concepts that are not generally understood outside the discipline. [10]

Disciplinary perspective: A discipline's unique view of reality that is like a lens through which it views the world. A discipline's perspective embraces, and in turn reflects, the ensemble of its defining elements that include the phenomena it prefers to study, its epistemology, assumptions, concepts, and favored theories and methods. [5]

Disciplinary reductionism: Reduces complex things to simpler or more fundamental things. [3]

Disciplinary research: Involves choosing from upward of a dozen or so specialized methods to study a particular phenomenon. [10]

Discipline: A branch of learning or body of knowledge such as physics, psychology, or history. [3]

Dualism: Belief that knowledge is objective, certain, and absolute. [7]

Empiricism: Holds that all knowledge is derived from our perceptions (transmitted by the five senses of touch, smell, taste, hearing, and sight), experience, and observation. [5]

Epistemic position: Understanding the nature of knowledge and how you determine truth. [7]

Epistemological pluralism: Rejects notions of absolute truth and embraces the ambiguity that arises out of conflict and difference. [6]

Epistemology: The study of the nature and basis of knowledge. [5]

Externalizing the problem: Drawing a picture of the problem. [11]

Generalist interdisciplinarians: Understand interdisciplinarity loosely to mean "any form of dialog or interaction between two or more disciplines," minimizing, obscuring, or rejecting altogether the role of integration. [6]

Inductive approach: Begins with making systematic observations, detecting patterns, formulating tentative hypotheses about these patterns, and then formulating a theory that explains the phenomenon in question. [5]

Informed borrowing: Selecting one path to understanding while "bracketing" others. [2]

Insights: Scholarly contributions to the clear understanding of a complex problem, object, or text. Insights may be found in published books or articles or in papers delivered at scholarly conferences. [3]

Instrumental interdisciplinarity: A pragmatic conception of interdisciplinarity that focuses on research, borrowing (from disciplines), and practical problem solving in response to the demands of society. [3]

Integration (interdisciplinary): The cognitive process of critically evaluating disciplinary insights and creating common ground among them to construct a more comprehensive understanding. The new understanding is the product or result of the integrative process. [6]

Integrationist interdisciplinarians: Regard integration as *the key distinguishing characteristic* of interdisciplinarity and *the goal* of fully interdisciplinary work. [6]

Integrative thinking: A defining characteristic of interdisciplinary learning that is the ability to knit together information from different sources to produce a more comprehensive understanding or create new meaning. [1]

Intellectual autobiography: The story of your academic or intellectual journey told from your point of view. [4]

Intellectual dexterity: The ability to speak to (if not from) a broad spectrum of knowledge and experience. [4]

Interdisciplinarity: The term used for interdisciplinary studies to identify the "intellectual essence" of the field that refers both to its "defining elements" and to the "process" it uses to engage in the scholarly enterprise. [3]

Interdisciplinary breadth: Basic knowledge about each potentially relevant discipline so that you can understand its perspective and access, translate, think critically about, and use its insights. [7]

Interdisciplinary creation: Involves putting elements together—integrating them—to produce some- thing that is new, coherent, and whole. [6]

Interdisciplinary perspective taking: The intellectual capacity to view a complex problem, phenomenon, or behavior from multiple perspectives, including disciplinary ones, in order to develop a more comprehensive understanding of it.

Interdisciplinary research: To study a topic or question that is inherently complex and whose parts are the focus of two or more disciplines, to integrate their insights, and to construct a more comprehensive understanding of the topic or question. [10]

Interrogate in an interdisciplinary sense: Ask critical and probing questions of each relevant discipline. [7]

Knowledge society: One in which the development and creative application of knowledge is the primary engine of economic growth, prosperity, and empowerment of all developing sectors of society. [1]

Links: The directional arrows that connect the nodes and indicate the relationships of nodes to each other. [11]

Metacognition: The awareness of your own learning and thinking processes, often described as "thinking about your thinking." [4]

Metaphor: A figure of speech in which a word or phrase, a story, or a picture is likened to the idea that you are trying to communicate. [3]

Methods: Particular procedures or processes or techniques used by a discipline's practitioners to conduct, organize, and present research. [5]

More comprehensive understanding: A cognitive advancement that results from integrating insights that produces a new whole that would not be possible using single disciplinary means. [9]

Multidisciplinarity: The placing side by side of insights from two or more disciplines without attempting to integrate them. [3]

Multiplicity: The ability to work effectively with several plausible yet contradictory explanations of the same phenomenon as opposed to one simple, clear-cut, unambiguous explanation. [7]

Nodes: The important concepts or the phenomena under study. [11]

Peer review: A process in which researchers scrutinize and critique each other's work in search of possible shortcomings or alternative explanations. [5]

Perceptual apparatus: A discipline's defining elements. [7]

Personal bias: Allowing your own point of view (e.g., your politics, faith tradition, cultural identity) to influence how you understand or approach the problem. [4]

Perspective in an interdisciplinary sense: Refers to a discipline's unique view of that part of reality that it is typically most interested in. [2]

Perspective taking (interdisciplinary): The intellectual capacity to view a complex problem, phenomenon, or behavior from multiple perspectives, including disciplinary ones, in order to develop a more comprehensive understanding of it. [4]

Potentially relevant: A discipline is considered potentially relevant when the problem falls within its research domain but it is not known whether the discipline's experts have written about the problem. [11]

Practical intelligence: The ability to apply an idea in an effective way, whether in business or in everyday life. [1]

Problem-centering approach: Also known as the instrumental approach to integration that uses issues of public debate, product development, or an intervention such as one designed to improve health and well- being as focal points for making connections between disciplines and integrating their insights. [9]

Problem-focused research: Distinct from what is called basic research (e.g., laboratory experiments or surveys) or pure theoretical research because it focuses on societal needs and practical problem solving. [10]

Reductionism: The strategy of "dividing a phenomenon into its constituent parts and studying them separately in the expectation that knowledge produced by narrow specialties can be readily combined into the understanding of the phenomenon as a whole" (Newell, 2004, p. 2). [6]

Relativism: Belief that there is no such thing as objective knowledge and that beliefs, theories, and values are inherently relative, contingent, and contextual. [7]

Relevant: A discipline is relevant to the problem if the discipline's experts have produced one or more insights into the problem. [11]

Research: The process of gathering information to understand how some aspect of the natural or human world functions. [10]

Researchable in an interdisciplinary sense: When experts from two or more disciplines have written about the problem. [10]

Rubric: An explicit set of criteria for evaluating a particular type of work or activity. [10]

Scope: Refers to the parameters of what is included or excluded from the study. [10]

Service learning: "A teaching and learning strategy that integrates meaningful community service with instruction and reflection to enrich the learning experience, teach civic responsibility, and strengthen communities" (www. servicelearning.org). [4]

Silo perspective: The tendency to see the university and the larger world through the narrow lens of a given disciplinary major. [1]

Simplistic epistemic positions: These positions, such as dualism and relativism, rest on the assumption the one already "knows what is true" about a given subject. [7]

Skewed: Refers to the degree to which an insight reflects the biases inherent in the discipline's perspective and thus the way an author understands the problem resulting from the author's deliberate decision or unconscious predisposition to omit certain information that pertains to the problem. [12]

Social content of disciplines: The community of scholars who engage in the work of the discipline. [5]

Sophisticated epistemic position: That of critical pluralism which sees multiple and conflicting perspectives as *partial understandings of the subject under study.* [7]

Stakeholder: A person or entity outside the academy who is interested in and may have a material stake in the outcome of a particular societal issue. [1]

"Strong sense" critical thinking: Directing your attention *inward*, causing you to examine the assumptions and premises you have used to construct the logical argument presented in your work. [4]

Subdisciplines: Branches of or specialties within disciplines. [5]

Successful intelligence: The ability to keep three types of intelligence in balance: creative intelligence, analytical intelligence, and practical intelligence. [1]

Systems thinking: The ability to break a problem down into its constituent parts to reveal internal and external factors, figure out how each of these parts relates to the others and to the problem as a whole, and identify which parts different disciplines address. [1]

Taxonomy: Grouping things according to their common characteristics. [5]

Theory: A generalized scholarly explanation about some aspect of the natural or human world, how it works, and how specific facts are related, that is, supported by data and research. [5]

Theory of conceptual integration: Explains the innate human ability to create new meaning by blending concepts. [6]

Transdisciplinarity: The cooperation of academics, stakeholders, and practitioners to solve a common complex societal or environmental problem of common interest with the goal of resolving it by designing and implementing public policy. [3]

REFERENCES

Agger, B. (1998). *Critical social theories: An introduction*. Boulder, CO: Westview Press.

Alba, R., & Nee, V. (2005). Rethinking assimilation theory for a new era of immigration. In M. M. Suarez-Orozco, C. Suarez-Orozco, & D. Baolin Qin (Eds.), *The new immigration: An interdisciplinary reader* (pp. 35–66). New York, NY: Routledge.

Alliance for Childhood. (1999). *Fool's gold: A critical look at computers in childhood*. Retrieved from **http://www.allianceforchildhood.net**

Alvesson, M., & Sköldberg, K. (2000). *Reflexive methodology: New vistas for qualitative research*. Thousand Oaks, CA: Sage.

Anderson, L. W., Krathwohl, D. R., Airasian, P. W., Cruikshank, K. A., Mayer, R. E., Pintrich, P. R., . . . Wittrock, M. (2001). *Taxonomy for learning, teaching, and assessing: A revision of Bloom's taxonomy of educational objectives*. New York, NY: Longman.

Association of American Colleges and Universities. (2004). *Greater expectations: A new vision for learning as a nation goes to college*. Washington, DC: Author.

Augsburg, T. (2003). Becoming interdisciplinary. The student portfolio in the bachelor of interdisciplinary studies program at Arizona State University. *Issues in Integrative Studies, 21*, 98–125.

Augsburg, T., & Chitewere, T. (2013). Starting with world views: A five-step preparatory approach to interdisciplinary learning. *Issues in Interdisciplinary Studies, 31*, 174–191.

Augsburg, T., & Henry, S. (Eds.). (2009). *The politics of interdisciplinary studies: Essays on transformations in American undergraduate programs*. Jefferson, NC: McFarland & Company.

Bailis, S. (2001). Contending with complexity: A response to William H. Newell's "A theory of interdisciplinary studies." *Issues in Integrative Studies, 19*, 27–42.

Bal, M. (1996). *Double exposures: The subject of cultural analyses*. New York, NY: Routledge.

Bal, M. (1999). Introduction. In M. Bal (Ed.), *The practice of cultural analysis: Exposing interdisciplinary interpretation* (pp. 1–14). Stanford, CA: Stanford University Press.

Bal, M. (2002). *Traveling concepts in the humanities: A rough guide*. Buffalo, NY: University of Toronto Press.

Bal, M. (2012). *Mektoub*: When art meets history, philosophy, and linguistics. In A. F. Repko, W. H. Newell, & R. Szostak (Eds.), *Case studies in interdisciplinary research* (pp. 91–122). Thousand Oaks, CA: Sage.

Baloche, L., Hynes, J. L., & Berger, H. A. (1996). Moving toward the integration of professional and general education. *Action in Teacher Education, 18*, 1–9.

Barnet, S. (2008). *A short guide to writing about art* (9th ed.). Upper Saddle River, NJ: Pearson Prentice Hall.

Baskin, P. (2012, February 13). National Science Foundation steps up its push for interdisciplinary research. *The Chronicle of Higher Education*. Retrieved from **http://chronicle.com/article/National-Science-Foundation/130757/**

Becher, T. (1989). *Academic tribes and territories: Intellectual enquiry and the cultures of disciplines*. Milton Keynes, England: Open University Press.

Beilin, R. (2012). Changing the landscape management paradigm with farmers: A story of community-based resource management in the "Heartbreak Hills," Victoria, Australia. In H. Bender & I. Lowe (Eds.), *Reshaping environments: An interdisciplinary approach to sustainability in a complex world* (pp. 66–113). Melbourne, Australia: Cambridge University Press.

Bender, T. (1997). Politics, intellect, and the American University, 1945–1995. In T. Bender & C. E. Schorske (Eds.), *American academic culture in transformation: Fifty years, four disciplines* (pp. 17–54). Princeton, NJ: Princeton University Press.

Bergmann, M., Jahn, T., Knobloch, T., Krohn, W., Pohl, C., & Schramm, E. (2012). *Methods for transdisciplinary research: A primer for practice*. Berlin, Germany: Campus Verlag.

Bernard, H. R. (2002). *Research methods in anthropology: Qualitative and quantitative methods* (3rd ed.). New York, NY: AltaMira Press.

Bestcolleges.com. (2016). *Best integrative studies programs*. Retrieved from **http://www.bestcolleges.com/features/top-integrative-studies-programs/**

Birken, M., & Coon, A. C. (2001, April). The pedagogical and epistemological uses of analogy in poetry and mathematics. *Consciousness, Literature and the Arts, 2*(1).

Blackburn, S. (1999). *Think: A compelling introduction to philosophy.* Oxford, England: Oxford University Press.

Blesser, G., & Salter, L. R. (2007). *Spaces speak, are you listening?* Cambridge, MA: MIT Press.

Boix Mansilla, V. (2005, January/ February). Assessing student work at disciplinary crossroads. *Change, 37,* 14–21.

Boix Mansilla, V., Dillon, D., & Middlebrooks, K. (n.d.). *Building bridges across disciplines: Organizational and individual qualities of exemplary interdisciplinary work* (Paper 16: GoodWork Project, Project Zero). Cambridge, MA: Harvard Graduate School of Education.

Boix Mansilla, V., Duraisingh, E. D., Wolfe, C., & Haynes, C. (2009, May/ June). Targeted assessment rubric: An empirically grounded rubric for interdisciplinary writing. *The Journal of Higher Education, 80*(3), 334–353.

Boix Mansilla, V., & Jackson, A. (2011). *Educating for global competence: Preparing our youth to engage the world.* New York, NY: Asia Society.

Boix Mansilla, V., Miller, W. C., & Gardner, H. (2000). On disciplinary lenses and interdisciplinary work. In S. Wineburg & P. Grossman (Eds.), *Interdisciplinary curriculum: Challenges to implementation* (pp. 17–38). New York, NY: Teachers College Press.

Booth, W. C., Columb, G. G., & Williams, J. M. (2008). *The craft of research* (3rd ed.). Chicago, IL: University of Chicago Press.

Boyer, E. I. (1981). The quest for common learning. In *Common learning: A Carnegie colloquium on general education* (pp. 3–21).

Washington, DC: The Carnegie Foundation for the Advancement of Learning.

Bradsford, J. D., Brown, A. L., & Cocking, R. R. (Eds.). (1999). *How people learn: Brain, mind, experience, and school.* Washington, DC: National Academy Press.

Brint, S. G., Turk-Bicakci, L., Proctor, K., & Murphy, S. P. (2009). Expanding the social frame of knowledge: Interdisciplinary, degree-granting fields in American colleges and universities, 1975–2000. *Review of Higher Education, 32*(2), 155–183.

Brookfield, S. D. (2012). *Teaching for critical thinking: Tools and techniques to help students question their assumptions.* San Francisco, CA: Jossey-Bass.

Bromme, R. (2000). Beyond one's own perspective: The psychology of cognitive interdisciplinarity. In P. Weingart & N. Stehr (Eds.), *Practising interdisciplinarity* (pp. 115–133). Toronto, Canada: University of Toronto Press.

Butterfield, A. K. J., & Korazim-Korosy, Y. (Eds.). (2007). *Interdisciplinary community development.* Binghamton, NY: Haworth Press.

Buzan, T. (2010). *The mind map book.* London, England: BBC Books.

Calhoun, C. (2002). *Dictionary of the social sciences.* Oxford, England: Oxford University Press.

Calhoun, C., & Rhoten, D. (2010). Integrating the social sciences: Theoretical knowledge, methodological tools, and practical applications. In R. Frodeman, J. T. Klein, & C. Mitcham (Eds.), *The Oxford handbook of interdisciplinarity* (pp. 103–118). New York, NY: Oxford University Press.

Carmichael, T., & LaPierre, Y. (2014). Interdisciplinary learning works: The results of a comprehensive assessment of students and student learning outcomes in an integrative learning community. *Issues in Interdisciplinary Studies, 32,* 53–78.

Casey, B. A. (2010). Administering interdisciplinary programs. In R. Frodeman, J. T. Klein, & C. Mitcham (Eds.), *The Oxford handbook of interdisciplinarity* (pp. 345–359). Oxford, England: Oxford University Press.

Clark, B. (1989). The academic life: Small worlds, different worlds. *Educational Researcher, 18*(5), 4–8.

Clark, H. H. (1996). *Using language.* Cambridge, MA: Cambridge University Press.

Clark, T. (2001). *Interdisciplinary problem solving in species and ecosystem conservation* (F&ES Bulletin 105). New Haven, CT: Yale University.

Cluck, N. A. (1980). Reflections on the interdisciplinary approaches to the humanities. *Liberal Education, 66*(1), 67–77.

Colwell, R. (1998, September 3). *The National Science Foundation's role in the Artic.* Retrieved from www.nsf.gov/news/speeches/colwell/rc80903.htm

Connor, M. A. (2012). The metropolitan problem in interdisciplinary perspective. In A. F. Repko, W. H. Newell, & R. Szostak (Eds.), *Case studies in interdisciplinary research* (pp. 53–122). Thousand Oaks, CA: Sage.

Cooke, N. J., & Hilton, M. L. (2015). *Enhancing the effectiveness of team science.* Washington, DC: National Research Council.

Crenshaw, K. (2014). *On intersectionality: The essential writings of Kimberle Crenshaw*. New York, NY: New Press.

Danserau, D. F., & Newbern, D. (1997). Using knowledge maps to enhance excellence. In W. E. Campbell & K. A. Smith, (Eds.), *New paradigms for college teaching* (pp. 127–148). Edina, MN: Interaction Book Company.

Davis, G. A. (1992). *Creativity is forever* (3rd ed.). Dubuque, IA: Kendall/Hunt.

Delph, J. B. (2005). *An integrative approach to the elimination of the "perfect crime."* Unpublished manuscript, University of Texas at Arlington.

de Saint-Exupéry, A. (2000). *The little prince*. New York, NY: Harcourt.

Dietrich, W. (1995). *Northwest passage: The great Columbia River*. Seattle: University of Washington Press.

Dhole, A. (n.d.). *Globalization and its effects on the environment*. Unpublished manuscript.

Donald, J. (2002). *Learning to think: Disciplinary perspectives*. San Francisco, CA: Jossey-Bass.

Donald, J. G. (2009). The commons: Disciplinary and interdisciplinary encounters. In Caroline Kreber (Ed.), *The university and its disciplines: Teaching and learning within and beyond disciplinary boundaries* (pp. 35–49). New York, NY: Routledge.

Dow, S. (2001). Modernism and postmodernism: A dialectical analysis. In S. Cullenberg, J. Amariglio, & D. F. Ruccio (Eds.), *Postmodernism, economics and knowledge* (pp. 61–101). New York, NY: Routledge.

Easton, D. (1991). The division, integration, and transfer of knowledge. In D. Easton & C. S. Schelling (Eds.), *Divided knowledge: Across disciplines, across cultures* (pp. 7–36). Newbury Park, CA: Sage.

Elliott, D. J. (2002). Philosophical perspectives on research. In R. Colwell & C. Richardson (Eds.), *The new handbook of research on music teaching and learning* (pp. 85–102). Oxford, England: Oxford University Press.

Fauconnier, G. (1994). *Mental spaces: Aspects of meaning construction in natural language*. Cambridge, England: Cambridge University Press.

Fischer, C. C. (1988). On the need for integrating occupational sex discrimination theory on the basis of causal variables. *Issues in Integrative Studies, 6*, 21–50.

Foucault, M. (1975). *Discipline and punish: The birth of the prison* (A. Sheridan, Trans.). New York, NY: Vintage Books.

Frankfort-Nachmias, C., & Nachmias, D. (2008). *Research and methods in the social sciences* (7th ed.). New York, NY: Worth.

Friedman, T. L., & Mandelbaum, M. (2011). *That used to be us: How American fell behind in the world it invented and how we can come back*. New York, NY: Farrar, Straus and Giroux.

Frodeman, R., & Mitcham, C. (2007). New directions in interdisciplinarity: Broad, deep, and critical. *Bulletin of Science, Technology & Society, 20*(10), 1–9.

Fuchsman, K. (2012). Interdisciplines and interdisciplinarity: Political psychology and psychohistory compared. *Issues in Integrative Studies, 30*, 128–154.

Funchess, K. D. (n.d.). *Globalization: An interdisciplinary approach to explain how western culture spreads around the world*. Unpublished manuscript.

Fussell, S. G., & Kraus, R. M. (1991). Accuracy and bias in estimates of others' knowledge. *European Journal of Social Psychology, 21*, 445–454.

Fussell, S. G., & Kraus, R. M. (1992). Coordination of knowledge in communication: Effects of speakers' assumptions about what others know. *Journal of Personality and Social Psychology, 62*, 378–391.

Galinsky, A. D., & Moskowitz, G. B. (2000). Perspective-taking: Decreasing stereotype expression, stereotype accessibility, and in-group favoritism. *Journal of Personality and Social Psychology, 78*(4), 708–724.

Gardner, H. (1989). *The unschooled mind: How children think and how schools should teach*. New York, NY: Basic Books.

Gardner, H. (2008). *Five minds for the future*. Boston, MA: Harvard Business Press.

Gibbons, M., Limoges, C., Nowotny, H., Schwartzman, S., Scott, P., & Trow, M. (1994). *The new production of knowledge*. London, England: Sage.

Golding, C. (2009). *Integrating the disciplines: Successful interdisciplinary subjects*. Melbourne, Australia: University of Melbourne, Centre for the Study of Higher Education. Available in electronic form **http://www.cshe .unimelb.edu.au/resources_teach/ curriculum_design/docs/ Interdisc_Guide.pdf**

Goodin, R. E., & Klingerman, H. D. (Eds.). (1996). *A new handbook of political science.* New York, NY: Oxford University Press.

Gorenflo, D. W., & Crano, W. D. (1998). The multiple perspectives inventory: A measure of perspective-taking. *Swiss Journal of Psychology, 57*(3), 163–177.

Griffin, G. (2005). Research methods for English studies: An introduction. In G. Griffin (Ed.), *Research methods for English studies* (pp. 1–16). Edinburgh, Scotland: Edinburgh University Press.

Growney, J. (2008). Mathematics influences poetry. *Journal of Mathematics and the Arts, 2*(1), 1–7.

Gutmann, M. P. (2011, June 2). Statement of Dr. Myron P. Gutmann, assistant director, Social, Behavioral, and Economic Sciences National Science Foundation before the Committee on Science, Space, and Technology Subcommittee on Research and Science Education, U.S. House of Representatives. Retrieved from **http://www.nsf.gov/about/congress/112/mg_sberesearch_110602.jsp**

Halpern, D. F. (1996). *Thought and knowledge* (3rd ed.). Mahwah, NJ: Erlbaum.

Halpern, D. F. (1999, Winter). Teaching for critical thinking: Helping college students develop the skills and dispositions of a critical thinker. *New Directions for Teaching and Learning, 80,* 69–74.

Halx, M., & Reybold, L. (2006). A pedagogy of force: Faculty perspectives of critical thinking capacity in undergraduate students. *Journal of General Education, 54*(4), 293–315.

Harman, J. (2012). *The chaos of financial order: An interdisciplinary perspective.* Unpublished manuscript.

Harris, J. (2001). *The new art history: A critical introduction.* New York, NY: Routledge.

Hatcher, D. (2006). Stand-alone versus integrated critical thinking courses. *Journal of General Education, 55*(3/4), 247–272.

Hershberg, T. (1981). The new urban history: Toward an interdisciplinary history of the city. In T. Hershberg (Ed.), *Philadelphia: Work, space, family, and group experience in the nineteenth century* (pp. 3–42). New York, NY: Oxford University Press.

Heuer, R. J., Jr. (2008). *Psychology of intelligence analysis.* Washington, DC: Center for the Study of Intelligence. Retrieved from **https://www.cia.gov/library/center-for-the-study-of-intelligence/csi-publications/books-and-monographs/psychology-of-intelligence-analysis/index.html**

Holley, K. A. (2009). Understanding interdisciplinary challenges and opportunities in higher education. *ASHE Higher Education Report, 35*(2).

Hoskin, K. W. (1993). Education and the genesis of disciplinarity: The unexpected reversal. In E. Messer-Davidow, D. R. Shumway, & D. J. Sylvan (Eds.), *Knowledges: Historical and critical studies in disciplinarity* (pp. 271–304). Charlottesville: University Press of Virginia.

Howell, M., & Prevenier, W. (2001). *From reliable sources: An introduction to historical methods.* Ithaca, NY: Cornell University Press.

Huber, M. T., Hutchings, P., & Gale, R. (2005). Integrative learning for liberal education. *Peer Review, 7*(4), 4–7.

Huber, M. T., Hutchings, P., Gale, R., Miller, R., & Breen, M. (2007, Spring). Leading initiatives for integrative learning. *Liberal Education, 93*(2). Retrieved October 31, 2012, from **http://www.aacu.org/liberaleducation/le-sp07/featurefour.cfm**

Hughes, J. (2007, October). *What works? Research in practice.* Retrieved from **http://www.edu.gov.on.ca/eng/literacynumeracy/inspire/research/Hughes.pdf**

Hughes, P. C., Munoz, J. S., & Tanner, M. (2015). *Perspectives in Interdisciplinary and Integrative Studies.* Lubbock: Texas Tech University Press.

Hutcheson, P. A. (1997). Structures and practices. In J. G. Gaff, J. L. Ratcliff, & Associates (Eds.), *Handbook of the undergraduate curriculum: A comprehensive guide to purpose, structures, practices, and change* (pp. 100–117). San Francisco, CA: Jossey-Bass.

Hyland, K. (2004). *Disciplinary discourses: Social interaction in academic writing.* Ann Arbor: University of Michigan Press.

Iggers, G. G. (1997). *Historiography in the twentieth century: From scientific objectivity to postmodern challenges.* Middletown, CT: Wesleyan University Press.

Ivanitkaya, L., Clark, D., Montgomery, G., & Primeau, R. (2002). Interdisciplinary learning: Process and outcomes. *Innovative Higher Education, 27*(2), 95–111.

Jones, P. C., & Merritt, Q. (1999). The TALESSI Project: Promoting active learning for interdisciplinarity, values awareness and critical thinking in environmental higher education. *Geography in Higher Education, 23*(3), 335–348.

Kafatos, F. C., & Eisner, T. (2004). Unification in the Century of Biology. *Science 202,* 1257.

Kann, M. (1979). The political culture of interdisciplinary explanation. *Humanities in Society, 2*(3), 185–300.

Katz, C. (2001). Disciplining interdisciplinarity. *Feminist Studies, 27*(2), 519–525.

Kaufman, G. (2012). "Losing yourself" in a fictional character can affect your real life. *The Ohio State Research and Innovations Communications.* Retrieved from **http://researchnews.osu.edu/archive/exptaking.htm**

Kelder, R. (1992). *Epistemology and determining critical thinking skills in the disciplines.* Paper presented at the annual conference of the Institute for Critical Thinking, Montclair, NJ.

Kelly, J. S. (1996). Wide and narrow interdisciplinarity. *The Journal of Education, 45*(2), 95–113.

King, A., & Brownell, J. (1966). *The curriculum and the disciplines of knowledge.* New York, NY: Wiley.

King, P. M., & Kitchener, K. S. (1994). *Developing reflective judgment: Understanding and promoting intellectual growth and critical thinking in adolescents and adults.* San Francisco, CA: Jossey-Bass.

Klein, J. T. (1990). *Interdisciplinarity: History, theory and practice.* Detroit, MI: Wayne State University Press.

Klein, J. T. (1996). *Crossing boundaries: Knowledge, disciplinarities, and interdisciplinarities.* Charlottesville: University Press of Virginia.

Klein, J. T. (2005). *Humanities, culture, and interdisciplinarity: The changing American academy.* Albany: State University of New York.

Klein, J. T. (2010). *Creating interdisciplinary campus cultures: A*

model for strength and sustainability. San Francisco, CA: Jossey-Bass.

Klein, J. T., & Newell, W. H. (1997). Advancing interdisciplinary studies. In J. G. Gaff, J. L. Ratcliff, & Associates (Eds.), *Handbook of the undergraduate curriculum: A comprehensive guide to purposes, structures, practices, and change* (pp. 393–415). San Francisco, CA: Jossey-Bass.

Lakoff, G. (1987). *Women, fire, and dangerous things. Case study I.* Chicago, IL: University of Chicago Press.

Lattuca, L. (2001). *Creating interdisciplinarity: Interdisciplinary research and reaching among college and university faculty.* Nashville, TN: Vanderbilt University Press.

Leary, M. R. (2004). *Introduction to behavioral research methods* (4th ed.). Boston, MA: Pearson Education.

Lederman, L. M., & Hill, C. T. (2011). *Quantum physics for poets.* Amherst, NY: Prometheus.

Lenhart, A., & Fox, S. (2006, July). *Bloggers. A portrait of the internet's new storytellers.* Retrieved from **http://www.pewinternet.org/files/old-media/Files/Reports/2006/PIP%20Bloggers%20Report%20July%2019%202006.pdf.pdf**

Levine, A. (1993). *Higher learning in America, 1980–2000.* Baltimore, MD: Johns Hopkins University Press.

Levy, F., & Cannon, C. (2016, February 9). *The Bloomberg Job Skills Report, 2016: What recruiters want.* Retrieved from **http://www.bloomberg.com/graphics/2016-job-skills-report/**

Lewis, B. (2003, Summer). Response to David DeGrazia. *Journal of Medical Humanities, 24*(1/2), pp. 73–78.

Lin, M. (2000). *Boundaries.* New York, NY: Simon & Schuster.

Longo, G. (2002). The constructed objectivity of the mathematics and the cognitive subject. In M. Mugur-Schachter & A. van der Merwe (Eds.), *Quantum mechanics, mathematics, cognition and action* (pp. 433–462). Boston, MA: Kluwer Academic.

Looney, C., Donovan, S., O'Rourke, M., Crowley, S., Eigenbrode, S. D., Rotschy, L., . . . Wulfhorst, J. D. (2014). Using Toolbox workshops to enhance cross-disciplinary communication. In M. O'Rourke, S. Crowley, S. D. Eigenbrode, & J. D Wulfhorst (Eds.), *Enhancing communication and collaboration in interdisciplinary research,* (pp. 220–243). Thousand Oaks, CA: Sage.

Magnus, D. (2000). Down the primrose path: Competing epistemologies in early twentieth century biology. In R. Creath & J. Maienschein (Eds.), *Biology and epistemology* (pp. 91–121). Cambridge, England: Cambridge University Press.

Marsh, D., & Furlong, P. (2002). A skin, not a sweater: Ontology and epistemology in political science. In D. Marsh & G. Stoker (Eds.), *Theory and methods in political science* (2nd ed., pp. 17–41). New York, NY: Palgrave Macmillan.

Marshall, D. G. (1992). Literary interpretation. In J. Gibaldi (Ed.), *Introduction to scholarship in modern languages and literatures* (pp. 159–182). New York, NY: Modern Language Association of America.

Maurer, B. (2004). Models of scientific inquiry and statistical practice: Implications for the structure of scientific knowledge.

In M. L. Taper & S. R. Lee (Eds.), *The nature of scientific evidence: Statistical, philosophical, and empirical considerations* (pp. 17–31). Chicago, IL: University of Chicago Press.

Mayville, W. V. (1978). *Interdisciplinarity: The mutable paradigm.* Washington, DC: The Association of American Colleges and Universities.

Martin, R., Thomas, G., Charles, K., Epitropaki, O., & McNamara, R. (2005). The role of leader-member exchanges in mediating the relationship between locus of control and work reactions. *Journal of Occupational and Organizational Psychology, 78,* 141–147.

McKay, K. A. (n.d.). *Nurse burnout: An integrative approach to a multidimensional problem.* Unpublished manuscript.

Menken, S., & Keestra, M. (Eds.). (2016). *An introduction to interdisciplinary research.* Amsterdam, the Netherlands: Amsterdam University Press.

Miller, M., & Boix Mansilla, V. (2004). *Thinking across perspectives and disciplines* (Interdisciplinary Studies Project, Project Zero, pp. 1–16). Cambridge, MA: Harvard Graduate School of Education.

Miller, T. R., Baird, T. D., Littlefield, C. M., Kofinas, G., Chapin, F., III, and Redman, C. L. (2008). Epistemological pluralism: reorganizing interdisciplinary research. *Ecology and Society, 13*(2), 46. Retrieved from http://www.ecologyandsociety.org/vol13/iss2/art46/

Mollinga, P. P. (2008). *The rational organization of dissent: Boundary concepts, boundary objects and boundary settings in the interdisciplinary study of natural resources management* (ZEF Working Paper No. 33). Bonn, Germany: University of Bonn, Center for Development Research, Department of Political and Cultural Change.

Moran, J. (2010). *Interdisciplinity* (2nd ed.). New York, NY: Routledge.

Morrison, J. L. (2003, October). Conceptual integration in online interdisciplinary study: Current perspective, theories, and implications for future research. *The International Review of Research in Open and Distance Learning, 4*(2), Retrieved May 26, 2012 from http://www.irrodl.org/index.php/irrodl/article/view/154/235

National Academy of Sciences, National Academy of Engineering, & Institute of Medicine. (2005). *Facilitating interdisciplinary research.* Washington, DC: Department of Education.

National Association of Colleges and Employers. (November, 2011). *Job outlook 2012.* Retrieved from http://www.sjsu.edu/careercenter/docs/job-outlook-survey-NACE_2012.pdf

National Center for Education Statistics. (2007, July). *Digest of education statistics, 2006.* Washington, DC: U.S. Department of Education. Retrieved on August 17, 2012, from http://nces.ed.gov/pubs2007/2007017.pdf

National Science Foundation & Directorate for Social, Behavioral and Economic Sciences. (2011). *Rebuilding the mosaic: Fostering research in the social, behavioral, and economic sciences at the National Science Foundation in the next decade.* Arlington, VA: National Science Foundation.

Newell, W. H. (1989). Strong sense critical thinking and interdisciplinary study. *CT News, 8*(1), 1–4.

Newell, W. H. (2001). A theory of interdisciplinary studies. *Issues in Integrative Studies, 19,* 1–25.

Newell, W. H. (2004). Complexity and interdisciplinarity. In D. Kiel (Ed.), *Encyclopedia of life support systems* (EOLSS). Retrieved from http://www.eolss.net

Newell, W. H. (2007). Decision making in interdisciplinary studies. In G. Morçöl (Ed.), *Handbook of decision making* (pp. 245–264). New York, NY: Marcel-Dekker.

Newell, W. H. (2010a). Educating for a complex world: Integrative learning and interdisciplinary studies. *Liberal Education, 96*(4), 6–11.

Newell, W. H. (2010b). Undergraduate general education. In Frodeman, R., Klein, J.T., and Mitcham, C. (Eds.), *The Oxford handbook of interdisciplinarity* (pp. 360–371). Oxford: Oxford University Press.

Newell, W. H. (2012). Conclusion. In A. F. Repko, W. H. Newell, & R. Szostak (Eds.), *Case studies in interdisciplinary research* (pp. 299–314). Thousand Oaks, CA: Sage.

Nikitina, S. (2006). Three strategies for interdisciplinary teaching: Contextualization, conceptualization, and problem-centering. *Journal of Curriculum Studies, 38*(3), 251–271.

Nissani, M. (1995). Fruits, salads, and smoothies: A working definition of interdisciplinarity. *Journal of Educational Thought, 29,* 119–126.

Novak, J. D. (1998). *Learning, creating, and using knowledge: Concept maps as facilitative tools in schools and corporations.* Mahwah, NJ: Erlbaum.

Novick, P. (1998). *That noble dream: The "objectivity question" and the American historical profession.* New York, NY: Cambridge University Press.

Paul, R. W. (1994). *Critical thinking: What every person needs to survive in a rapidly changing world* (Rev. 3rd ed.). Melbourne, Australia: Hawker Brownlow Education.

Perry, W. G. (1981). Cognitive and ethical growth: The making of meaning. In A. W. Chickering (Ed.), *The modern American college* (pp. 76–116). San Francisco, CA: Jossey-Bass.

Petrie, H. G. (1976). Do you see what I see? The epistemology of interdisciplinary inquiry. *Journal of American Education, 10,* 29–43.

Pieters R., & Baumgartner, H. (2002). Who talks to whom? Intra- and interdisciplinary communication of economics journals. *Journal of Economic Literature, 40,* 483–509.

Prescott, A. (2012). An electric current of the imagination: What the digital humanities are and what they might become. *Journal of Digital Humanities, 1.* Retrieved from **http://journalofdigitalhumanities .org/1-2/an-electric-current-of-the-imagination-by-andrew-prescott/**

Razmak, J., & Bélanger, C. (2016). Interdisciplinary approach: A lever to business innovation. *International Journal of Higher Education, 5,* 173–182.

Remler, D. K., & Van Ryzin, G. G. (2011). *Research methods in practice: Strategies for description and causation.* Thousand Oaks, CA: Sage.

Repko, A. F. (2008). *Interdisciplinary research: Process and theory.* Thousand Oaks, CA: Sage.

Repko, A. F. (2012). Integrating theory-based insights on the causes of suicide terrorism. In A. F. Repko, W. H. Newell, and R. Szostak (Eds.), *Case studies in interdisciplinary*

research (pp. 125–157). Thousand Oaks, CA: Sage.

Repko, A. F., & Szostak, R. (2016). *Interdisciplinary research: Process and theory* (3rd ed.). Thousand Oaks, CA: Sage.

Rescher, N. (2003). *Epistemology: An introduction to the theory of knowledge.* Albany: State University of New York Press.

Rhoten, D., Boix-Mansilla, V., Chun, M., & Klein, J. T. (2006). *Interdisciplinary education at liberal arts institutions.* Brooklyn, NY: Social Science Research Council, 2006. **www.teaglefoundation.org/learning/ pdf/2006_ssrc_whitepaper.pdf**

Rivkin, J. (2005). The strategic importance of integrative skills. *Rotman Magazine* (Winter), pp. 42–43.

Root-Bernstein, R. (1989). *Discovery.* Cambridge, MA: Harvard University Press.

Rosenau, P. M. (1992). *Post-modernism and the social sciences: Insights, inroads, and intrusions.* Princeton, NJ: Princeton University Press.

Rosenberg, A. (2000). *Philosophy of science* (2nd ed.). New York, NY: Routledge.

Ross, A. (2012, February 1). [Transcript]. National Public Radio.

Saffle, M. (2005). The humanities. In M. K. Herndon (Ed.), *An introduction to interdisciplinary studies* (pp. 11–27). Dubuque, IA: Kendall/Hunt.

Saxe, J. G. (1963). *The blind men and the elephant.* New York, NY: McGraw-Hill.

Schneider, C. G. (2003). Liberal education and integrative learning. *Issues in Integrative Studies, 21,* 1–8.

Schommer, M. (1994). Synthesizing epistemological belief research:

Tentative understandings and provocative conclusions. *Educational Psychology Review, 6*(4), 293–319.

Sill, D. (1996). Integrative thinking, synthesis, and creativity in interdisciplinary studies. *Journal of General Education, 45*(2), 129–151.

Snow, C. P. (1964). *The two cultures.* London, England: Cambridge University Press.

Stefani, L., Mason, R., & Pegler, C. (2008). *The educational potential of e-portfolios. Supporting personal development and reflective learning.* London, England: Routledge.

Sternberg, R. J. (1996). *Successful intelligence: How practical and creative intelligence determine success in life.* New York, NY: The Penguin Group.

Stone, J. R. (1998). Introduction. In J. R. Stone (Ed.), *The craft of religious studies* (pp. 1–17). New York, NY: St. Martin's Press.

Sturgeon, S., Martin, M. G. F., & Grayling, A. C. (1995). Epistemology. In A. C. Grayling (Ed.), *Philosophy 1: A guide through the subject* (pp. 7–60). New York, NY: Oxford University Press.

Swoboda, W. W. (1979). Disciplines and interdisciplinarity: A historical perspective. In J. J. Kockelmans (Ed.), *Interdisciplinarity and higher education* (pp. 49–92). University Park: Pennsylvania State University Press.

Szostak, R. (2002). How to do interdisciplinarity: Integrating the debate. *Issues in Integrative Studies, 20,* 103–137.

Szostak, R. (2003). "Comprehensive" curricular reform: Providing students with an overview of the scholarly enterprise." *Journal of General Education, 52*(1), 27–49.

Szostak, R. (2004). *Classifying science: Phenomena, data, theory, method, practice*. Dordrecht, the Netherlands: Springer.

Szostak, R. (2009). *The causes of economic growth: Interdisciplinary perspectives*. Berlin, Germany: Springer.

Taffel, A. (1992). *Physics: Its methods and meanings* (6th ed.). Upper Saddle River, NJ: Prentice Hall.

Tayler, M. R. (2012). Jewish marriage as an expression of Israel's conflicted identity. In A. F. Repko, W. H. Newell, & R. Szostak (Eds.), *Case studies in interdisciplinary research* (pp. 23–51). Thousand Oaks, CA: Sage.

Tayler, M. R. (2014). The transformation from multidisciplinarity to interdisciplinarity: A case study of a course involving the status of Arab citizens in Israel. *Issues in Interdisciplinary Studies, 32*, 28–52.

Terpstra, J. L., Best, A., Abrams, D. B., & Moor, G. (2010). Health sciences and health services. In R. Frodeman, J. T. Klein, & C. Mitcham (Eds.), *The Oxford handbook of interdisciplinarity* (pp. 508–521). Oxford, England: Oxford University Press.

Toynton, R. (2005). Degrees of disciplinarity in equipping students in higher education for engagement and success in lifelong learning. *Active Learning in Higher Education, 6*(2), 106–117.

Transdisciplinary Net. (2009). *Transdisciplinary research*. Available at http://www.transdiscipliarity .ch/e/Transdisciplinarity/index .php

Tress, B., Tress, G., & Fry, G. (2005). Defining concepts and process of knowledge production in integrative research. In B. Tress, G. Tress, G. Fry, & P. Opdam (Eds.), *From landscape research to landscape planning: Aspects of integration, education and application* (pp. 13–26). Heidelberg, Germany: Springer.

Tress, G., Tress, B., & Fry, G. (2007). Analysis of the barriers to integration in landscape research projects, *Land Use Policy*, (24), pp. 374–385.

Tsui, L. (2007). Cultivating critical thinking: Insights from an elite liberal arts college. *Journal of General Education, 56*(3/4), 200–227.

Turner, M. (2001). *Cognitive dimensions of social science*. New York, NY: Oxford University Press.

U.S. National Institutes of Health Common Fund (2012). Interdisciplinary research. Retrieved from https://commonfund.nih.gov/ interdisciplinary/overview.aspx)

van der Lecq, R. (2012). Why we talk: An interdisciplinary approach to the evolutionary origins of language. In A. F. Repko, W. H. Newell, & R. Szostak (Eds.), *Case studies in interdisciplinary research* (pp. 191–224). Thousand Oaks, CA: Sage.

Veysey, L. (1965). *The emergence of the American university*. Chicago, IL: University of Chicago Press.

Vickers, J. (1998). "[U]nframed in open, unmapped fields": Teaching the practice of interdisciplinarity. *Arachne: An Interdisciplinary Journal in the Humanities, 4*(2), 11–42.

Wallace, R. A., & Wolf, A. (2006). *Contemporary sociological theory: Expanding the classical tradition* (6th ed.). Upper Saddle River, NJ: Pearson.

Wasserstrom, J. N. (2006, January 20). Expanding on the I-Word. *The Chronicle of Higher Education*, Section B, B5.

Wheeler, L., & Miller, E. (1970, October 6). *Multidisciplinary approach to planning*. Paper presented at Council of Education Facilities Planners 47th Annual Conference in Oklahoma City, OK, 6 October, 1976. (ERIC Document Reproduction Service No. ED044814)

Weingart, P. (2000). Introduction. In P. Weingart & N. Stehr (Eds.), *Practising interdisciplinarity* (pp. xi–xvi). Toronto, Canada: University of Toronto Press.

Welch, J., IV. (2011). The emergence of interdisciplinarity from epistemological thought. *Issues in Integrative Studies, 29*, 1–39.

Willard-Traub, M. K. (2007). Scholarly autobiography: An alternative intellectual practice. *Feminist Studies, 33*(1), 188–206.

Wolfe, C., & Haynes, C. (2003). Interdisciplinary writing assessment profiles. *Issues in Integrative Studies, 21*, 126–169.

Yassin, S. F. M., Rahman, S., & Yamat, H. (2010). Interdisciplinary integration through problem-based learning with ICT in pre-service teacher education. *EABR & ETLC Conference Proceedings*, 377–385.

Zajonic, A. (1993). *Catching the light: The entwined history of light and mind*. New York, NY: Bantam.

Zerhouni, E. (2003, October 3). NIH roadmap of medical research. *Science*, New Series, 302(5642), 63–64, 72.

INDEX